PRAISE FOR THE *MANGA G*

"Highly recommended."
—CHOICE MAGAZINE ON *THE MANGA GUIDE TO DATABASES*

"The *Manga Guides* definitely have a place on my bookshelf."
—SMITHSONIAN MAGAZINE

"The art is charming and the humor engaging. A fun and fairly painless lesson on what many consider to be a less-than-thrilling subject."
—SCHOOL LIBRARY JOURNAL ON *THE MANGA GUIDE TO STATISTICS*

"Stimulus for the next generation of scientists."
—SCIENTIFIC COMPUTING ON *THE MANGA GUIDE TO MOLECULAR BIOLOGY*

"The series is consistently good. A great way to introduce kids to the wonder and vastness of the cosmos."
—DISCOVERY.COM

"Absolutely amazing for teaching complex ideas and theories . . . excellent primers for serious study of physics topics."
—PHYSICS TODAY ON *THE MANGA GUIDE TO PHYSICS*

"A great fit of form and subject. Recommended."
—OTAKU USA MAGAZINE ON *THE MANGA GUIDE TO PHYSICS*

"I found the cartoon approach of this book so compelling and its story so endearing that I recommend that every teacher of introductory physics, in both high school and college, consider using it."
—AMERICAN JOURNAL OF PHYSICS ON *THE MANGA GUIDE TO PHYSICS*

"This is really what a good math text should be like. Unlike the majority of books on subjects like statistics, it doesn't just present the material as a dry series of pointless-seeming formulas. It presents statistics as something *fun* and something enlightening."
—GOOD MATH, BAD MATH ON *THE MANGA GUIDE TO STATISTICS*

"A single tortured cry will escape the lips of every thirty-something biochem major who sees *The Manga Guide to Molecular Biology*: 'Why, oh why couldn't this have been written when I was in college?'"
—THE SAN FRANCISCO EXAMINER

"A lot of fun to read. The interactions between the characters are lighthearted, and the whole setting has a sort of quirkiness about it that makes you keep reading just for the joy of it."
—HACKADAY ON *THE MANGA GUIDE TO ELECTRICITY*

"The *Manga Guide to Databases* was the most enjoyable tech book I've ever read."
—RIKKI KITE, LINUX PRO MAGAZINE

"*The Manga Guide to Electricity* makes accessible a very intimidating subject, letting the reader have fun while still delivering the goods."
—GEEKDAD

"If you want to introduce a subject that kids wouldn't normally be very interested in, give it an amusing storyline and wrap it in cartoons."
—MAKE ON *THE MANGA GUIDE TO STATISTICS*

"A clever blend that makes relativity easier to think about—even if you're no Einstein."
—STARDATE, UNIVERSITY OF TEXAS, ON *THE MANGA GUIDE TO RELATIVITY*

"This book does exactly what it is supposed to: offer a fun, interesting way to learn calculus concepts that would otherwise be extremely bland to memorize."
—DAILY TECH ON *THE MANGA GUIDE TO CALCULUS*

"Scientifically solid . . . entertainingly bizarre."
—CHAD ORZEL, SCIENCEBLOGS, ON *THE MANGA GUIDE TO RELATIVITY*

"Makes it possible for a 10-year-old to develop a decent working knowledge of a subject that sends most college students running for the hills."
—SKEPTICBLOG ON *THE MANGA GUIDE TO MOLECULAR BIOLOGY*

"*The Manga Guide to the Universe* does an excellent job of addressing some of the biggest science questions out there, exploring both the history of cosmology and the main riddles that still challenge physicists today."
—ABOUT.COM

"*The Manga Guide to Calculus* is an entertaining comic with colorful characters and a fun strategy to teach its readers calculus."
—DR. DOBB'S

THE MANGA GUIDE™ TO CRYPTOGRAPHY

THE MANGA GUIDE™ TO
CRYPTOGRAPHY

MASAAKI MITANI,
SHINICHI SATO,
IDERO HINOKI AND
VERTE CORP.

The Manga Guide to Cryptography is a translation of the Japanese original, *Manga de wakaru angou*, published by Ohmsha, Ltd. of Tokyo, Japan, © 2007 by Masaaki Mitani, Shinichi Sato, Idero Hinoki, and Verte Corp.

This English edition is co-published by No Starch Press, Inc. and Ohmsha, Ltd.

Printed in USA
Second printing

23 22 21 20 19 2 3 4 5 6 7 8 9

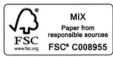

MIX
Paper from responsible sources
FSC® C008955
www.fsc.org

ISBN-10: 1-59327-742-3
ISBN-13: 978-1-59327-742-0

Publisher: William Pollock
Production Editor: Laurel Chun
Authors: Masaaki Mitani and Shinichi Sato
Illustrator: Idero Hinoki
Producer: Verte Corp.
Developmental Editor: Jan Cash
Translators: Raechel Dumas and Asumi Shibata
Technical Reviewer: Erik Lopez
Additional Technical Reviewers: Jean-Philippe Aumasson and Ron Henry
Copyeditor: Paula L. Fleming
Compositors: Laurel Chun and David Van Ness
Proofreader: Lisa Devoto Farrell
Indexer: BIM Creatives, LLC

For information on distribution, translations, or bulk sales, please contact No Starch Press, Inc. directly:
No Starch Press, Inc.
245 8th Street, San Francisco, CA 94103
phone: 1.415.863.9900; info@nostarch.com; http://www.nostarch.com/

Library of Congress Cataloging-in-Publication Data
Names: Mitani, Masaaki, author. | Sato, Shinichi (Professor of engineering), author. | Hinoki, Idero, author. | Verte Corp., author.
Title: The manga guide to cryptography / Masaaki Mitani, Shinichi Sato, Idero Hinoki, and Verte Corp.
Other titles: Manga de wakaru angou. English
Description: San Francisco : No Starch Press, Inc., [2018] | Translation of Manga de wakaru angou, published by Ohmsha, Ltd. of Tokyo, Japan, 2007.
Identifiers: LCCN 2018017805 (print) | LCCN 2018018420 (ebook) | ISBN 9781593278502 (epub) | ISBN 1593278500 (epub) | ISBN 9781593277420 (pbk.) | ISBN 1593277423 (pbk.)
Subjects: LCSH: Public key cryptography--Comic books, strips, etc. | Telecommunication--Security measures--Comic books, strips, etc. | Graphic novels.
Classification: LCC TK5102.94 (ebook) | LCC TK5102.94 .M5813 2018 (print) | DDC 652/.8--dc23
LC record available at https://lccn.loc.gov/2018017805

CONTENTS

4
PRACTICAL APPLICATIONS OF ENCRYPTION

PREFACE

When thinking about information societies, which rely on networks that function with the internet at their core, we can see how many aspects of our lives have become more convenient. In addition to now being able to search for information on the web and communicate via email, other network services like online shopping and internet banking have become widespread.

While the age of networking comes with many benefits, we also encounter phrases like, "safe and secure," "information security," "protection of personal information," "encryption," and so on that have a somewhat unpleasant ring to them. These words are everywhere—not a day goes by without seeing them. Why is such talk so prevalent?

Networks require a variety of information to be exchanged, and this includes information that could cause problems when in the hands of others and information that we wish to keep secret. We must take measures to protect information in order to prevent important data such as our credit card numbers, bank account numbers, medical histories, loan debts, and email addresses from easily leaking to outsiders. This information can be abused, and as such there is no doubt that protecting information is the most important issue that faces us in the age of networking. In our connected society, where there are so many unreliable factors, the ability to distinguish authentic information and provide protection from dangers such as fraud, forgery, revision, and interception is crucial. *Cryptography* is the core technology we use to create network services that the public can use safely.

Cryptographic technology has evolved rapidly in recent years. It is no longer just the domain of information security specialists, and is now necessary knowledge for the users themselves, who up until now have used convenient network services without a thought.

So how then does cryptography work? How does it actually provide information security and protect personal information?

Using manga, this book explains how cryptography works and what it does. The complex math is broken down into friendly explanations. We've done our best to make this an effortless learning experience where you can enjoy the story. Of course, there are also ciphertexts worked into the story, so do your best to decipher them while having fun. By the time you've finished reading this book, you'll no doubt have a thorough understanding of the fundamentals of cryptography and security.

Lastly, we'd like to express our most sincere gratitude to those who helped us publish this book, first to the folks at Ohmsha, Ltd. and also to Mr. Idero Hinoki who provided the illustrations.

MASAAKI MITANI AND SHINICHI SATO
APRIL, 2007

PROLOGUE

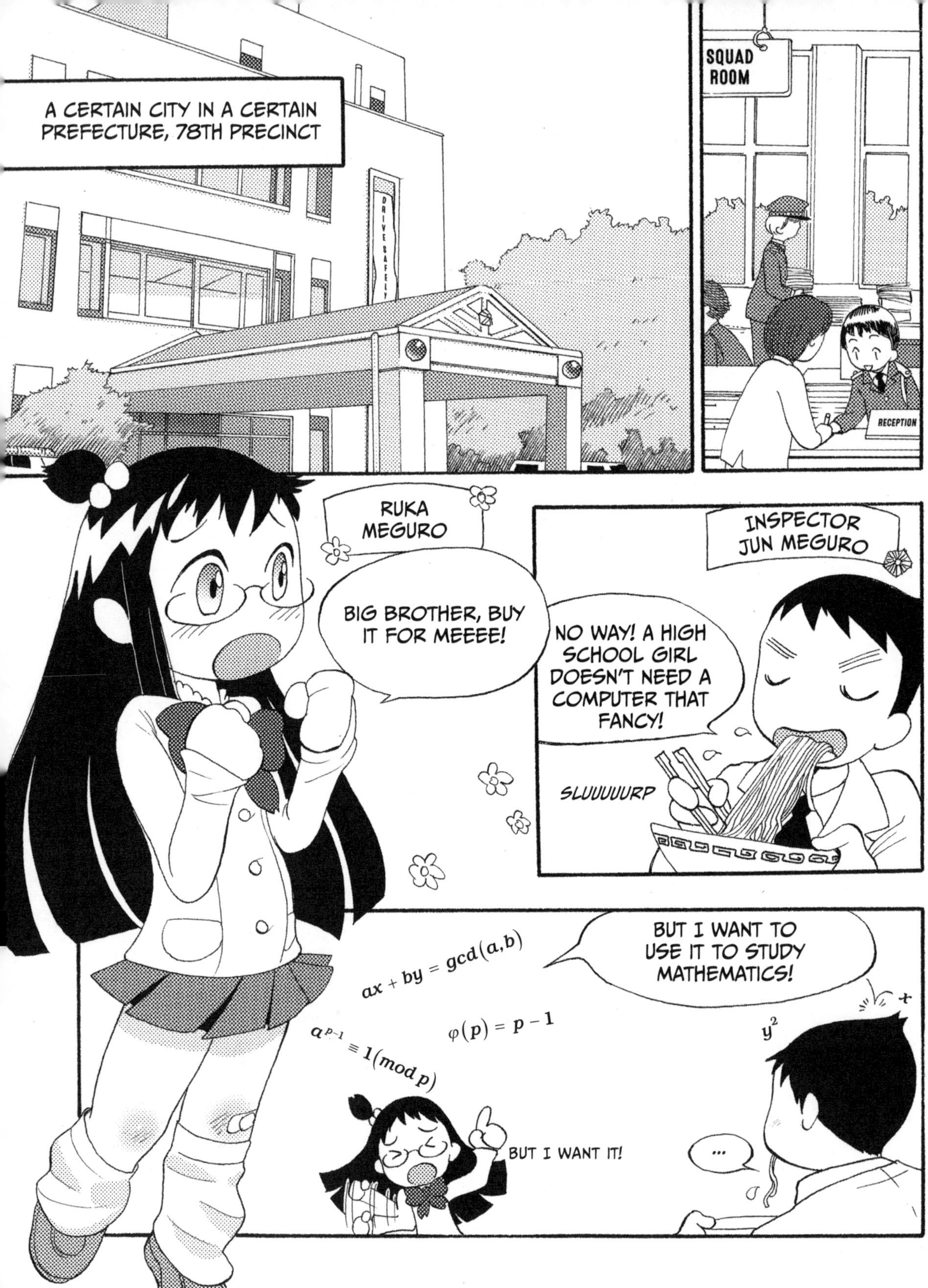
A CERTAIN CITY IN A CERTAIN PREFECTURE, 78TH PRECINCT
DRIVE SAFELY
SQUAD ROOM
RECEPTION
RUKA MEGURO
BIG BROTHER, BUY IT FOR MEEEE!
INSPECTOR JUN MEGURO
NO WAY! A HIGH SCHOOL GIRL DOESN'T NEED A COMPUTER THAT FANCY!
SLUUUUURP
BUT I WANT TO USE IT TO STUDY MATHEMATICS!
$ax + by = gcd(a,b)$
$\varphi(p) = p - 1$
$a^{p-1} \equiv 1(mod\ p)$
BUT I WANT IT!
y^2
x
...

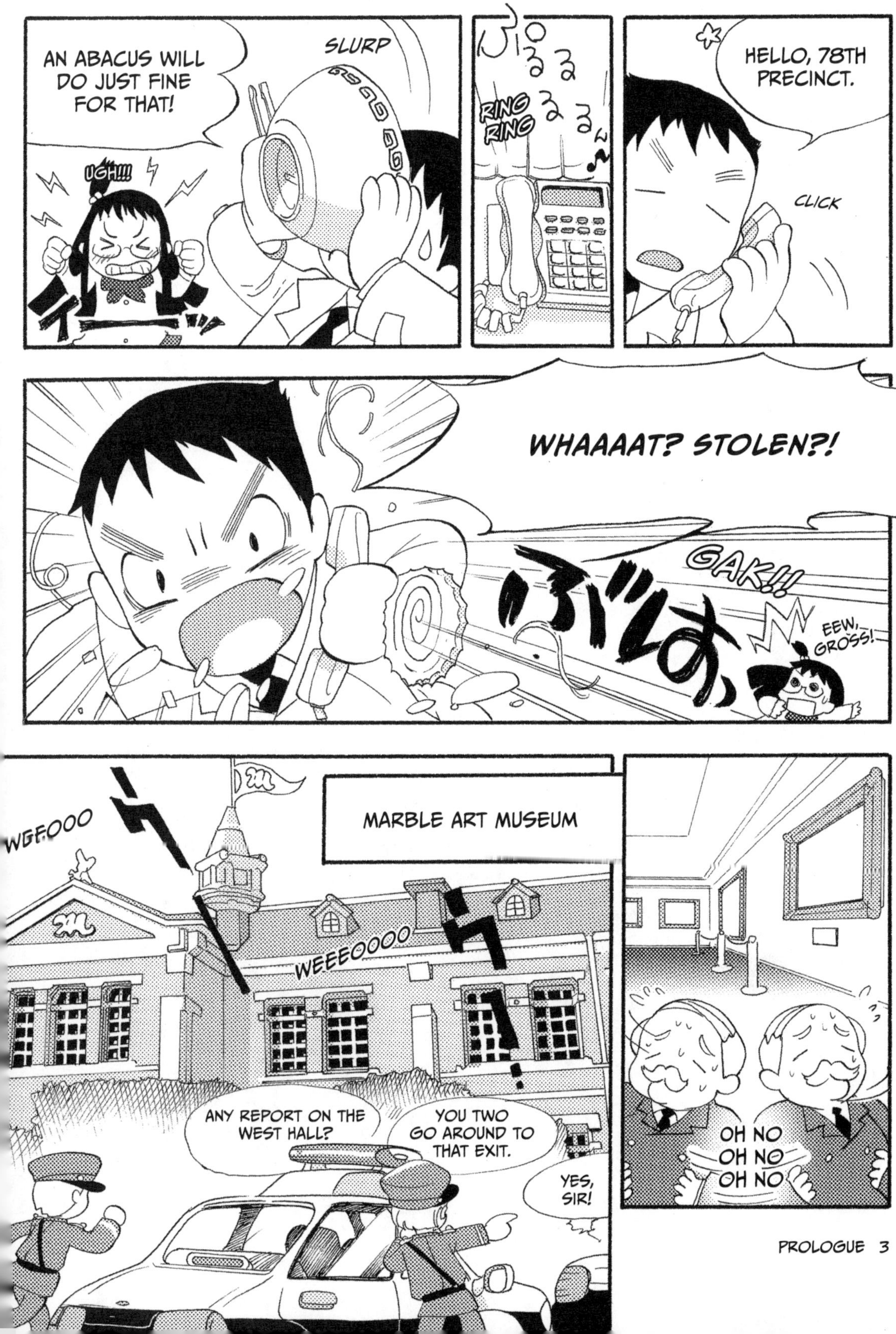
AN ABACUS WILL DO JUST FINE FOR THAT!
SLURP
UGH!!!
RING RING
ぷるるるるるるん
HELLO, 78TH PRECINCT.
CLICK
WHAAAAT? STOLEN?!
GAK!!
ぶはっ
EEW, GROSS!
MARBLE ART MUSEUM
WEEOOO
WEEEOOOO
ANY REPORT ON THE WEST HALL?
YOU TWO GO AROUND TO THAT EXIT.
YES, SIR!
OH NO
OH NO
OH NO

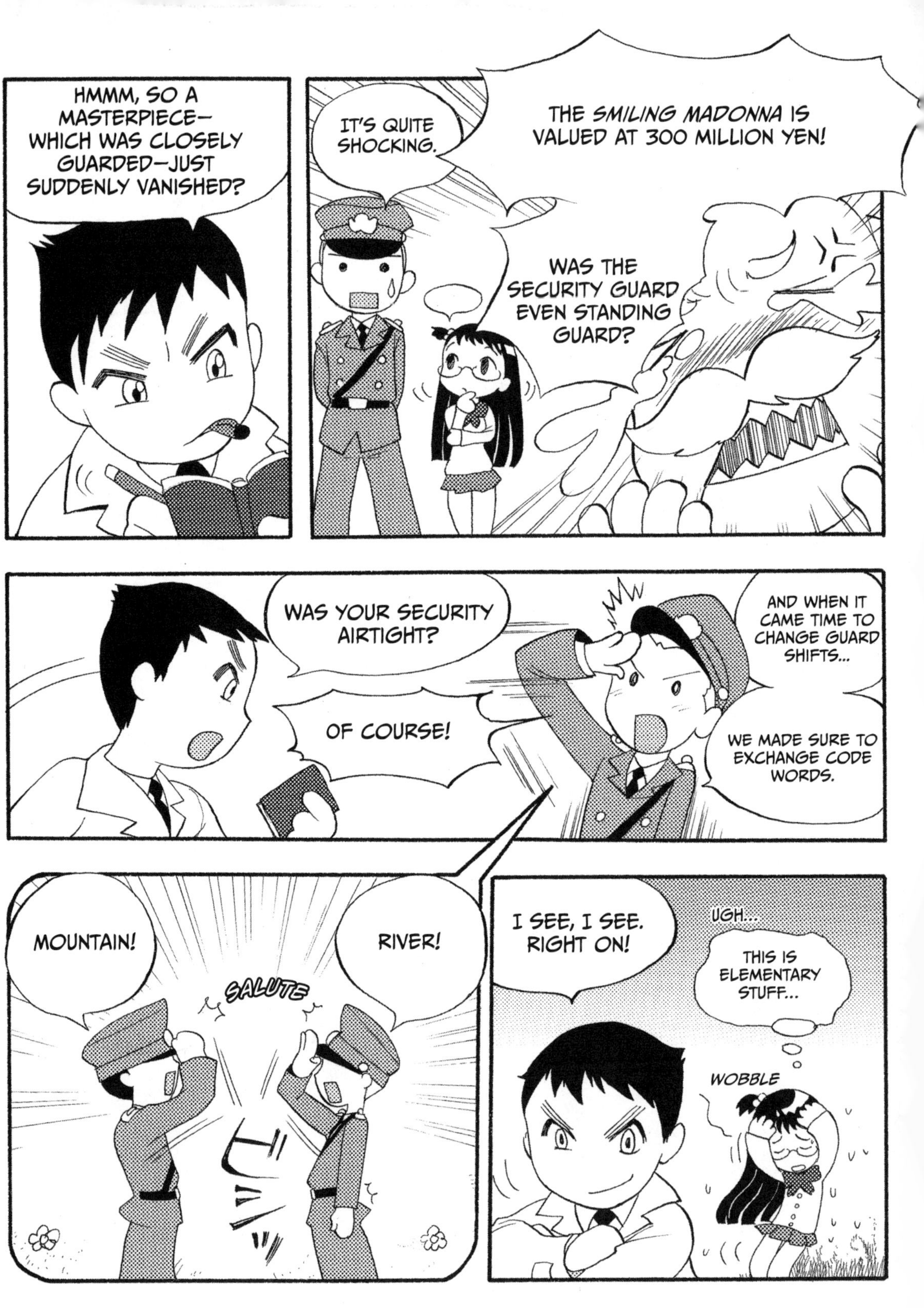
HMMM, SO A MASTERPIECE—WHICH WAS CLOSELY GUARDED—JUST SUDDENLY VANISHED?
IT'S QUITE SHOCKING.
THE *SMILING MADONNA* IS VALUED AT 300 MILLION YEN!
WAS THE SECURITY GUARD EVEN STANDING GUARD?
WAS YOUR SECURITY AIRTIGHT?
OF COURSE!
AND WHEN IT CAME TIME TO CHANGE GUARD SHIFTS...
WE MADE SURE TO EXCHANGE CODE WORDS.
MOUNTAIN!
RIVER!
SALUTE
I SEE, I SEE. RIGHT ON!
UGH...
THIS IS ELEMENTARY STUFF...
WOBBLE

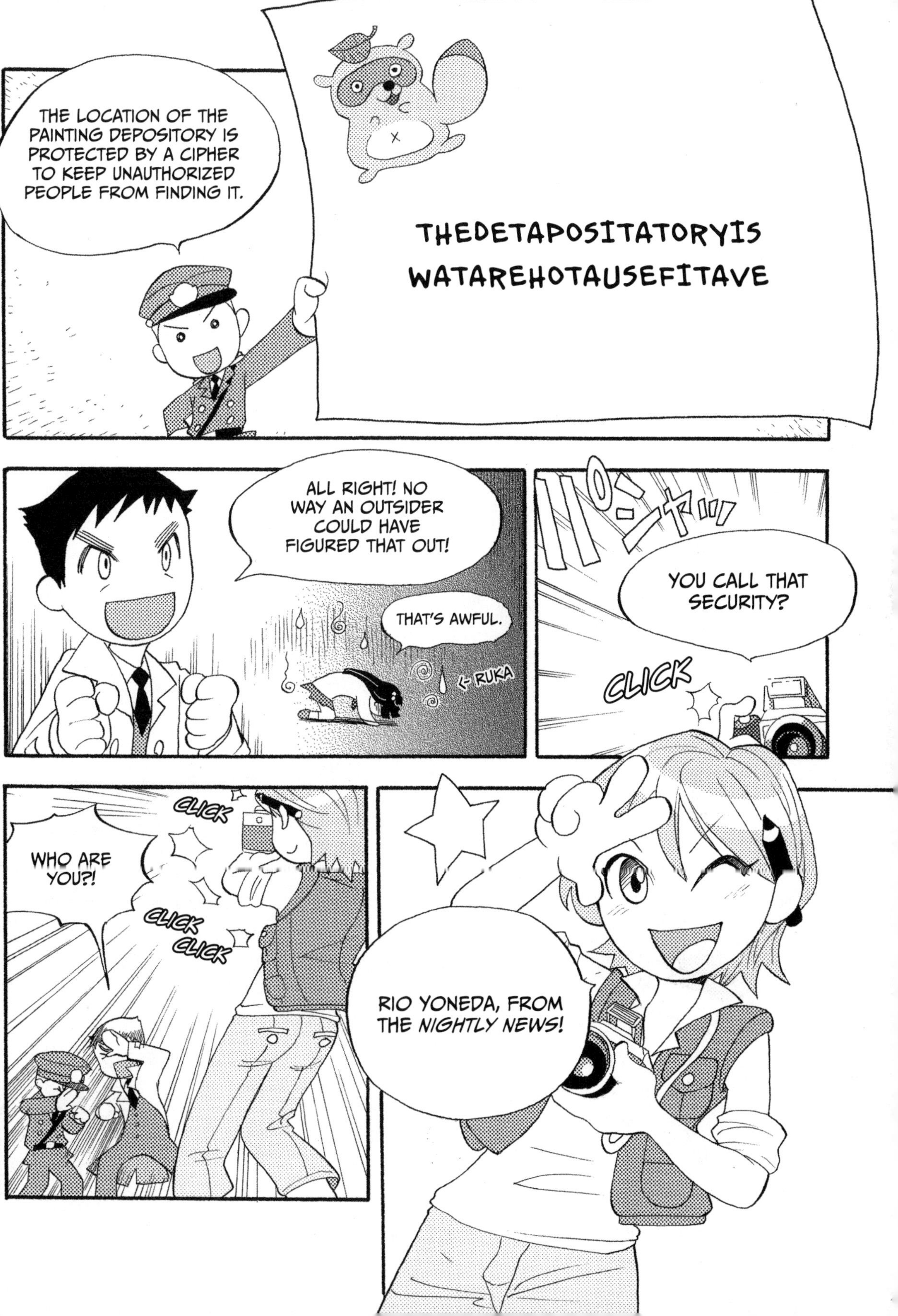
THE LOCATION OF THE PAINTING DEPOSITORY IS PROTECTED BY A CIPHER TO KEEP UNAUTHORIZED PEOPLE FROM FINDING IT.
THEDETAPOSITATORYIS
WATAREHOTAUSEFITAVE
ALL RIGHT! NO WAY AN OUTSIDER COULD HAVE FIGURED THAT OUT!
THAT'S AWFUL.
← RUKA
YOU CALL THAT SECURITY?
CLICK
CLICK
WHO ARE YOU?!
CLICK
CLICK
RIO YONEDA, FROM THE *NIGHTLY NEWS*!

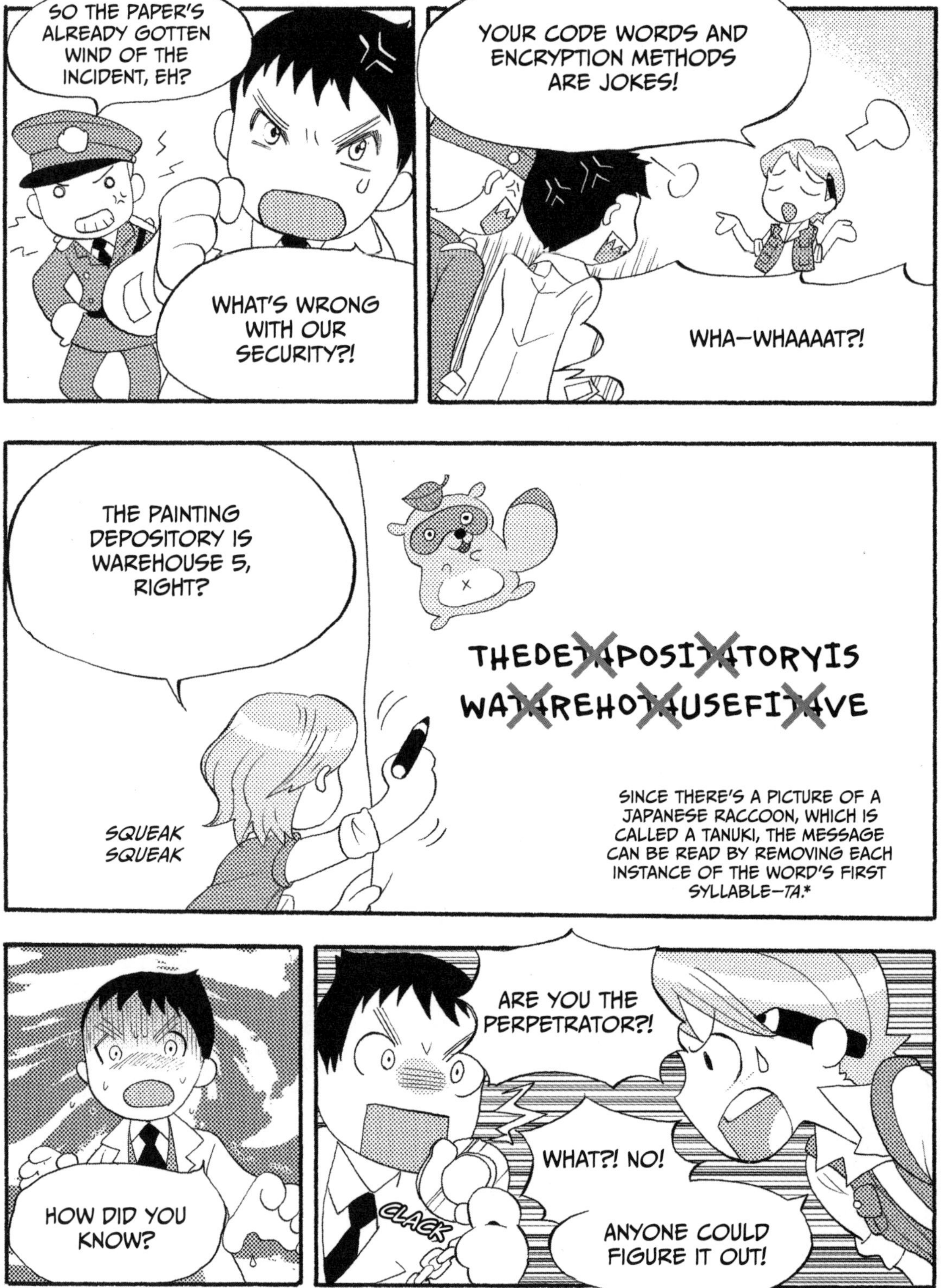
SO THE PAPER'S ALREADY GOTTEN WIND OF THE INCIDENT, EH?
WHAT'S WRONG WITH OUR SECURITY?!
YOUR CODE WORDS AND ENCRYPTION METHODS ARE JOKES!
WHA–WHAAAAT?!
THE PAINTING DEPOSITORY IS WAREHOUSE 5, RIGHT?
SQUEAK SQUEAK
THEDETAPOSITATORYIS
WATAREHOTAUSEFITAVE
SINCE THERE'S A PICTURE OF A JAPANESE RACCOON, WHICH IS CALLED A TANUKI, THE MESSAGE CAN BE READ BY REMOVING EACH INSTANCE OF THE WORD'S FIRST SYLLABLE—*TA*.*
HOW DID YOU KNOW?
ARE YOU THE PERPETRATOR?!
WHAT?! NO!
CLACK
ANYONE COULD FIGURE IT OUT!

* THE TANUKI CIPHER IS A COMMON WORDPLAY GAME IN JAPAN. THE CIPHER IS BASED ON A PUN OF THE WORD *TANUKI*, WHICH CAN MEAN "RACCOON" OR "OMIT THE TA'S."

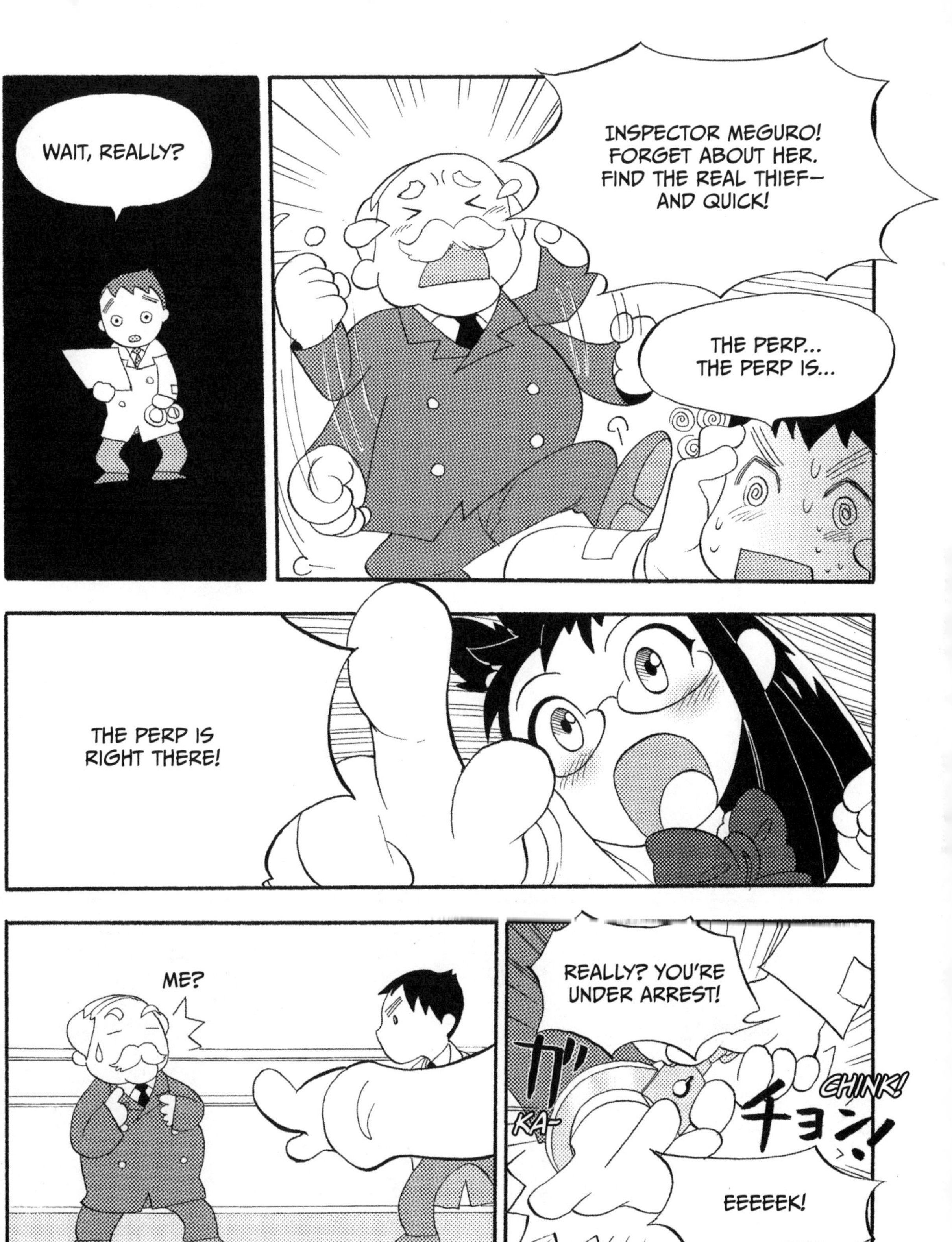
WAIT, REALLY?
INSPECTOR MEGURO! FORGET ABOUT HER. FIND THE REAL THIEF—AND QUICK!
THE PERP... THE PERP IS...
THE PERP IS RIGHT THERE!
ME?
REALLY? YOU'RE UNDER ARREST!
ガ
KA-
CHINK!
チョン!
EEEEEK!

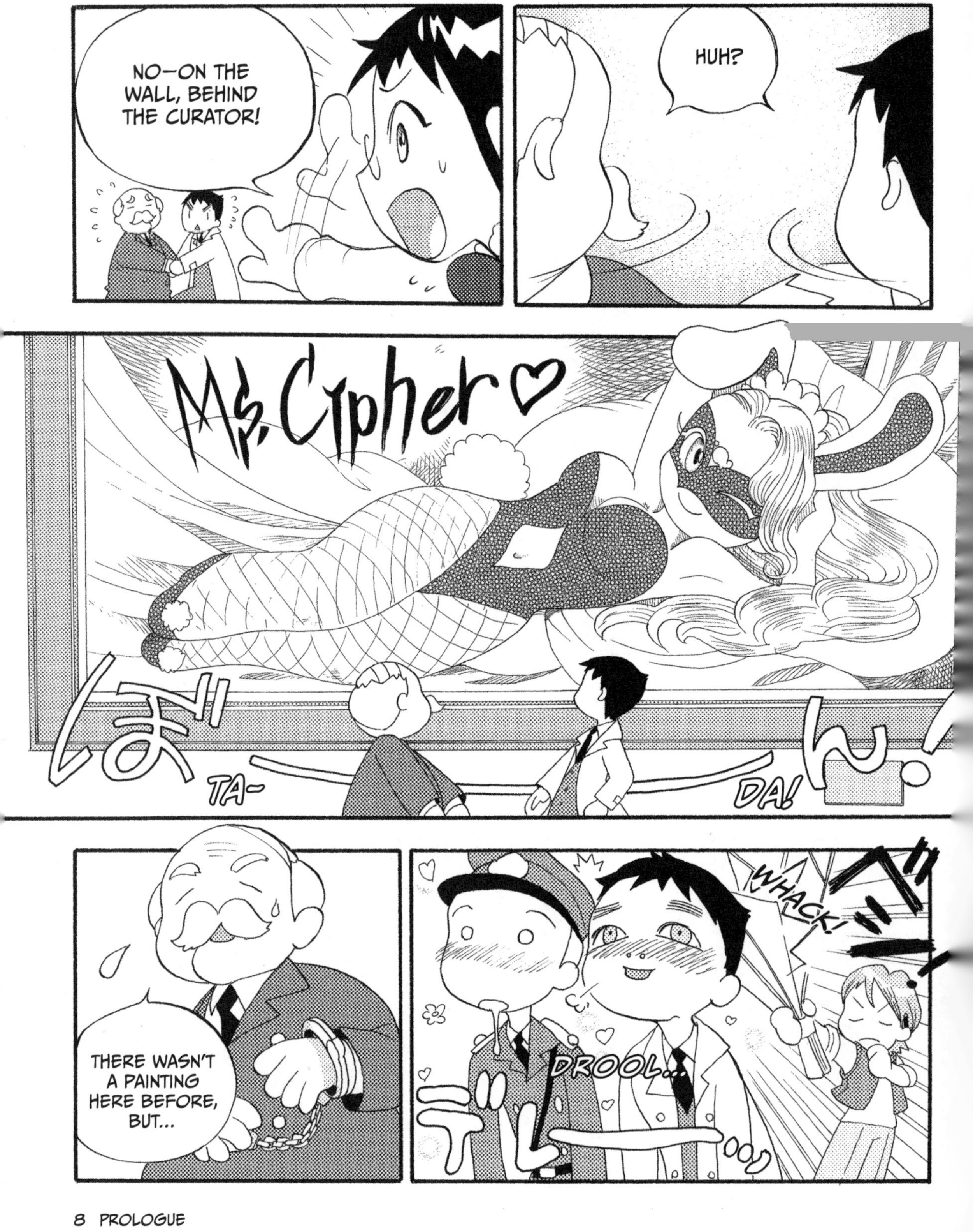
NO—ON THE WALL, BEHIND THE CURATOR!
HUH?
Ms. Cipher ♡
TA-
DA!
THERE WASN'T A PAINTING HERE BEFORE, BUT...
DROOL...
WHACK!

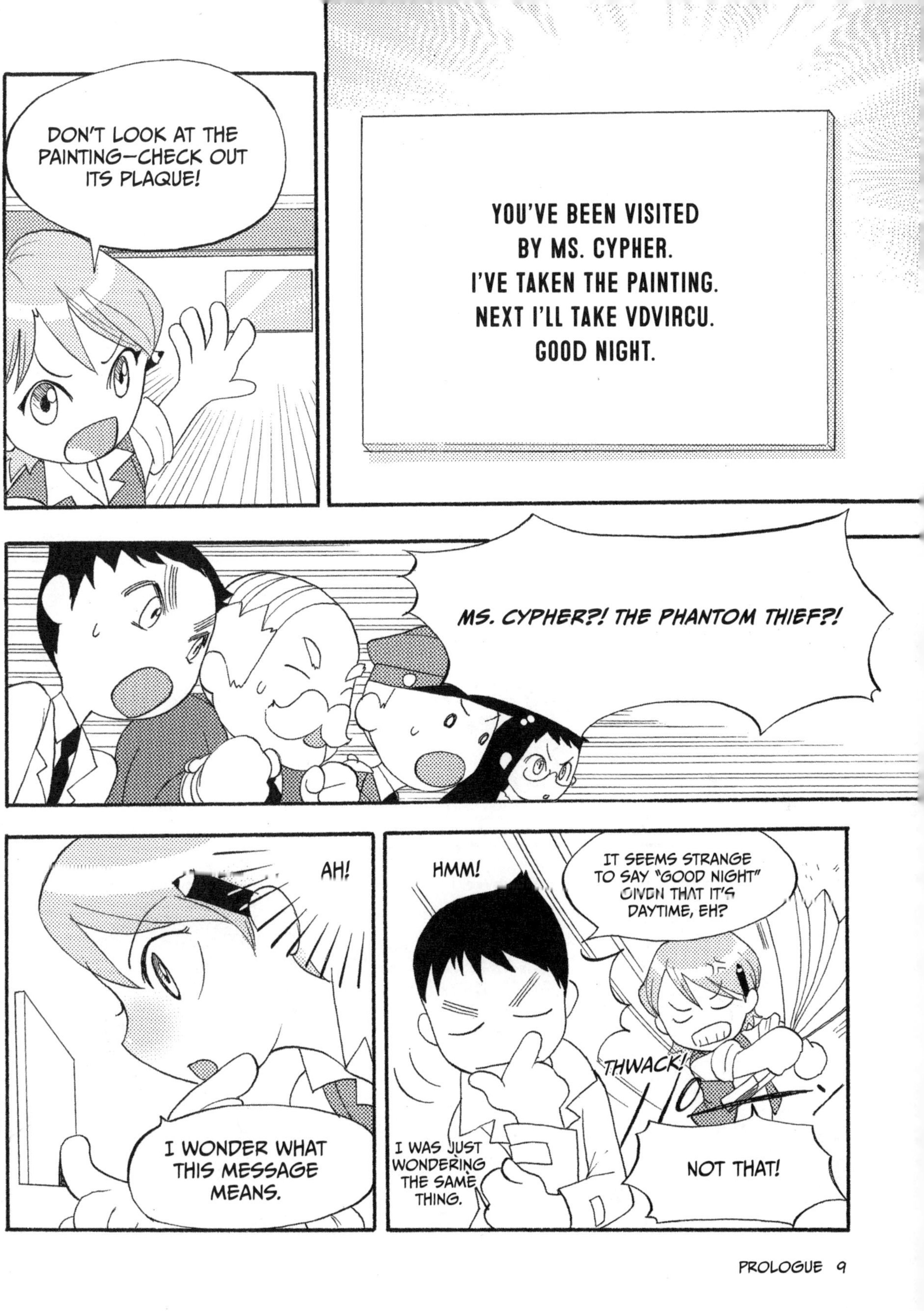
DON'T LOOK AT THE PAINTING—CHECK OUT ITS PLAQUE!
YOU'VE BEEN VISITED
BY MS. CYPHER.
I'VE TAKEN THE PAINTING.
NEXT I'LL TAKE VDVIRCU.
GOOD NIGHT.
MS. CYPHER?! THE PHANTOM THIEF?!
AH!
I WONDER WHAT THIS MESSAGE MEANS.
HMM!
IT SEEMS STRANGE TO SAY "GOOD NIGHT" GIVEN THAT IT'S DAYTIME, EH?
THWACK!
I WAS JUST WONDERING THE SAME THING.
NOT THAT!

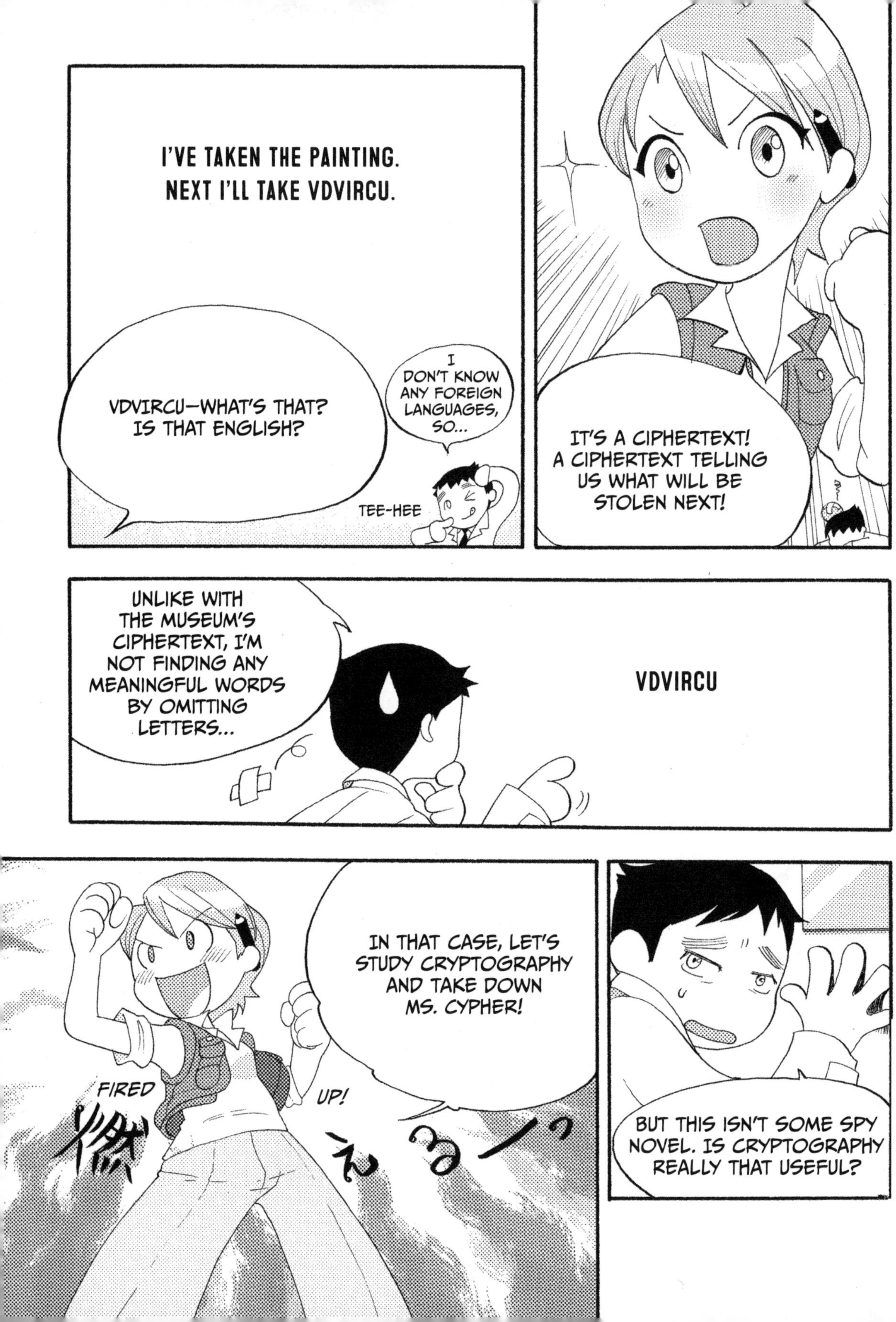
I'VE TAKEN THE PAINTING.
NEXT I'LL TAKE VDVIRCU.
VDVIRCU—WHAT'S THAT? IS THAT ENGLISH?
I DON'T KNOW ANY FOREIGN LANGUAGES, SO...
TEE-HEE
IT'S A CIPHERTEXT! A CIPHERTEXT TELLING US WHAT WILL BE STOLEN NEXT!
UNLIKE WITH THE MUSEUM'S CIPHERTEXT, I'M NOT FINDING ANY MEANINGFUL WORDS BY OMITTING LETTERS...
VDVIRCU
FIRED
UP!
燃えるーっ
IN THAT CASE, LET'S STUDY CRYPTOGRAPHY AND TAKE DOWN MS. CYPHER!
BUT THIS ISN'T SOME SPY NOVEL. IS CRYPTOGRAPHY REALLY THAT USEFUL?

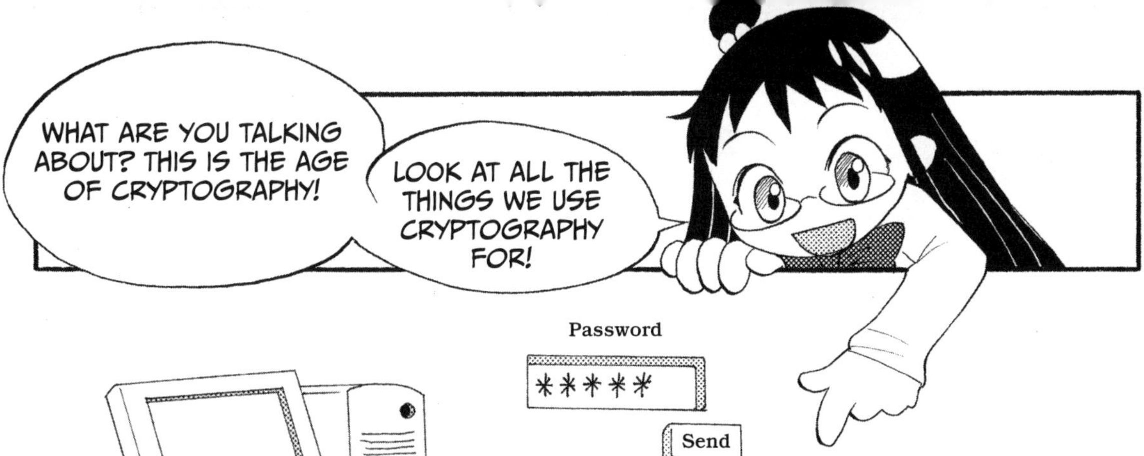
WHAT ARE YOU TALKING ABOUT? THIS IS THE AGE OF CRYPTOGRAPHY!
LOOK AT ALL THE THINGS WE USE CRYPTOGRAPHY FOR!

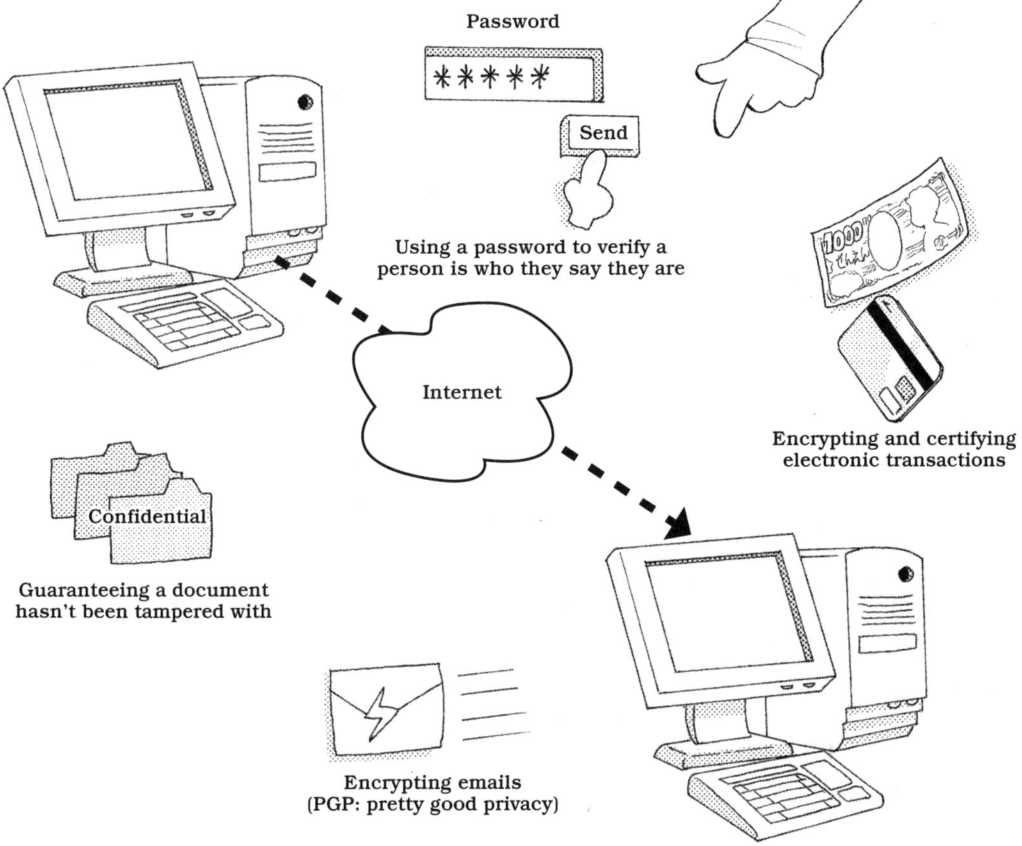
Password
*****
Send
Using a password to verify a person is who they say they are
Internet
Encrypting and certifying electronic transactions
Confidential
Guaranteeing a document hasn't been tampered with
Encrypting emails (PGP: pretty good privacy)

In the computer age, cryptography has become essential to protecting against the falsification, destruction, and interception of information.

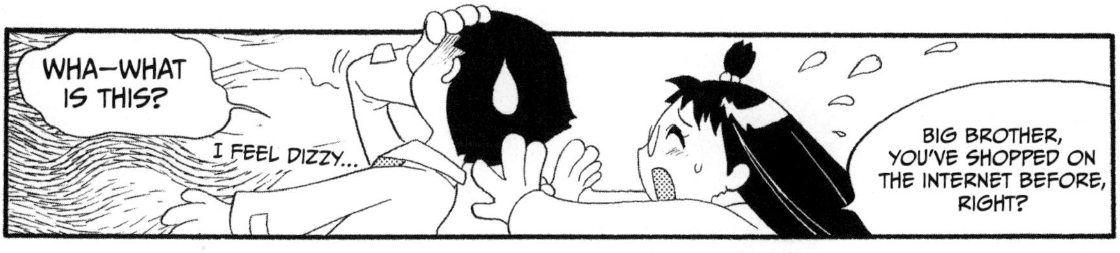
WHA-WHAT IS THIS?
I FEEL DIZZY...
BIG BROTHER, YOU'VE SHOPPED ON THE INTERNET BEFORE, RIGHT?

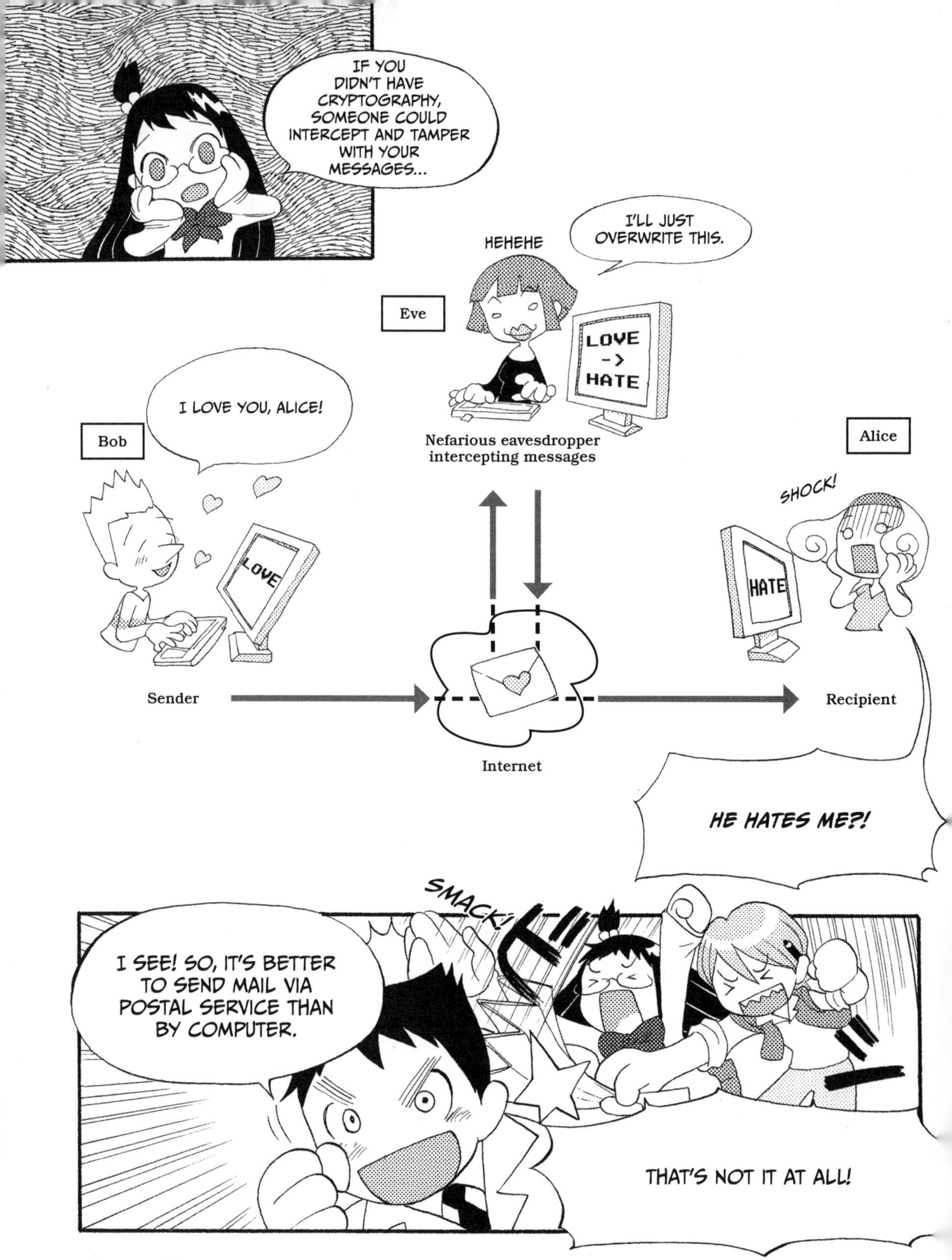
IF YOU DIDN'T HAVE CRYPTOGRAPHY, SOMEONE COULD INTERCEPT AND TAMPER WITH YOUR MESSAGES...
HEHEHE
I'LL JUST OVERWRITE THIS.
Eve
LOVE -> HATE
I LOVE YOU, ALICE!
Bob
LOVE
Nefarious eavesdropper intercepting messages
Alice
SHOCK!
HATE
Sender
Recipient
Internet
HE HATES ME?!
SMACK!
I SEE! SO, IT'S BETTER TO SEND MAIL VIA POSTAL SERVICE THAN BY COMPUTER.
THAT'S NOT IT AT ALL!

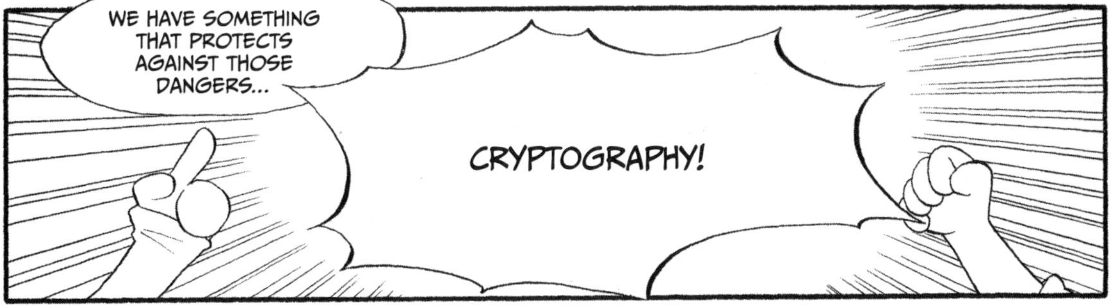
WE HAVE SOMETHING THAT PROTECTS AGAINST THOSE DANGERS...
CRYPTOGRAPHY!

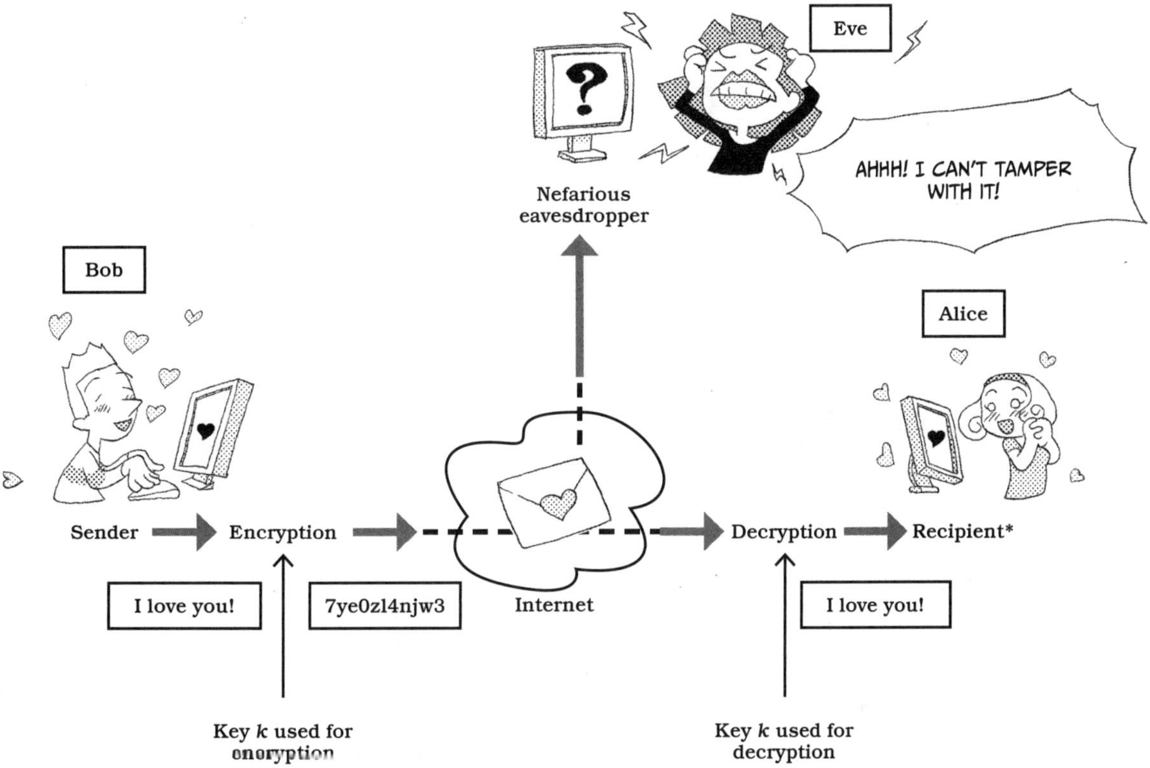
Eve
AHHH! I CAN'T TAMPER WITH IT!
Nefarious eavesdropper
Bob
Alice
Sender
Encryption
Internet
Decryption
Recipient*
I love you!
7ye0zl4njw3
I love you!
Key k used for encryption
Key k used for decryption

* The recipient doesn't have to be a person. It could instead be a hard disk, computer memory, or some other type of storage media.

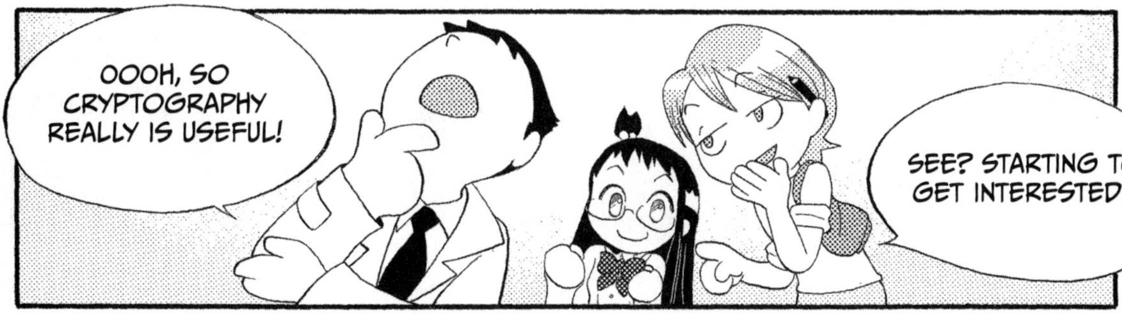
OOOH, SO CRYPTOGRAPHY REALLY IS USEFUL!
SEE? STARTING TO GET INTERESTED?

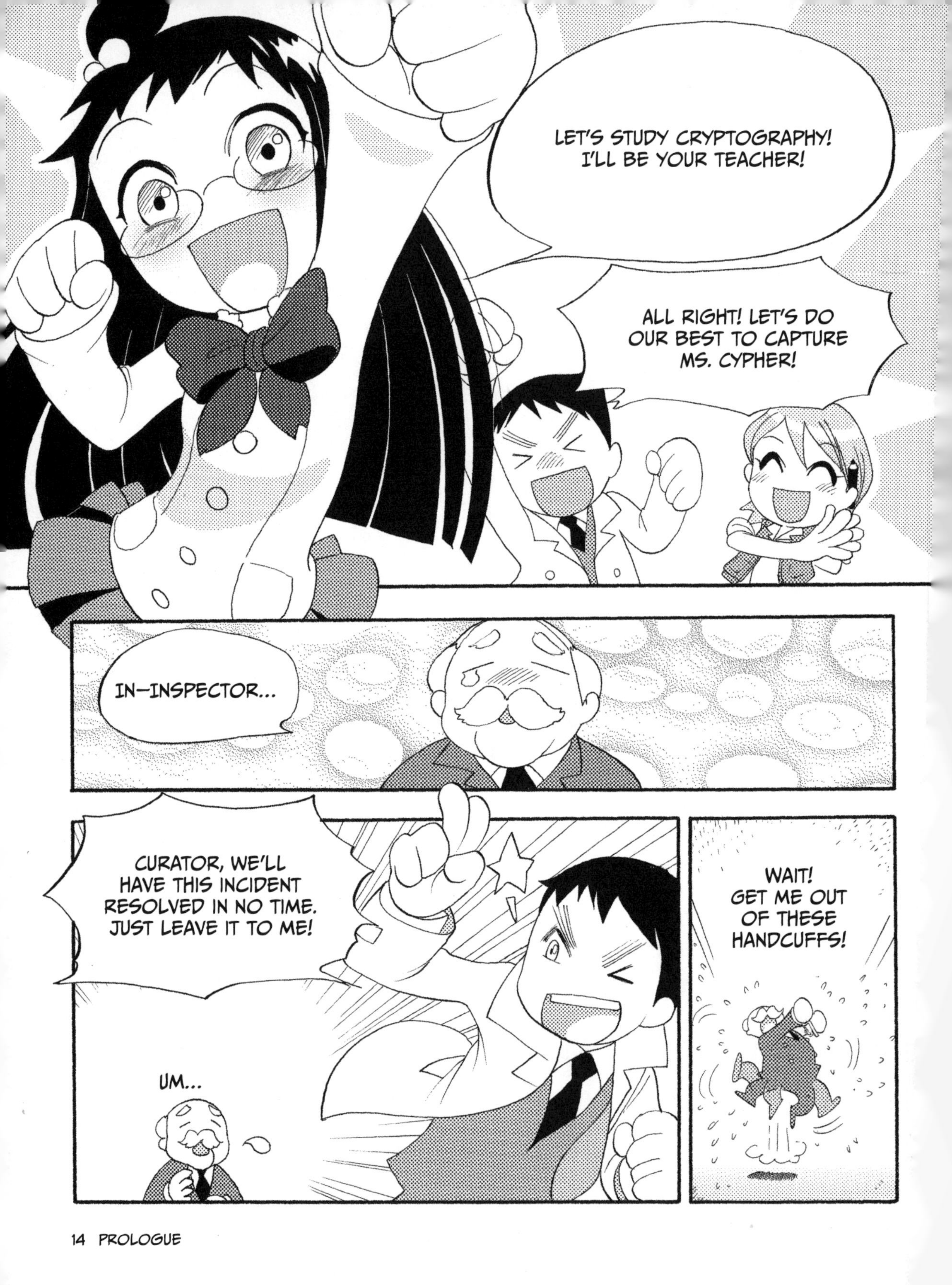
LET'S STUDY CRYPTOGRAPHY! I'LL BE YOUR TEACHER!
ALL RIGHT! LET'S DO OUR BEST TO CAPTURE MS. CYPHER!
IN—INSPECTOR...
CURATOR, WE'LL HAVE THIS INCIDENT RESOLVED IN NO TIME. JUST LEAVE IT TO ME!
UM...
WAIT! GET ME OUT OF THESE HANDCUFFS!

1

THE FOUNDATIONS OF ENCRYPTION

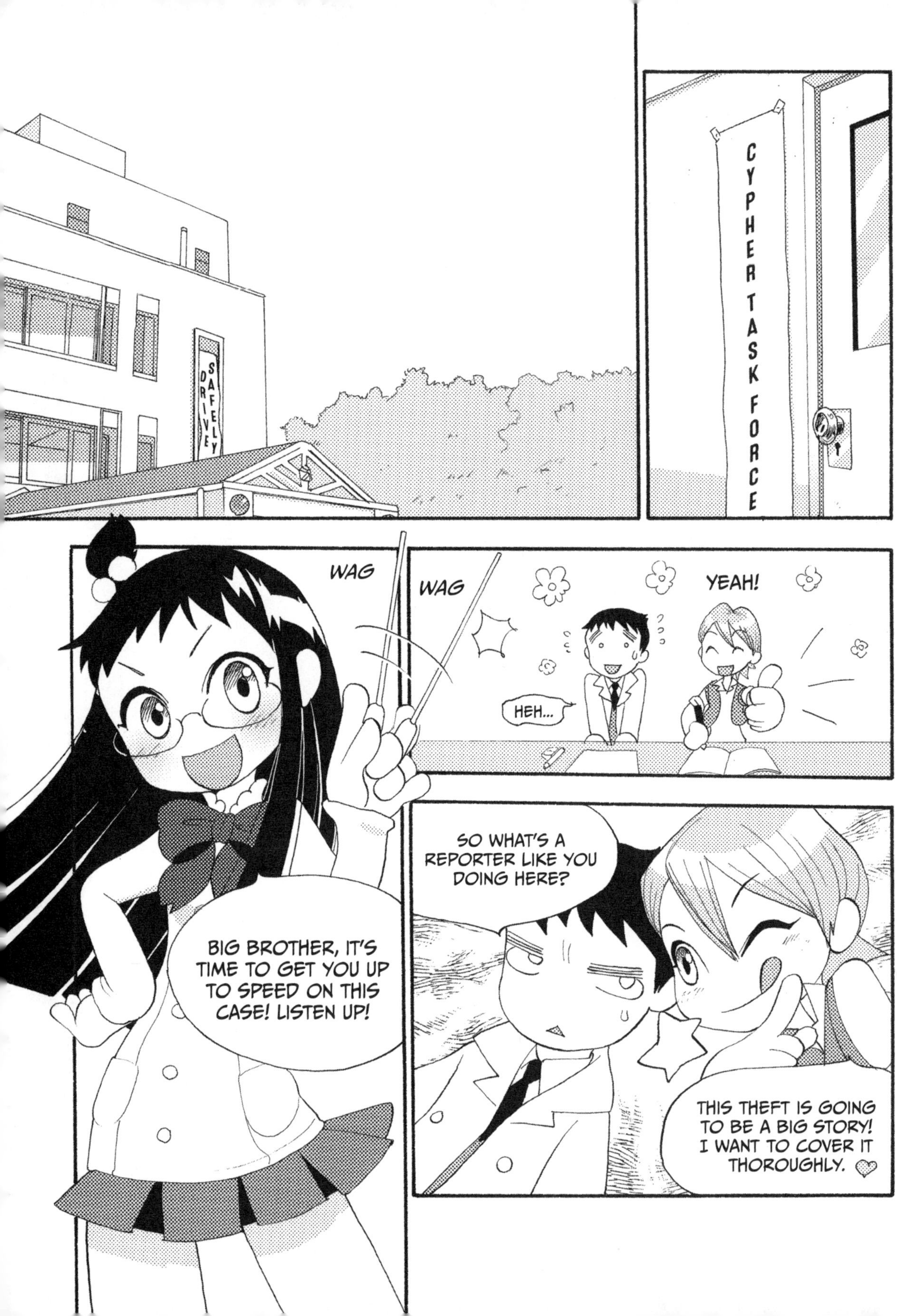
DRIVE SAFELY
CYPHER TASK FORCE
WAG
BIG BROTHER, IT'S TIME TO GET YOU UP TO SPEED ON THIS CASE! LISTEN UP!
WAG
YEAH!
HEH...
SO WHAT'S A REPORTER LIKE YOU DOING HERE?
THIS THEFT IS GOING TO BE A BIG STORY! I WANT TO COVER IT THOROUGHLY. ♡

WHAT IS A CIPHER?

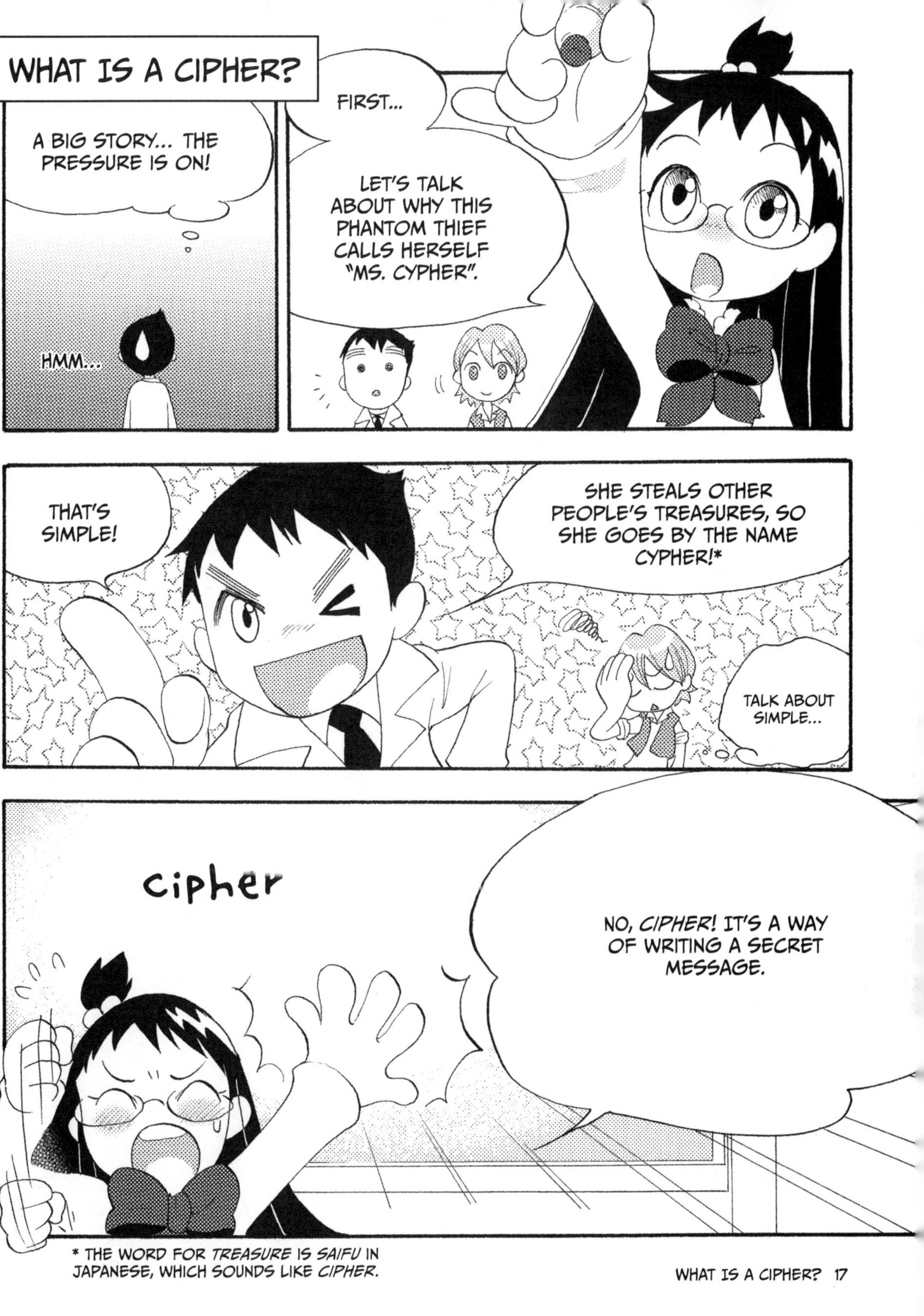
A BIG STORY... THE PRESSURE IS ON!
HMM...
FIRST...
LET'S TALK ABOUT WHY THIS PHANTOM THIEF CALLS HERSELF "MS. CYPHER".
THAT'S SIMPLE!
SHE STEALS OTHER PEOPLE'S TREASURES, SO SHE GOES BY THE NAME CYPHER!*
TALK ABOUT SIMPLE...
cipher
NO, *CIPHER*! IT'S A WAY OF WRITING A SECRET MESSAGE.

* THE WORD FOR *TREASURE* IS *SAIFU* IN JAPANESE, WHICH SOUNDS LIKE *CIPHER*.

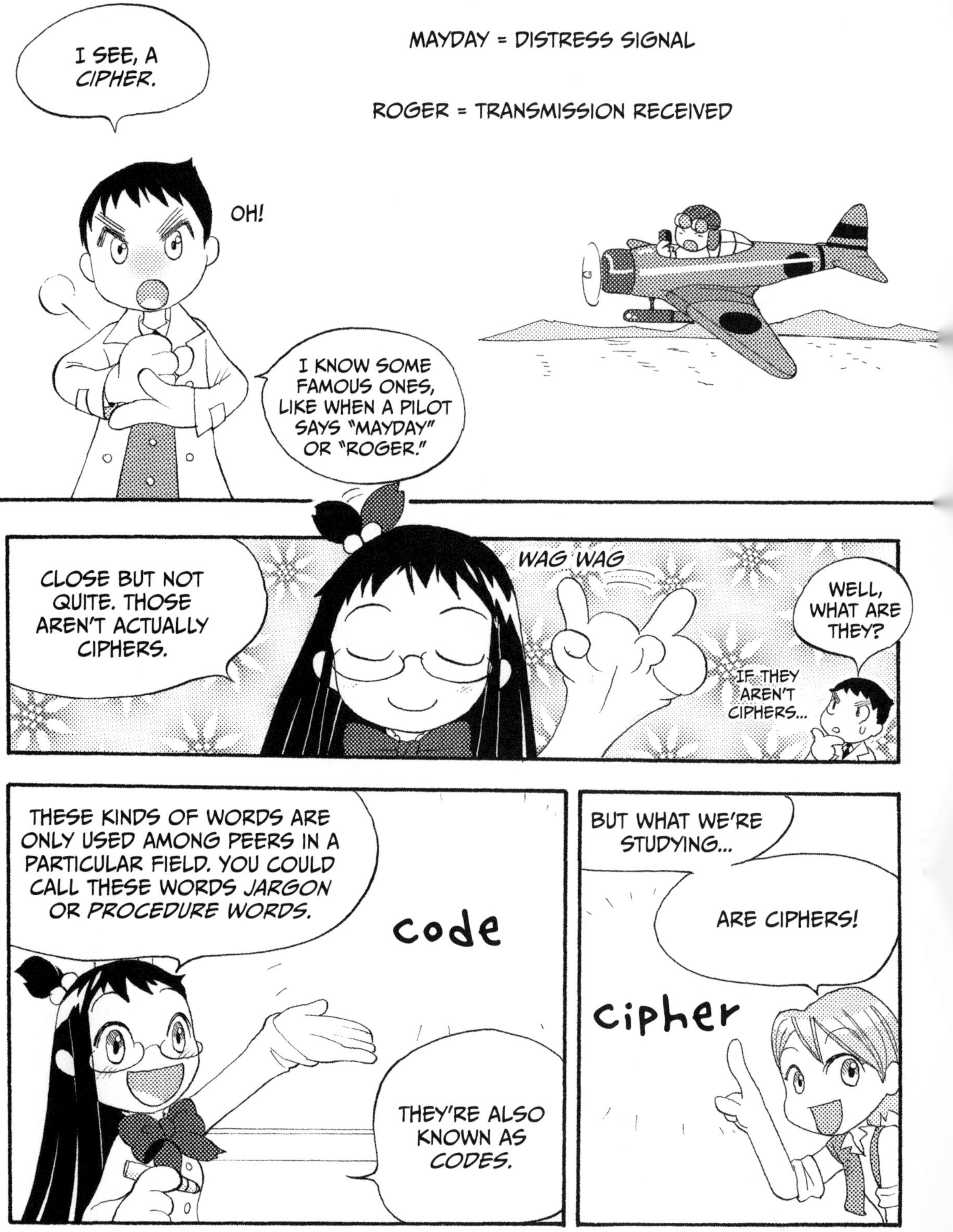
I SEE, A *CIPHER.*
OH!
I KNOW SOME FAMOUS ONES, LIKE WHEN A PILOT SAYS "MAYDAY" OR "ROGER."
MAYDAY = DISTRESS SIGNAL
ROGER = TRANSMISSION RECEIVED
CLOSE BUT NOT QUITE. THOSE AREN'T ACTUALLY CIPHERS.
WAG WAG
WELL, WHAT ARE THEY?
IF THEY AREN'T CIPHERS...
THESE KINDS OF WORDS ARE ONLY USED AMONG PEERS IN A PARTICULAR FIELD. YOU COULD CALL THESE WORDS *JARGON* OR *PROCEDURE WORDS.*
code
THEY'RE ALSO KNOWN AS *CODES.*
BUT WHAT WE'RE STUDYING...
ARE CIPHERS!
cipher

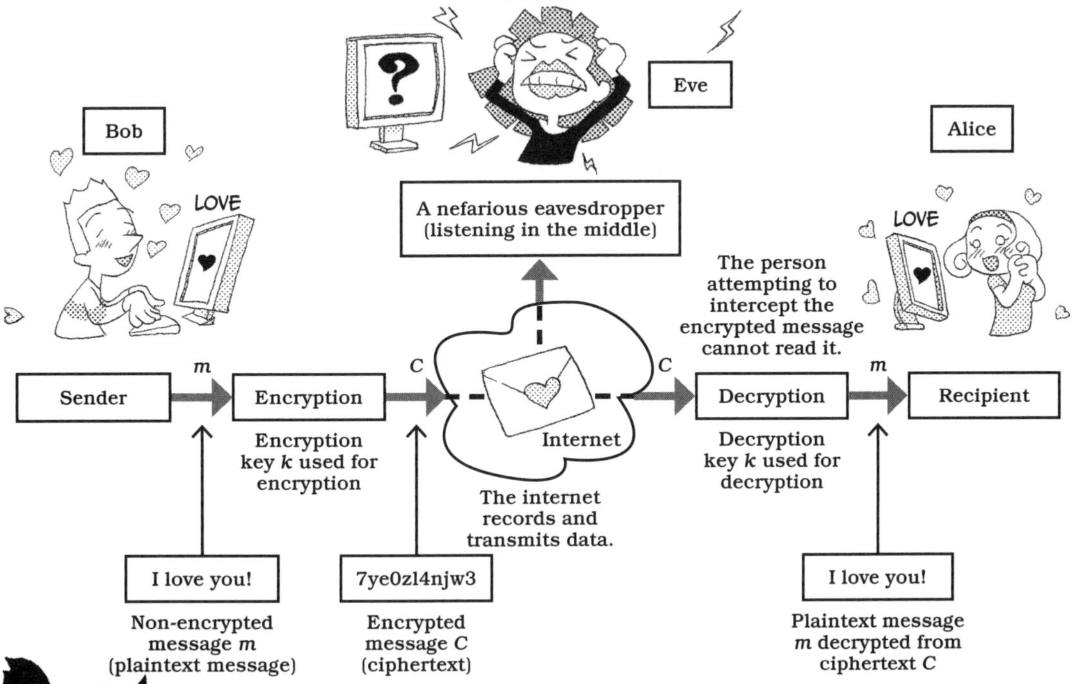
Eve
Bob
Alice
LOVE
A nefarious eavesdropper
(listening in the middle)
LOVE
The person attempting to intercept the encrypted message cannot read it.
Sender
m
Encryption
C
Internet
C
Decryption
m
Recipient
Encryption key k used for encryption
The internet records and transmits data.
Decryption key k used for decryption
I love you!
Non-encrypted message m (plaintext message)
7ye0zl4njw3
Encrypted message C (ciphertext)
I love you!
Plaintext message m decrypted from ciphertext C

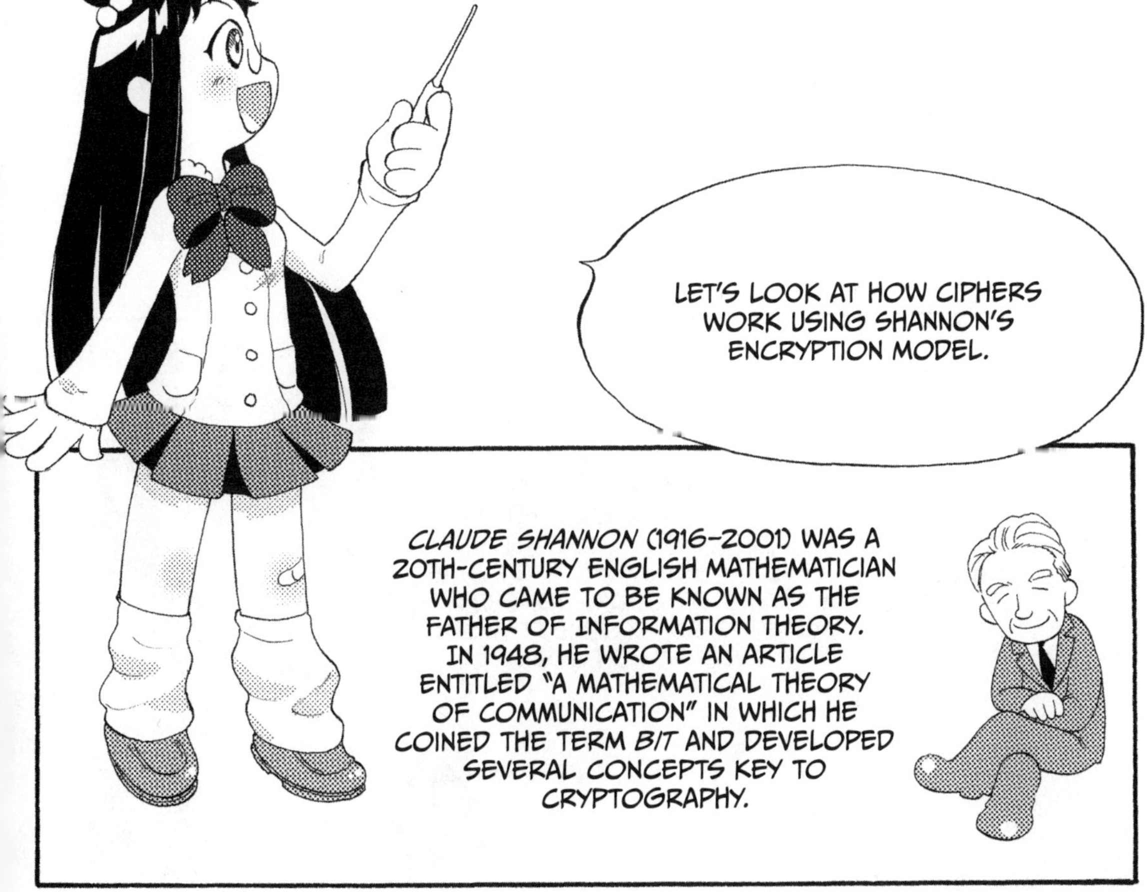
LET'S LOOK AT HOW CIPHERS WORK USING SHANNON'S ENCRYPTION MODEL.
CLAUDE SHANNON (1916–2001) WAS A 20TH-CENTURY ENGLISH MATHEMATICIAN WHO CAME TO BE KNOWN AS THE FATHER OF INFORMATION THEORY. IN 1948, HE WROTE AN ARTICLE ENTITLED "A MATHEMATICAL THEORY OF COMMUNICATION" IN WHICH HE COINED THE TERM *BIT* AND DEVELOPED SEVERAL CONCEPTS KEY TO CRYPTOGRAPHY.

SHANNON'S ENCRYPTION MODEL

Here's what the process looks like, broken down into steps.

You start with a *plaintext (m)*, which is just an unencrypted, normal message.

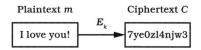

Plaintext m = | I love you!

You end up with *ciphertext (C)*, which is the encrypted message.

Ciphertext C = | 7ye0zl4njw3

Encryption is the process that transforms the plaintext to a ciphertext:

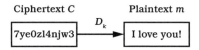

| Plaintext m | | Ciphertext C |
| I love you! | $\xrightarrow{E_k}$ | 7ye0zl4njw3 |

where E_k is encryption using an encryption key k.

Decryption is the process that restores the plaintext from a ciphertext:

| Ciphertext C | | Plaintext m |
| 7ye0zl4njw3 | $\xrightarrow{D_k}$ | I love you! |

where D_k is decryption using a decryption key k.

WHY DO YOU NEED A KEY TO MAKE A CIPHER?

WHICH ONE IS IT?

IT'S NOT AN ACTUAL KEY!

THE *ENCRYPTION KEY (K)* IS THE SECRET DATA (THE ENCRYPTION ALGORITHM) THAT THE CIPHER USES TO PROTECT THE PLAINTEXT. AN *ALGORITHM* IS A SERIES OF OPERATIONS THAT ACHIEVES SOME OBJECTIVE OR SOLVES SOME PROBLEM.

DATA

ENCRYPTION KEY K

HERE'S THE ENCRYPTION ALGORITHM AND ENCRYPTION KEY *K* FROM THE TANUKI CIPHER (SEE PAGE 6):
THE ENCRYPTION ALGORITHM ADDS EXTRA LETTERS TO THE PLAINTEXT.
IN THIS CASE, THE ENCRYPTION KEY *K* IS JUST ADDING THE LETTERS *TA*.

THAT'S RIGHT!
AND VICE VERSA, THE *DECRYPTION KEY* (*K*) IS A DECODING ALGORITHM THAT REVEALS THE PLAINTEXT. IN THE TANUKI CIPHER, DECRYPTION REMOVES THE EXTRA LETTERS—*TA*—FROM THE CIPHERTEXT!
KEY *K*
TA

THE RELATIONSHIP BETWEEN THE ENCRYPTION KEY AND THE DECRYPTION KEY

The sender encrypts their message. Using the sender's plaintext message m and encryption key k on the encryption algorithm results in ciphertext C.

Encryption key k
Plaintext m
Encryption
Ciphertext C

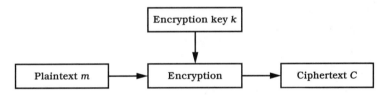

The recipient decodes the ciphertext. Ciphertext C is decrypted into plaintext m by using the ciphertext C and decryption key k on the decryption algorithm.

Decryption key k
Ciphertext C
Decryption
Plaintext m

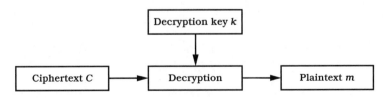

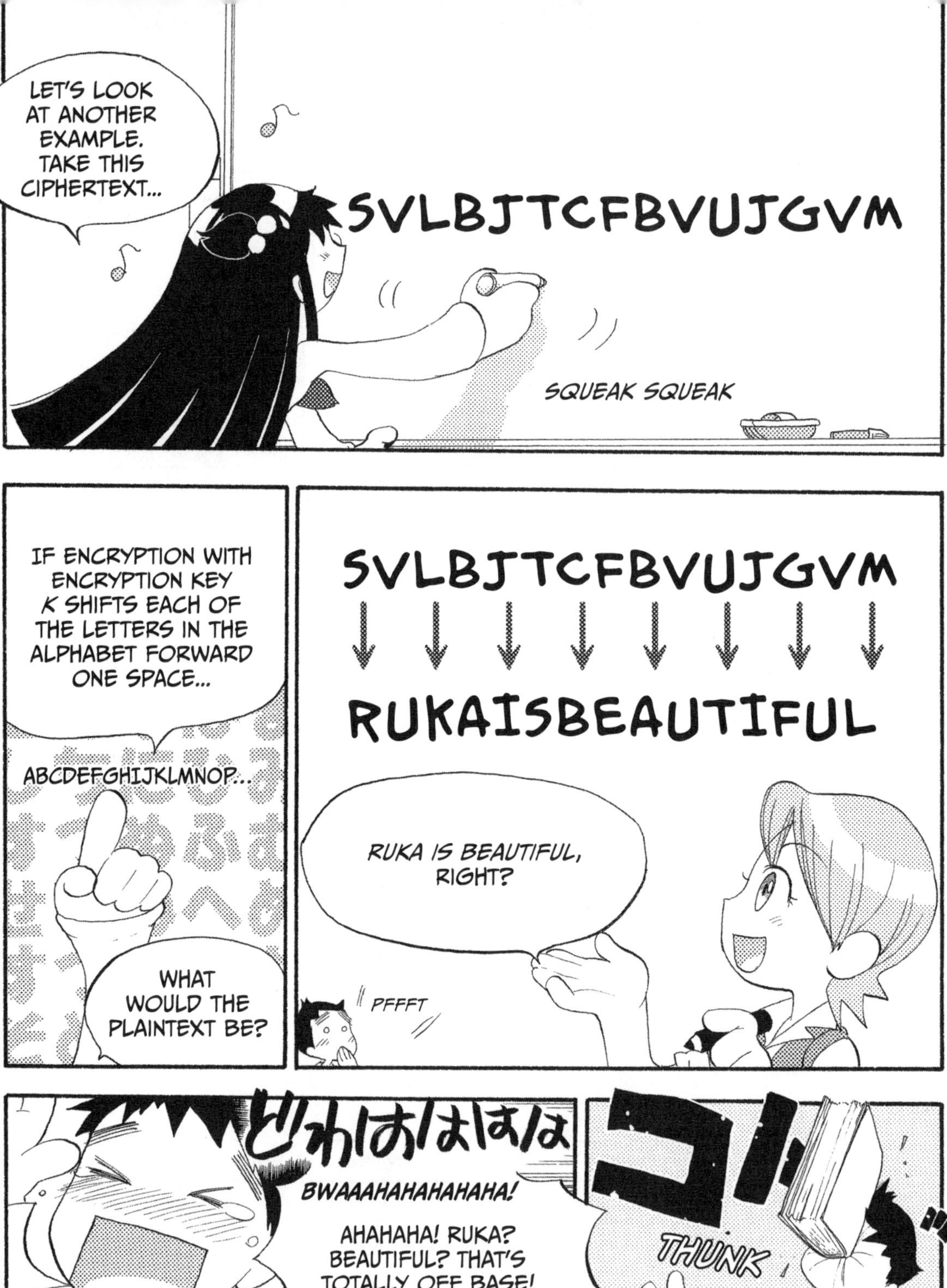
LET'S LOOK AT ANOTHER EXAMPLE. TAKE THIS CIPHERTEXT...
SVLBJTCFBVUJGVM
SQUEAK SQUEAK
IF ENCRYPTION WITH ENCRYPTION KEY K SHIFTS EACH OF THE LETTERS IN THE ALPHABET FORWARD ONE SPACE...
ABCDEFGHIJKLMNOP...
WHAT WOULD THE PLAINTEXT BE?
SVLBJTCFBVUJGVM
RUKAISBEAUTIFUL
RUKA IS BEAUTIFUL, RIGHT?
PFFFT
BWAAAHAHAHAHAHA!
AHAHAHA! RUKA? BEAUTIFUL? THAT'S TOTALLY OFF BASE!
THUNK

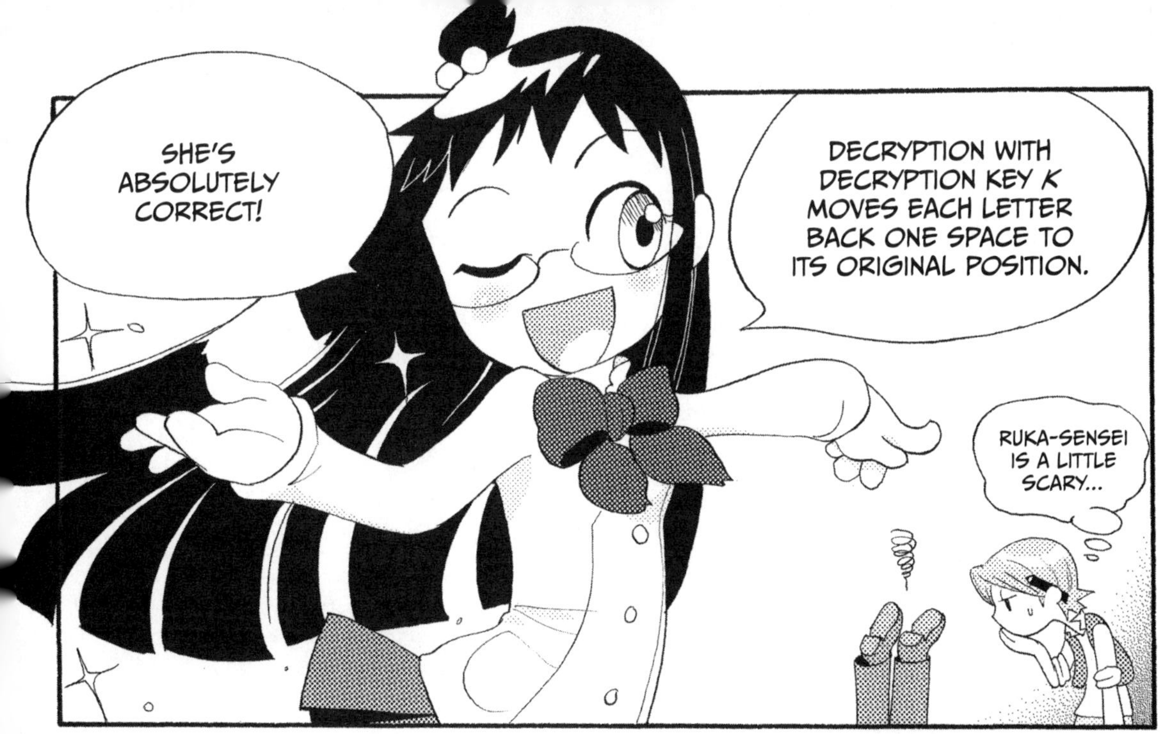
SHE'S ABSOLUTELY CORRECT!
DECRYPTION WITH DECRYPTION KEY K MOVES EACH LETTER BACK ONE SPACE TO ITS ORIGINAL POSITION.
RUKA-SENSEI IS A LITTLE SCARY...
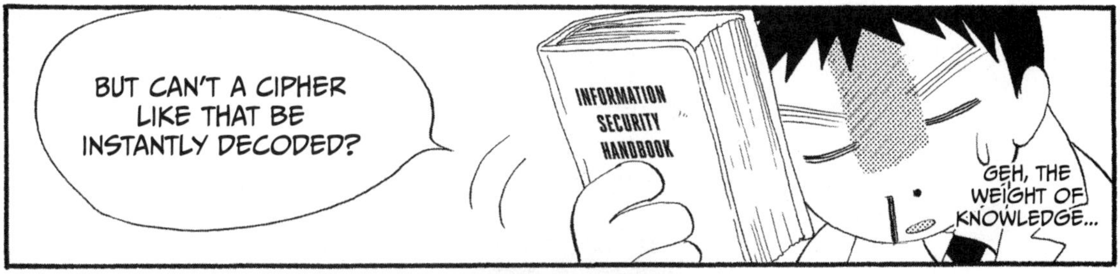
BUT CAN'T A CIPHER LIKE THAT BE INSTANTLY DECODED?
INFORMATION SECURITY HANDBOOK
GEH, THE WEIGHT OF KNOWLEDGE...
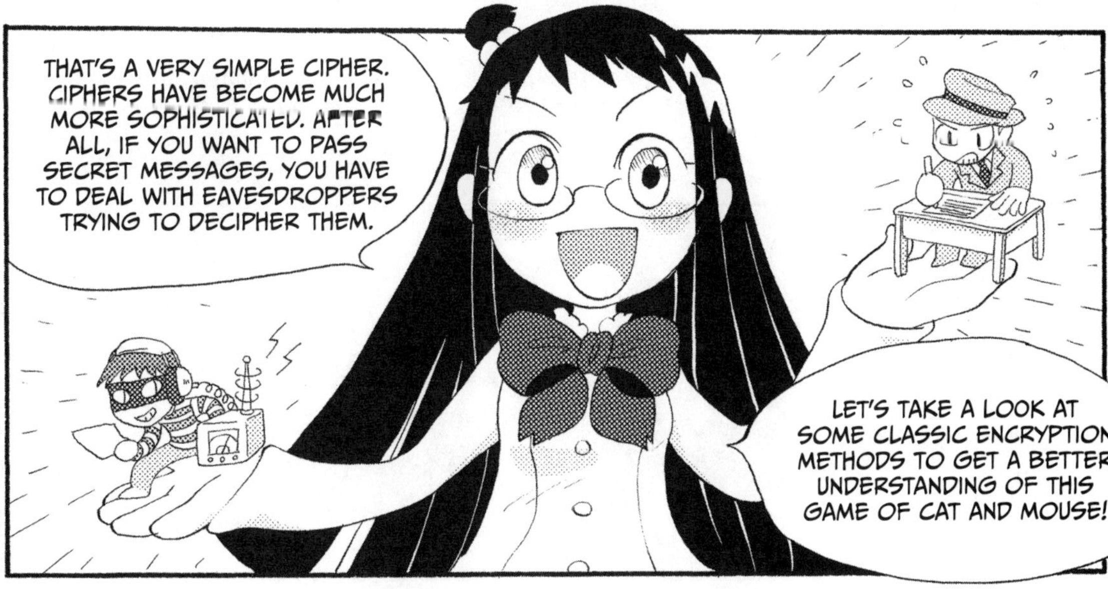
THAT'S A VERY SIMPLE CIPHER. CIPHERS HAVE BECOME MUCH MORE SOPHISTICATED. AFTER ALL, IF YOU WANT TO PASS SECRET MESSAGES, YOU HAVE TO DEAL WITH EAVESDROPPERS TRYING TO DECIPHER THEM.
LET'S TAKE A LOOK AT SOME CLASSIC ENCRYPTION METHODS TO GET A BETTER UNDERSTANDING OF THIS GAME OF CAT AND MOUSE!

CLASSIC ENCRYPTION METHODS

Although classic encryption methods are no longer used because they're not secure, they're still useful for learning how encryption works. Let's look at how some of these historical ciphers worked in practice.

CAESAR CIPHER

In the previous example, you saw the Caesar cipher in action. The *Caesar cipher* uses an algorithm that creates the ciphertext by shifting each letter of plaintext *n* letters. By way of example, let's try to encrypt the title of the Japanese fairytale *Momotaro*. If $n = 3$, we would move each letter forward by three.

. . . L [M] N O [P] Q R . . .

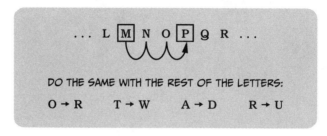

DO THE SAME WITH THE REST OF THE LETTERS:

O → R T → W A → D R → U

Once you've done this, a ciphertext is formed.

MOMOTARO Plaintext *m*

↓

PRPRWDUR Ciphertext *C*

Letters at the end of the alphabet just wrap around to the beginning.

X → A Y → B Z → C

This cipher is named after the Roman soldier and statesman Julius Caesar (Gaius Iulius, 100–44 BCE). Caesar used this cipher during the Gallic Wars to correspond with his allies unbeknownst to his rivals.

JULIUS CAESAR SAID, "THE DIE IS CAST!" WHEN HE CROSSED THE RUBICON.
WHAM
REALLY?!*

* IN JAPANESE, *DIE* SOUNDS THE SAME AS *RHINO*.

SUBSTITUTION CIPHER

It's pretty easy to decrypt a plain Caesar cipher, which is a type of *substitution cipher*. Substitution ciphers that replace one letter of the plaintext with another letter to make the ciphertext, as the Caesar cipher does, are called simple substitution ciphers.

Let's look at a *simple substitution cipher* to get a handle on it.

Assume that the 26 letters of the English alphabet have been converted as follows:

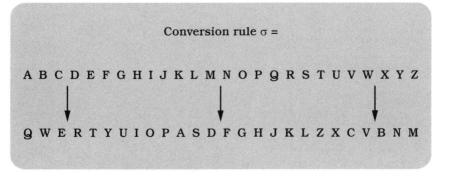

Conversion rule σ =

A B C D E F G H I J K L M N O P Q R S T U V W X Y Z

Q W E R T Y U I O P A S D F G H J K L Z X C V B N M

Thus, a cipher is formed as follows:

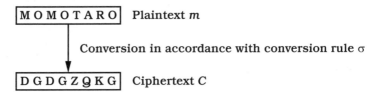

| M O M O T A R O | Plaintext *m*

Conversion in accordance with conversion rule σ

| D G D G Z Q K G | Ciphertext *C*

In this cipher, the conversion of letters is the algorithm, and the "letter-by-letter replacement method"—in other words, the conversion rule σ—is the encryption key *k*.

σ? HOW DO YOU SAY THAT?

THAT'S THE GREEK LETTER SIGMA.

POLYALPHABETIC CIPHER

A cipher that divides the plaintext into fixed-size blocks of *n* letters and varies the number of positions each letter shifts within each block is known as a *polyalphabetic cipher*. This makes a substitution cipher even sneakier.

Here we see conversion rule δ (delta) in action for a block of four letters (*n* = 4):

Conversion rule δ =

First letter ➤ Move by 2 letters

Second letter ➤ Move by 5 letters

Third letter ➤ Move by 3 letters

Fourth letter ➤ Move by 1 letter

The resulting cipher works like this:

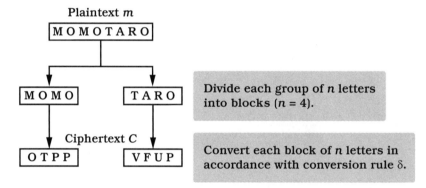

Plaintext *m*

| M O M O T A R O |

| M O M O | | T A R O |

Divide each group of *n* letters into blocks (*n* = 4).

Ciphertext *C*

| O T P P | | V F U P |

Convert each block of *n* letters in accordance with conversion rule δ.

The process to decrypt the ciphertext works the same way, just in reverse.

TRANSPOSITION CIPHER

A cipher that divides the plaintext into fixed-size blocks of *n* letters and then changes the sequence of the letters in each block is called a *transposition cipher*. For example, if *n* = 4, the substitution rule τ (tau) gives us the following:

$$\tau = \begin{pmatrix} 1234 \\ 2413 \end{pmatrix}$$

Here's what is going on in this transposition cipher:

> **Substitution rule τ =**
>
> First letter ▸ Becomes second letter
>
> Second letter ▸ Becomes fourth letter
>
> Third letter ▸ Becomes first letter
>
> Fourth letter ▸ Becomes third letter

Thus, the following cipher is born:

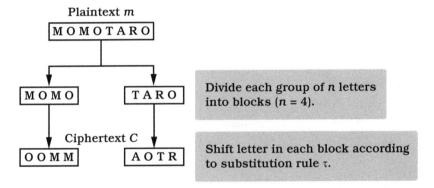

Plaintext *m*

MOMOTARO

MOMO   TARO

Divide each group of *n* letters into blocks (*n* = 4).

Ciphertext *C*

OOMM   AOTR

Shift letter in each block according to substitution rule τ.

In this cipher, the rearrangement of the letters makes up the algorithm, and the number of letters per block and the substitution rule τ are the encryption key.

δ IS THE GREEK LETTER DELTA, AND τ IS THE GREEK LETTER TAU.

I SEE.

CIPHER SECURITY

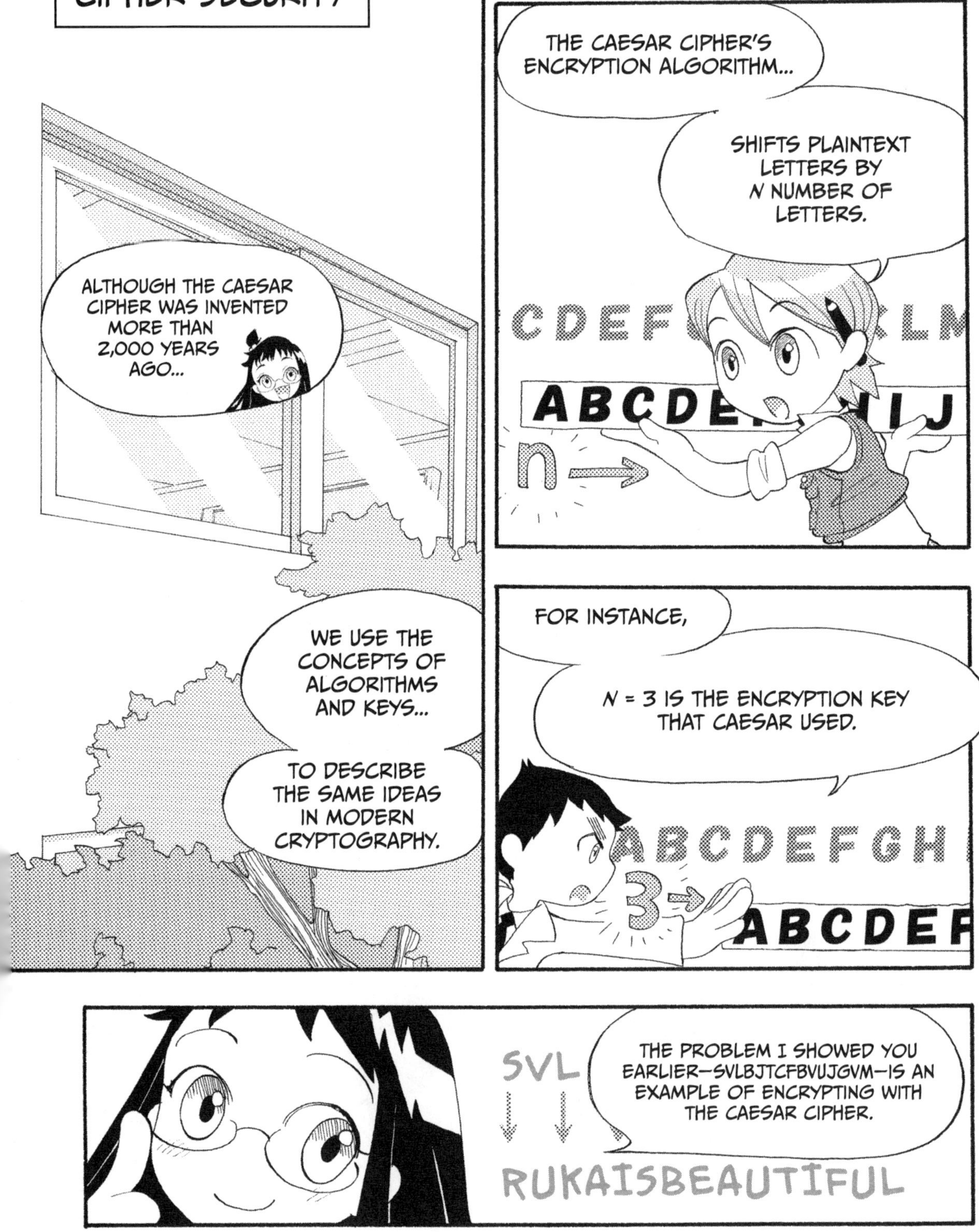
ALTHOUGH THE CAESAR CIPHER WAS INVENTED MORE THAN 2,000 YEARS AGO...
WE USE THE CONCEPTS OF ALGORITHMS AND KEYS...
TO DESCRIBE THE SAME IDEAS IN MODERN CRYPTOGRAPHY.
THE CAESAR CIPHER'S ENCRYPTION ALGORITHM...
SHIFTS PLAINTEXT LETTERS BY *N* NUMBER OF LETTERS.
CDEF
LM
ABCDE
IJ
n
FOR INSTANCE,
N = 3 IS THE ENCRYPTION KEY THAT CAESAR USED.
ABCDEFGH
3
ABCDEF
SVL
THE PROBLEM I SHOWED YOU EARLIER—SVLBJTCFBVUJGVM—IS AN EXAMPLE OF ENCRYPTING WITH THE CAESAR CIPHER.
RUKAISBEAUTIFUL

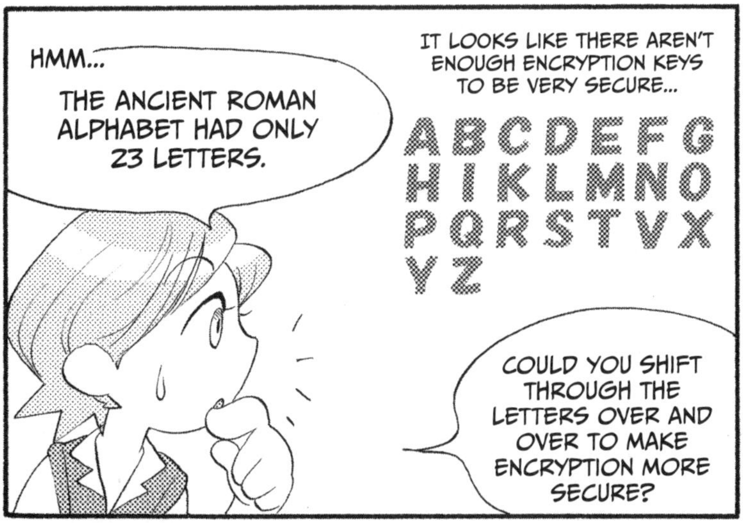
HMM...
THE ANCIENT ROMAN ALPHABET HAD ONLY 23 LETTERS.
IT LOOKS LIKE THERE AREN'T ENOUGH ENCRYPTION KEYS TO BE VERY SECURE...
A B C D E F G H I K L M N O P Q R S T V X Y Z
COULD YOU SHIFT THROUGH THE LETTERS OVER AND OVER TO MAKE ENCRYPTION MORE SECURE?

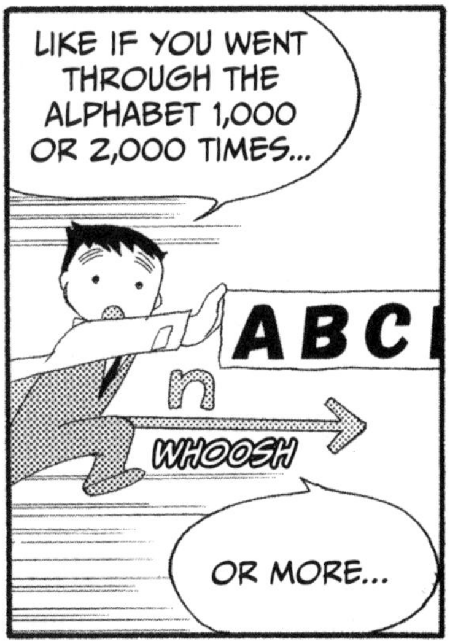
LIKE IF YOU WENT THROUGH THE ALPHABET 1,000 OR 2,000 TIMES...
ABC
n
WHOOSH
OR MORE...

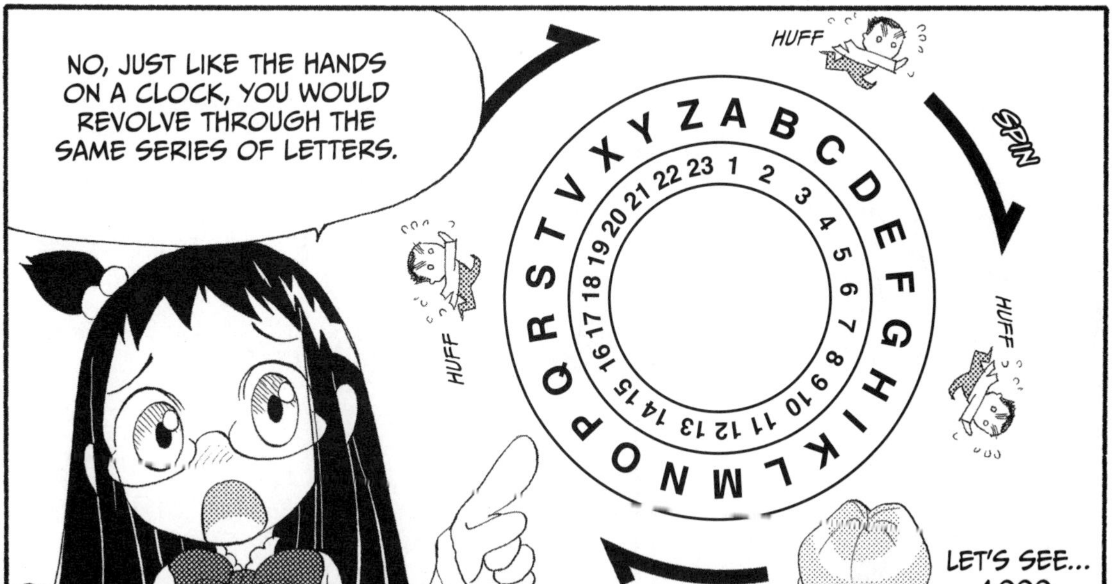
NO, JUST LIKE THE HANDS ON A CLOCK, YOU WOULD REVOLVE THROUGH THE SAME SERIES OF LETTERS.
HUFF
SPIN
Z A B C D E F G H I K L M N O P Q R S T V X Y
1 2 3 4 5 6 7 8 9 10 11 12 13 14 15 16 17 18 19 20 21 22 23
HUFF
HUFF
SPIN
LET'S SEE... 1,000, 2,000...

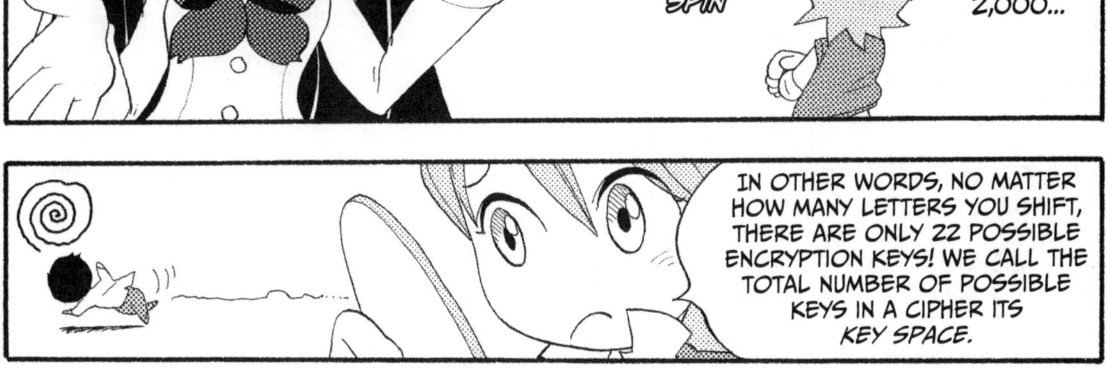
IN OTHER WORDS, NO MATTER HOW MANY LETTERS YOU SHIFT, THERE ARE ONLY 22 POSSIBLE ENCRYPTION KEYS! WE CALL THE TOTAL NUMBER OF POSSIBLE KEYS IN A CIPHER ITS *KEY SPACE*.

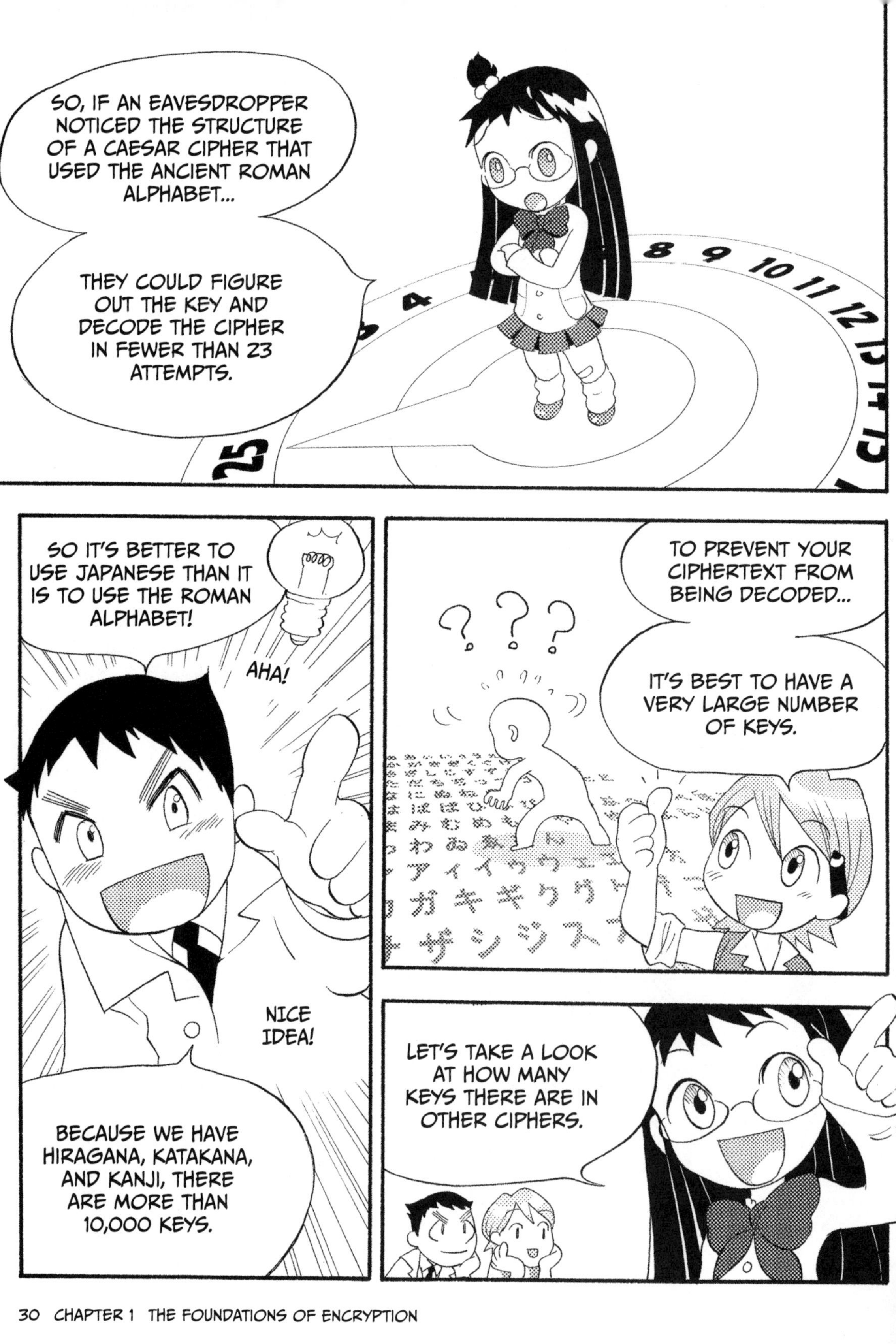
SO, IF AN EAVESDROPPER NOTICED THE STRUCTURE OF A CAESAR CIPHER THAT USED THE ANCIENT ROMAN ALPHABET...
THEY COULD FIGURE OUT THE KEY AND DECODE THE CIPHER IN FEWER THAN 23 ATTEMPTS.
SO IT'S BETTER TO USE JAPANESE THAN IT IS TO USE THE ROMAN ALPHABET!
AHA!
NICE IDEA!
BECAUSE WE HAVE HIRAGANA, KATAKANA, AND KANJI, THERE ARE MORE THAN 10,000 KEYS.
TO PREVENT YOUR CIPHERTEXT FROM BEING DECODED...
IT'S BEST TO HAVE A VERY LARGE NUMBER OF KEYS.
LET'S TAKE A LOOK AT HOW MANY KEYS THERE ARE IN OTHER CIPHERS.

THE SUBSTITUTION CIPHER'S KEY SPACE

Let's think more about how many potential keys there might be for substitution ciphers and how easy such a cipher would be to break. You saw that a Caesar cipher using the ancient Roman alphabet had only 22 possible keys (a *key space* of 22), so breaking it wouldn't be too hard. The key space of the Caesar cipher is limited because it depends on shifting the alphabet to determine the plaintext letter's ciphertext substitution. In Caesar's version of the Caesar cipher, the substitution letters are simply the alphabet shifted by three positions, but you could take a different approach by scrambling the positions of the letters entirely.

Instead of shifting the letters to determine letter substitutions, you could substitute each letter of the alphabet with any other letter as long as each plaintext letter corresponds with one unique substitution. Your plaintext letters would be the alphabet in order:

ABCDEFGHIJKLMNOPQRSTUVWXYZ

Then one example of a substitution with a scrambled alphabet could be written out like this:

QWERTYUIOPASDFGHJKLZXCVBNM

Each letter of the alphabet would be substituted with a corresponding letter in the scrambled version of the alphabet. You can simply substitute according to the position of the letters in the alphabet, so *A* would be substituted as *Q*, *B* as *W*, and so on. The scrambled alphabet would be the cipher's key.

If we used our modern alphabet with 26 letters, we would have a large number of ways to potentially arrange those letters for a key:

$$_{26}P_{26} = 26! = 26 \times 25 \times 24 \times \ldots \times 3 \times 2 \times 1 \approx 4.03291461 \times 10^{26}$$

The letter *P* is used to represent a *permutation*, which is a unique arrangement of letters in a sequence. The subscript number before the *P* means that there are 26 total characters, and the subscript number after the *P* means we are using all 26 of them. The exclamation mark means *factorial*, or the product of the integer and all the positive integers less than it. This formula makes sense if you think about it this way:

- The first letter could be assigned any of the 26 letters, so there are 26 to choose from.

- The second letter could be any of the remaining 25 letters, so there are 25 to choose from. For two letters, there are 26 × 25 possibilities.

- The third letter could be any of the remaining 24 letters.

  And so on until . . .

- The last letter will be whichever letter remains—there is one option for the last letter.

Given $4.03291461 \times 10^{26}$ possible permutations of letters, if a computer were asked to generate all these arrangements until it found the correct key to break the cipher, then, even if it were to perform an exhaustive search at a rate of 100,000,000 keys per second, it could take a preposterous period of up to 128,000,000,000 years.

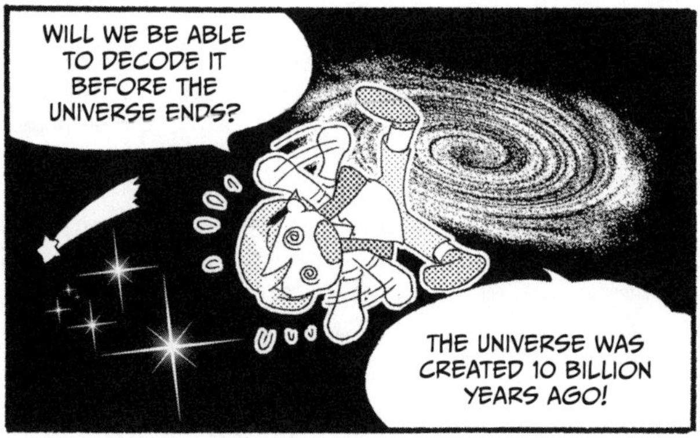
WILL WE BE ABLE TO DECODE IT BEFORE THE UNIVERSE ENDS?
THE UNIVERSE WAS CREATED 10 BILLION YEARS AGO!

PERMUTATION, COMBINATION, AND FREQUENCY ANALYSIS

Let's look at permutations in more detail. A *permutation*, expressed as P, is a method of selecting r things from n possibilities and putting them into unique arrangements. By unique arrangements, we mean that, for instance, ABCDE is not the same as EDCBA. Those are considered two different arrangements.

If we selected 5 letters out of the 26 letters of the alphabet, r would be 5 and n would be 26. Then we would use this formula to find the number of arrangements of 5 letters selected from 26:

$${}_nP_r = n \times (n-1) \times (n-2) \times \ldots \times (n-r+1) = \frac{n!}{(n-r)!}$$

Thus,

$${}_{26}P_5 = \frac{26!}{(26-5)!} = \frac{26!}{21!}$$

Because all the factors in 21! are in 26!, you can cancel out the numbers up to and including 21:

$$\frac{26!}{21!} = 26 \times 25 \times 24 \times 23 \times 22 = 7,893,000$$

In contrast, if r things are selected from n possibilities and order does not matter, this is called *combination* and is expressed as C in the combination formula:

$$_{n}C_{r} = \frac{_{n}P_{r}}{r!} = \frac{n!}{(n-r)! \times r!}$$

If we're still selecting 5 letters out of 26 possible letters, we would get this:

$$\frac{26!}{(21! \times 5!)}$$

The factors would cancel like in the permutation example, which would leave you with this:

$$\frac{(26 \times 25 \times 24 \times 23 \times 22)}{(1 \times 2 \times 3 \times 4 \times 5)} = 65,780$$

Because order does not matter, the arrangements ABCDE and EDCBA would be considered the same, meaning that there are fewer possible arrangements when using combinations rather than permutations.

Searching for the correct key within the large space of $4.03291461 \times 10^{26}$ permutations is theoretically possible, but in practical terms, it's a *computationally infeasible problem*. That said, these types of ciphers are susceptible to a cryptographic attack known as *frequency analysis*, which assumes that the frequency of letters that appear in the plaintext and the frequency of letters that appear in the ciphertext are consistent.

For example, the letter *E* is the most common letter in English. That means if *Z* is the most common letter in the encrypted text, you can reasonably assume that the corresponding letter in the plaintext is *E*. Frequency analysis attacks are one of the most effective attacks on simple substitution ciphers.

THE POLYALPHABETIC CIPHER'S KEY SPACE

Let's assume that a given block is n characters long. Because we don't know how many spaces the first letter has been shifted, we make 26 attempts to figure it out. Each letter shift in the block is independent from the other shifts, so the second letter could also take 26 attempts, same with the third letter, and so on, until we arrive at the nth letter.

Using what we just learned about permutations, combinations, and frequency analysis, r would be block size n, and the possible correct values for n would be the 26 letters of the alphabet and would apply to each letter. Because of this, the total number of keys is as follows:

$$26 \times 26 \times ... \times 26 \times 26 = 26^{n}$$

If $n = 4$, then the key space would be the following:

$$26^4 = 26 \times 26 \times 26 \times 26 = 456{,}976$$

As n grows larger, the number of keys rapidly increases. When $n = 10$, the number of possible keys surpasses 140 trillion.

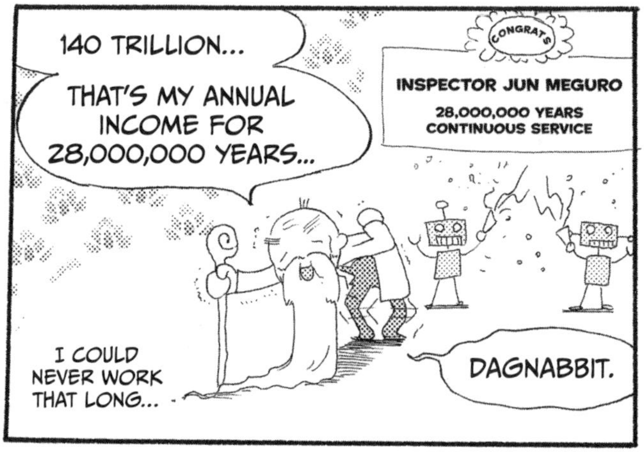
140 TRILLION...
THAT'S MY ANNUAL INCOME FOR 28,000,000 YEARS...
CONGRATS
INSPECTOR JUN MEGURO
28,000,000 YEARS CONTINUOUS SERVICE
I COULD NEVER WORK THAT LONG...
DAGNABBIT.

THE TRANSPOSITION CIPHER'S KEY SPACE

The total number of keys for a block of n characters is expressed as follows:

$${}_nP_n = n \times (n-1) \times (n-2) \times \ldots \times 3 \times 2 \times 1 = n!$$

So when there are four letters in one block ($n = 4$), the total number of keys k is as follows:

$$4! = 4 \times 3 \times 2 \times 1 = 24$$

As with other ciphers, the key space increases as n becomes larger, and the security of the encryption becomes stronger. Note that $n = 26$ would give the same key space as the substitution cipher.

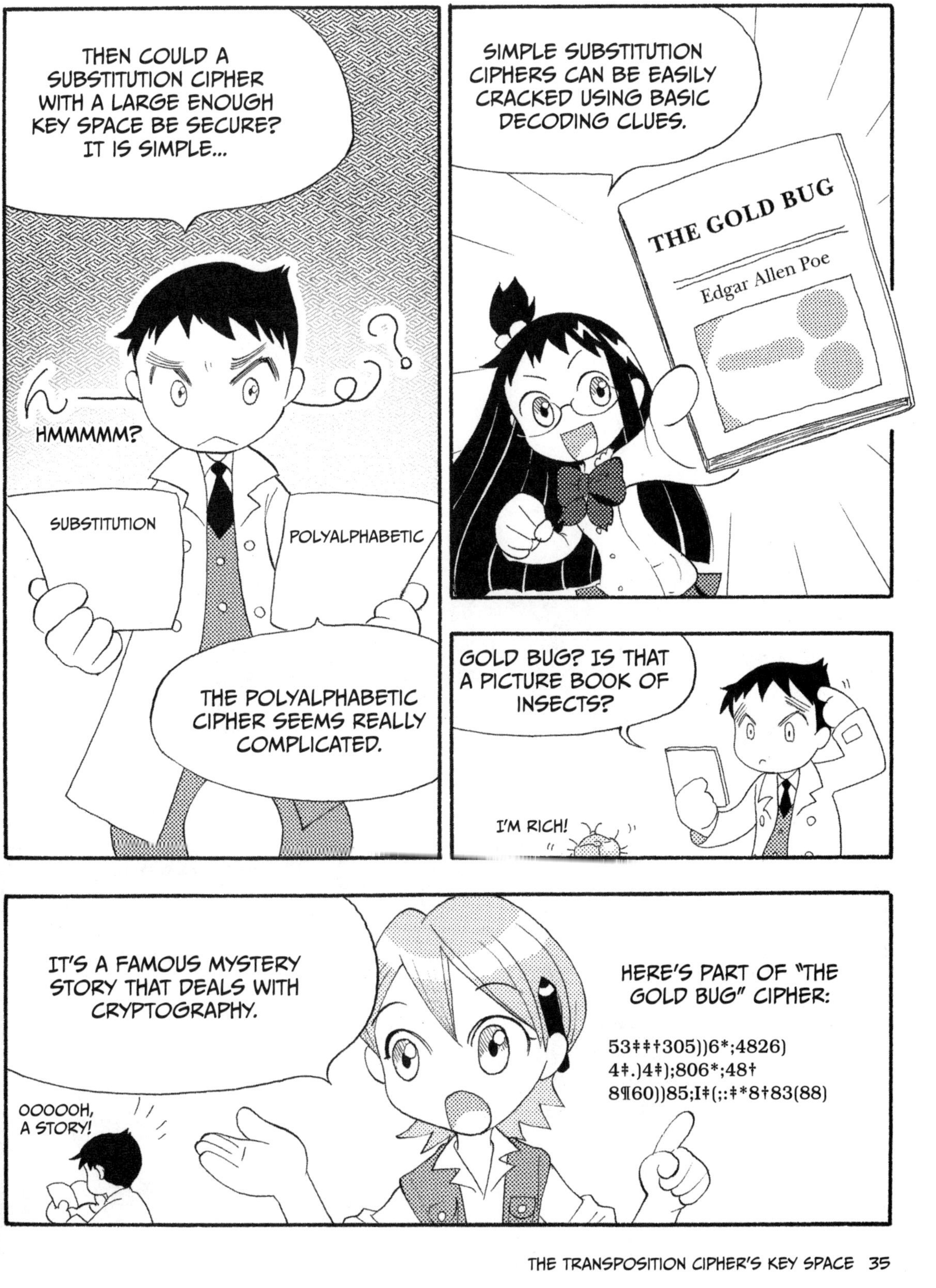
THEN COULD A SUBSTITUTION CIPHER WITH A LARGE ENOUGH KEY SPACE BE SECURE? IT IS SIMPLE...
HMMMMM?
SUBSTITUTION
POLYALPHABETIC
THE POLYALPHABETIC CIPHER SEEMS REALLY COMPLICATED.
SIMPLE SUBSTITUTION CIPHERS CAN BE EASILY CRACKED USING BASIC DECODING CLUES.
THE GOLD BUG
Edgar Allen Poe
GOLD BUG? IS THAT A PICTURE BOOK OF INSECTS?
I'M RICH!
IT'S A FAMOUS MYSTERY STORY THAT DEALS WITH CRYPTOGRAPHY.
OOOOOH, A STORY!
HERE'S PART OF "THE GOLD BUG" CIPHER:
53‡‡†305))6*;4826)
4‡.)4‡);806*;48†
8¶60))85;1‡(;:‡*8†83(88)

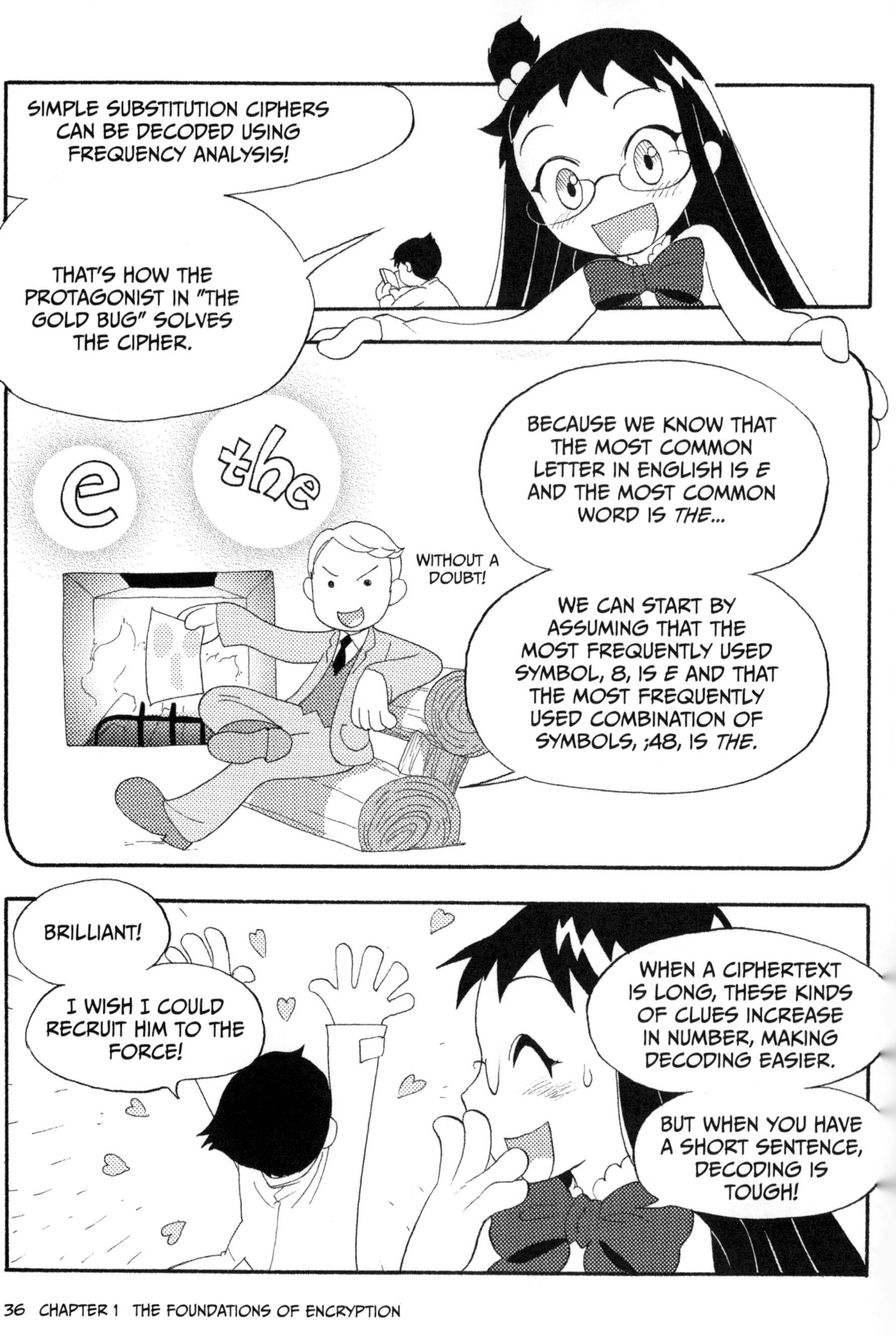
SIMPLE SUBSTITUTION CIPHERS CAN BE DECODED USING FREQUENCY ANALYSIS!
THAT'S HOW THE PROTAGONIST IN "THE GOLD BUG" SOLVES THE CIPHER.
e
the
WITHOUT A DOUBT!
BECAUSE WE KNOW THAT THE MOST COMMON LETTER IN ENGLISH IS *E* AND THE MOST COMMON WORD IS *THE*...
WE CAN START BY ASSUMING THAT THE MOST FREQUENTLY USED SYMBOL, 8, IS *E* AND THAT THE MOST FREQUENTLY USED COMBINATION OF SYMBOLS, ;48, IS *THE*.
BRILLIANT!
I WISH I COULD RECRUIT HIM TO THE FORCE!
WHEN A CIPHERTEXT IS LONG, THESE KINDS OF CLUES INCREASE IN NUMBER, MAKING DECODING EASIER.
BUT WHEN YOU HAVE A SHORT SENTENCE, DECODING IS TOUGH!

AH!
BUT IF THIS GUY WEREN'T RECRUITED BY A COP, BUT INSTEAD BY BAD GUYS...
THE GOLD BUG
IS THERE A SECURE CIPHER THAT EVEN THE PROTAGONIST OF "THE GOLD BUG" ABSOLUTELY COULDN'T DECODE?
UMM...
THERE IS!
STOP PANICKING AND I'LL TELL YOU!

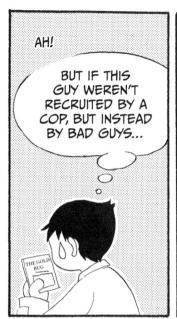

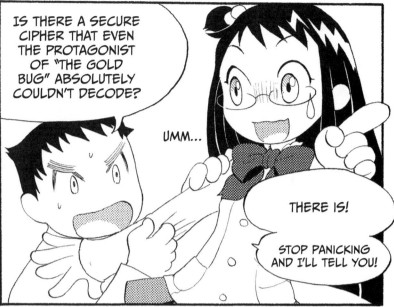

WHEN BREAKING CLASSICAL ENCRYPTION IS POSSIBLE

Typically, breaking classical encryption is possible under these conditions:

1. When you understand the encryption algorithm
2. When there is data about the statistical properties of the encrypted plaintext; for example, the frequency with which a letter or word appears
3. When you have a large number of encrypted example sentences

PERFECTLY SECURE ENCRYPTION

By generating a random number to use as a one-time pad—a key that is as long as the plaintext, is used once, and is then discarded—you can produce a cipher that is computationally secure. More specifically, you would be generating a ciphertext by applying a string of random numbers to plaintext *m* that is the same length as the plaintext. This ciphertext cannot be decrypted without knowledge of the key. Unfortunately, a one-time pad is not practical because it is difficult to distribute the one-time pad to all the communicating parties ahead of time.

Gilbert Vernam devised a cipher that uses a one-time pad, the Vernam cipher, in 1917 and patented it a couple of years later. During World War II, Claude Shannon (see page 19) established that this cipher is unbreakable and in 1949 publicly published his mathematical proof.

Here is a simple example of a Vernam cipher. You start by converting the alphabet to numerical values in a process known as *character encoding*:

A	B	C	D	E	F	G	H	I	J	K	L	M
0	1	2	3	4	5	6	7	8	9	10	11	12

N	O	P	Q	R	S	T	U	V	W	X	Y	Z
13	14	15	16	17	18	19	20	21	22	23	24	25

1. Convert each letter to a numerical value (e.g., A becomes 0).

Plaintext

M	O	M	O	T	A	R	O
↓	↓	↓	↓	↓	↓	↓	↓
12	14	12	14	19	0	17	14

2. Add each number in the sequence to the corresponding one-time use number.

Random number sequence (encryption key)

12	14	12	14	19	0	17	14
+	+	+	+	+	+	+	+
9	20	15	23	27	2	15	8
=	=	=	=	=	=	=	=
21	34	27	37	46	2	32	22

3. Calculate the remainder when each number is divided by 26.

21	34	27	37	46	2	32	22
÷	÷	÷	÷	÷	÷	÷	÷
26	26	26	26	26	26	26	26
=	=	=	=	=	=	=	=
21	8	1	11	20	2	6	22

4. Convert the numbers to letters using the character encoding.

21	8	1	11	20	2	6	22
↓	↓	↓	↓	↓	↓	↓	↓
V	I	B	L	U	C	G	W

Ciphertext

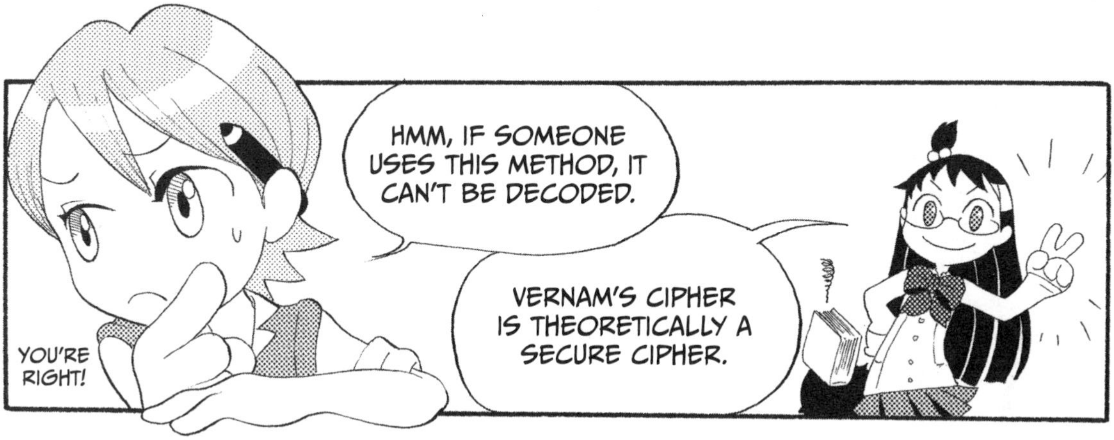
HMM, IF SOMEONE USES THIS METHOD, IT CAN'T BE DECODED.
VERNAM'S CIPHER IS THEORETICALLY A SECURE CIPHER.
YOU'RE RIGHT!

SECURE CIPHERS

1. Fail-safe ciphers

   A fail-safe cipher like Vernam's cipher is theoretically unbreakable.

2. Computationally secure ciphers

   Although computationally secure ciphers can be decoded, doing so is computationally infeasible because it's so time and labor intensive that it isn't worth trying. These ciphers are what we use today.

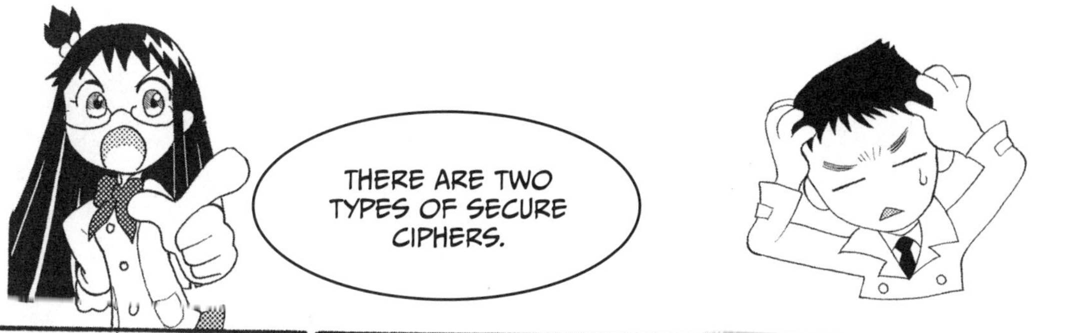
THERE ARE TWO TYPES OF SECURE CIPHERS.

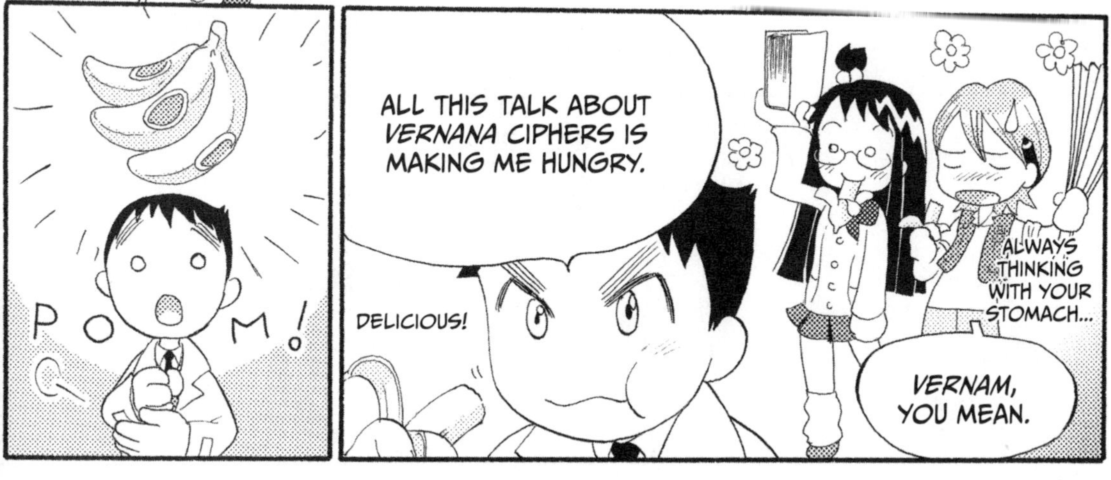
POM!
ALL THIS TALK ABOUT *VERNANA* CIPHERS IS MAKING ME HUNGRY.
ALWAYS THINKING WITH YOUR STOMACH...
DELICIOUS!
VERNAM, YOU MEAN.

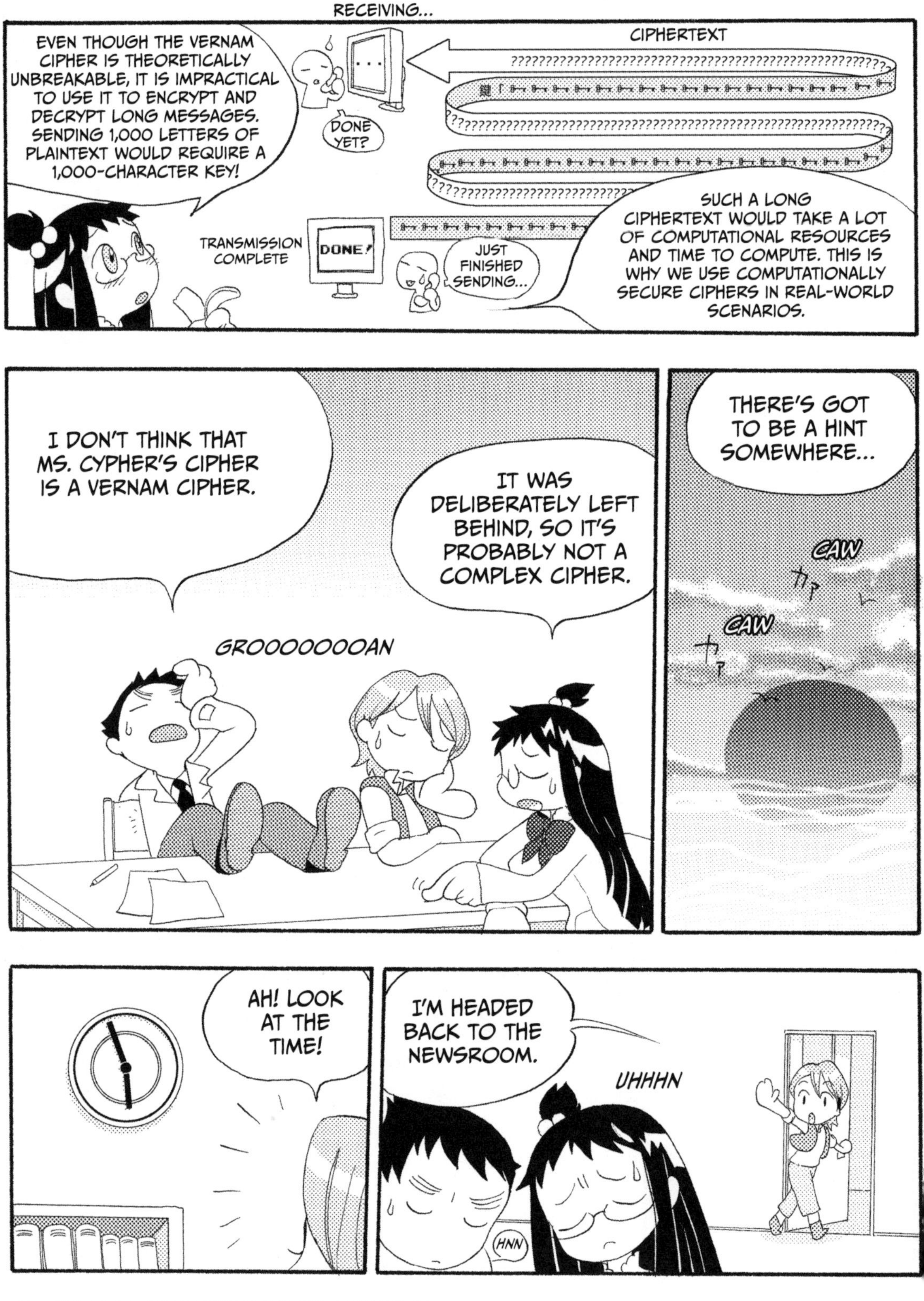
RECEIVING...
EVEN THOUGH THE VERNAM CIPHER IS THEORETICALLY UNBREAKABLE, IT IS IMPRACTICAL TO USE IT TO ENCRYPT AND DECRYPT LONG MESSAGES. SENDING 1,000 LETTERS OF PLAINTEXT WOULD REQUIRE A 1,000-CHARACTER KEY!
CIPHERTEXT
DONE YET?
TRANSMISSION COMPLETE
DONE!
JUST FINISHED SENDING...
SUCH A LONG CIPHERTEXT WOULD TAKE A LOT OF COMPUTATIONAL RESOURCES AND TIME TO COMPUTE. THIS IS WHY WE USE COMPUTATIONALLY SECURE CIPHERS IN REAL-WORLD SCENARIOS.
I DON'T THINK THAT MS. CYPHER'S CIPHER IS A VERNAM CIPHER.
IT WAS DELIBERATELY LEFT BEHIND, SO IT'S PROBABLY NOT A COMPLEX CIPHER.
GROOOOOOOAN
THERE'S GOT TO BE A HINT SOMEWHERE...
CAW
CAW
AH! LOOK AT THE TIME!
I'M HEADED BACK TO THE NEWSROOM.
UHHHN
HNN

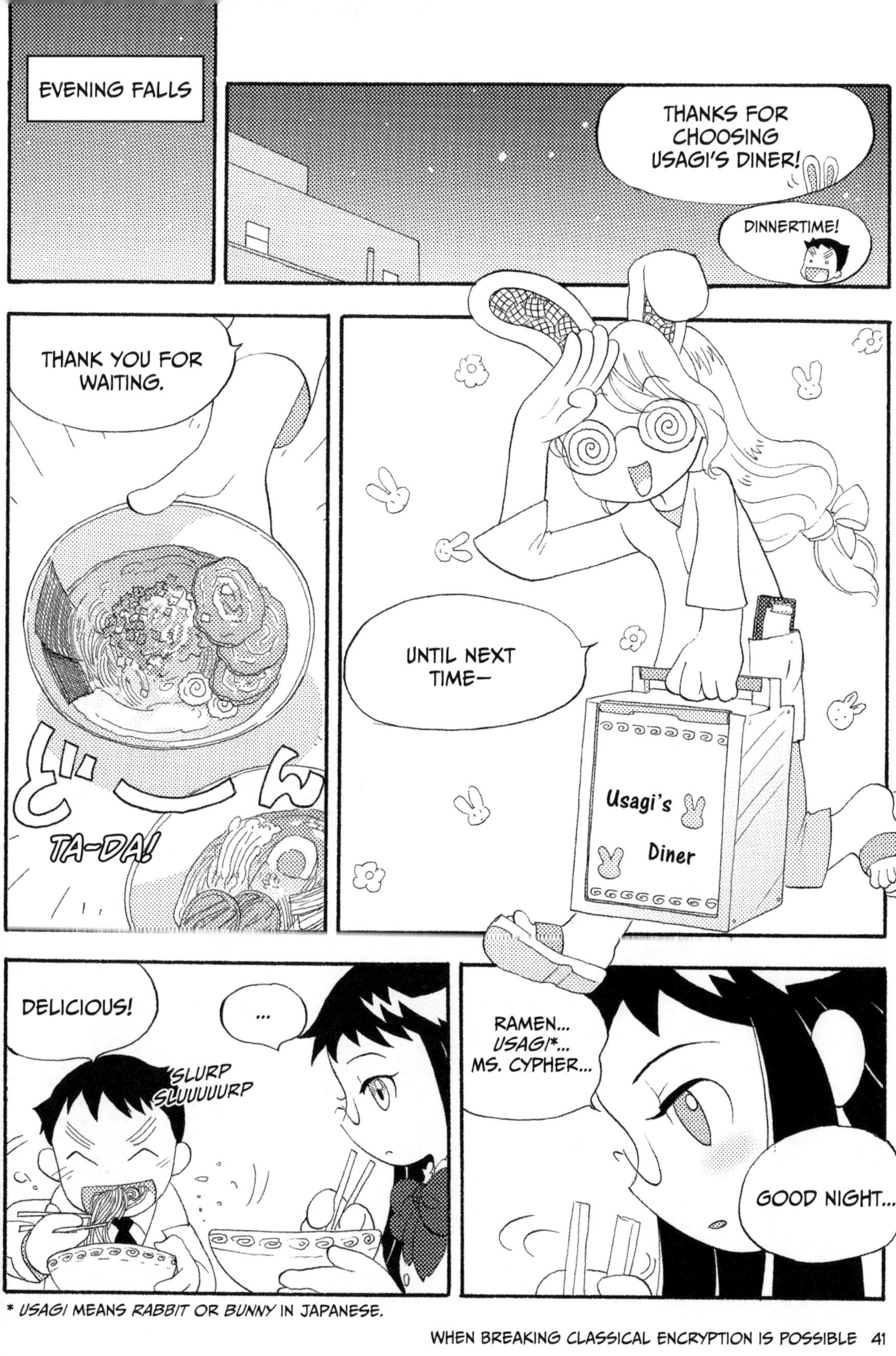
EVENING FALLS
THANKS FOR CHOOSING USAGI'S DINER!
DINNERTIME!
THANK YOU FOR WAITING.
どーん
TA-DA!
UNTIL NEXT TIME—
Usagi's Diner
DELICIOUS!
...
SLURP SLUUUUURP
RAMEN... USAGI*... MS. CYPHER...
GOOD NIGHT...

* *USAGI* MEANS *RABBIT* OR *BUNNY* IN JAPANESE.

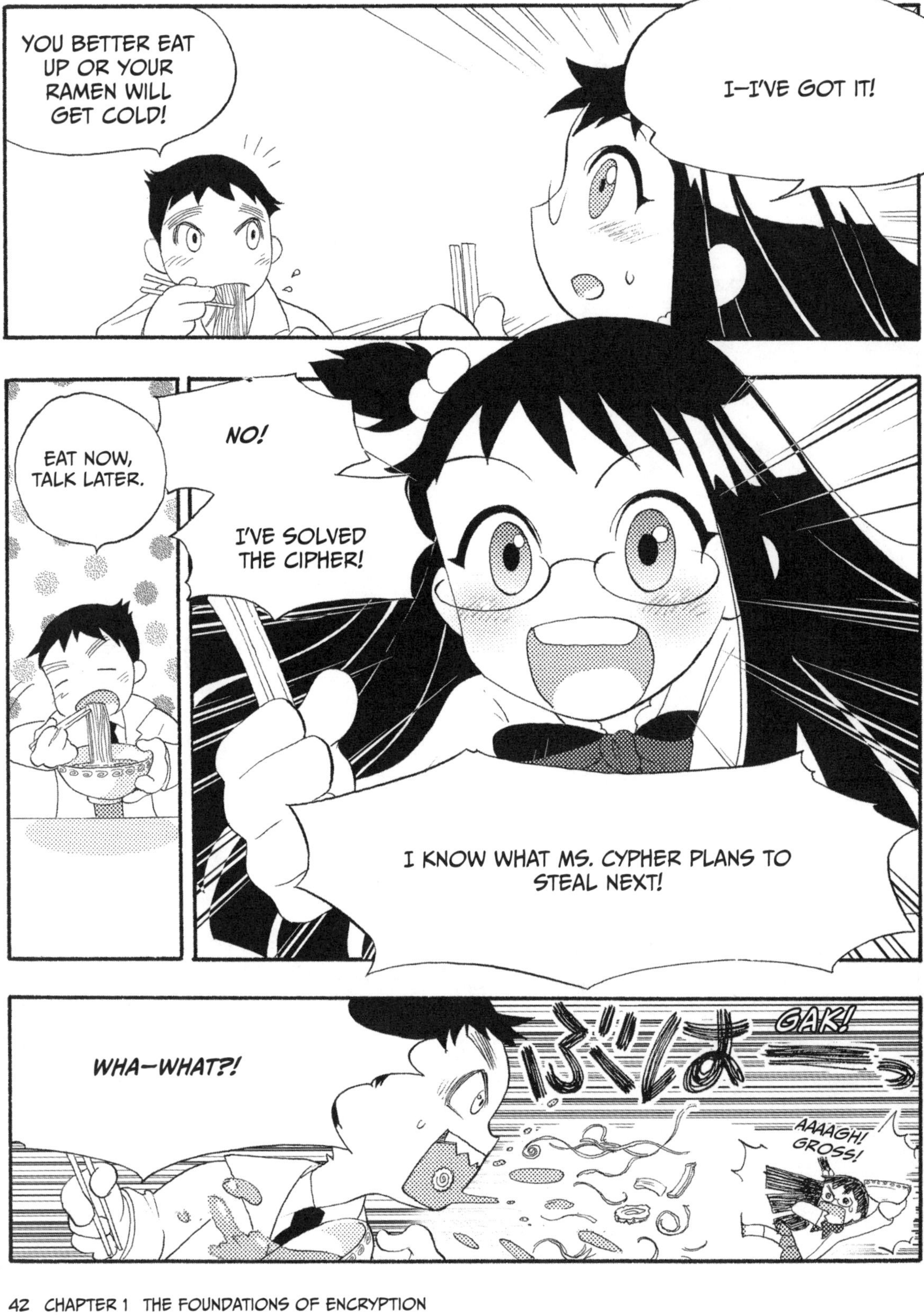
YOU BETTER EAT UP OR YOUR RAMEN WILL GET COLD!
I—I'VE GOT IT!
EAT NOW, TALK LATER.
NO!
I'VE SOLVED THE CIPHER!
I KNOW WHAT MS. CYPHER PLANS TO STEAL NEXT!
WHA-WHAT?!
ぶはーっ
GAK!
AAAAGH! GROSS!

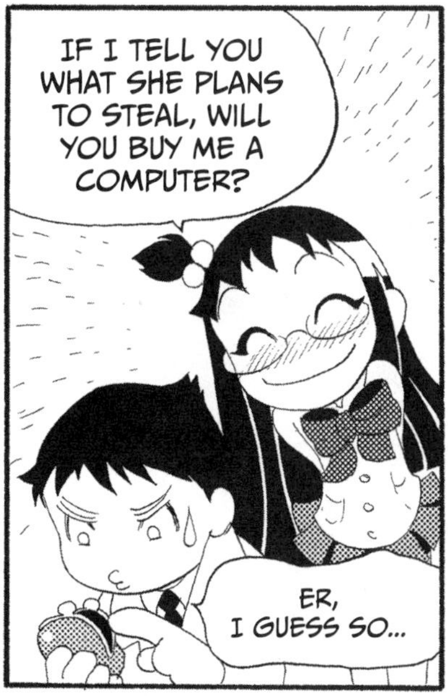
IF I TELL YOU WHAT SHE PLANS TO STEAL, WILL YOU BUY ME A COMPUTER?
ER, I GUESS SO...

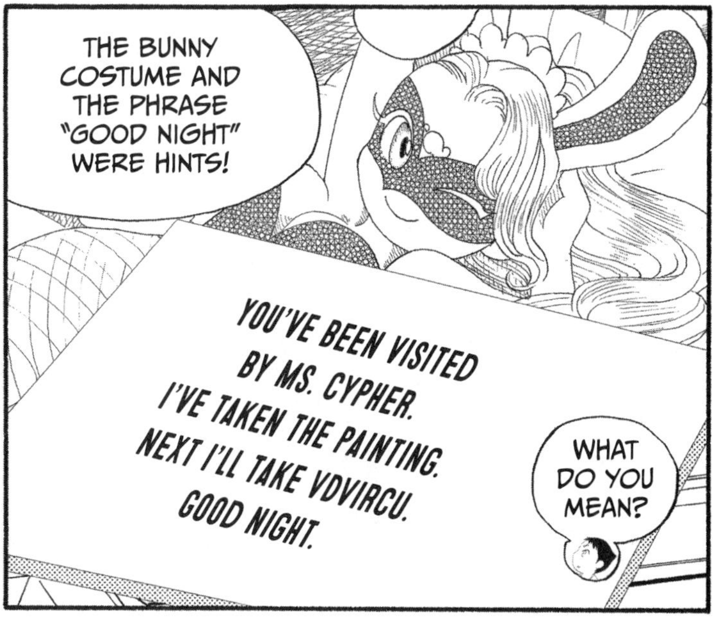
THE BUNNY COSTUME AND THE PHRASE "GOOD NIGHT" WERE HINTS!
YOU'VE BEEN VISITED BY MS. CYPHER. I'VE TAKEN THE PAINTING. NEXT I'LL TAKE VDVIRCU. GOOD NIGHT.
WHAT DO YOU MEAN?

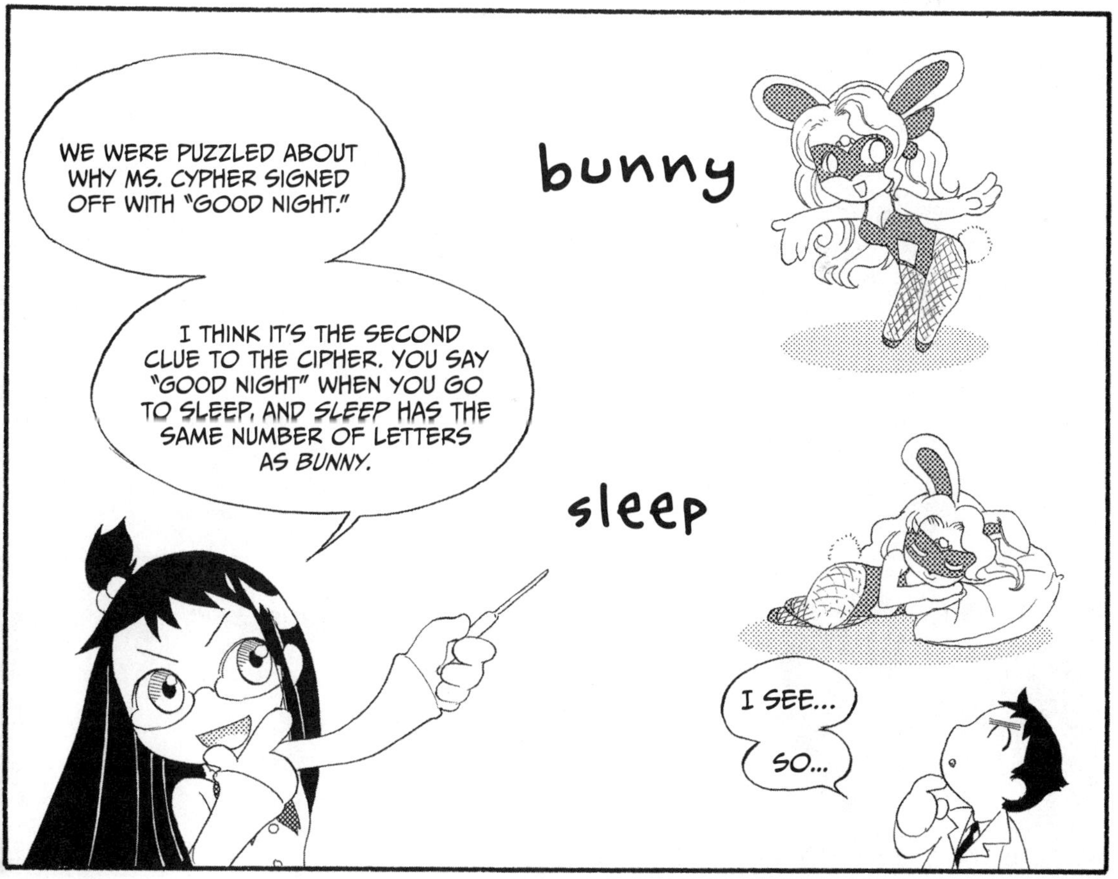
WE WERE PUZZLED ABOUT WHY MS. CYPHER SIGNED OFF WITH "GOOD NIGHT."
bunny
I THINK IT'S THE SECOND CLUE TO THE CIPHER. YOU SAY "GOOD NIGHT" WHEN YOU GO TO SLEEP, AND *SLEEP* HAS THE SAME NUMBER OF LETTERS AS *BUNNY*.
sleep
I SEE...
SO...

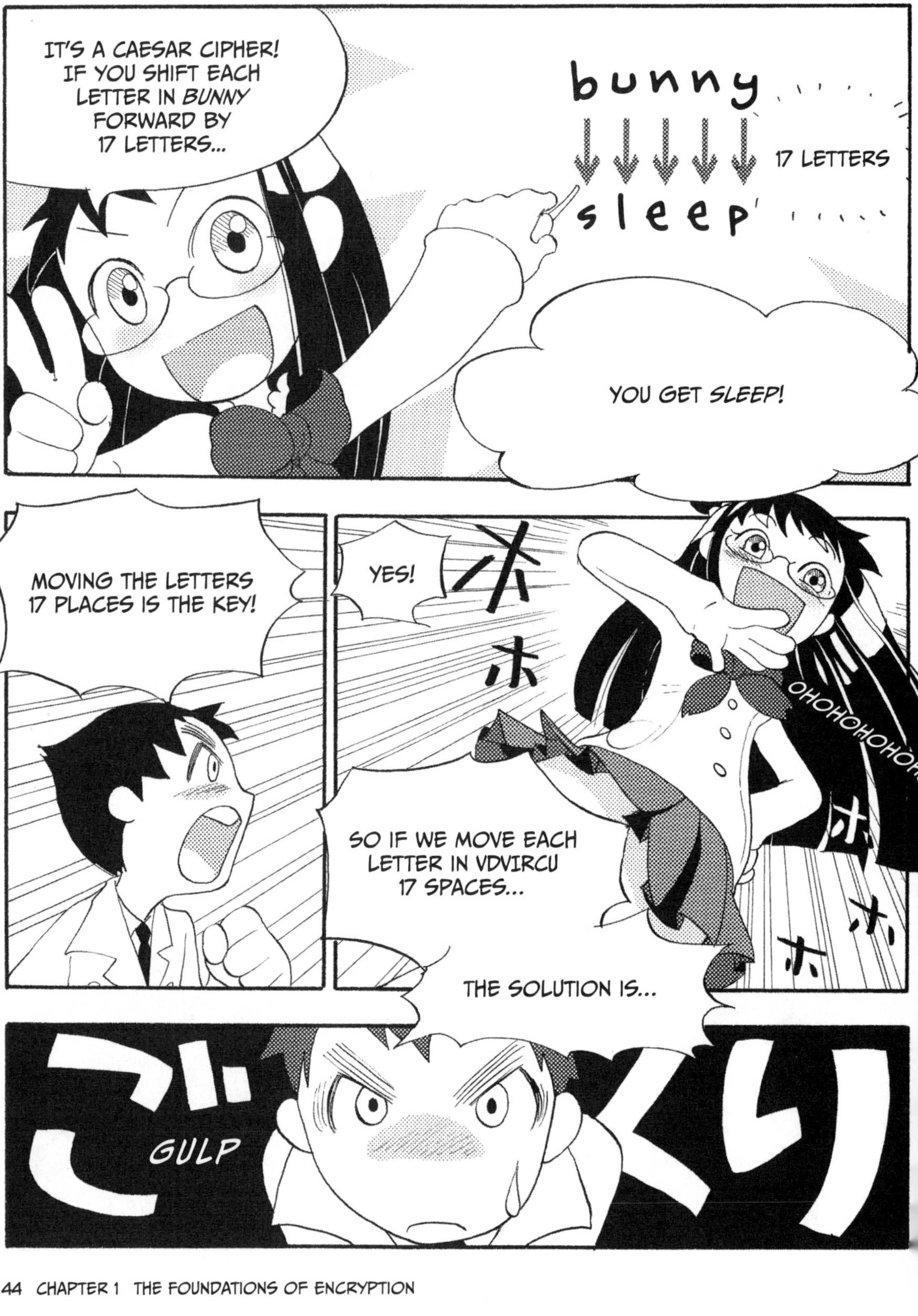
IT'S A CAESAR CIPHER! IF YOU SHIFT EACH LETTER IN *BUNNY* FORWARD BY 17 LETTERS...
bunny
17 LETTERS
sleep
YOU GET *SLEEP!*
MOVING THE LETTERS 17 PLACES IS THE KEY!
YES!
OHOHOHOHOHOHO
SO IF WE MOVE EACH LETTER IN VDVIRCU 17 SPACES...
THE SOLUTION IS...
ごくり
GULP

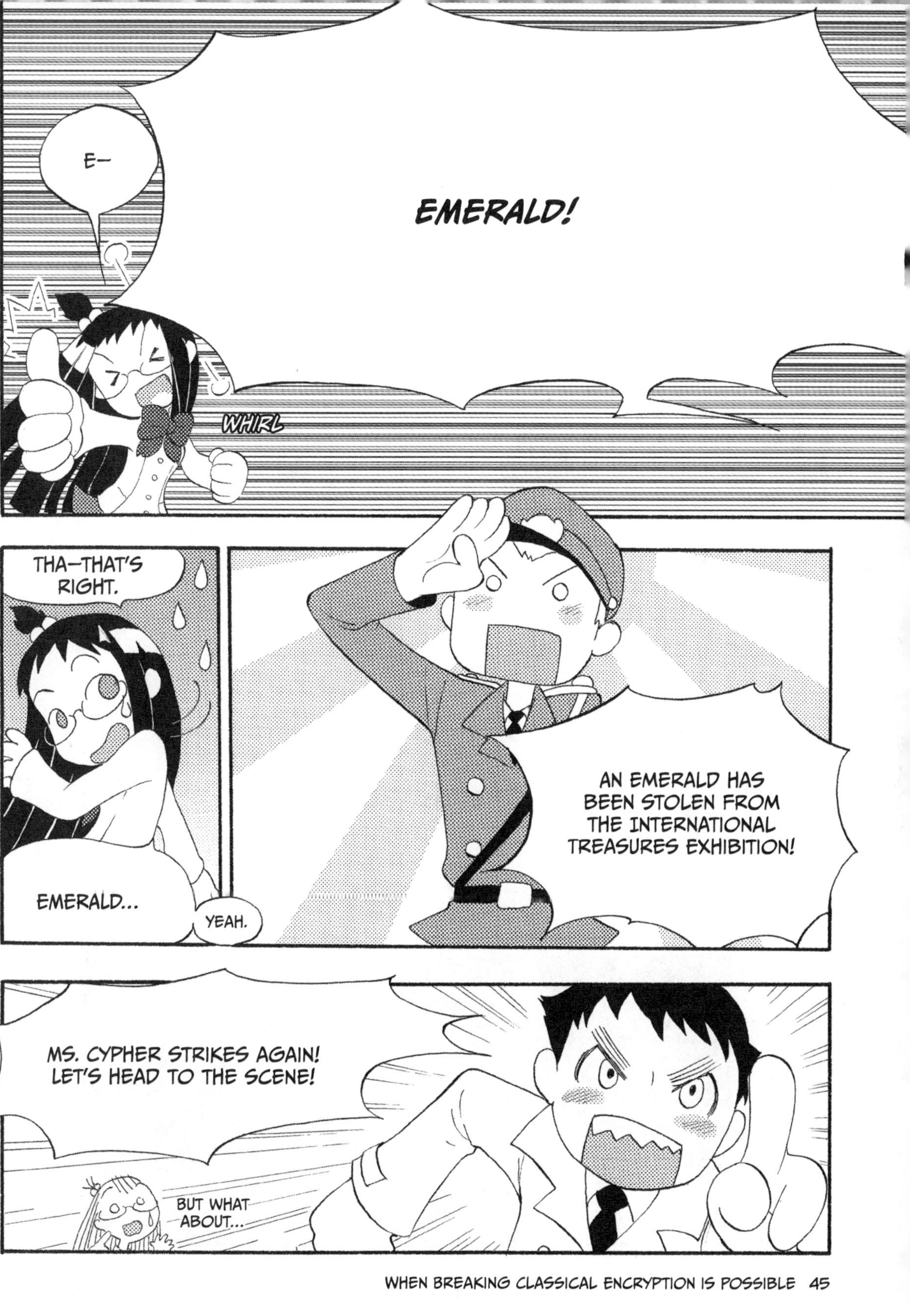
E–
EMERALD!
WHIRL
THA–THAT'S RIGHT.
EMERALD...
YEAH.
AN EMERALD HAS BEEN STOLEN FROM THE INTERNATIONAL TREASURES EXHIBITION!
MS. CYPHER STRIKES AGAIN! LET'S HEAD TO THE SCENE!
BUT WHAT ABOUT...

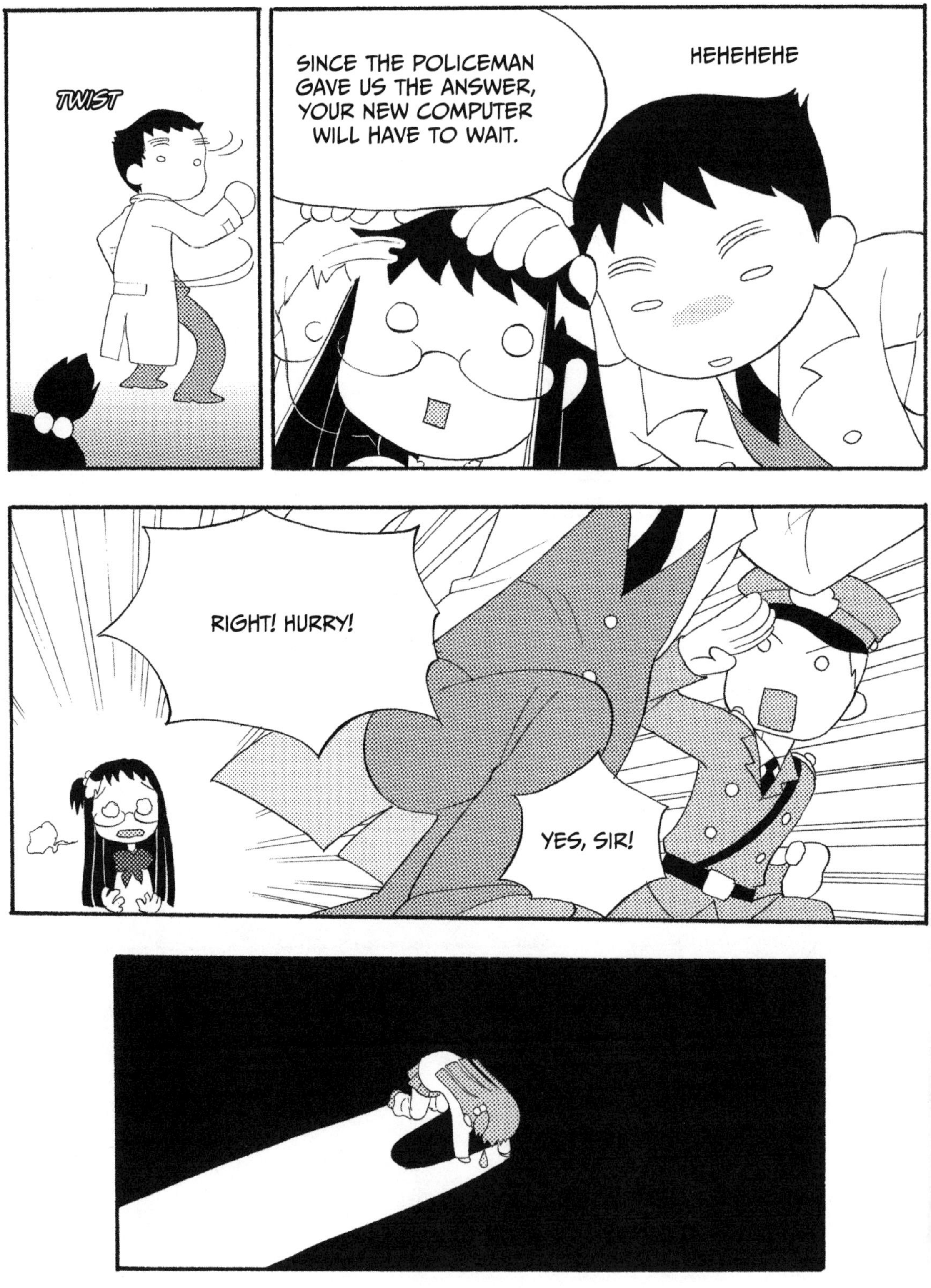
TWIST
SINCE THE POLICEMAN GAVE US THE ANSWER, YOUR NEW COMPUTER WILL HAVE TO WAIT.
HEHEHEHE
RIGHT! HURRY!
YES, SIR!

2

SYMMETRIC-KEY
ALGORITHMS

BINARY DIGITS AND LOGICAL OPERATORS

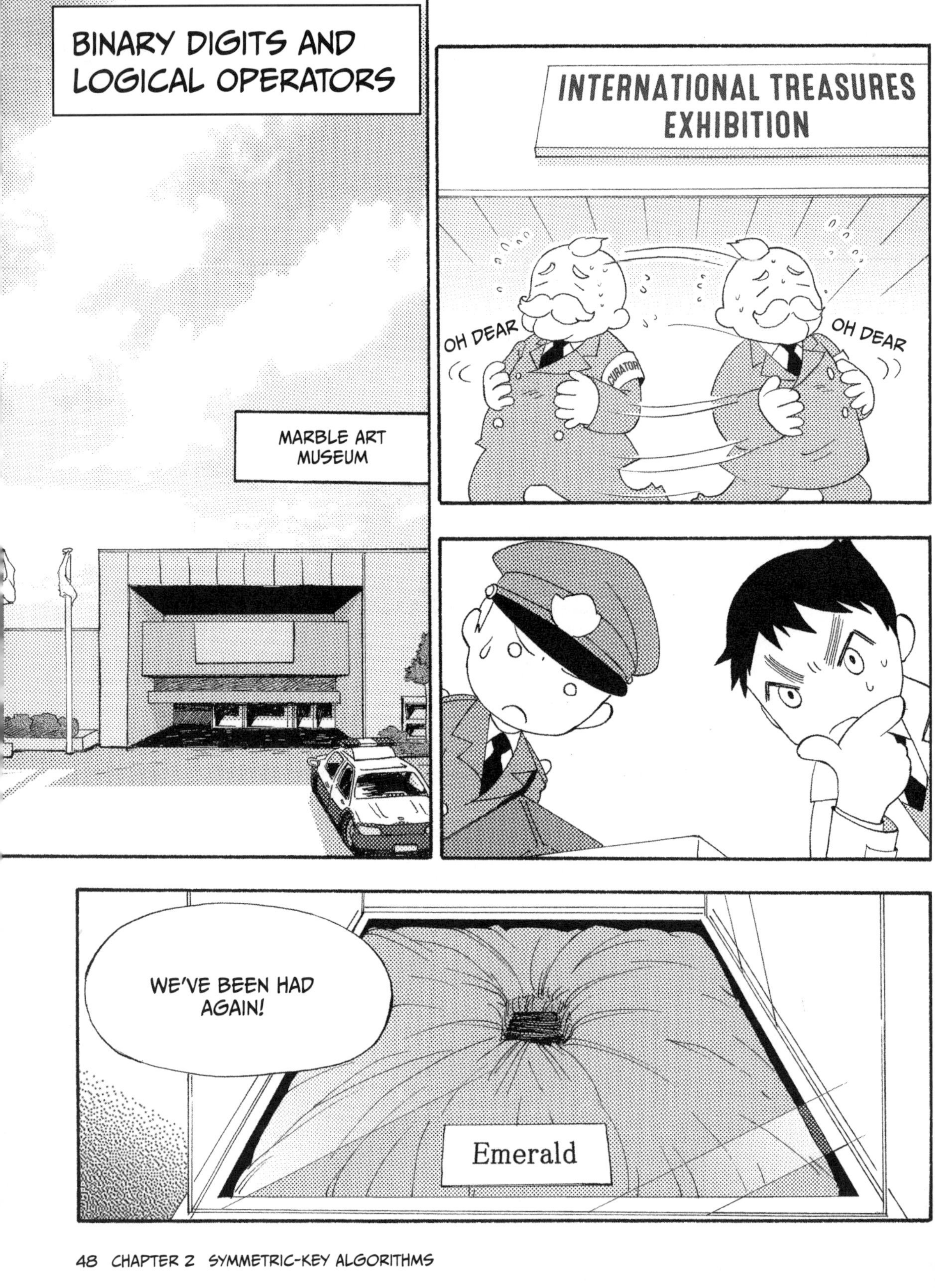
MARBLE ART MUSEUM
INTERNATIONAL TREASURES EXHIBITION
OH DEAR
CURATOR
OH DEAR
WE'VE BEEN HAD AGAIN!
Emerald

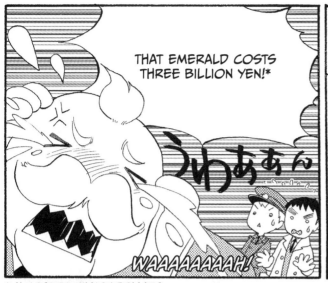

THAT EMERALD COSTS THREE BILLION YEN!*
うわああん
WAAAAAAAAAH!
WAS THE EXHIBITION CASE LOCKED?
OF COURSE! BUT—
IT MUST HAVE BEEN OPENED AT SOME POINT. BECAUSE YOUR PRECIOUS GEM WAS REELED RIGHT UP FROM THE CEILING.
HI!
YOU AGAIN!
HOW DO YOU KNOW THE THIEF'S MODUS OPERANDI?
FWIP
THIS WAS DELIVERED TO THE NEWSROOM!

* ALMOST 30 MILLION DOLLARS

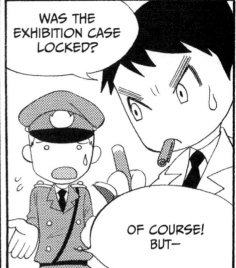

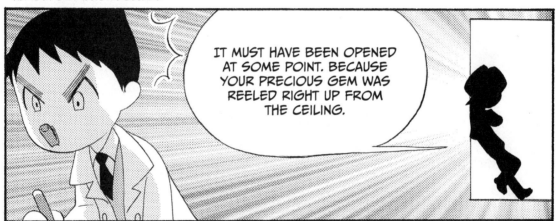

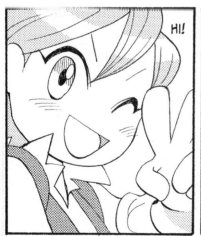

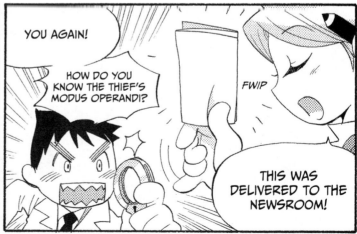

WHAT? WHAT IS IT?

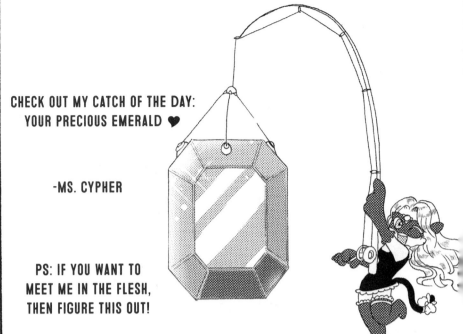

CHECK OUT MY CATCH OF THE DAY: YOUR PRECIOUS EMERALD ❤

-MS. CYPHER

PS: IF YOU WANT TO MEET ME IN THE FLESH, THEN FIGURE THIS OUT!

00110001   00101011   00110001   00111101   00110000

SO IT'S A NEW CIPHERTEXT...

HMMMMM

I'LL GET RUKA'S HELP—PRONTO!

WAIT FOR ME!

WAIT! WHAT ABOUT THE EMERALD?

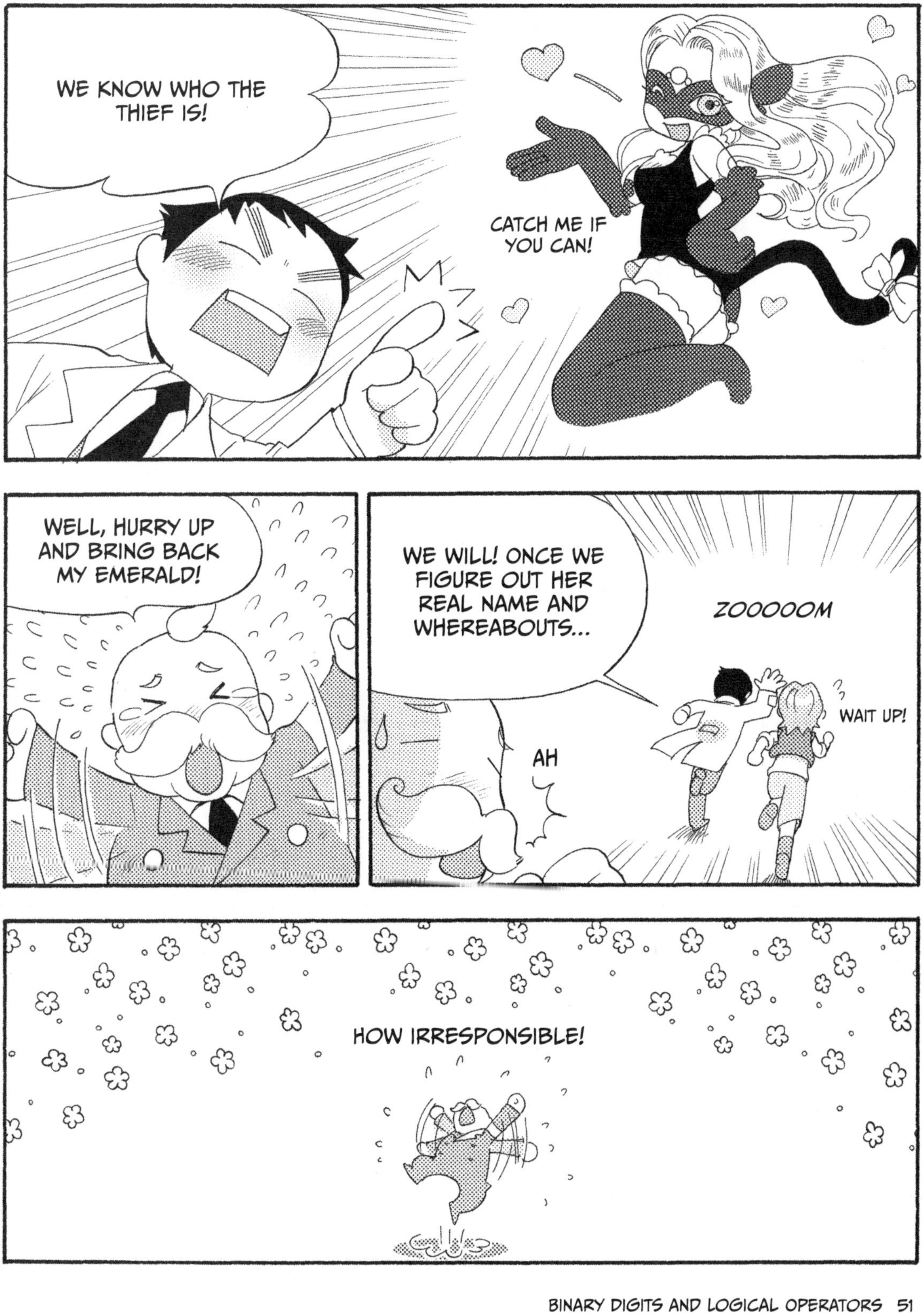
WE KNOW WHO THE THIEF IS!
CATCH ME IF YOU CAN!
WELL, HURRY UP AND BRING BACK MY EMERALD!
WE WILL! ONCE WE FIGURE OUT HER REAL NAME AND WHEREABOUTS...
ZOOOOOM
WAIT UP!
AH
HOW IRRESPONSIBLE!

CYPHER
TASK
FORCE

HMMMM

00110001   00101011   00110001   00111101   00110000

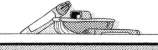

THIS TIME IT'S A BUNCH OF 1s AND 0s.

WHAT COULD IT MEAN?

AHA!

IT'S BINARY!

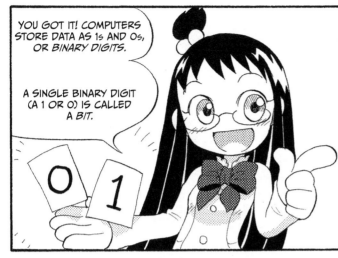

YOU GOT IT! COMPUTERS STORE DATA AS 1s AND 0s, OR *BINARY DIGITS*.

A SINGLE BINARY DIGIT (A 1 OR 0) IS CALLED A *BIT*.

We usually use the base-10 decimal number system, but the binary system is in base 2, which uses only two numbers to count.

When you count past 1 in binary, you run out of digits and must carry the 1 to the next largest place value. For example, the number 2 is 10 in binary.

A group of eight bits in a row is called a *byte*. Each bit represents a 0 or 1, so a byte has a total of $2^8 = 256$ possible combinations. Each combination represents a different piece of information.

Binary number	Decimal number	Hexadecimal number	Binary number	Decimal number	Hexadecimal number
0000	0	0	1000	8	8
0001	1	1	1001	9	9
0010	2	2	1010	10	A
0011	3	3	1011	11	B
0100	4	4	1100	12	C
0101	5	5	1101	13	D
0110	6	6	1110	14	E
0111	7	7	1111	15	F

0 IS 0, 1 IS 1, 2 IS 10...

As numbers become larger, the number of digits required to represent them in binary grows rapidly, so *hexadecimal notation* is often used instead. Hexadecimal notation is in base 16, using digits 0 through 9 and letters A through F, as shown in this table. This means that after you count up to 9, you use A instead of 10, B instead of 11, and so on up to F. The prefix 0x is added to hexadecimal numbers, so for example, the decimal number 10 is 0xA in hexadecimal.

UNLIKE HISTORICAL CIPHERS, WHICH OPERATE ON LETTERS, MODERN ENCRYPTION METHODS OPERATE ON BINARY NUMBERS.

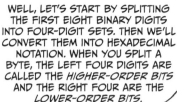

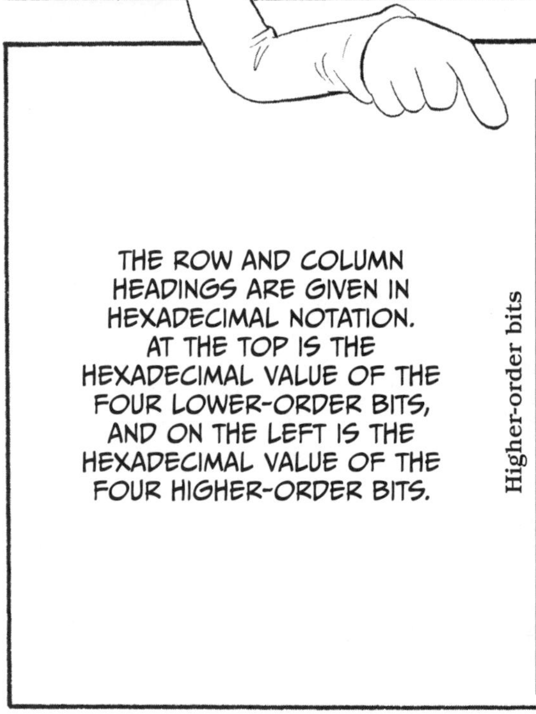

Lower-order bits (columns) / Higher-order bits (rows)

	0	1	2	3	4	5	6	7
0	NUL	DLE	space	0	@	P	`	p
1	SOH	DC1	!	1	A	Q	a	q
2	STX	DC2	"	2	B	R	b	r
3	ETX	DC3	#	3	C	S	c	s
4	EOT	DC4	$	4	D	T	d	t
5	ENQ	NAK	%	5	E	U	e	u
6	ACK	SYN	&	6	F	V	f	v
7	BEL	ETB	'	7	G	W	g	w
8	BS	CAN	(	8	H	X	h	x
9	HT	EM	)	9	I	Y	i	y
A	LF	SUB	*	:	J	Z	j	z
B	VT	ESC	+	;	K	[	k	{
C	FF	FS	,	<	L	\	l		
D	CR	GS	-	=	M	]	m	}
E	SO	RS	.	>	N	^	n	~
F	SI	US	/	?	O	_	o	del

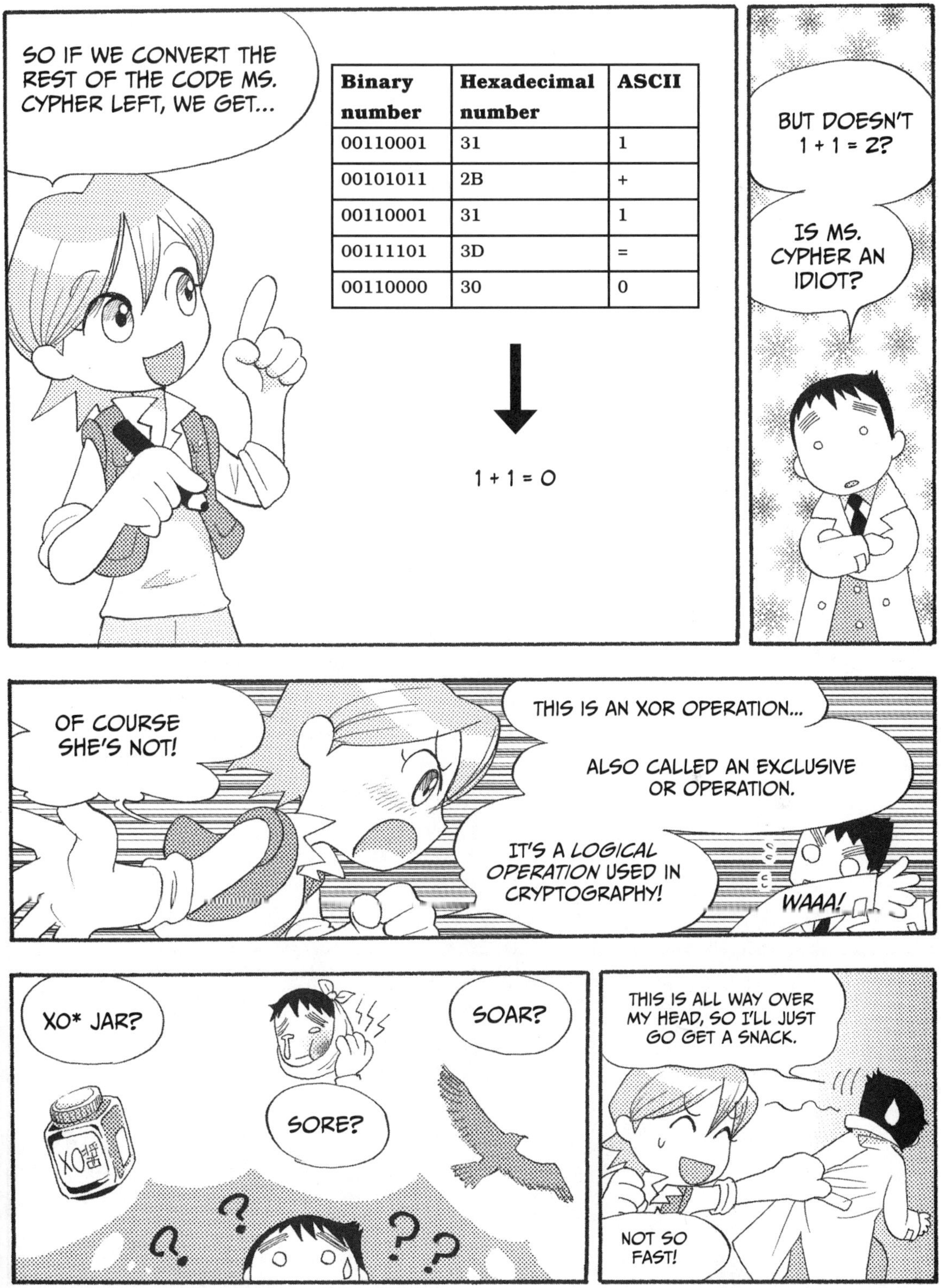
SO IF WE CONVERT THE REST OF THE CODE MS. CYPHER LEFT, WE GET...

Binary number	Hexadecimal number	ASCII
00110001	31	1
00101011	2B	+
00110001	31	1
00111101	3D	=
00110000	30	0

1 + 1 = 0
BUT DOESN'T 1 + 1 = 2?
IS MS. CYPHER AN IDIOT?
OF COURSE SHE'S NOT!
THIS IS AN XOR OPERATION...
ALSO CALLED AN EXCLUSIVE OR OPERATION.
IT'S A *LOGICAL OPERATION* USED IN CRYPTOGRAPHY!
WAAA!
XO* JAR?
SORE?
SOAR?
XO醤
THIS IS ALL WAY OVER MY HEAD, SO I'LL JUST GO GET A SNACK.
NOT SO FAST!

* XO SAUCE IS A CHINESE CONDIMENT.

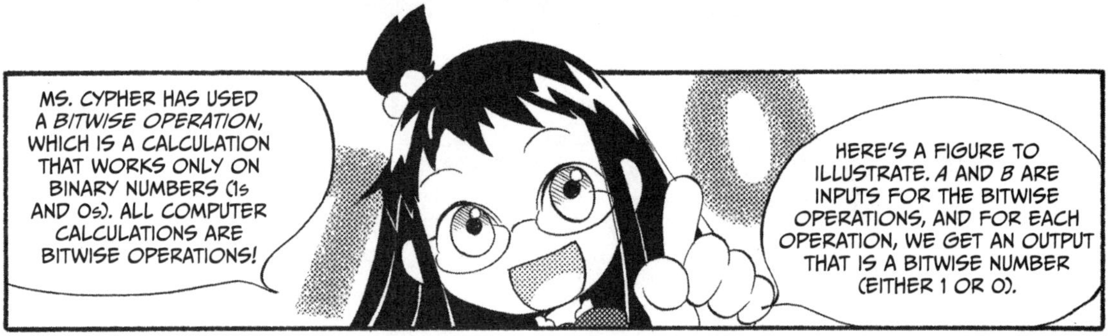
MS. CYPHER HAS USED A *BITWISE OPERATION*, WHICH IS A CALCULATION THAT WORKS ONLY ON BINARY NUMBERS (1s AND 0s). ALL COMPUTER CALCULATIONS ARE BITWISE OPERATIONS!
HERE'S A FIGURE TO ILLUSTRATE. *A* AND *B* ARE INPUTS FOR THE BITWISE OPERATIONS, AND FOR EACH OPERATION, WE GET AN OUTPUT THAT IS A BITWISE NUMBER (EITHER 1 OR 0).

AND operations are sometimes referred to as conjunction logic, and OR operations are sometimes referred to as disjunction logic. XOR operations are a combination of conjunction and disjunction logic.

OR operation

$A + B$

A	B	$A + B$
0	0	0
1	0	1
0	1	1
1	1	1

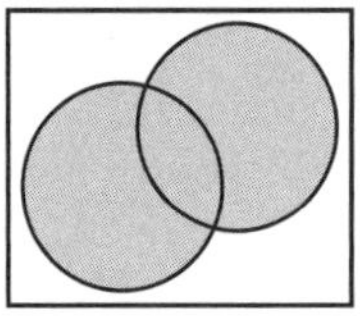

If either A or B is a 1, the output is 1.

AND operation

$A \cdot B$

A	B	$A \cdot B$
0	0	0
1	0	0
0	1	0
1	1	1

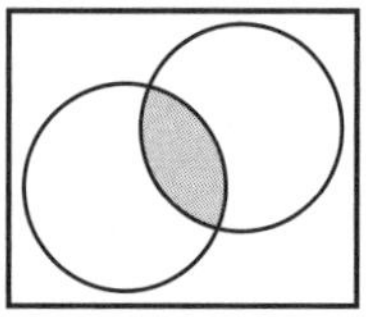

If both A and B are 1, the output is 1.

NOT operation

$\overline{A}$

A	$\overline{A}$
1	0
0	1

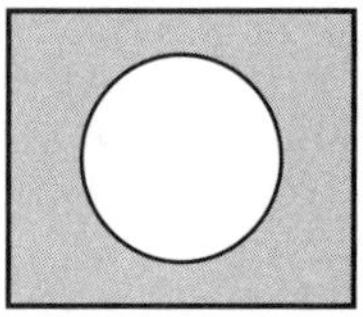

The output is the opposite of A. If A is 1, the output is 0; if A is 0, the output is 1.

NAND operation

$\overline{A \cdot B}$

A	B	$\overline{A \cdot B}$
0	0	1
1	0	1
0	1	1
1	1	0

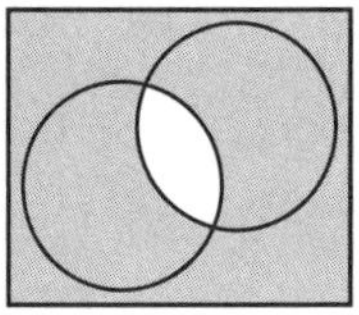

If either A or B is 0, the output is 1; otherwise it is 0.

NOR operation

$\overline{A + B}$

A	B	$\overline{A + B}$
0	0	1
1	0	0
0	1	0
1	1	0

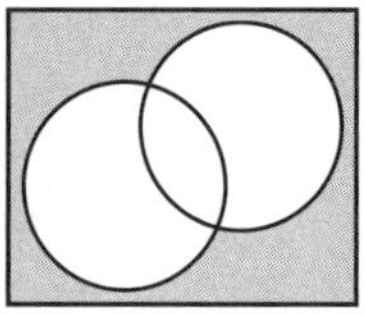

If both A and B are 0, the output is 1; otherwise it is 0.

XOR operation

$A \cdot \overline{B} + A \cdot \overline{B} = (A \oplus B)$

A	B	$A \oplus B$
0	0	0
1	0	1
0	1	1
1	1	0

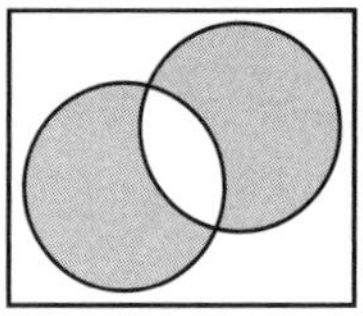

If A and B are different, the output is 1; otherwise it is 0.

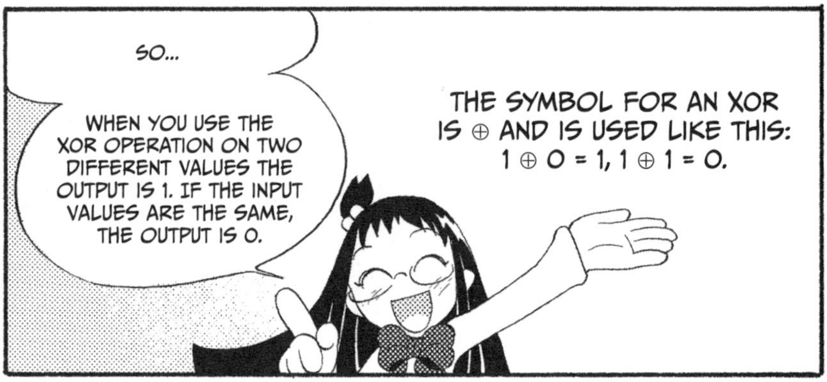
SO...
WHEN YOU USE THE XOR OPERATION ON TWO DIFFERENT VALUES THE OUTPUT IS 1. IF THE INPUT VALUES ARE THE SAME, THE OUTPUT IS 0.
THE SYMBOL FOR AN XOR IS ⊕ AND IS USED LIKE THIS: 1 ⊕ 0 = 1, 1 ⊕ 1 = 0.

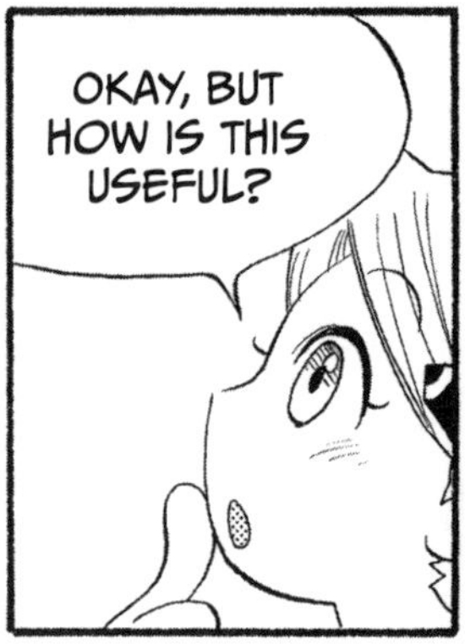
OKAY, BUT HOW IS THIS USEFUL?

WE CAN USE IT TO DECIPHER CODES!

As an example, let's perform an XOR operation using the plaintext 1101 and the encryption key 1001.

$$1101 \oplus 1001 = 0100$$

Plaintext   Encryption   Ciphertext
key

The result of the operation is the ciphertext 0100. Next, we'll perform an XOR operation using the ciphertext 0100 and the decryption key 1001.

$$0100 \oplus 1001 = 1101$$

Ciphertext   Decryption   Plaintext
key

The result of the operation is the plaintext 1101. When you perform the XOR operation using the ciphertext 0100 and the plaintext 1101, you get the encryption/decryption key:

$$0100 \oplus 1101 = 1001$$

Ciphertext   Plaintext   Decryption key = Encryption key

This means that as long as we have two of the three pieces of data—the plaintext, encryption/decryption key, or ciphertext—we can derive the remaining piece of data.

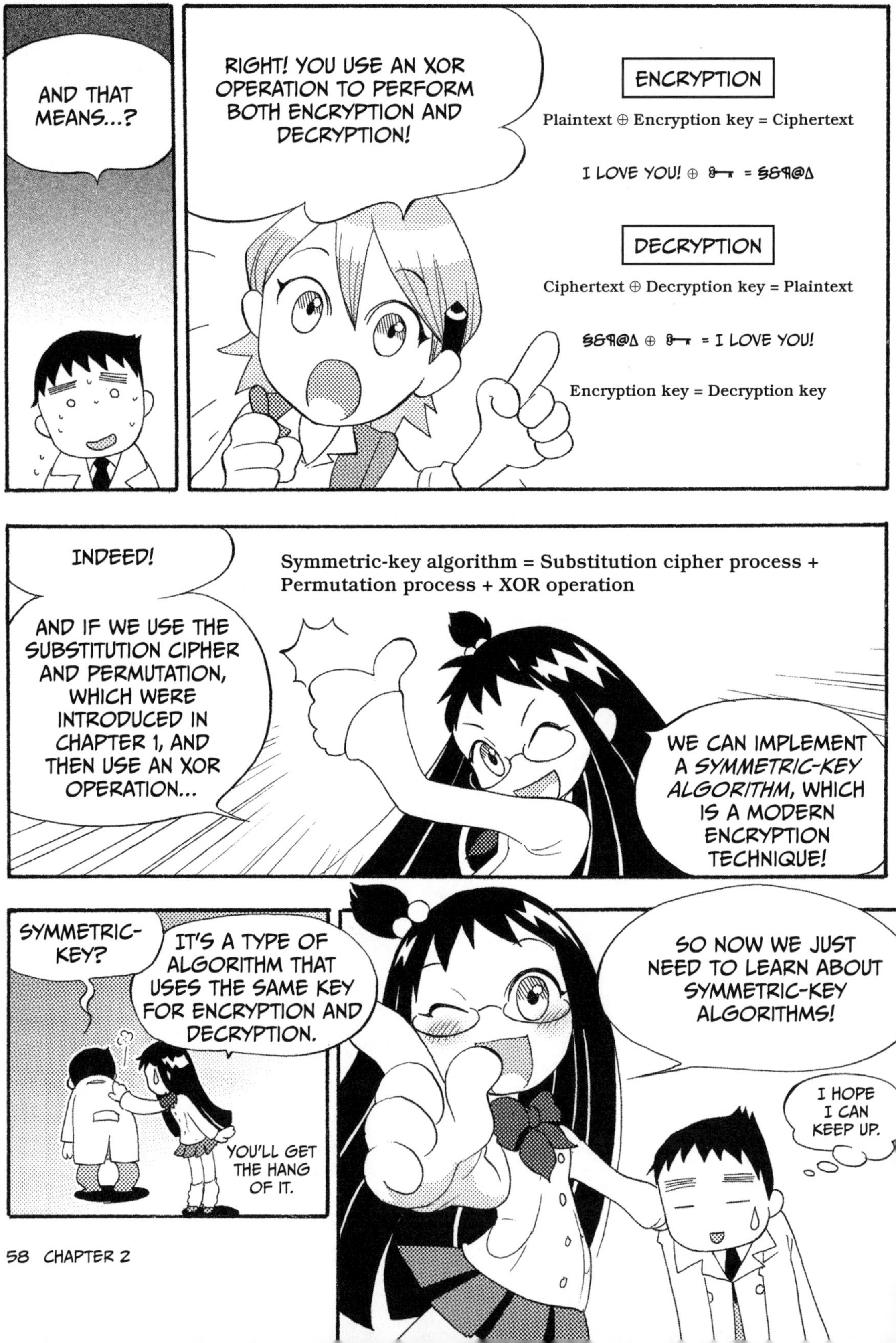
AND THAT MEANS...?
RIGHT! YOU USE AN XOR OPERATION TO PERFORM BOTH ENCRYPTION AND DECRYPTION!
ENCRYPTION
Plaintext ⊕ Encryption key = Ciphertext
I LOVE YOU! ⊕
DECRYPTION
Ciphertext ⊕ Decryption key = Plaintext
⊕ = I LOVE YOU!
Encryption key = Decryption key
INDEED!
Symmetric-key algorithm = Substitution cipher process + Permutation process + XOR operation
AND IF WE USE THE SUBSTITUTION CIPHER AND PERMUTATION, WHICH WERE INTRODUCED IN CHAPTER 1, AND THEN USE AN XOR OPERATION...
WE CAN IMPLEMENT A *SYMMETRIC-KEY ALGORITHM*, WHICH IS A MODERN ENCRYPTION TECHNIQUE!
SYMMETRIC-KEY?
IT'S A TYPE OF ALGORITHM THAT USES THE SAME KEY FOR ENCRYPTION AND DECRYPTION.
YOU'LL GET THE HANG OF IT.
SO NOW WE JUST NEED TO LEARN ABOUT SYMMETRIC-KEY ALGORITHMS!
I HOPE I CAN KEEP UP.

SYMMETRIC-KEY ALGORITHMS

SLUUUURP

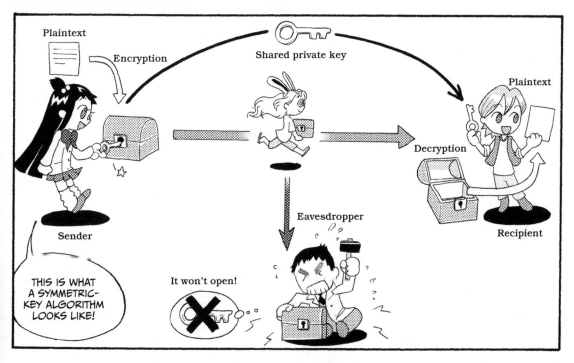

Plaintext

Encryption

Shared private key

Plaintext

Decryption

Sender

Recipient

Eavesdropper

THIS IS WHAT A SYMMETRIC-KEY ALGORITHM LOOKS LIKE!

It won't open!

THE CIPHER'S SENDER AND RECIPIENT USE THE SAME KEY...

HMMM...

THAT'S UNKNOWN TO ANYONE ELSE TO PERFORM BOTH ENCRYPTION AND DECRYPTION.

BECAUSE BOTH PARTIES SHARE THE SAME KEY, SYMMETRIC-KEY CRYPTOGRAPHY IS ALSO KNOWN AS *SHARED-KEY CRYPTOGRAPHY* OR *SECRET-KEY CRYPTOGRAPHY*. MOST TRADITIONAL ENCRYPTION SCHEMES USE A SHARED KEY.

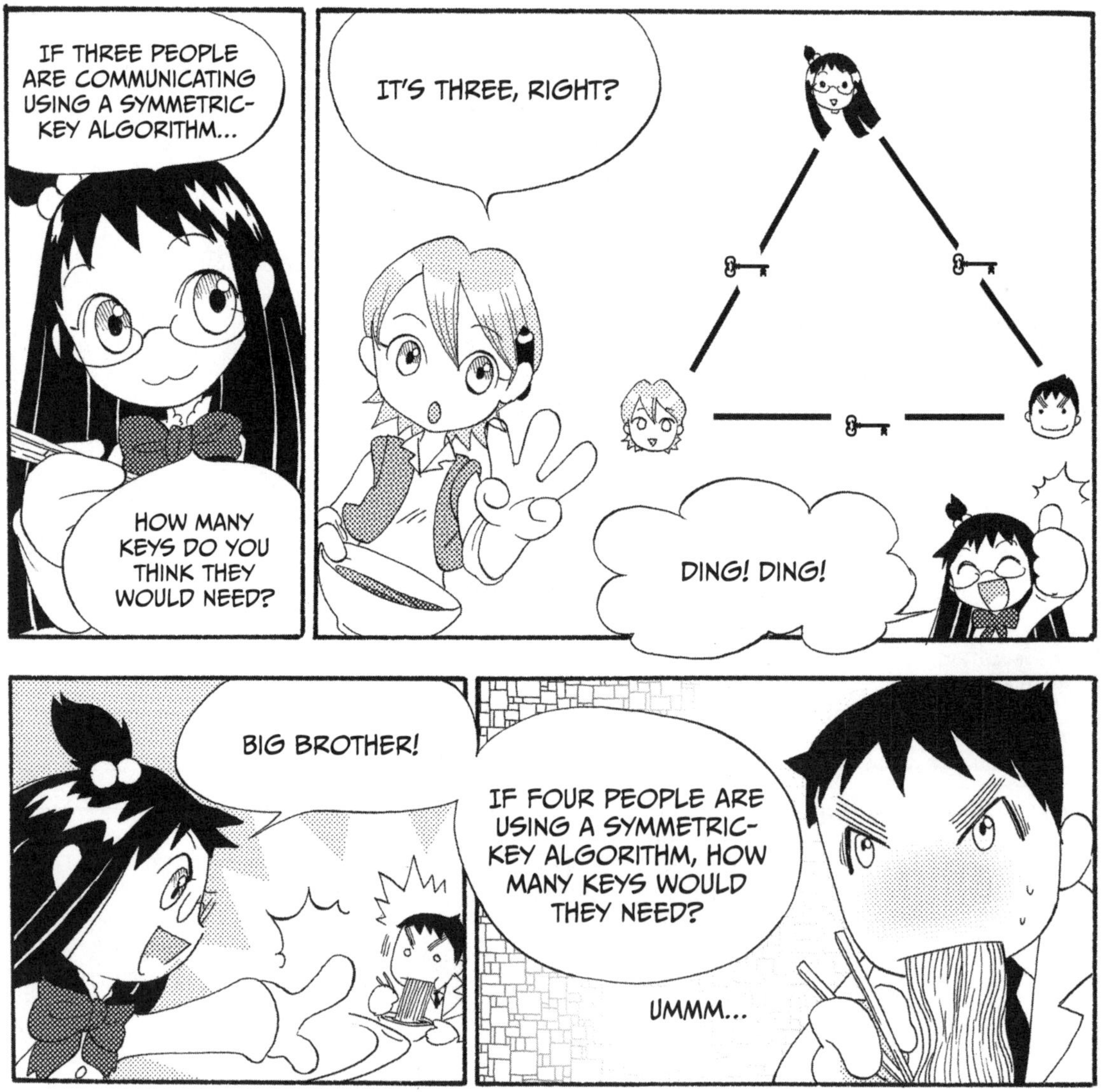
IF THREE PEOPLE ARE COMMUNICATING USING A SYMMETRIC-KEY ALGORITHM...
HOW MANY KEYS DO YOU THINK THEY WOULD NEED?
IT'S THREE, RIGHT?
DING! DING!
BIG BROTHER!
IF FOUR PEOPLE ARE USING A SYMMETRIC-KEY ALGORITHM, HOW MANY KEYS WOULD THEY NEED?
UMMM...

IF THREE PEOPLE NEED THREE KEYS...

FOUR PEOPLE WOULD NEED FOUR, RIGHT?

WOMP WOOOOOOMP.

IT'S AN EASY MISTAKE TO MAKE, BUT THE ANSWER IS SIX.

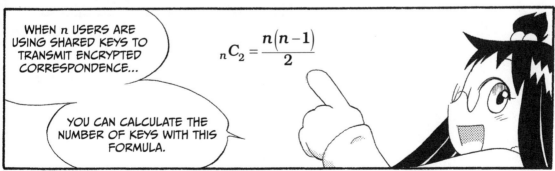

WHEN n USERS ARE USING SHARED KEYS TO TRANSMIT ENCRYPTED CORRESPONDENCE...

YOU CAN CALCULATE THE NUMBER OF KEYS WITH THIS FORMULA.

$$_nC_2 = \frac{n(n-1)}{2}$$

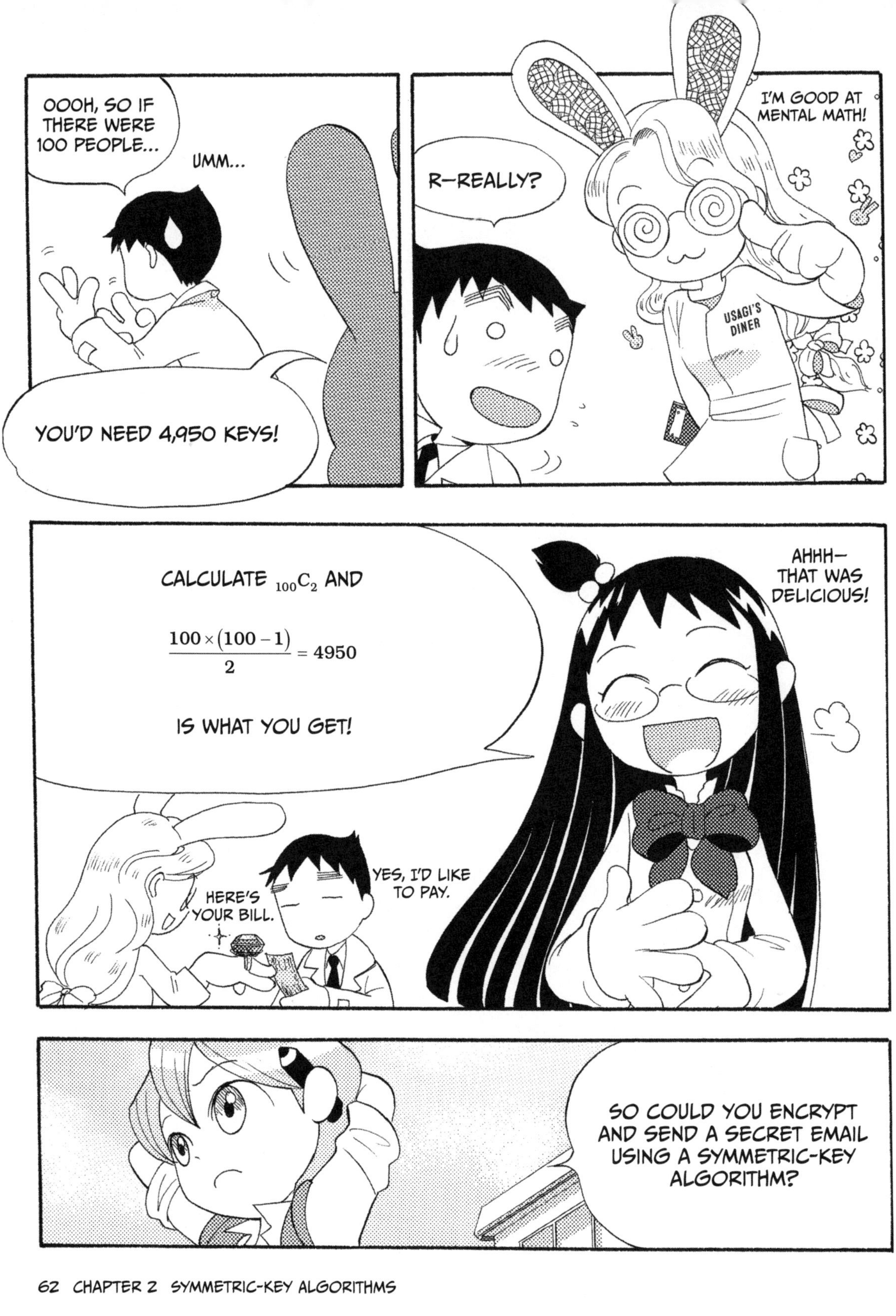
OOOH, SO IF THERE WERE 100 PEOPLE...
UMM...
YOU'D NEED 4,950 KEYS!
R—REALLY?
I'M GOOD AT MENTAL MATH!
USAGI'S DINER
CALCULATE $_{100}C_2$ AND
$$\frac{100 \times (100-1)}{2} = 4950$$
IS WHAT YOU GET!
AHHH— THAT WAS DELICIOUS!
HERE'S YOUR BILL.
YES, I'D LIKE TO PAY.
SO COULD YOU ENCRYPT AND SEND A SECRET EMAIL USING A SYMMETRIC-KEY ALGORITHM?

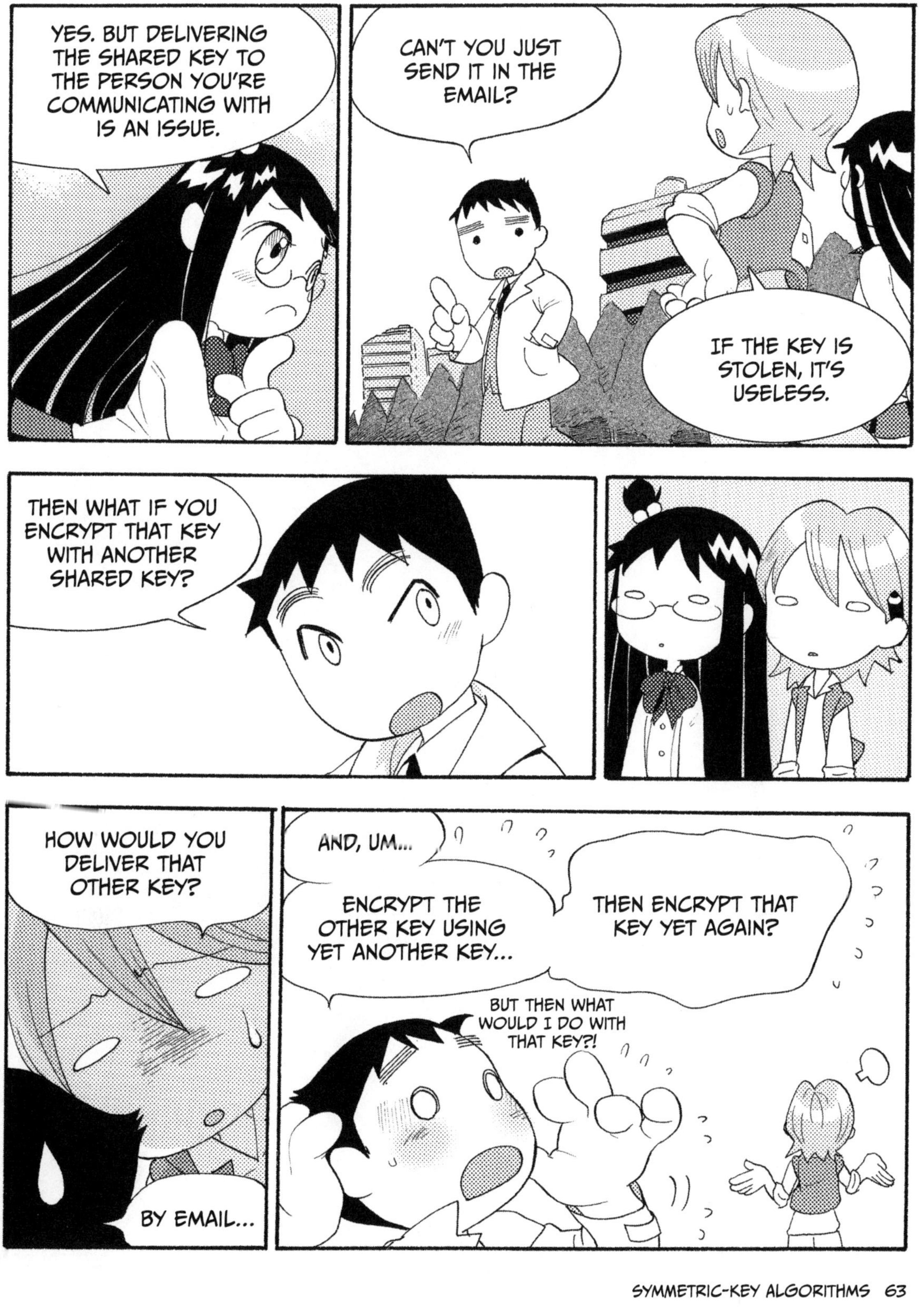
YES. BUT DELIVERING THE SHARED KEY TO THE PERSON YOU'RE COMMUNICATING WITH IS AN ISSUE.
CAN'T YOU JUST SEND IT IN THE EMAIL?
IF THE KEY IS STOLEN, IT'S USELESS.
THEN WHAT IF YOU ENCRYPT THAT KEY WITH ANOTHER SHARED KEY?
HOW WOULD YOU DELIVER THAT OTHER KEY?
BY EMAIL...
AND, UM...
ENCRYPT THE OTHER KEY USING YET ANOTHER KEY...
THEN ENCRYPT THAT KEY YET AGAIN?
BUT THEN WHAT WOULD I DO WITH THAT KEY?!

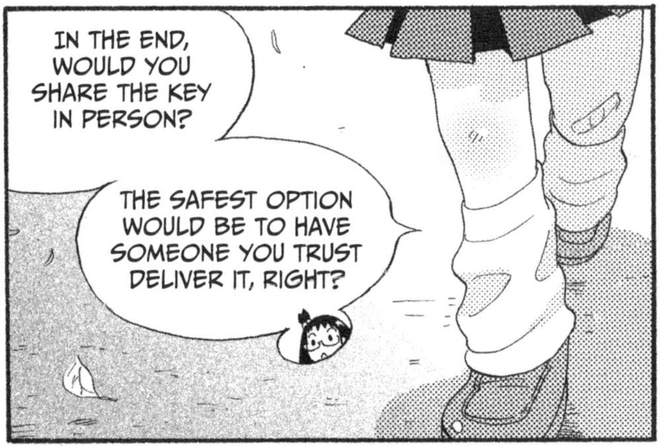
IN THE END, WOULD YOU SHARE THE KEY IN PERSON?
THE SAFEST OPTION WOULD BE TO HAVE SOMEONE YOU TRUST DELIVER IT, RIGHT?

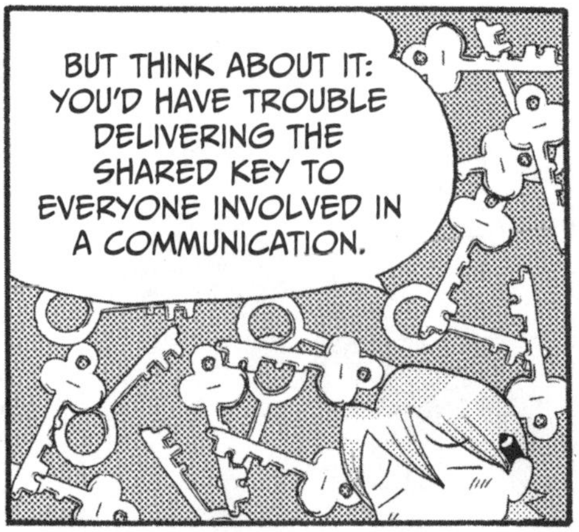
BUT THINK ABOUT IT: YOU'D HAVE TROUBLE DELIVERING THE SHARED KEY TO EVERYONE INVOLVED IN A COMMUNICATION.

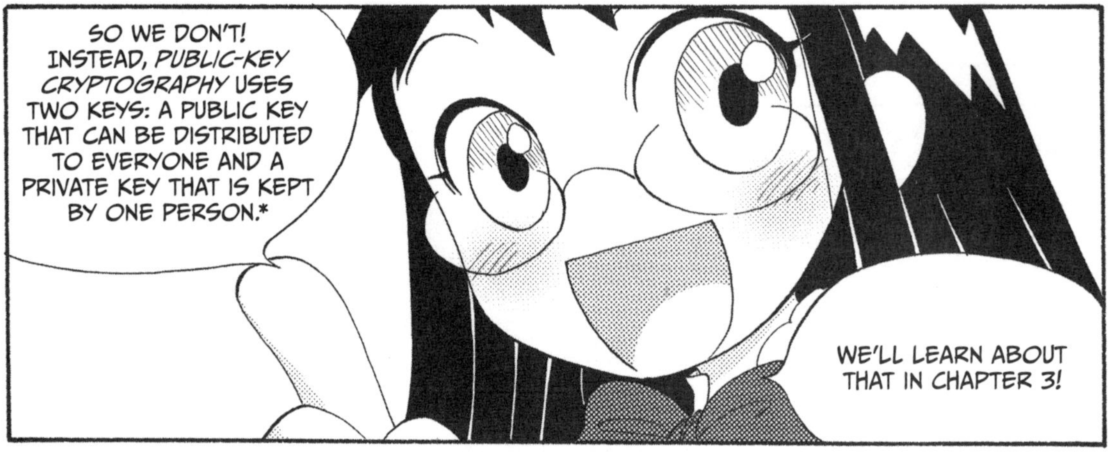
SO WE DON'T! INSTEAD, *PUBLIC-KEY CRYPTOGRAPHY* USES TWO KEYS: A PUBLIC KEY THAT CAN BE DISTRIBUTED TO EVERYONE AND A PRIVATE KEY THAT IS KEPT BY ONE PERSON.*
WE'LL LEARN ABOUT THAT IN CHAPTER 3!

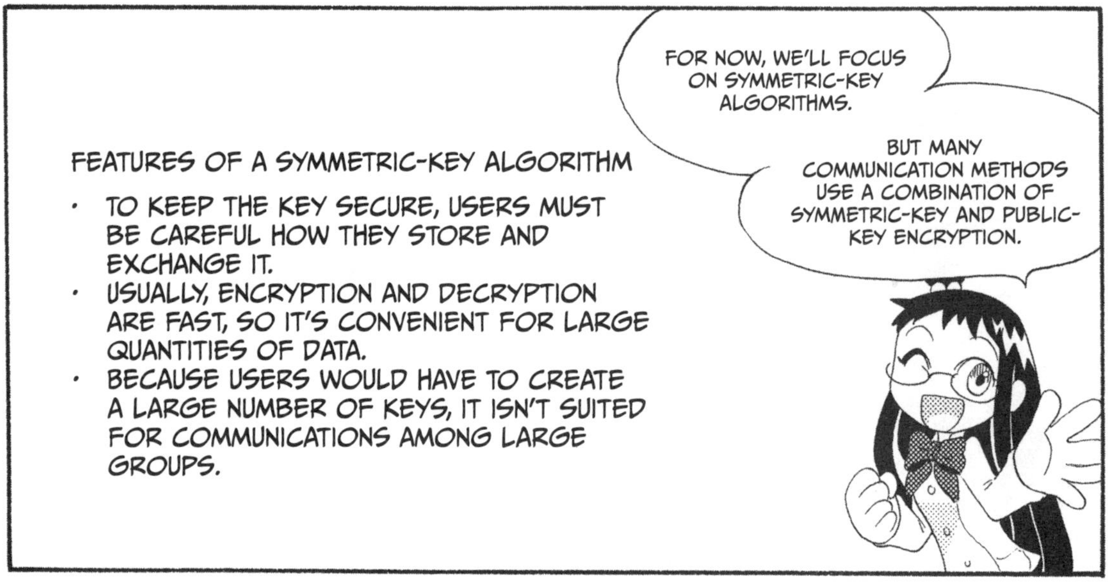
FEATURES OF A SYMMETRIC-KEY ALGORITHM
· TO KEEP THE KEY SECURE, USERS MUST BE CAREFUL HOW THEY STORE AND EXCHANGE IT.
· USUALLY, ENCRYPTION AND DECRYPTION ARE FAST, SO IT'S CONVENIENT FOR LARGE QUANTITIES OF DATA.
· BECAUSE USERS WOULD HAVE TO CREATE A LARGE NUMBER OF KEYS, IT ISN'T SUITED FOR COMMUNICATIONS AMONG LARGE GROUPS.
FOR NOW, WE'LL FOCUS ON SYMMETRIC-KEY ALGORITHMS.
BUT MANY COMMUNICATION METHODS USE A COMBINATION OF SYMMETRIC-KEY AND PUBLIC-KEY ENCRYPTION.

* PUBLIC-KEY ENCRYPTION USES SEPARATE BUT MATHEMATICALLY PAIRED KEYS FOR ENCRYPTION AND DECRYPTION. THIS IS DIFFERENT FROM SYMMETRIC-KEY ENCRYPTION, WHERE THE SAME KEY IS USED TO BOTH ENCRYPT AND DECRYPT A MESSAGE.

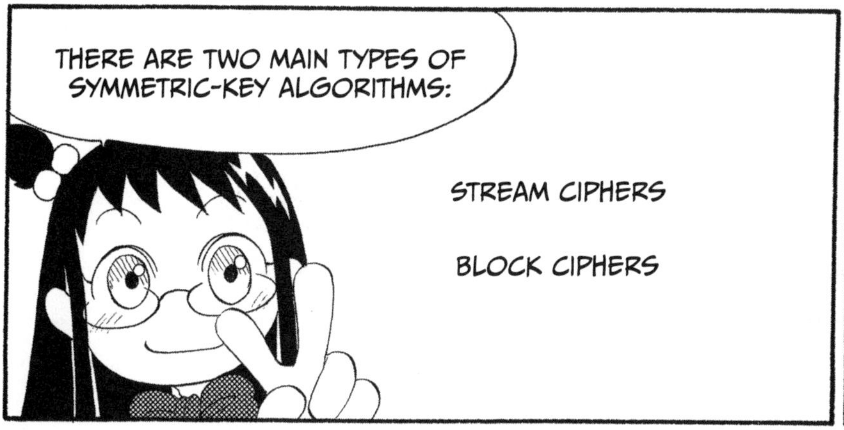
THERE ARE TWO MAIN TYPES OF SYMMETRIC-KEY ALGORITHMS:
STREAM CIPHERS
BLOCK CIPHERS

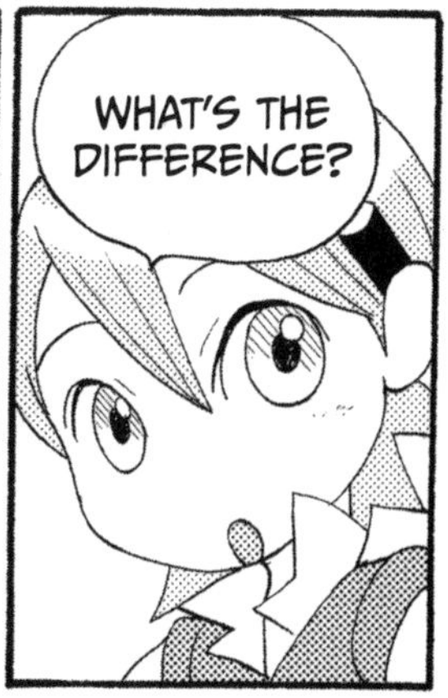
WHAT'S THE DIFFERENCE?

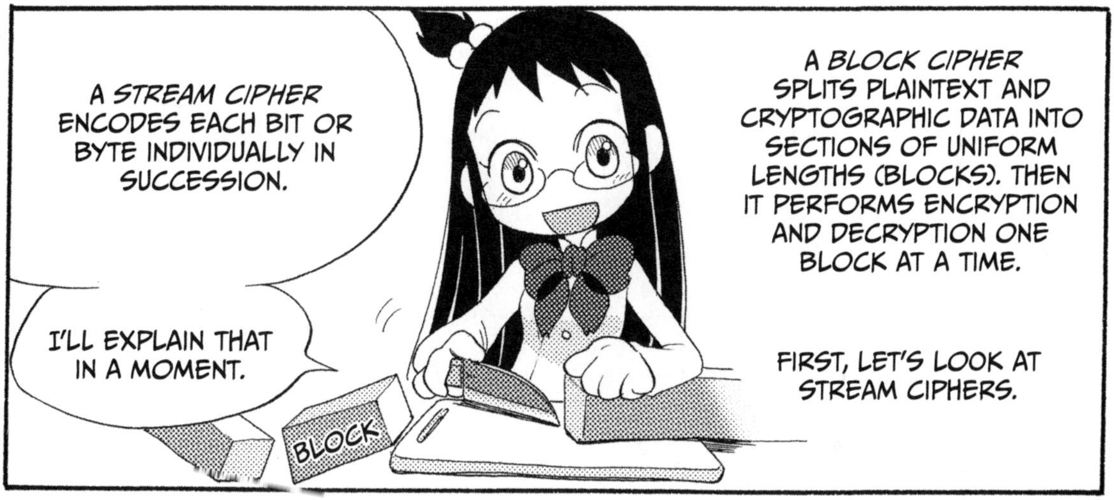
A *STREAM CIPHER* ENCODES EACH BIT OR BYTE INDIVIDUALLY IN SUCCESSION.
I'LL EXPLAIN THAT IN A MOMENT.
BLOCK
A *BLOCK CIPHER* SPLITS PLAINTEXT AND CRYPTOGRAPHIC DATA INTO SECTIONS OF UNIFORM LENGTHS (BLOCKS). THEN IT PERFORMS ENCRYPTION AND DECRYPTION ONE BLOCK AT A TIME.
FIRST, LET'S LOOK AT STREAM CIPHERS.

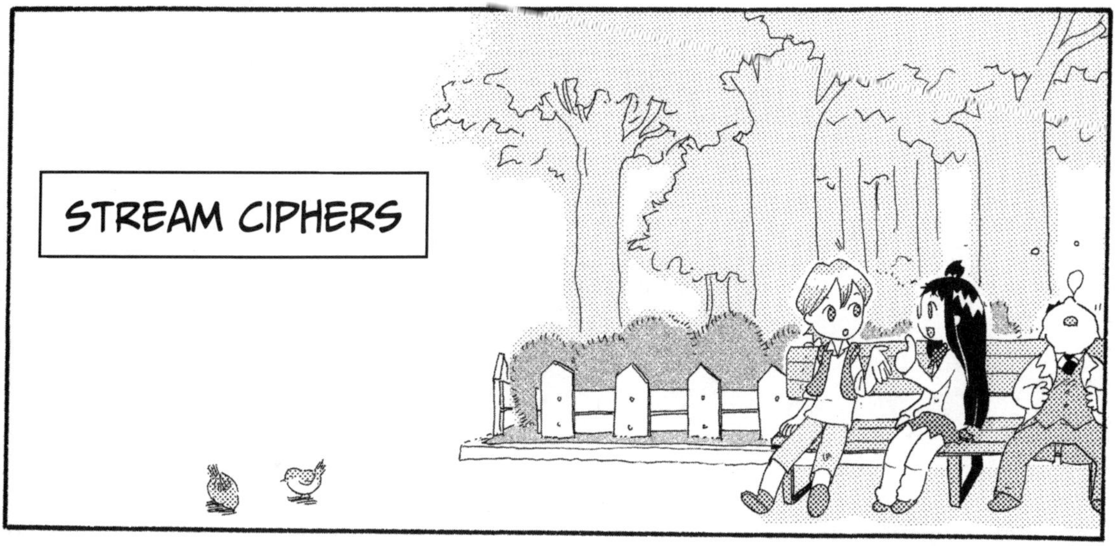
STREAM CIPHERS

LET'S SEE HOW STREAM CIPHERS PERFORM ENCRYPTION.

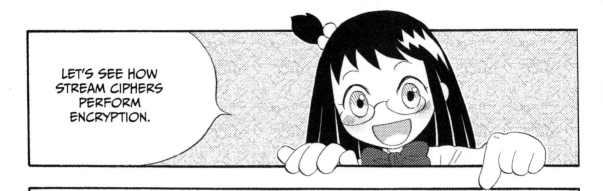

In a stream cipher, the key is a long, pseudorandom sequence of numbers. You can encrypt or decrypt with the key by performing XOR operations on each bit or byte data, as shown in the following figure. Stream ciphers are generally less computationally intensive than block ciphers. Some examples of stream ciphers include RC4 and SEAL.

Start
End
1 bit
Plaintext
1
1
0
0
1
. . .
Encrypt 1 bit or group of bits at a time.
Key
1
0
1
1
0
. . .
Ciphertext
1

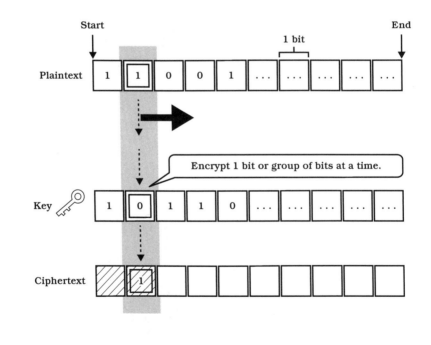

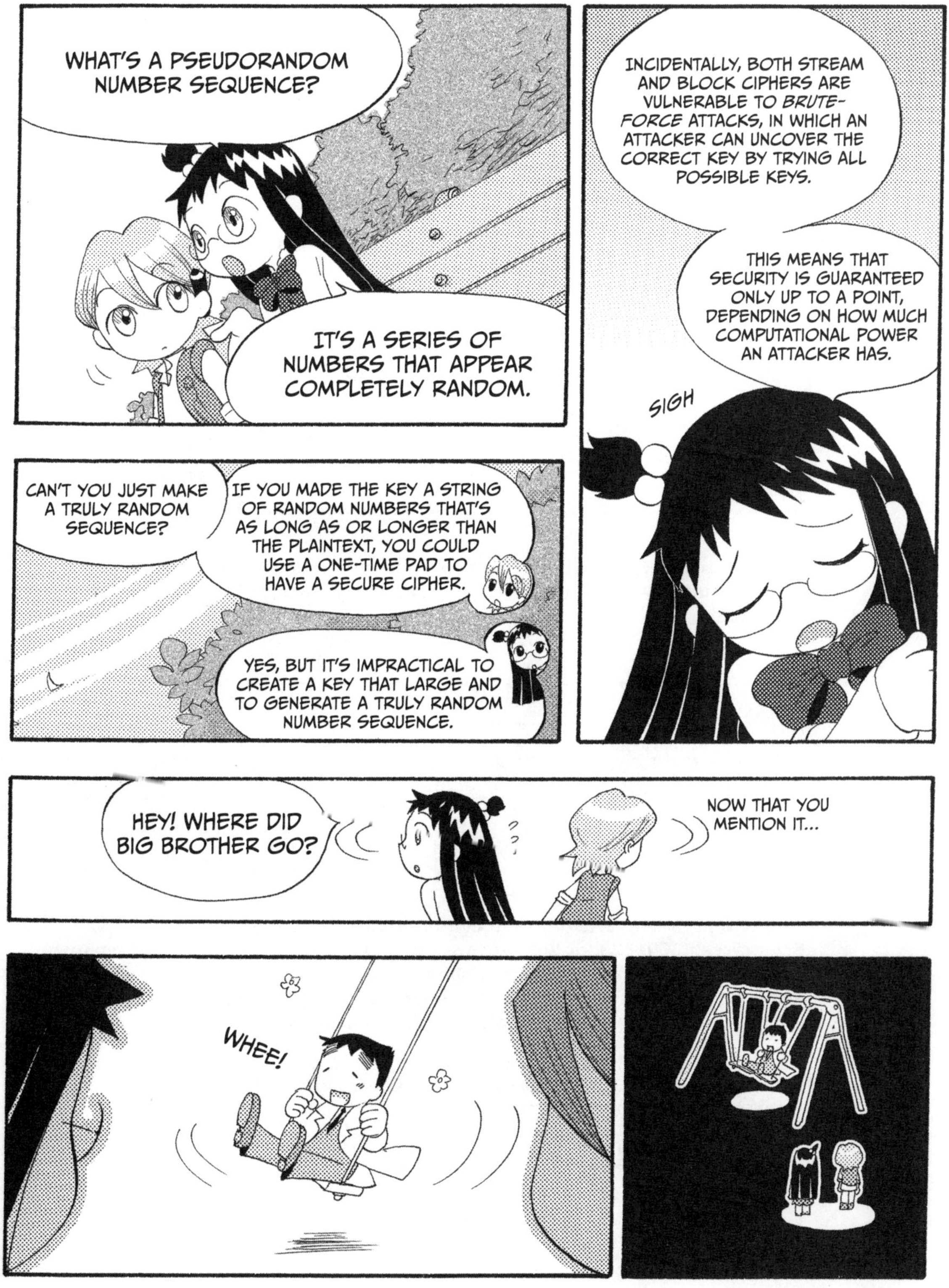

WHAT'S A PSEUDORANDOM NUMBER SEQUENCE?
IT'S A SERIES OF NUMBERS THAT APPEAR COMPLETELY RANDOM.
INCIDENTALLY, BOTH STREAM AND BLOCK CIPHERS ARE VULNERABLE TO *BRUTE-FORCE* ATTACKS, IN WHICH AN ATTACKER CAN UNCOVER THE CORRECT KEY BY TRYING ALL POSSIBLE KEYS.
THIS MEANS THAT SECURITY IS GUARANTEED ONLY UP TO A POINT, DEPENDING ON HOW MUCH COMPUTATIONAL POWER AN ATTACKER HAS.
SIGH
CAN'T YOU JUST MAKE A TRULY RANDOM SEQUENCE?
IF YOU MADE THE KEY A STRING OF RANDOM NUMBERS THAT'S AS LONG AS OR LONGER THAN THE PLAINTEXT, YOU COULD USE A ONE-TIME PAD TO HAVE A SECURE CIPHER.
YES, BUT IT'S IMPRACTICAL TO CREATE A KEY THAT LARGE AND TO GENERATE A TRULY RANDOM NUMBER SEQUENCE.
HEY! WHERE DID BIG BROTHER GO?
NOW THAT YOU MENTION IT...
WHEE!

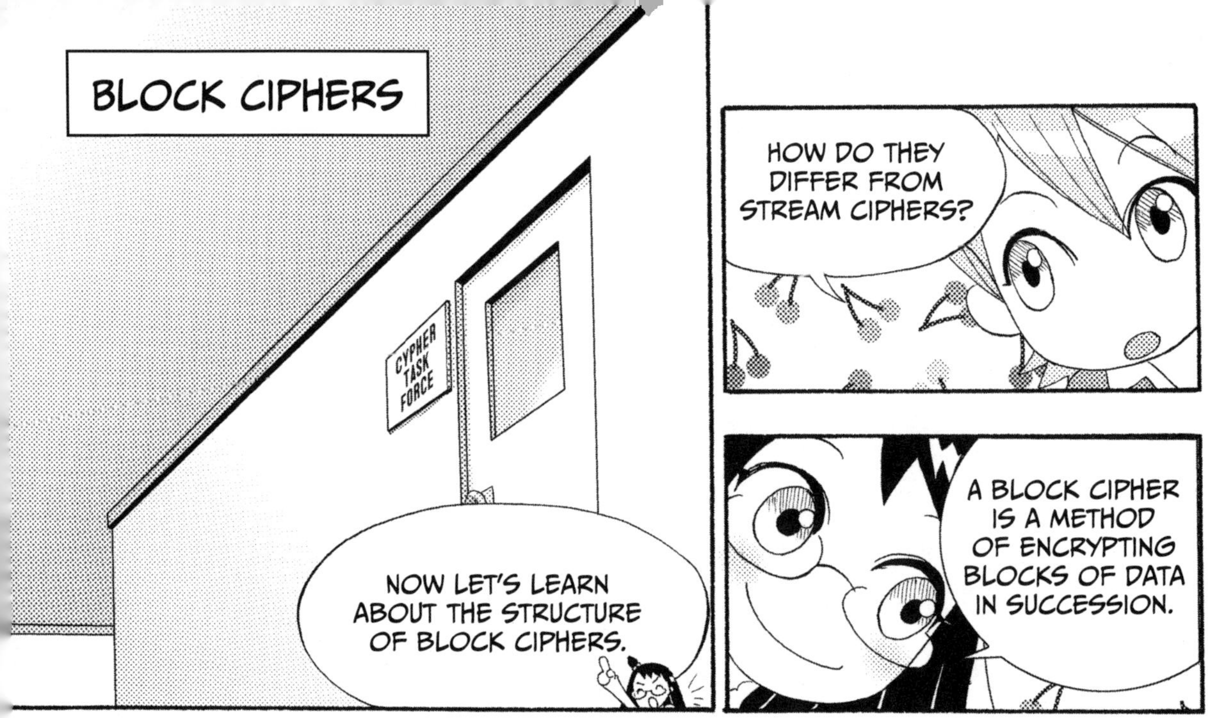
BLOCK CIPHERS
CYPHER TASK FORCE
NOW LET'S LEARN ABOUT THE STRUCTURE OF BLOCK CIPHERS.
HOW DO THEY DIFFER FROM STREAM CIPHERS?
A BLOCK CIPHER IS A METHOD OF ENCRYPTING BLOCKS OF DATA IN SUCCESSION.

Unlike a stream cipher, which encrypts each bit in succession, a block cipher splits data into blocks of uniform length and then encrypts each block, as shown here.

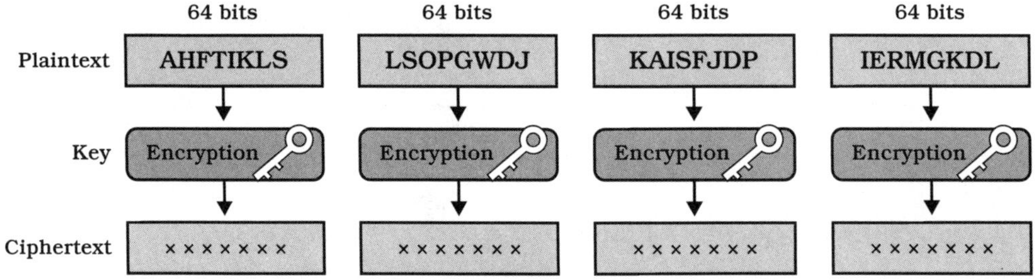
64 bits
64 bits
64 bits
64 bits
Plaintext
AHFTIKLS
LSOPGWDJ
KAISFJDP
IERMGKDL
Key
Encryption
Encryption
Encryption
Encryption
Ciphertext
×××××××
×××××××
×××××××
×××××××

The length of a given block depends on the structure of the cipher used. Block sizes of 64, 128, or 256 bits are the most common for ciphers. Because 1 byte is composed of 8 contiguous bits, it would be reasonable to use 64-bit blocks because you could use 8 characters to satisfy the block size. Using 64-bit blocks allows for faster calculations on a computer.

Name of cipher	Block length (bits)	Key length (bits)
DES	64	64
AES	128	128 192 256

Emerald
7 letters × 8 bits/letter = 56 bits
HOLD ON!
THE WORD *EMERALD* HAS 7 LETTERS. SINCE IT TAKES 1 BYTE (8 BITS) TO ENCRYPT EACH OF THOSE LETTERS...
DON'T WE NEED ONLY 56 BITS TO REPRESENT *EMERALD*?
WHEN THE LENGTH OF A BLOCK IS 64 BITS (8 BYTES)...
56 BITS
8 BITS
64 BITS
THE WORD WOULD BE 8 BITS (1 BYTE) SHORT.
IN THAT SITUATION, WE HAVE TO ADD SOME EXTRA NUMBERS TO THE END OF THE BLOCK UNTIL WE HAVE THE RIGHT BLOCK LENGTH. THIS IS CALLED *PADDING*.

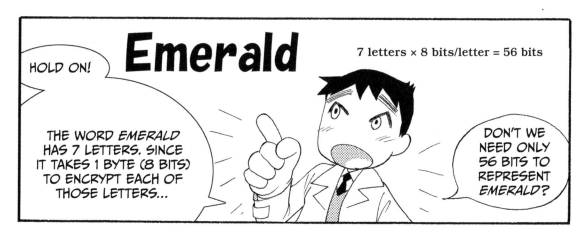

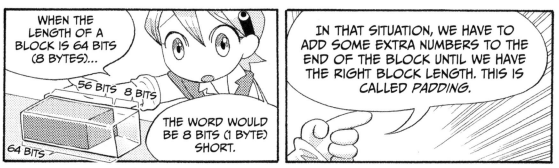

Here's how you would create a block with a length of 64 bits.

Plaintext							
E	m	e	r	a	l	d	

↓ Character encoding in hexadecimal notation

56 bits							
8 bits	8 bits	8 bits	8 bits	8 bits	8 bits	8 bits	8 bits short
0x45	0x6D	0x65	0x72	0x61	0x6C	0x64	

↓ Padding to create 64-bit block length

64 bits							
8 bits	8 bits	8 bits	8 bits	8 bits	8 bits	8 bits	8 bits
0x45	0x6D	0x65	0x72	0x61	0x6C	0x64	0x08

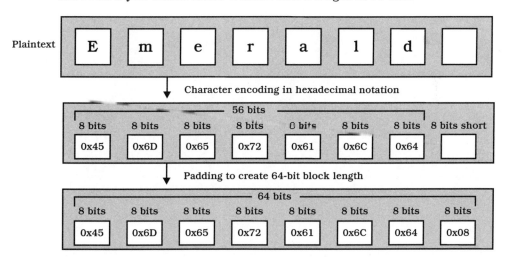

Remember: digits that have the prefix 0x are numbers in hexadecimal notation.

The value 0x08 is added to the end of the block so that the block length is 64 bits (8 bytes). The padding is 0x08 because that is the amount of padding that should be removed when the message is decrypted. This is just one way to pad blocks.

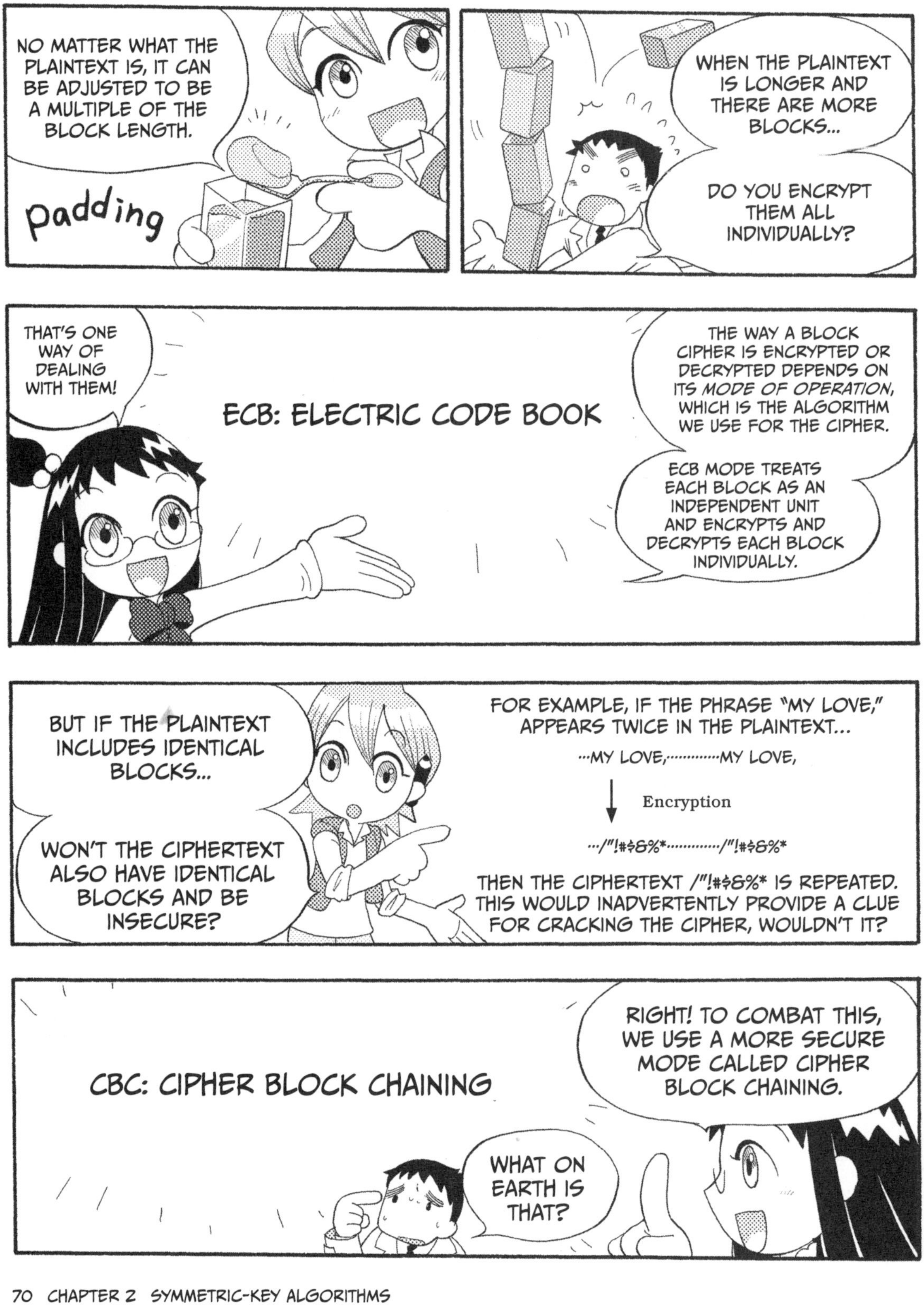
NO MATTER WHAT THE PLAINTEXT IS, IT CAN BE ADJUSTED TO BE A MULTIPLE OF THE BLOCK LENGTH.
padding
WHEN THE PLAINTEXT IS LONGER AND THERE ARE MORE BLOCKS...
DO YOU ENCRYPT THEM ALL INDIVIDUALLY?
THAT'S ONE WAY OF DEALING WITH THEM!
ECB: ELECTRIC CODE BOOK
THE WAY A BLOCK CIPHER IS ENCRYPTED OR DECRYPTED DEPENDS ON ITS *MODE OF OPERATION*, WHICH IS THE ALGORITHM WE USE FOR THE CIPHER.
ECB MODE TREATS EACH BLOCK AS AN INDEPENDENT UNIT AND ENCRYPTS AND DECRYPTS EACH BLOCK INDIVIDUALLY.
BUT IF THE PLAINTEXT INCLUDES IDENTICAL BLOCKS...
WON'T THE CIPHERTEXT ALSO HAVE IDENTICAL BLOCKS AND BE INSECURE?
FOR EXAMPLE, IF THE PHRASE "MY LOVE," APPEARS TWICE IN THE PLAINTEXT...
···MY LOVE,············MY LOVE,
Encryption
···/"!#$&%*············/"!#$&%*
THEN THE CIPHERTEXT /"!#$&%* IS REPEATED. THIS WOULD INADVERTENTLY PROVIDE A CLUE FOR CRACKING THE CIPHER, WOULDN'T IT?
CBC: CIPHER BLOCK CHAINING
RIGHT! TO COMBAT THIS, WE USE A MORE SECURE MODE CALLED CIPHER BLOCK CHAINING.
WHAT ON EARTH IS THAT?

CBC MODE

CBC mode outputs different ciphertexts even in cases where the plaintext is the same.

Once the plaintext is cut into blocks, the first block is XORed with an *initialization vector* (an additional cipher block, which is a value known to everyone), and then it's encrypted using a block cipher with a key. The next plaintext block is XORed with the most recently encrypted block and then also encrypted using the block cipher with a key.

This process is done on all of the blocks, making it practically impossible for any connection to be made between blocks. In the following figure, the previous ciphertext block C_{i-1} and the next plaintext block P_i are XORed to produce X_i. In other words, X_i is calculated by using the following formula:

$$X_i = C_i \oplus P_i$$

With this method, even if there are blocks of identical plaintext data, there are no identical blocks in the ciphertext.

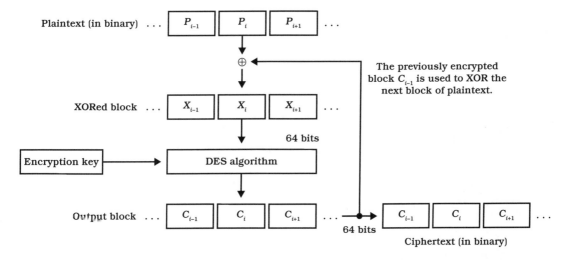

Plaintext (in binary) . . .
P_{i-1}
P_i
P_{i+1}
. . .
The previously encrypted block C_{i-1} is used to XOR the next block of plaintext.
XORed block . . .
X_{i-1}
X_i
X_{i+1}
. . .
64 bits
Encryption key
DES algorithm
Output block . . .
C_{i-1}
C_i
C_{i+1}
. . .
64 bits
C_{i-1}
C_i
C_{i+1}
. . .
Ciphertext (in binary)

CBC and ECB are two of the most well-known modes of operation. ECB is no longer used because it is insecure. Other common modes are OFB (output feedback) and CFB (cipher feedback).

THIS IS GETTING TOUGH.

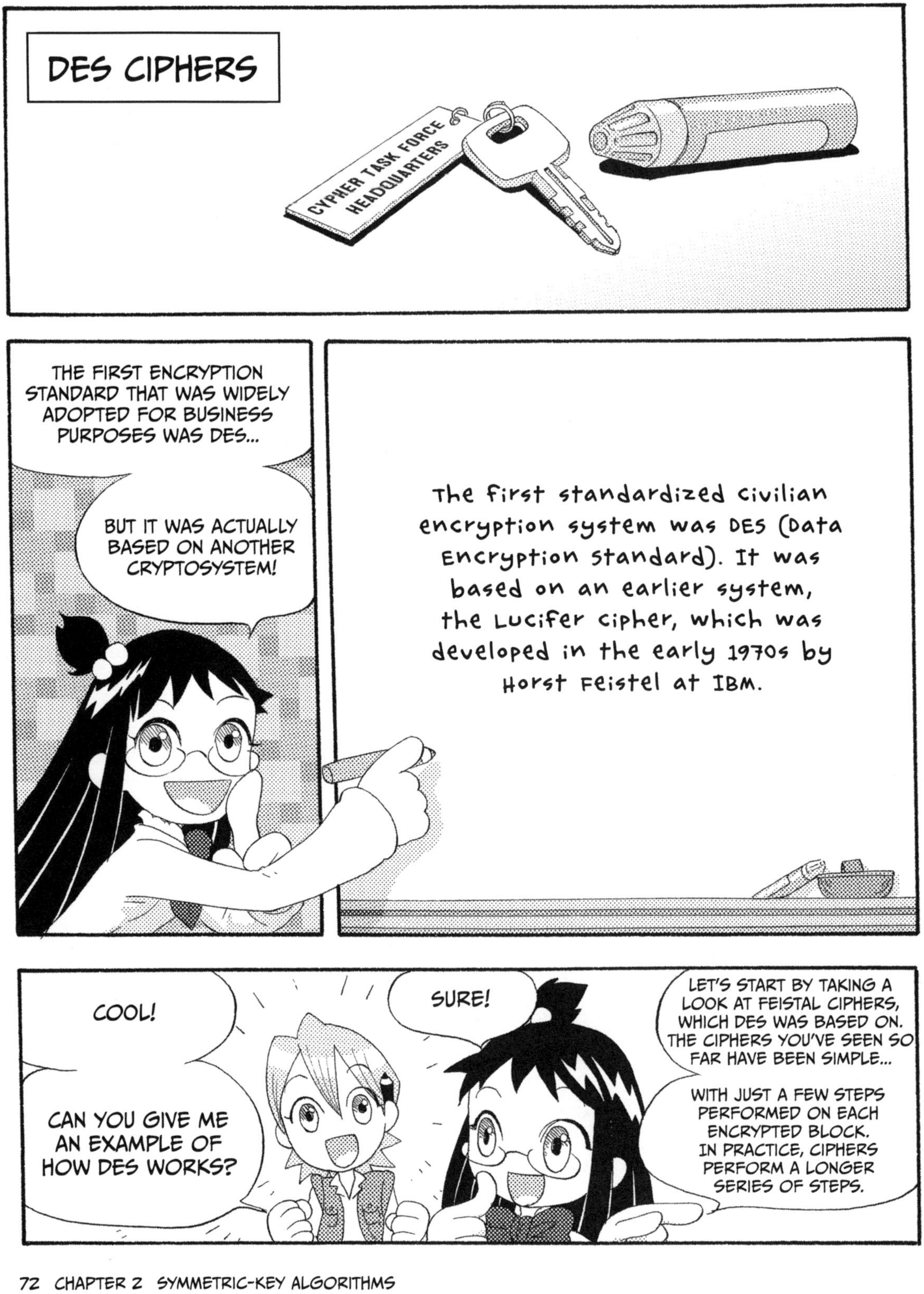
DES CIPHERS
CYPHER TASK FORCE HEADQUARTERS
THE FIRST ENCRYPTION STANDARD THAT WAS WIDELY ADOPTED FOR BUSINESS PURPOSES WAS DES...
BUT IT WAS ACTUALLY BASED ON ANOTHER CRYPTOSYSTEM!
The first standardized civilian encryption system was DES (Data Encryption Standard). It was based on an earlier system, the Lucifer cipher, which was developed in the early 1970s by Horst Feistel at IBM.
COOL!
CAN YOU GIVE ME AN EXAMPLE OF HOW DES WORKS?
SURE!
LET'S START BY TAKING A LOOK AT FEISTAL CIPHERS, WHICH DES WAS BASED ON. THE CIPHERS YOU'VE SEEN SO FAR HAVE BEEN SIMPLE...
WITH JUST A FEW STEPS PERFORMED ON EACH ENCRYPTED BLOCK. IN PRACTICE, CIPHERS PERFORM A LONGER SERIES OF STEPS.

THE BASIC CONFIGURATION OF A FEISTEL CIPHER

Each set of steps is called a *round*, and rounds are performed multiple times on a block. The series of steps performed each round is the *round function*. The Feistel cipher uses multiple rounds and subkeys that are derived from one initial key. The following figure outlines Feistel's method of encryption; we'll discuss the details of each round and how the subkeys are created later.

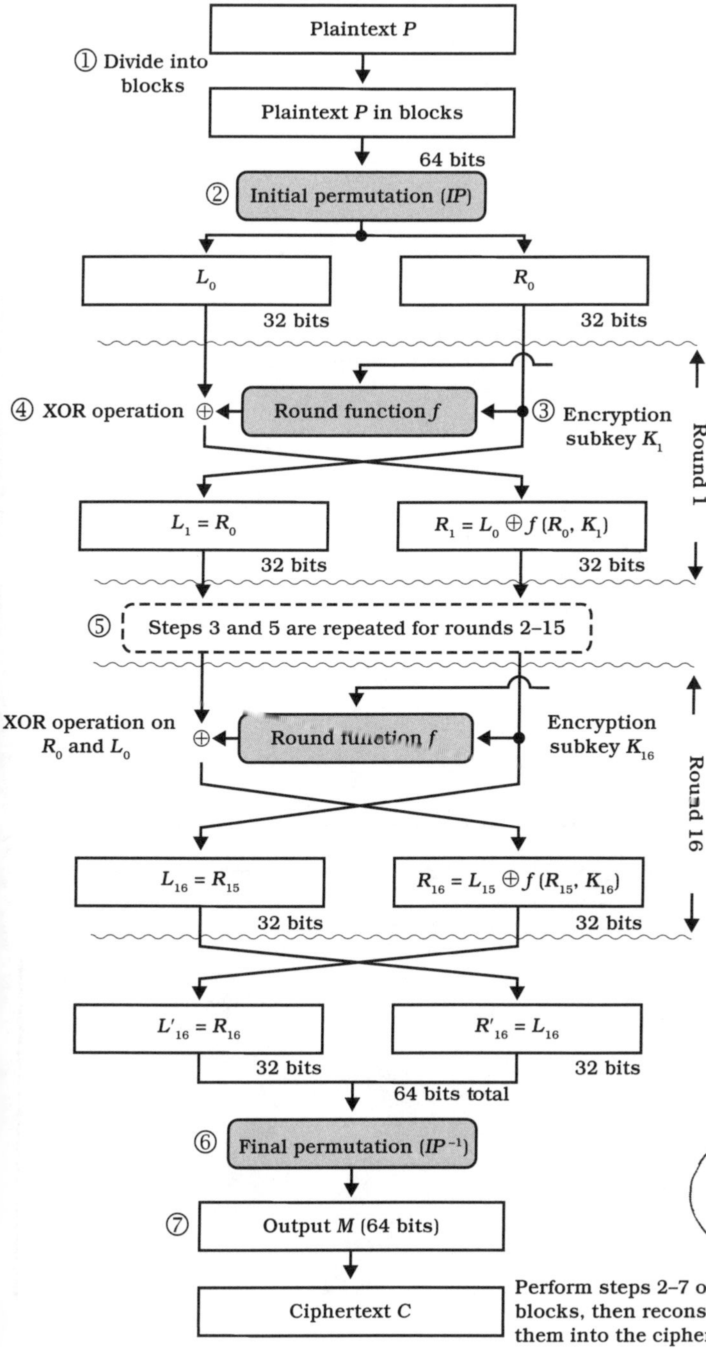

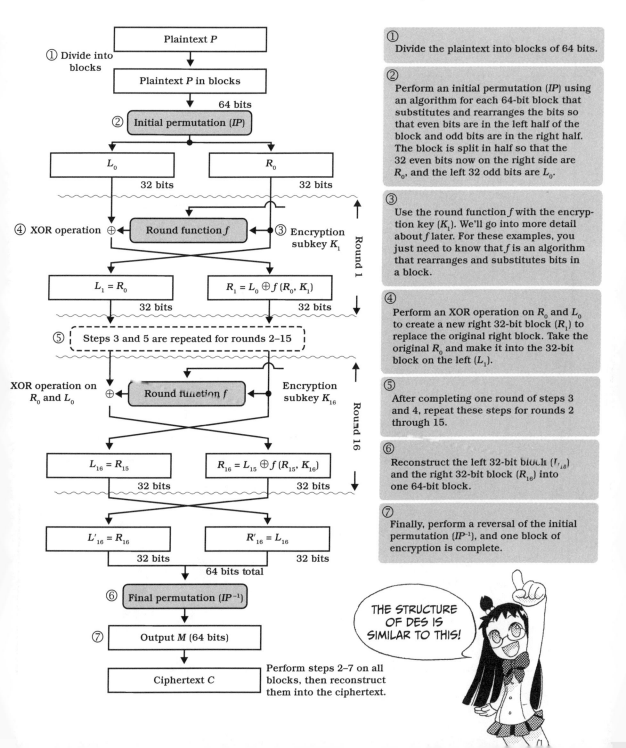

Plaintext P
① Divide into blocks
Plaintext P in blocks
64 bits
② Initial permutation (IP)
L_0
R_0
32 bits
32 bits
④ XOR operation
Round function f
③ Encryption subkey K_1
Round 1
$L_1 = R_0$
$R_1 = L_0 \oplus f(R_0, K_1)$
32 bits
32 bits
⑤ Steps 3 and 5 are repeated for rounds 2–15
XOR operation on R_0 and L_0
Round function f
Encryption subkey K_{16}
Round 16
$L_{16} = R_{15}$
$R_{16} = L_{15} \oplus f(R_{15}, K_{16})$
32 bits
32 bits
$L'_{16} = R_{16}$
$R'_{16} = L_{16}$
32 bits
32 bits
64 bits total
⑥ Final permutation (IP^{-1})
⑦ Output M (64 bits)
Ciphertext C
Perform steps 2–7 on all blocks, then reconstruct them into the ciphertext.

①
Divide the plaintext into blocks of 64 bits.

②
Perform an initial permutation (*IP*) using an algorithm for each 64-bit block that substitutes and rearranges the bits so that even bits are in the left half of the block and odd bits are in the right half. The block is split in half so that the 32 even bits now on the right side are R_0, and the left 32 odd bits are L_0.

③
Use the round function *f* with the encryption key (K_1). We'll go into more detail about *f* later. For these examples, you just need to know that *f* is an algorithm that rearranges and substitutes bits in a block.

④
Perform an XOR operation on R_0 and L_0 to create a new right 32-bit block (R_1) to replace the original right block. Take the original R_0 and make it into the 32-bit block on the left (L_1).

⑤
After completing one round of steps 3 and 4, repeat these steps for rounds 2 through 15.

⑥
Reconstruct the left 32-bit block (L_{16}) and the right 32-bit block (R_{16}) into one 64-bit block.

⑦
Finally, perform a reversal of the initial permutation (IP^{-1}), and one block of encryption is complete.

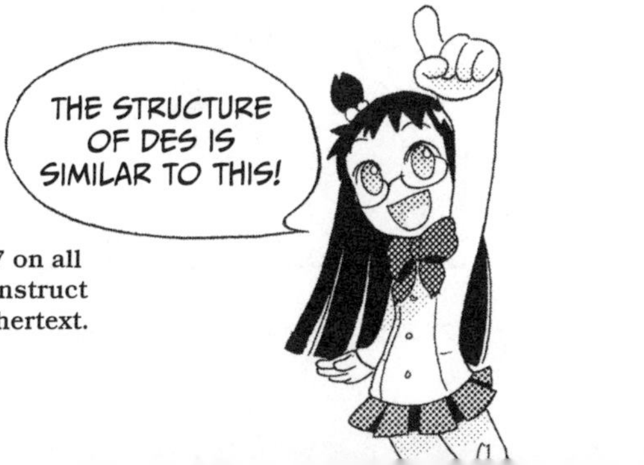

THE STRUCTURE OF DES IS SIMILAR TO THIS!

CREATING A CIPHER HAS SO MANY COMPLEX STEPS!

KEEP AT IT, BIG BROTHER.

THE PROCESS OF DECRYPTING THE CIPHERTEXT...

IS CALLED AN INVOLUTION.

INVOLUTION

An involution is a function that is its own inverse, which means that if you apply the function twice, you will return the input to its original state. For example, consider a function in which 1 becomes 4, 2 becomes 3, 3 becomes 2, and 4 becomes 1. The values in the list after the conversion are the same as the values before.

	First conversion		Second conversion	
1	→	4	→	1
2	→	3	→	2
3	→	2	→	3
4	→	1	→	4

By applying the function twice, we return to all of the original values in the same order.

FEISTEL'S CIPHER IS AWESOME, ISN'T IT?

AWW SHUCKS!

THE FEISTEL CIPHER INFLUENCED THE EVOLUTION OF BLOCK CIPHERS.

IT'S ALSO CALLED A FEISTEL NETWORK.

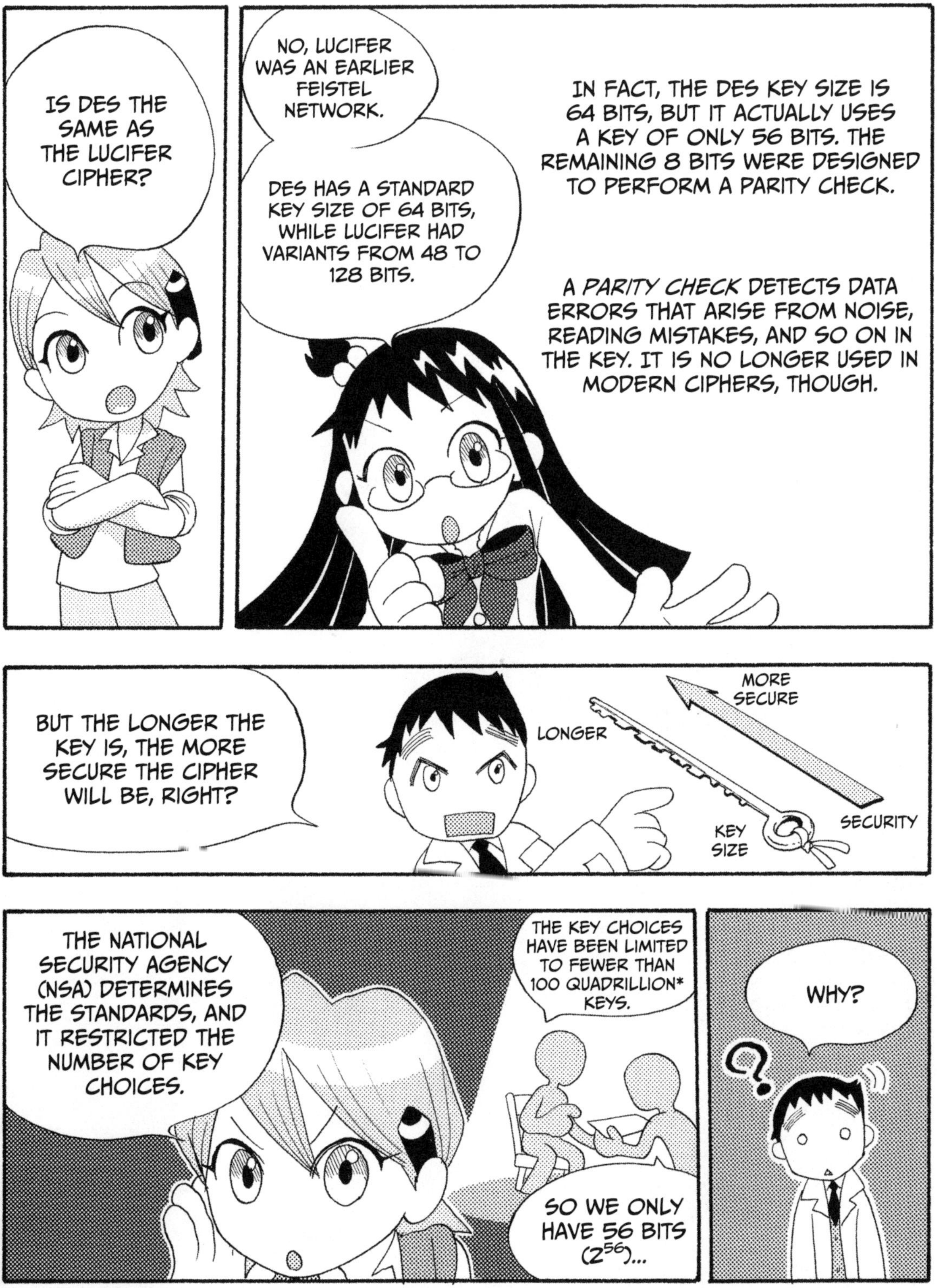
IS DES THE SAME AS THE LUCIFER CIPHER?
NO, LUCIFER WAS AN EARLIER FEISTEL NETWORK.
DES HAS A STANDARD KEY SIZE OF 64 BITS, WHILE LUCIFER HAD VARIANTS FROM 48 TO 128 BITS.
IN FACT, THE DES KEY SIZE IS 64 BITS, BUT IT ACTUALLY USES A KEY OF ONLY 56 BITS. THE REMAINING 8 BITS WERE DESIGNED TO PERFORM A PARITY CHECK.
A *PARITY CHECK* DETECTS DATA ERRORS THAT ARISE FROM NOISE, READING MISTAKES, AND SO ON IN THE KEY. IT IS NO LONGER USED IN MODERN CIPHERS, THOUGH.
BUT THE LONGER THE KEY IS, THE MORE SECURE THE CIPHER WILL BE, RIGHT?
MORE SECURE
LONGER
KEY SIZE
SECURITY
THE NATIONAL SECURITY AGENCY (NSA) DETERMINES THE STANDARDS, AND IT RESTRICTED THE NUMBER OF KEY CHOICES.
THE KEY CHOICES HAVE BEEN LIMITED TO FEWER THAN 100 QUADRILLION* KEYS.
SO WE ONLY HAVE 56 BITS (2^{56})...
WHY?

* ONE HUNDRED MILLION = 10^8, ONE TRILLION = 10^{12}, TEN QUADRILLION = 10^{16}, ONE HUNDRED QUINTILLION = 10^{20}

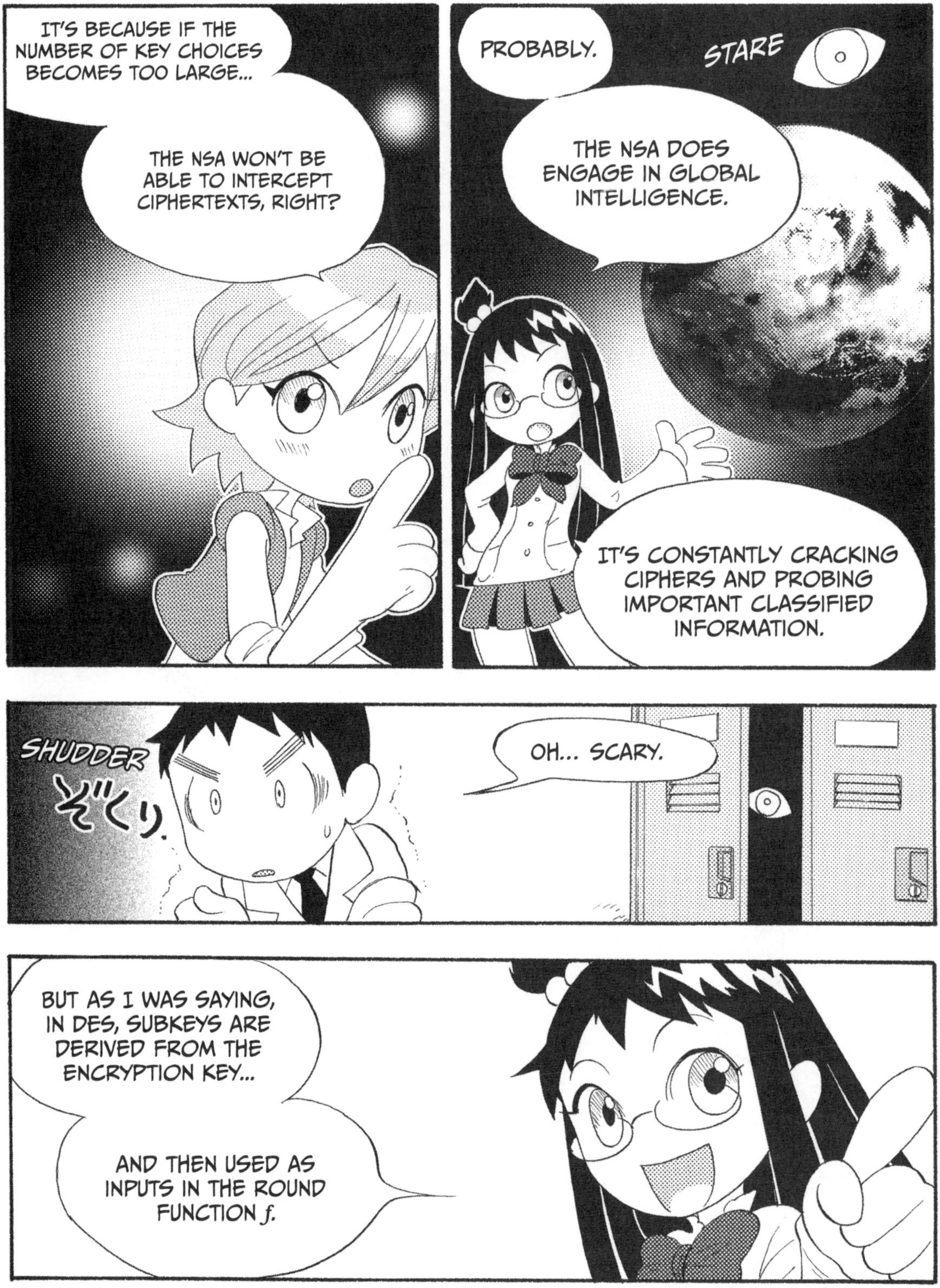
IT'S BECAUSE IF THE NUMBER OF KEY CHOICES BECOMES TOO LARGE...
THE NSA WON'T BE ABLE TO INTERCEPT CIPHERTEXTS, RIGHT?
PROBABLY.
STARE
THE NSA DOES ENGAGE IN GLOBAL INTELLIGENCE.
IT'S CONSTANTLY CRACKING CIPHERS AND PROBING IMPORTANT CLASSIFIED INFORMATION.
SHUDDER
ぞくり
OH... SCARY.
BUT AS I WAS SAYING, IN DES, SUBKEYS ARE DERIVED FROM THE ENCRYPTION KEY...
AND THEN USED AS INPUTS IN THE ROUND FUNCTION *f*.

GENERATING DES ENCRYPTION SUBKEYS

In DES, a different key is used for each round of encryption, so 16 subkeys—K_1, K_2, K_3, . . . , K_{16}—need to be created from the encryption key for each of the 16 rounds. This is the method used to derive subkeys:

Secret key K (initial key)
64 bits
①
Permuted choice PC–1
56 bits
②
28 bits
28 bits
C_0
D_0
③
Left circular shift (LS_1)
Left circular shift (LS_1)
28 bits
28 bits
C_1
D_1
Round 1
④
Compression permutation PC–2
48 bits
Subkey K_1
⑤
Steps 3 and 4 are repeated in rounds 2–15
48 bits
Subkeys K_2–K_{15}
Left circular shift (LS_{16})
Left circular shift (LS_{16})
28 bits
28 bits
C_{16}
D_{16}
Round 16
Compression permutation PC–2
48 bits
Subkey K_{16}

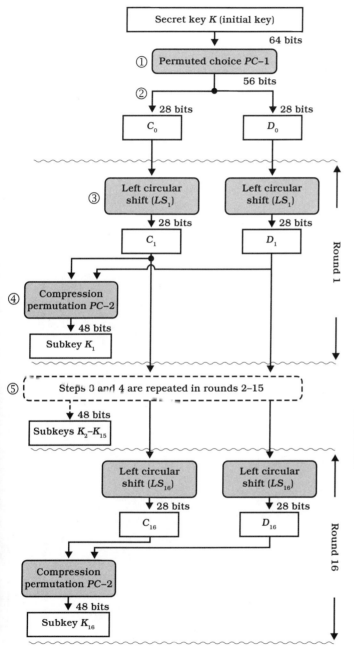

①
A permutation called permuted choice 1 (PC–1) is performed on the 56 nonparity bits of the initial key. Permuted choice 1 is a special permutation method that transposes each of the 56 bits into specific positions. We won't cover the details of it here.

②
The 56 bits are divided into a 28-bit left block (C_0) and a 28-bit right block (D_0).

③
The bits in C_0 and D_0 are left-circular shifted to create C_1 and D_1. A left-circular shift moves every bit a certain number of places to the left, and the bits at the beginning of the block are shifted to the very end, as though the block's beginning and end were connected as in a circle.

④
C_1 and D_1 are joined. Then subkey K_1 is made through another permutation, permuted choice 2 (PC–2). PC–2 is applied to all 56 bits of C_1 and D_1 except for the 8 parity bits, resulting in a compressed 48-bit subkey.

⑤
Steps 3 and 4 are repeated for each round to generate each subkey K_n. Each of these subkeys will then be used for each round in DES.

To generate the decryption subkeys, the bits are right-circular shifted instead. When the initial key is used for decryption, the subkeys are obtained in reverse order from K_{16} to K_1.

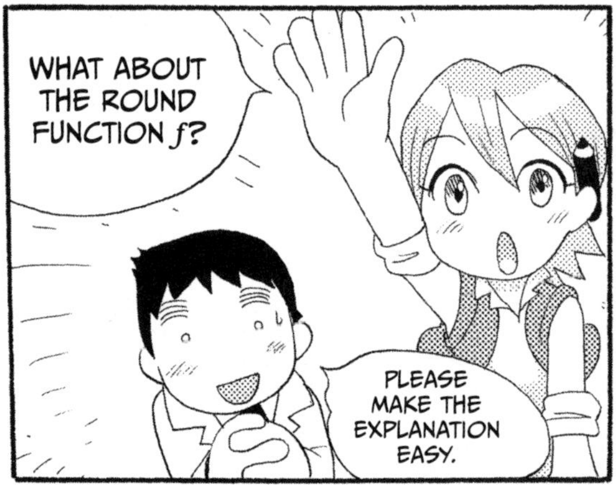
WHAT ABOUT THE ROUND FUNCTION *f*?
PLEASE MAKE THE EXPLANATION EASY.

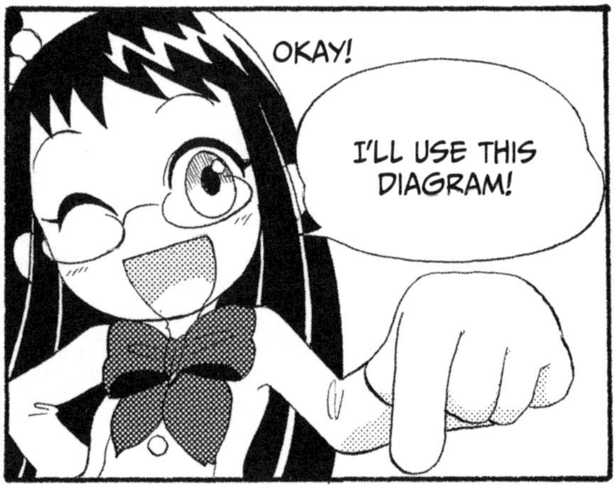
OKAY!
I'LL USE THIS DIAGRAM!

THE DES ROUND FUNCTION F

In a round function, you use an *S-box (substitution box)* to perform substitutions on an input to make a new output. Each S-box in this diagram contains a different permutation for creating the substitutions.

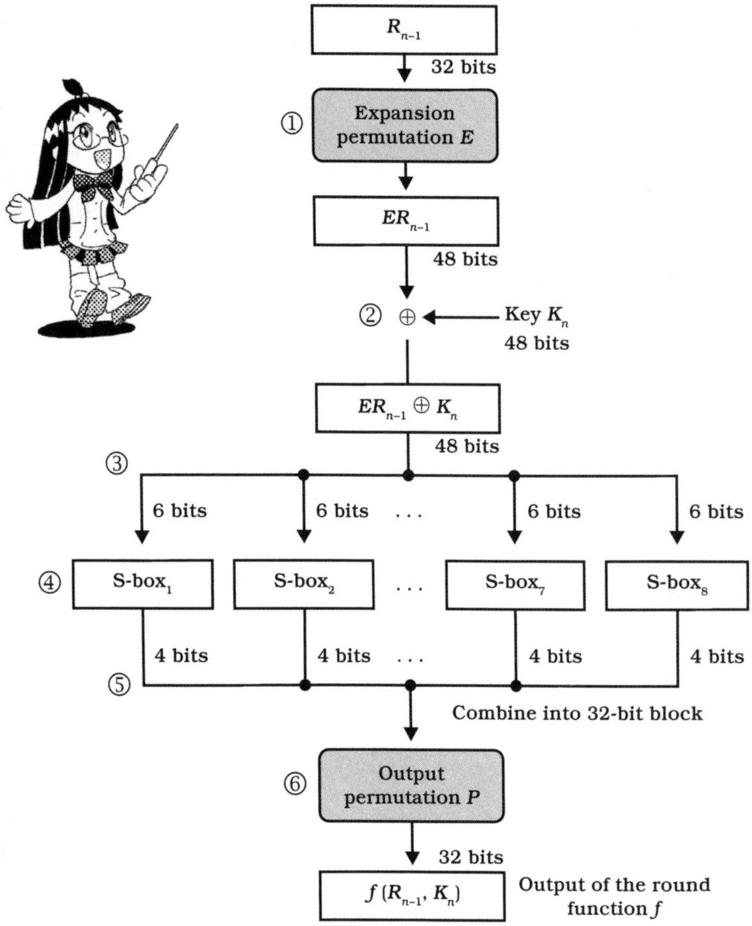
R_{n-1}
32 bits
①
Expansion permutation E
ER_{n-1}
48 bits
②
Key K_n
48 bits
$ER_{n-1} \oplus K_n$
48 bits
③
6 bits
6 bits
. . .
6 bits
6 bits
④
S-box$_1$
S-box$_2$
. . .
S-box$_7$
S-box$_8$
4 bits
4 bits
. . .
4 bits
4 bits
⑤
Combine into 32-bit block
⑥
Output permutation P
32 bits
$f(R_{n-1}, K_n)$
Output of the round function f

①
The DES function only works on 48-bit blocks, so the rightmost block of data, which is only 32 bits, needs to be expanded using a 48-bit expansion permutation E. This results in the output ER_{n-1}, which is a 48-bit block.

②
Perform an XOR operation on the data and the subkey.

③
Separate the result of the operation into eight sets of 6-bit blocks each.

④
Substitute each 6-bit set of data with 4 bits using S-boxes 1 through 8.

⑤
Combine the S-box output data sequentially to produce a 32-bit block.

⑥
Finally, apply permutation P to the data to yield the output of function f.

THE FULL STRUCTURE OF DES ENCRYPTION AND DECRYPTION

The full DES encryption and decryption processes with all the steps we've covered are shown here. The plaintext encryption process and the cipher decryption process are opposite each other.

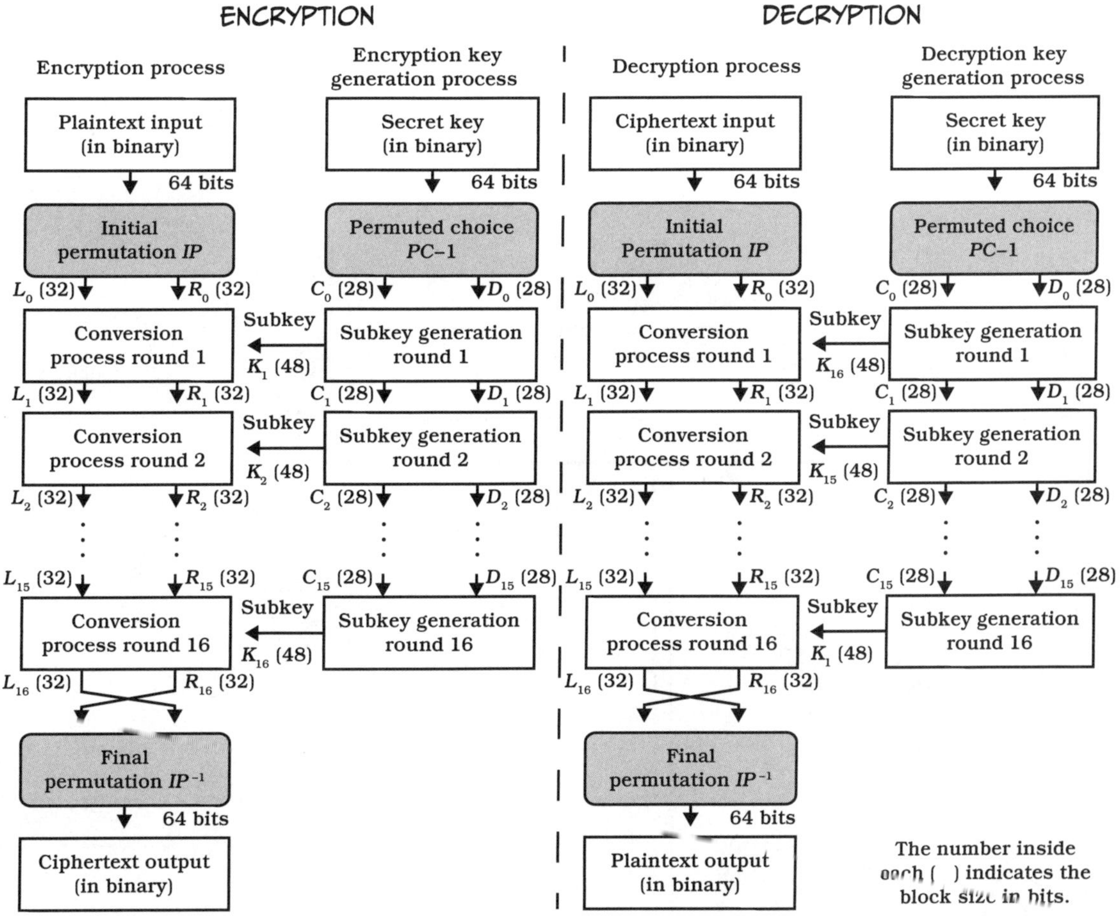

ENCRYPTION
Encryption process
Encryption key generation process
Plaintext input (in binary)
64 bits
Initial permutation IP
Secret key (in binary)
64 bits
Permuted choice PC–1
L0 (32)
R0 (32)
C0 (28)
D0 (28)
Conversion process round 1
Subkey K1 (48)
Subkey generation round 1
L1 (32)
R1 (32)
C1 (28)
D1 (28)
Conversion process round 2
Subkey K2 (48)
Subkey generation round 2
L2 (32)
R2 (32)
C2 (28)
D2 (28)
L15 (32)
R15 (32)
C15 (28)
D15 (28)
Conversion process round 16
Subkey K16 (48)
Subkey generation round 16
L16 (32)
R16 (32)
Final permutation IP^-1
64 bits
Ciphertext output (in binary)
DECRYPTION
Decryption process
Decryption key generation process
Ciphertext input (in binary)
64 bits
Initial Permutation IP
Secret key (in binary)
64 bits
Permuted choice PC–1
L0 (32)
R0 (32)
C0 (28)
D0 (28)
Conversion process round 1
Subkey K16 (48)
Subkey generation round 1
L1 (32)
R1 (32)
C1 (28)
D1 (28)
Conversion process round 2
Subkey K15 (48)
Subkey generation round 2
L2 (32)
R2 (32)
C2 (28)
D2 (28)
L15 (32)
R15 (32)
C15 (28)
D15 (28)
Conversion process round 16
Subkey K1 (48)
Subkey generation round 16
L16 (32)
R16 (32)
Final permutation IP^-1
64 bits
Plaintext output (in binary)
The number inside each ( ) indicates the block size in bits.

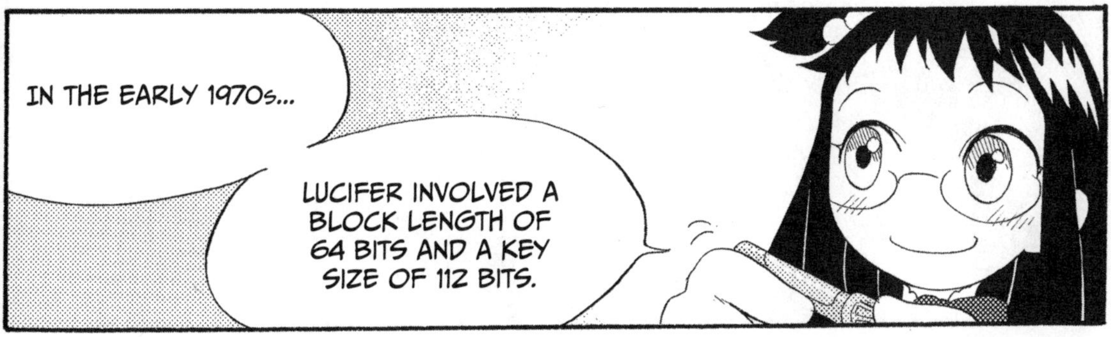

IN THE EARLY 1970s...
LUCIFER INVOLVED A BLOCK LENGTH OF 64 BITS AND A KEY SIZE OF 112 BITS.

3-DES ENCRYPTION AND AES ENCRYPTION

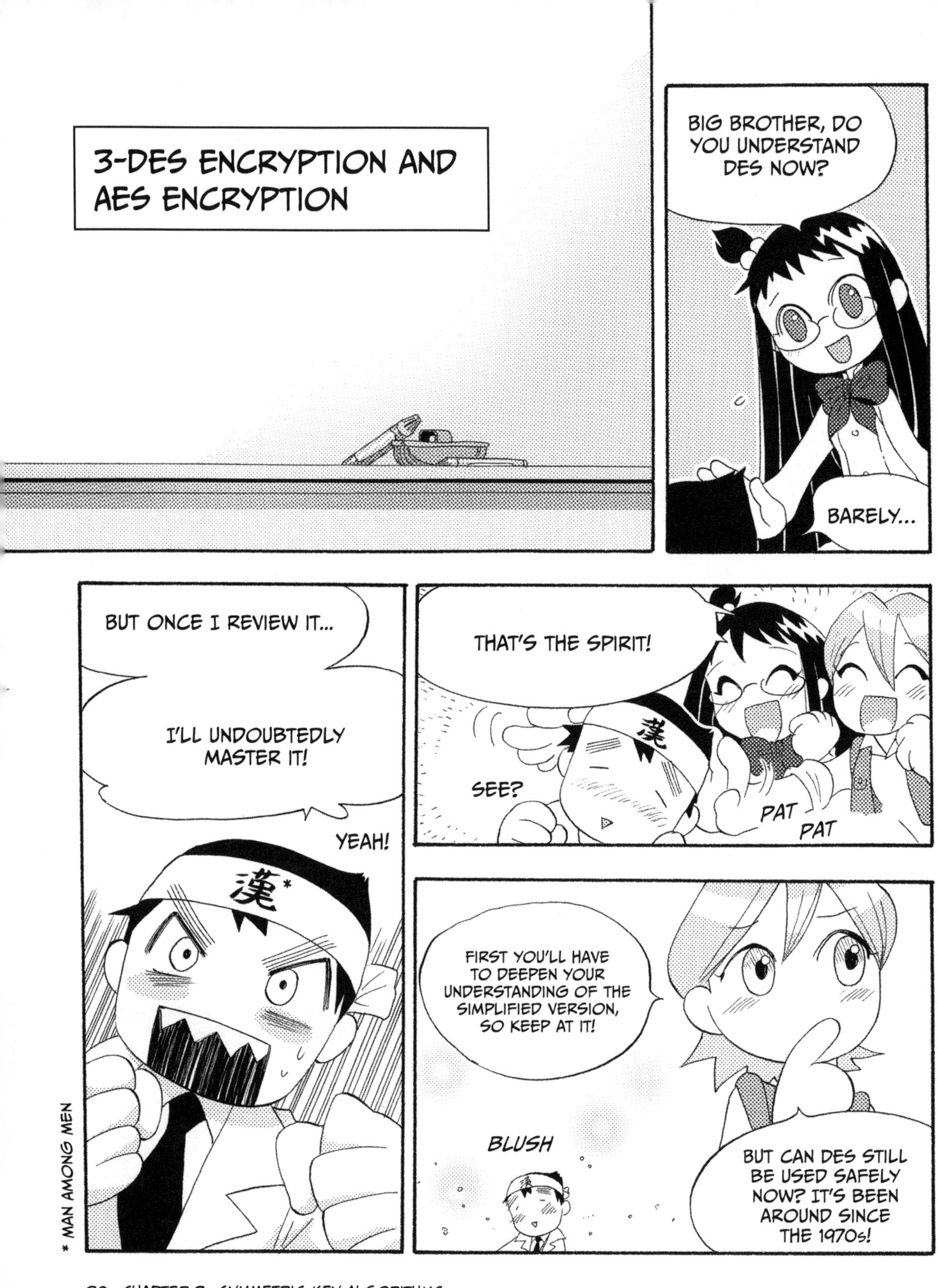
BIG BROTHER, DO YOU UNDERSTAND DES NOW?
BARELY...
BUT ONCE I REVIEW IT...
I'LL UNDOUBTEDLY MASTER IT!
YEAH!
漢*
THAT'S THE SPIRIT!
漢
SEE?
PAT PAT
FIRST YOU'LL HAVE TO DEEPEN YOUR UNDERSTANDING OF THE SIMPLIFIED VERSION, SO KEEP AT IT!
BLUSH
BUT CAN DES STILL BE USED SAFELY NOW? IT'S BEEN AROUND SINCE THE 1970s!

* MAN AMONG MEN

YES... DES HAS BECOME INSECURE DUE TO ADVANCEMENT IN COMPUTERS AND NOW CAN BE EASILY CRACKED.

THE DRAWBACKS OF DES

- SHORT KEY SIZE: THE SHORTER THE KEY, THE SMALLER THE NUMBER OF POSSIBLE KEYS AVAILABLE AND THE MORE FEASIBLE IT IS TO UNCOVER THE SECRET KEY.
- OUTDATED DESIGN: THE STRUCTURAL DESIGN OF DES IS CONSIDERED OBSOLETE AND IS NO LONGER USED. NONRIGOROUS IMPLEMENTATIONS OF CRYPTOGRAPHY COMMONLY APPEAR ON THE MARKET AND ARE EASIER TO CRACK THAN ALREADY ESTABLISHED ONES.

HOW IS IT DONE?

GLOW

CAN EVEN I DO IT?

ABSOLUTELY...

IMPOSSIBLE.

WHAM!

HERE ARE A FEW METHODS FOR CRACKING A BLOCK CIPHER!

Exhaustive search algorithm	Searching for the key by trying every possible key (brute forcing)
Differential cryptanalysis	Searching for vulnerabilities in the cipher by looking for any correlation between its inputs and outputs
Linear cryptanalysis	Searching for vulnerabilities in the cipher by looking for mathematical weaknesses in the cipher structure

IN THE 1990s, DES ENCRYPTION...

BECAME CRACKABLE USING COMPUTING POWER TO BRUTE-FORCE THE KEY.

HUH? BUT I WORKED SO HARD TO LEARN IT!

IT'S HOPELESS!

GAAAAAHHH!

THANKFULLY, 3-DES TOOK ITS PLACE!

3-DES

3-DES IS ALSO KNOWN AS TRIPLE-DES.

BASED ON THE NAME, IT USES DES, RIGHT?

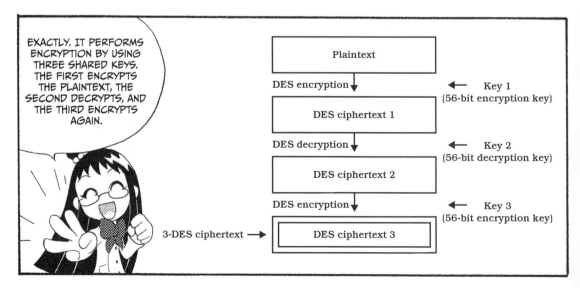

EXACTLY. IT PERFORMS ENCRYPTION BY USING THREE SHARED KEYS. THE FIRST ENCRYPTS THE PLAINTEXT, THE SECOND DECRYPTS, AND THE THIRD ENCRYPTS AGAIN.

Plaintext

DES encryption →

DES ciphertext 1

← Key 1 (56-bit encryption key)

DES decryption →

DES ciphertext 2

← Key 2 (56-bit decryption key)

DES encryption →

3-DES ciphertext →

DES ciphertext 3

← Key 3 (56-bit encryption key)

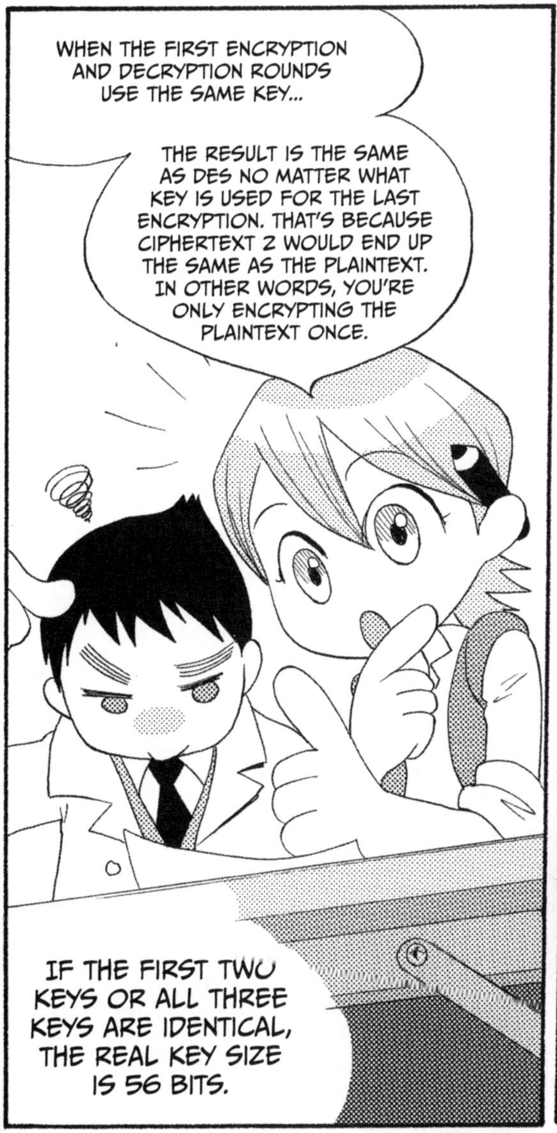
WHEN THE FIRST ENCRYPTION AND DECRYPTION ROUNDS USE THE SAME KEY...
THE RESULT IS THE SAME AS DES NO MATTER WHAT KEY IS USED FOR THE LAST ENCRYPTION. THAT'S BECAUSE CIPHERTEXT 2 WOULD END UP THE SAME AS THE PLAINTEXT. IN OTHER WORDS, YOU'RE ONLY ENCRYPTING THE PLAINTEXT ONCE.
IF THE FIRST TWO KEYS OR ALL THREE KEYS ARE IDENTICAL, THE REAL KEY SIZE IS 56 BITS.
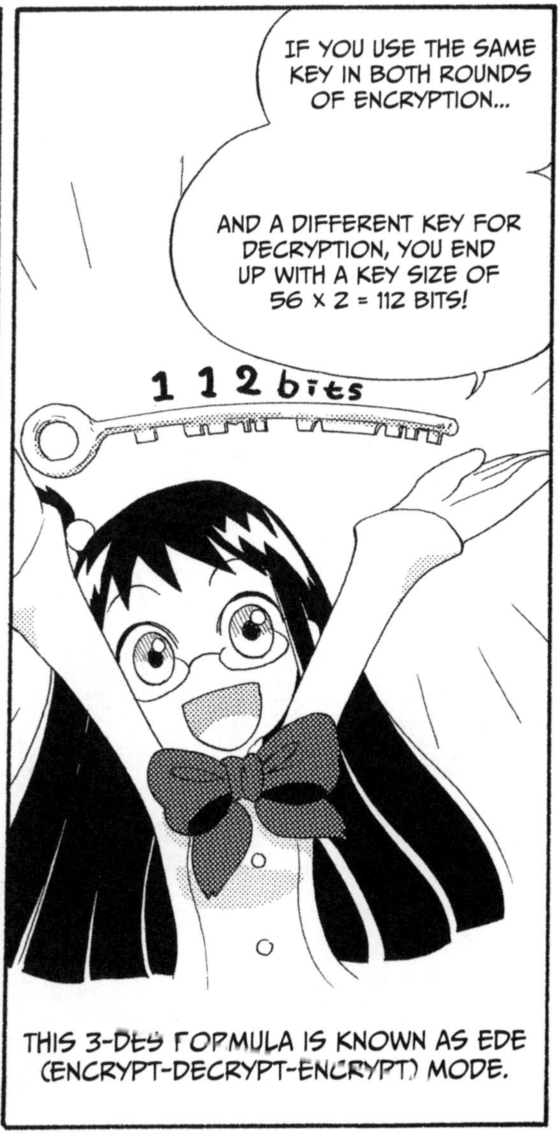
IF YOU USE THE SAME KEY IN BOTH ROUNDS OF ENCRYPTION...
AND A DIFFERENT KEY FOR DECRYPTION, YOU END UP WITH A KEY SIZE OF 56 x 2 = 112 BITS!
1 1 2 bits
THIS 3-DES FORMULA IS KNOWN AS EDE (ENCRYPT-DECRYPT-ENCRYPT) MODE.
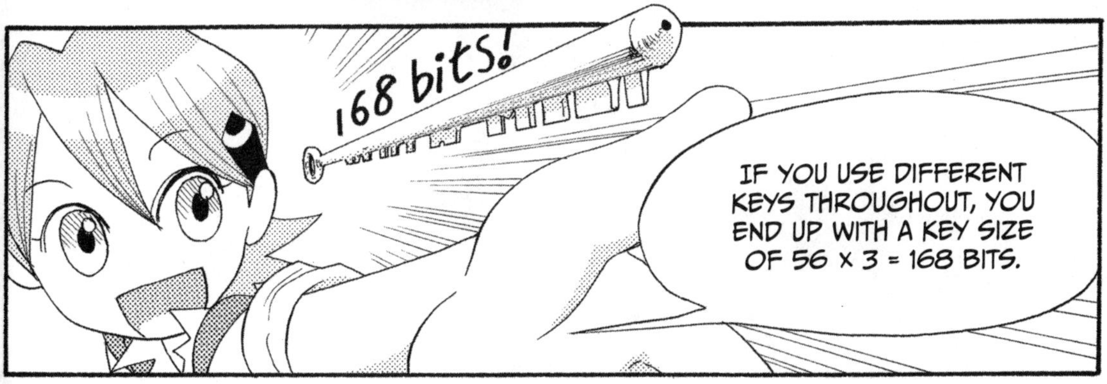
168 bits!
IF YOU USE DIFFERENT KEYS THROUGHOUT, YOU END UP WITH A KEY SIZE OF 56 x 3 = 168 BITS.

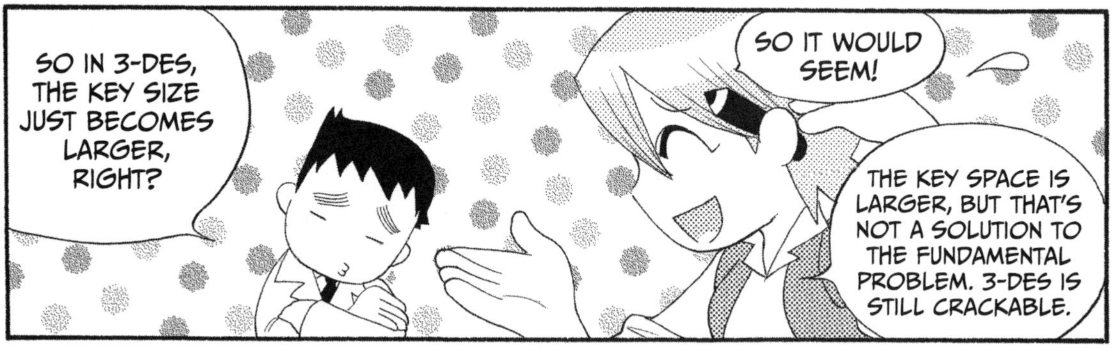
SO IN 3-DES, THE KEY SIZE JUST BECOMES LARGER, RIGHT?
SO IT WOULD SEEM!
THE KEY SPACE IS LARGER, BUT THAT'S NOT A SOLUTION TO THE FUNDAMENTAL PROBLEM. 3-DES IS STILL CRACKABLE.
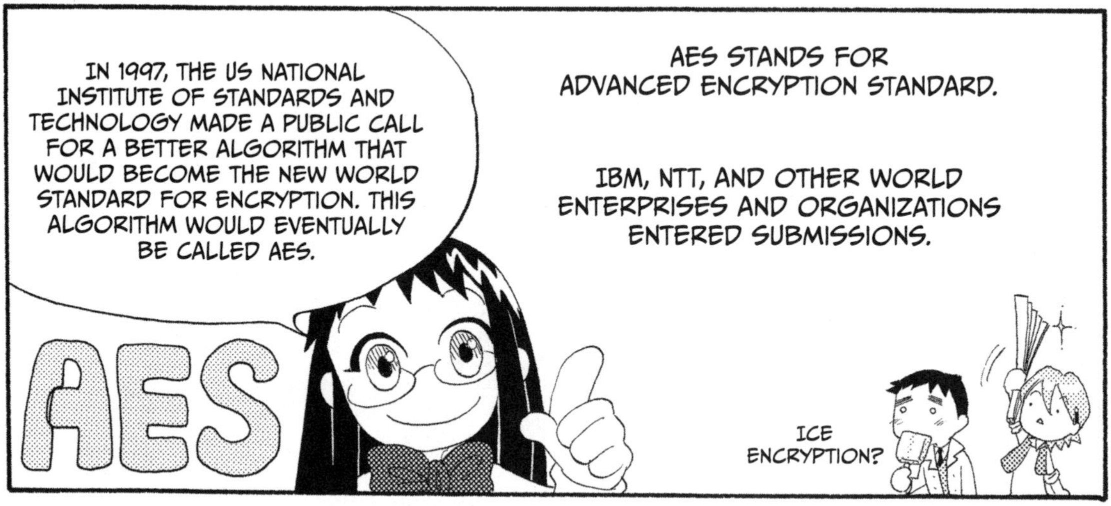
IN 1997, THE US NATIONAL INSTITUTE OF STANDARDS AND TECHNOLOGY MADE A PUBLIC CALL FOR A BETTER ALGORITHM THAT WOULD BECOME THE NEW WORLD STANDARD FOR ENCRYPTION. THIS ALGORITHM WOULD EVENTUALLY BE CALLED AES.
AES STANDS FOR ADVANCED ENCRYPTION STANDARD.
IBM, NTT, AND OTHER WORLD ENTERPRISES AND ORGANIZATIONS ENTERED SUBMISSIONS.
AES
ICE ENCRYPTION?
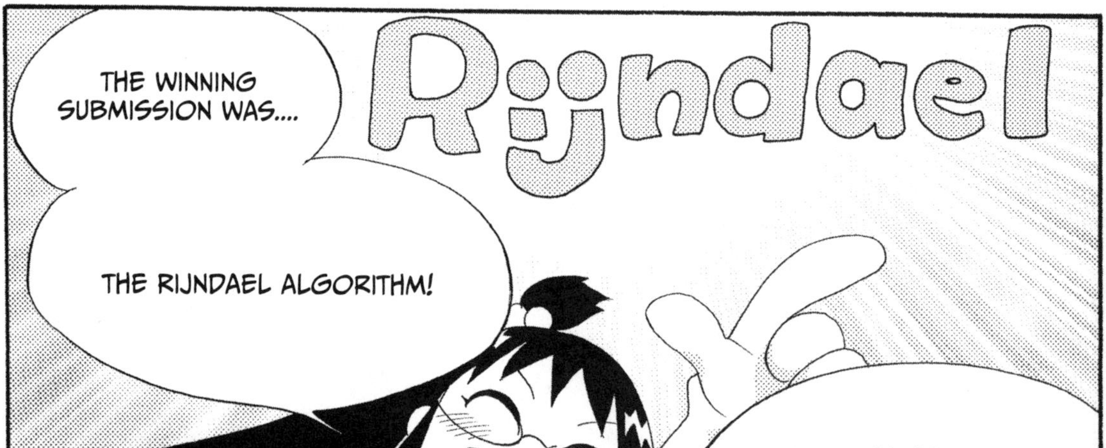
THE WINNING SUBMISSION WAS....
Rijndael
THE RIJNDAEL ALGORITHM!
NOW, IT'S USED TO ENCRYPT THE AMERICAN GOVERNMENT'S CONFIDENTIAL DOCUMENTS!

AN OUTLINE OF AES

In 2000, Rijndael was renamed AES and published as a Federal Information-tion Processing Standard (FIPS). The name Rijndael is derived from the names of its developers, Joan Daemen and Vincent Rijmen, researchers at Belgium's Catholic University of Leuven.

As shown in the following table, in AES there are three possible key sizes.

Type	Key size (bits)	Block size (bits)	Number of rounds
AES-128	128	128	10
AES-192	192	128	12
AES-256	256	128	14

The encryption strength increases with respect to the key size and the number of operations required. The block cipher structure of AES doesn't use a Feistel network but instead uses an SPN (substitution-permutation network). To give a superficial explanation of what an SPN is, imagine the substitution portion as an XOR operation that is performed on each block and subkey while the permutation is some function that simply scrambles the input bits. These two are performed simultaneously, usually for some number of rounds (just as in a Feistel network).

From here on out, we'll leave DES behind and discuss AES.

IS AES THAT STRONG?

IF A DES CIPHERTEXT CAN BE CRACKED IN 1 SECOND...

HOW LONG DO YOU THINK IT WOULD TAKE TO CRACK AN AES CIPHERTEXT?

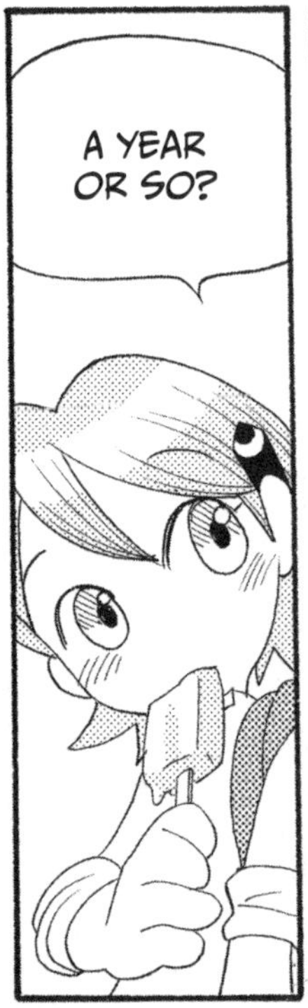
A YEAR OR SO?
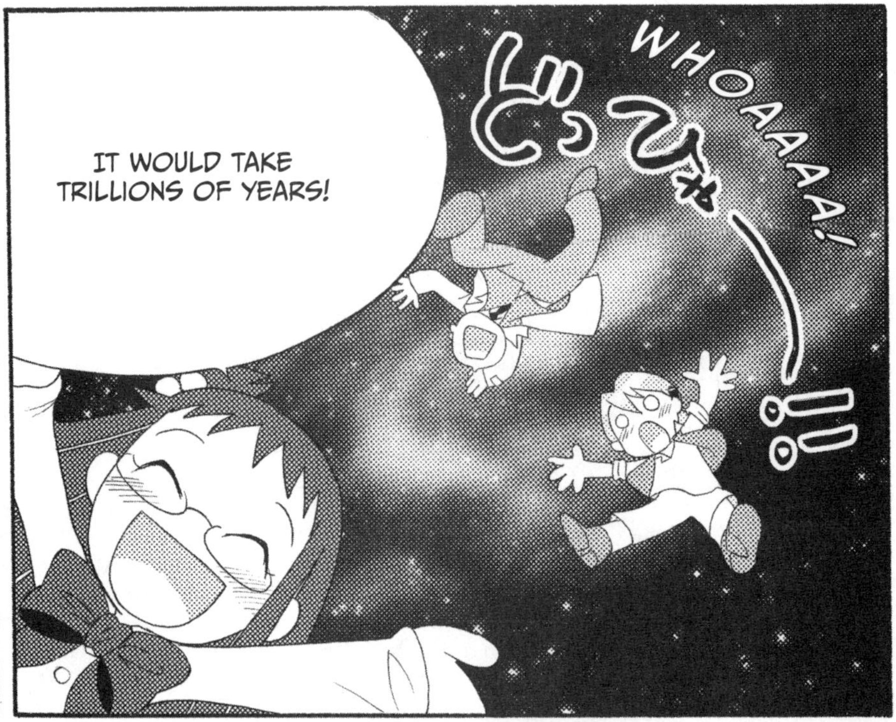
IT WOULD TAKE TRILLIONS OF YEARS!
WHOAAAAA!
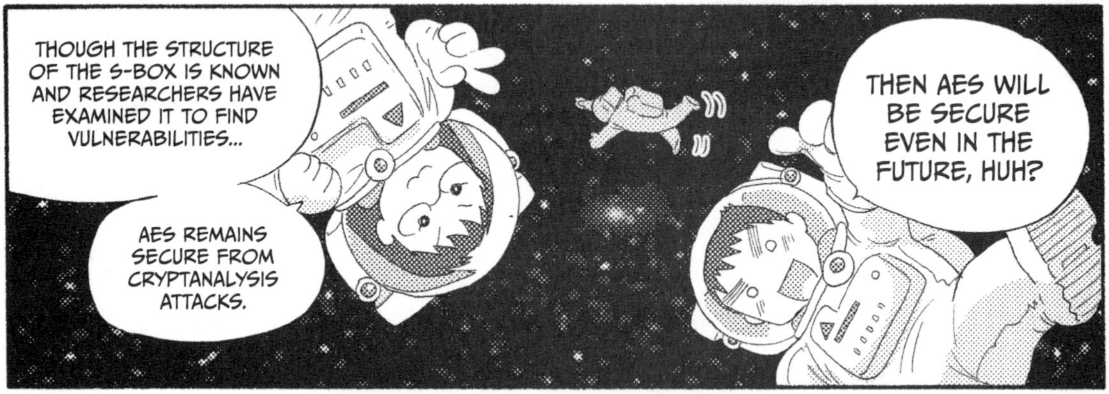
THOUGH THE STRUCTURE OF THE S-BOX IS KNOWN AND RESEARCHERS HAVE EXAMINED IT TO FIND VULNERABILITIES...
AES REMAINS SECURE FROM CRYPTANALYSIS ATTACKS.
THEN AES WILL BE SECURE EVEN IN THE FUTURE, HUH?
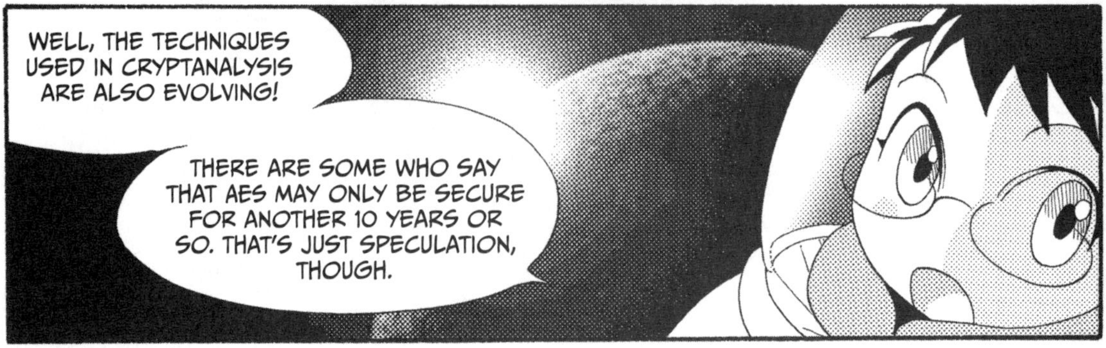
WELL, THE TECHNIQUES USED IN CRYPTANALYSIS ARE ALSO EVOLVING!
THERE ARE SOME WHO SAY THAT AES MAY ONLY BE SECURE FOR ANOTHER 10 YEARS OR SO. THAT'S JUST SPECULATION, THOUGH.

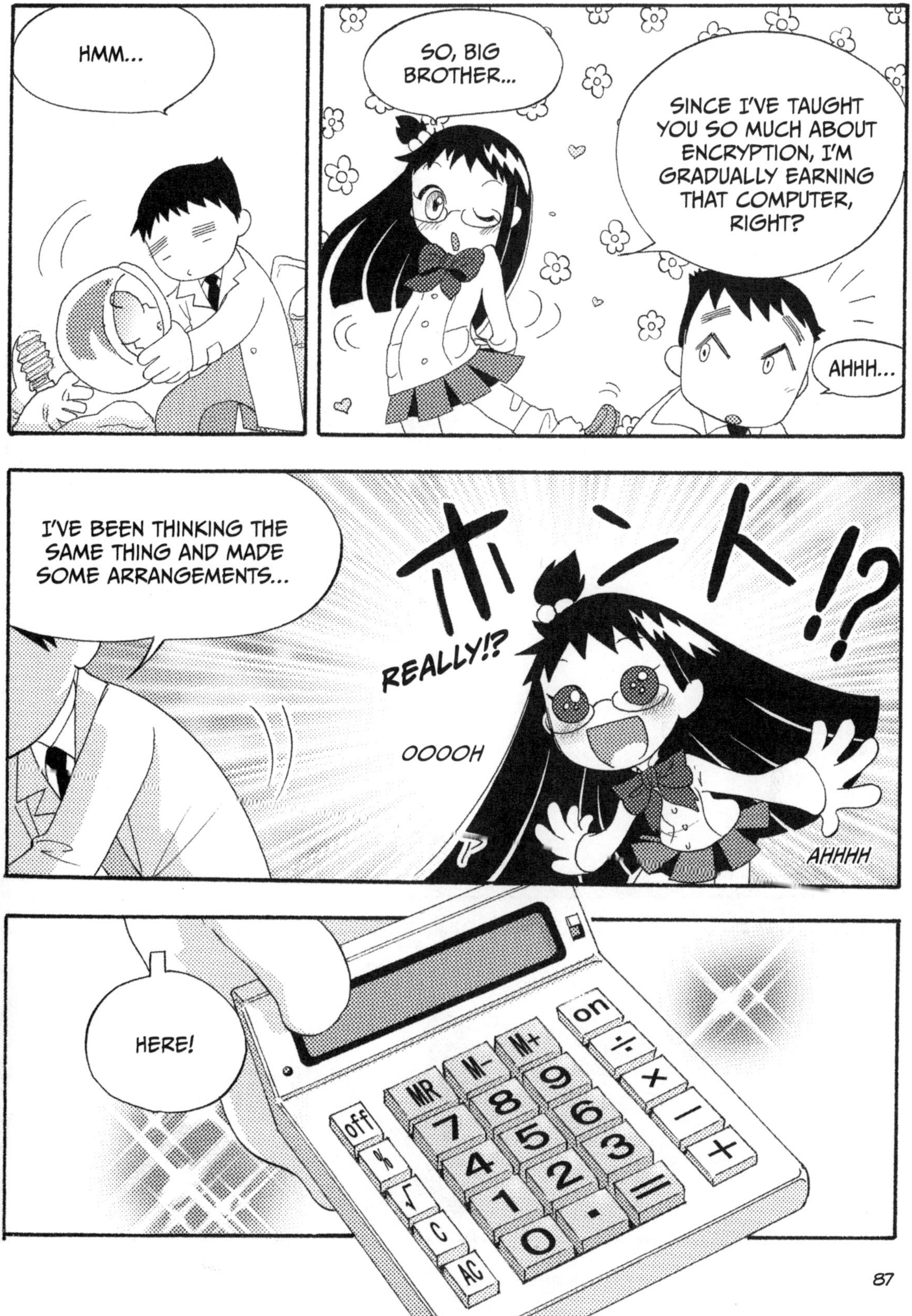
HMM...
SO, BIG BROTHER...
SINCE I'VE TAUGHT YOU SO MUCH ABOUT ENCRYPTION, I'M GRADUALLY EARNING THAT COMPUTER, RIGHT?
AHHH...
I'VE BEEN THINKING THE SAME THING AND MADE SOME ARRANGEMENTS...
ホント!?
REALLY!?
OOOOH
AHHHH
HERE!

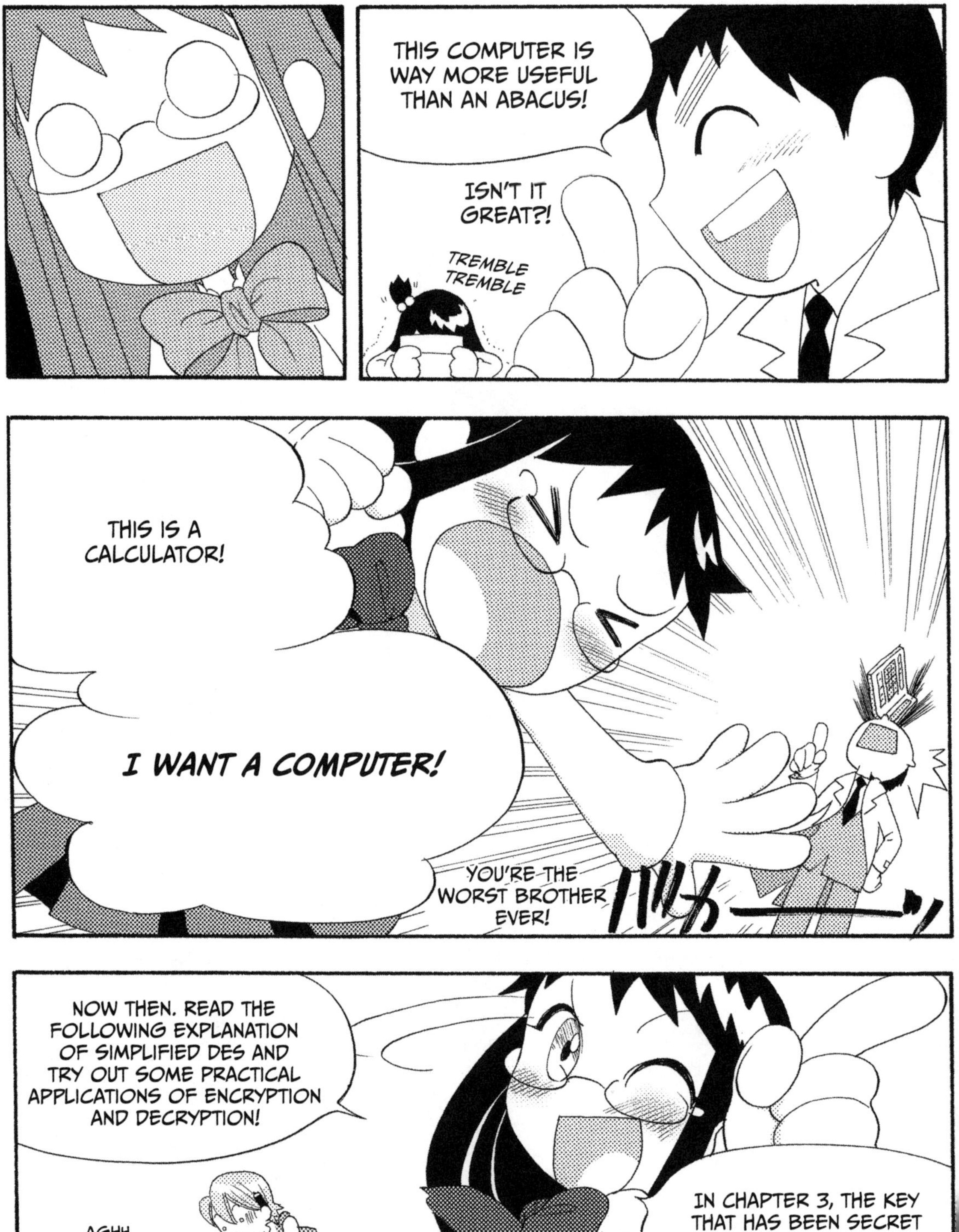
THIS COMPUTER IS WAY MORE USEFUL THAN AN ABACUS!
ISN'T IT GREAT?!
TREMBLE TREMBLE
THIS IS A CALCULATOR!
I WANT A COMPUTER!
YOU'RE THE WORST BROTHER EVER!
NOW THEN. READ THE FOLLOWING EXPLANATION OF SIMPLIFIED DES AND TRY OUT SOME PRACTICAL APPLICATIONS OF ENCRYPTION AND DECRYPTION!
AGHH
IN CHAPTER 3, THE KEY THAT HAS BEEN SECRET UNTIL NOW WILL BE REVEALED, SO ENJOY!

SIMPLIFIED DES ENCRYPTION AND DECRYPTION

How are encryption and decryption performed in DES? We will work on a reduced version of the DES algorithm to get an idea of what real DES is like. The adaptation of DES that we'll use here to help you solidify your understanding of the concepts imitates DES but with fewer steps and smaller block sizes (input/output sizes).

CONVERTING DATA INTO BINARY

Because modern-day algorithms—including DES and others—deal with binary data, we need to be able to convert plaintext messages composed of letters and numbers into binary. Table 2-1 illustrates 16 characters converted to 4-bit binary numbers.

TABLE 2-1: CHARACTERS REPRESENTED IN BINARY

Characters	Binary
A	0000
B	0001
C	0010
D	0011
E	0100
F	0101
G	0110
H	0111
I	1000
J	1001
K	1010
L	1011
M	1100
N	1101
O	1110
discarded character	1111

The encoding in Table 2-1 is a simple conversion we will use for the purposes of this book and is not based on any particular encoding used in cryptography. Likewise, the following conversions do not reflect actual binary representations of letters and numbers done in practice (which we saw earlier with ASCII encoding), but rather serve as simple examples of how characters may be converted to binary numbers.

GENERATING A DES CIPHERTEXT

In DES encryption, a block is 64 bits. However, for the purposes of this book, we will use an 8-bit block in our reduced DES cipher example, as shown in Figure 2-1. Our reduced DES cipher algorithm is composed of two steps—a *key schedule* (which generates a larger key from the key we use) and actual encryption using the generated keys. DES is not the only block cipher to require a key schedule procedure. It is common for block ciphers to perform a key schedule prior to or in parallel with encryption and decryption.

Plaintext input (binary digits)
Initial permutation *IP*
4 bits
4 bits
L_0
R_0
6 bits
$f(R_0, K_1)$
4 bits
$E(R_0)$
6 bits
Key K_1 (key K_2 at the time of decryption)
Round 1
$L_1 = R_0$
$R_1 = L_0 \oplus f(E(R_0), K_1)$
6 bits
$f(R_1, K_2)$
4 bits
$E(R_1)$
6 bits
Key K_2 (key K_1 at the time of decryption)
Round 2
$L_2 = R_1$
$L_2 = R_1 \oplus f(E(R_1), K_2)$
4 bits
4 bits
$L_2' = R_2$
$R_2' = L_2$
Final permutation *FP*
8 bits
Ciphertext output
(L_2'', R_2'')

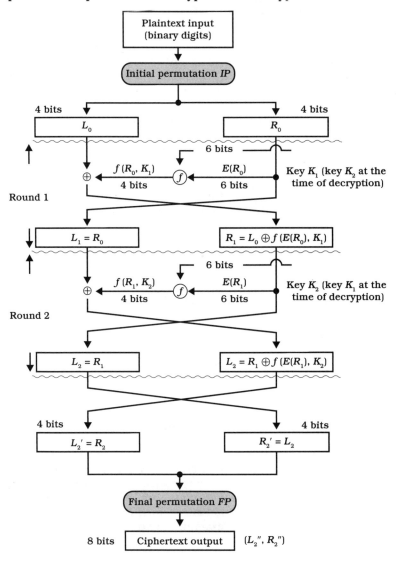

Figure 2-1: Simplified process of generating a DES ciphertext (excluding the key scheduler)

Though it is not shown in Figure 2-1, the plaintext we want to encrypt is first converted into 0s and 1s, using Table 2-1, so that we can work with binary data.

The two binary keys we'll use to perform reduced DES are as follows:

$$K_1 = (110001)_2,\ K_2 = (111000)_2$$

NOTE: *The notations ($)_2$ and ($)_{10}$ represent binary digits and decimal numbers, respectively.*

These keys have already been generated through the key schedule. We'll discuss how a key is generated through the key schedule later; for now, let's focus on the encryption process of truncated DES.

We'll encrypt the character string "MC" into a ciphertext using the truncated version of DES, so we'll start by expressing these two inputted characters as a block of 8 bits. Based on Table 2-1, "MC" in binary is expressed as 11000010.

PERFORM THE INITIAL PERMUTATION

We first convert the plaintext to binary, and then we perform the initial permutation on the binary data according to Table 2-2. *IP* permutes the 8-bit binary data by rearranging the input bit positions.

TABLE 2-2: INITIAL PERMUTATION *IP*

Input bits (original position)	b_1	b_2	b_3	b_4	b_5	b_6	b_7	b_8
Output bits (using original input positions)	b_2	b_4	b_6	b_8	b_1	b_3	b_5	b_7

In Table 2-2, the subscript of each bit indicates its original position, so these numbers are in order in the first row. Then the bit is translated, so for example, the first bit of input data (b_1) is transposed to be the fifth bit of output data, and the second bit of input data (b_2) is transposed to be the first bit of the output data. Figure 2-2 shows "MC", represented in binary, undergoing the initial permutation.

MC
1 1 0 0 0 0 1 0
Initial permutation IP
Permutation output data
1 0 0 0
1 0 0 1
L0
R0

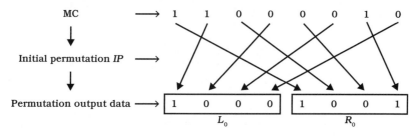

Figure 2-2: Initial permutation of the plaintext "MC"

SEPARATE DATA INTO HIGHER- AND LOWER-ORDER BITS

We separate the permutation's output data into higher-order and lower-order bits. The higher-order bits are denoted L_0, and the lower-order bits are denoted R_0. Based on Figure 2-2, this yields the following:

$$L_0 = (1000)_2$$
$$R_0 = (1001)_2$$

FEISTEL ROUNDS VARIANT

Now we begin going through rounds in a Feistel network. The Feistel network performs a specific set of steps that "mix bits" to create a new L and R. Since we're using a reduced form of DES, we'll mix the bits using a less rigorous method than with real DES. (In real DES, the network mixes the bits in a way that ensures pseudorandomness.) The following represents what a round of the Feistel network looks like in notation form:

$$L_i = R_{i-1}$$
$$R_i = L_{i-1} \oplus f(K_i, R_{i-1})$$

Each generation of a new L and R is a round, and i is equal to the round number. The process represented in Figure 2-2 is one round.

L_1 will be equal to R_0, but the process to derive R_1 requires much more work; R_0 and key K_1 are input into function f. In our reduced DES, there will be only 2 rounds, but real DES has 16 rounds.

Let's walk through how $f(K_1, R_0)$ works.

ROUND 1

The first operation in f is to apply the expansion function E from Table 2-3 on R_0.

TABLE 2-3: EXPANSION FUNCTION E

Input bits (original position)	b_1	b_2	b_3	b_4		
Output bits (using original input positions)	b_3	b_4	b_1	b_2	b_3	b_4

This means that we duplicate the third and fourth bits of R_0 and append them to the beginning of R_0 to form a new R_0 that is 6 bits long:

$$R_0 = (1001)_2 \xrightarrow{\;E\;} R_0 = (011001)_2$$

We next XOR the expansion permutation R_0 and the key $K_1 = (110001)_2$, as shown in Figure 2-3.

R_0
1 0 0 1
Expansion permutation E
$E(R_0)$
0 1 1 0 0 1
⊕ ⊕ ⊕ ⊕ ⊕ ⊕
K_1
1 1 0 0 0 1
$E(R_0) \oplus K_1$
1 0 1 0 0 0

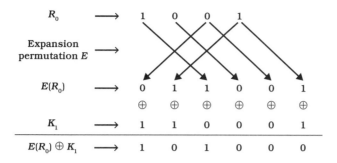

Figure 2-3: Visual representation of XORing $E(R_0)$ *and* K_1

The process shown in Figure 2-3 can be represented by the following equation:

$$E(R_0) \oplus K_1 = (011001)_2 \oplus (110001)_2 = (101000)_2$$

Now we put $R_0 \oplus K_1$ through the substitution box (S-box) in Table 2-4, which compresses and substitutes the bits from $R_0 \oplus K_1$ to create a 4-bit output. We'll label the bits from $R_0 \oplus K_1$ as $b_1b_2b_3b_4b_5b_6$.

TABLE 2-4: SUBSTITUTION BOX (S-BOX)

		Column numbers															
		0	1	2	3	4	5	6	7	8	9	10	11	12	13	14	15
Row numbers	0	14	4	13	1	2	15	11	8	3	10	6	12	5	9	0	7
	1	0	15	7	4	14	2	13	1	10	6	12	11	9	5	3	8
	2	4	1	14	8	13	6	2	11	15	12	9	7	3	10	5	0
	3	15	12	8	2	4	9	1	7	5	11	3	14	10	0	6	13

In the S-box shown in Table 2-4, four substitutions are available and labeled with row numbers starting with 0 and going up to 3. We determine which substitution to use based on the value of the bits $b_1b_2b_3b_4b_5b_6$. We convert the first and last bits, b_1 and b_6, to their base-10 equivalent and use those two numbers to determine which row of the S-box we use. We then also convert the remaining bits, $b_2b_3b_4b_5$, to base 10 to determine which column we will use.

For example, in $(101000)_2$, we select row 2 because b_1 is 1 and b_6 is 0 and $(10)_2 = (2)_{10}$. Then, bits $b_2b_3b_4b_5$ are also converted to base 10 to determine the column number we select. Since $(0100)_2 = (4)_{10}$, we select column 4 in this case, which contains the value $(13)_{10}$ (the position that is boxed in Table 2-4). After we find the corresponding table entry, we convert it into binary: $(1101)_2$.

The resulting binary, $(1101)_2$, then undergoes the permutation *PS* (Table 2-5).

TABLE 2-5: PERMUTATION *PS*

Input bits (original position)	b_1	b_2	b_3	b_4
Output bits (using original input positions)	b_3	b_4	b_1	b_2

When the permutation *PS* from Table 2-5 is applied to our working example, the process looks like Figure 2-4.

$R_0 \oplus K_1$
1 0 1 0 0 0
S-box $(R_0 \oplus K_1)$
1 1 0 1
Output of *PS*
$f(R_0, K_1)$
0 1 1 1

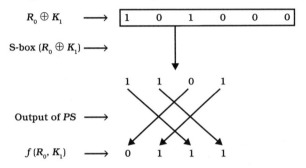

Figure 2-4: The calculation process of PS

The result is $(1111)_2$.We've now finished the permutation process. That is to say, we've done all the steps involved in the function *f*. All of these steps together are written with this notation:

$$f(K_1, R_0) = (0111)_2$$

This is the last step in the first round of the Feistel network (see Figure 2-1). In this step, we switch the sides of the bits to create L_1 and R_1. The four lower-order bits on the right side (R_0) that we got in "Separate Data into Higher- and Lower-Order Bits" on page 92 are assigned to L_1 so that they become the higher-order bits. L_0 is assigned to R_1 and becomes the lower-order bits. We can summarize the flip by assigning L_1 to the equation that produced R_0 and assigning R_1 to the equation in "Perform the Initial Permutation" on page 91. Using the equation from "Feistel Rounds Variant" on page 92, we will do the following:

$$L_1 = R_0 = (1001)_2$$
$$R_1 = L_0 \oplus f(K_1, R_0) = (1000)_2 \oplus (0111)_2 = (1111)_2$$

In order to complete a second round, we repeat these steps on R_1 and L_1. Since the steps in round 2 are identical to those in round 1, we'll only show the calculations involved, without detailed explanations.

ROUND 2

The expansion function from Table 2-3 is applied to R_1:

$$R_1 = (1111)_2 \xrightarrow{\ E\ } R_1 = (111111)_2$$

We then XOR R_1 with key $K_2 = (111000)_2$:

$$R_1 \oplus K_2 = (111111)_2 \oplus (111000)_2 = (000111)_2$$

Then we use the permutation in Table 2-5 to rearrange the position of the bits, resulting in this:

$$(0100)_2 \rightarrow (0001)_2$$

We'll apply the equation we use to express XORing R_1 and K_2 and process the result with the S-box:

$$f(K_2, R_1) = (0001)_2$$

For the final step of round 2 (see Figure 2-1 again), we will do the following:

$$L_2 = R_1 = (1111)_2$$
$$R_2 = L_1 \oplus f(K_2, R_1) = (1001)_2 \oplus (0001)_2 = (1000)_2$$

SWAP THE HIGHER- AND LOWER-ORDER BITS

After round 2 is completed, we swap the higher-order bits L_2 and lower-order bits R_2 again to get L_2' and R_2':

$$L_2' = R_2 = (1000)_2$$
$$R_2' = L_2 = (1111)_2$$

This swap is shown in Figure 2-5.

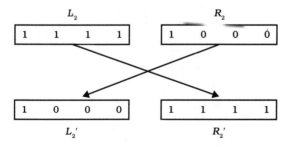

Figure 2-5: Swapping the higher- and lower-order bits

PERFORM THE FINAL PERMUTATION

Based on the final permutation *FP* in Table 2-6, we transpose each bit to a new position.

TABLE 2-6: FINAL PERMUTATION *FP*

Input bits (original position)	b_1	b_2	b_3	b_4	b_5	b_6	b_7	b_8
Output bits (using original input positions)	b_5	b_1	b_6	b_2	b_7	b_3	b_8	b_4

For example, if you look at Table 2-2, you'll see that the fifth input bit (b_5) becomes the seventh bit in the output. When the seventh bit (b_7) is processed in Table 2-6, it becomes the fifth bit in the output, which means the bit reverts to its initial position. Figure 2-6 shows the initial and final permutations.

Input bit position
1 2 3 4 5 6 7 8
Initial permutation IP
1 2 3 4 5 6 7 8
Final permutation FP
1 2 3 4 5 6 7 8
Output bit position

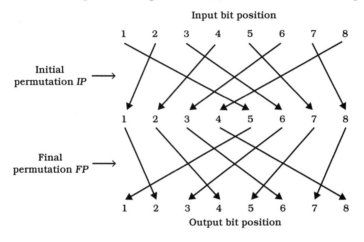

Figure 2-6: The process of putting an 8-bit block through IP *and* FP. *The initial permutation* IP *and final permutation* FP *are inverses of one another.*

The process shown in Table 2-6 results in L_2'' and R_2'', which when combined result in our 8-bit ciphertext:

$$L_2'' = (1000)_2$$
$$R_2'' = (1111)_2$$

The resulting ciphertext is $(11101010)_2$, as shown in Figure 2-7.

L_2'
R_2'
1 0 0 0
1 1 1 1
Final permutation FP
Ciphertext
1 1 1 0
1 0 1 0
L_2''
R_2''

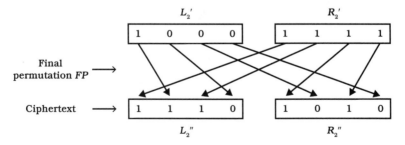

Figure 2-7: The resulting ciphertext from the final permutation FP

DECRYPTING A DES CIPHERTEXT

Now, we'll try to decrypt the DES ciphertext from Figure 2-7 into its original plaintext. For decryption, you apply the same steps shown in Figure 2-1.

PERFORM THE INITIAL PERMUTATION

The ciphertext is made up of its left and right sides, L_2'' and R_2''. In the initial permutation, both sides of the ciphertext's bits (11101010) were rearranged according to the initial permutation chart in Table 2-2.

SEPARATE DATA INTO HIGHER- AND LOWER-ORDER BITS

The permutated bits are separated into four higher-order bits (left side) L_0 and four lower-order bits (right side) R_0. These bits are the same as L_2' and R_2'. In equation form, this is the opposite of the final permutation when encrypting with DES:

$$L_0 = (1000)_2 \; (= L_2')$$
$$R_0 = (1111)_2 \; (= R_2')$$

Figure 2-8 shows the initial permutation and separation processes together.

L_2''
R_2''
Ciphertext
1 1 0 0
0 0 1 0
Initial permutation *IP*
Output from permutation
1 0 0 0
1 0 0 1
$L_2' = L_0$
$R_2' = R_0$

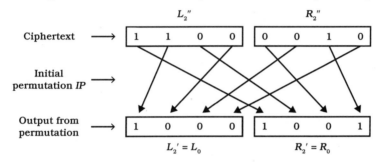

Figure 2-8: Output after applying the initial permutation IP *to the ciphertext*

ROUND 1

The first round of decryption inverts the last round of encryption, so we start by applying the expansion function E from Table 2-3 on R_0. The expansion function duplicates the first two bits of R_0 and attaches them to the end of R_0:

$$R_0 = (1111)_2 \xrightarrow{E} R_0 = (111111)_2$$

We calculate the XOR of R_0 and key K_2. As a reminder, K_2 is $(111000)_2$.

$$R_0 \oplus K_2 = (111111)_2 \oplus (111000)_2 = (000111)_2$$

We then compress and substitute the result from the previous step $(000111)_2$ using the S-box in Table 2-4. We select the first and last bits of the result, $(000111)_2$; combine those two bits into one binary number, $(01)_2$;

and convert the number to decimal, $(01)_2 = (1)_{10}$. We then convert the remaining four bits from the original binary number $(0011)_2$ to decimal, $(0011)_2 = (3)_{10}$. In Table 2-4, we find where the two decimal values intersect. The column number is 3 and the row is 1, so the intersecting value is $(4)_{10}$ (the position that is circled in Table 2-4). The intersecting value is converted into binary to produce $(0100)_2$. Then we use the permutation PS from Table 2-5 on this binary number, so $(0100)_2$ becomes $(0001)_2$. Finally, this function can be expressed as follows:

$$f(K_2, R_0) = (0001)_2$$

So far, we've found the output for the four higher-order bits L_1 and calculated $f(K_2, R_0) = (0001)_2$. With this information, we can also derive R_1. We first take L_1 and set it equal to R_0. Then, we derive R_1 by XORing L_0 and $f(K_2, R_0)$. We'll find the output for the four lower-order bits R_1 as follows:

$$L_1 = R_0 = (1111)_2$$
$$R_1 = L_0 \oplus f(K_2, R_0) = (1000)_2 + (0001)_2 = (1001)_2$$

Now that we have finished the first round, we'll perform the second round.

ROUND 2

As we did in all the previous rounds, we first find $f(K_1, R_2)$ by applying the expansion function E from Table 2-3 on R_1:

$$R_1 = (1001)_2 \xrightarrow{\ E\ } R_1 = (011001)_2$$

We calculate the XOR of R_1 and the key K_1. The key K_1 is equal to $(110001)_2$.

$$R_1 \oplus K_1 = (011001)_2 \oplus (110001)_2 = (101000)_2$$

Then we put $R_1 \oplus K_1$ through the S-box using the permutation PS from Table 2-5. Doing so rearranges the position of the binary number's bits so that it becomes the following:

$$(1101)_2 \rightarrow (0111)_2$$

Finally, this whole process is expressed in equation form as this:

$$f(K_1, R_2) = (0111)_2$$

In Figure 2-12, the output of round 2 is the four higher-order bits (left side) L_2 and four lower-order bits (right side) R_2, which are found using the following equations:

$$L_2 = R_1 = (1001)_2$$
$$R_2 = L_1 \oplus f(K_1, R_1) = (1111)_2 \oplus (0111)_2 = (1000)_2$$

L_2 is set equal to R_1, which in this case is the binary value 1001. R_2 is found by XORing L_1 and $f(K_1, R_1)$.

In the final stage of the process in Figure 2-1, we swap the higher-order bits, L_2, and lower-order bits, R_2, to find L_2' and R_2', as seen in Figure 2-9.

L_2
R_2
1 0 0 1
1 0 0 0
1 0 0 0
1 0 0 1
L_2'
R_2'

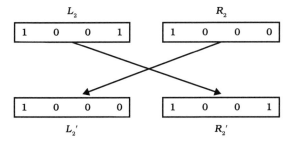

Figure 2-9: Swapping the left and right bits

This swap is represented by the following equations:

$$L_2' = R_2 = (1000)_2$$
$$R_2' = L_2 = (1001)_2$$

L_2'' and R_2'' are found by performing the final permutation *FP* from Table 2-6 on L_2' and R_2'. Using Table 2-1, L_2'' is then converted from binary to the character "M", and R_2'' is converted to "C".

$$L_2'' = (1100)_2$$
$$R_2'' = (0010)_2$$

You can see this process in Figure 2-10.

L_2'
R_2'
1 0 0 0
1 0 0 1
Final permutation *FP*
Plaintext
1 1 0 0
0 0 1 0
L_2'' ("M")
R_2'' ("C")

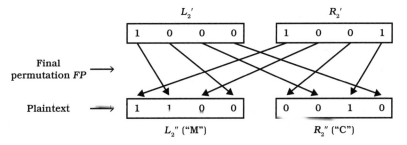

Figure 2-10: The final permutation performed on the bits of L_2'' *and* R_2''

The plaintext is 1100 0010, which is the character string "MC".

We can see that the resulting 8-bit output data corresponds with the original plaintext, so the ciphertext has been decrypted. As you can see, decryption is the same process as encryption, just with the order of keys reversed. The relationship between encryption and decryption processes is shown in Figure 2-11.

Encryption process
① Plaintext (11000010)
② Initial permutation (10001001)
③ L_0 (1000) R_0 (1001)
Key K_1
④ L_1 (1001) R_1 (1111)
Key K_2
⑤ L_2 (1111) R_2 (1000)
⑥ L_2' (1000) R_2' (1111)
⑦ Final permutation (11101010) ciphertext
Decryption process
Ciphertext (11101010) ❶
Initial permutation (10001111) ❷
L_0 (1000) R_0 (1111) ❸
Key K_2
L_1 (1111) R_1 (1001) ❹
Key K_1
L_2 (1001) R_2 (1000) ❺
L_2' (1000) R_2' (1001) ❻
Final permutation (11000010) plaintext ❼
① ⟷ ❼
② ⟷ ❻
③ ⟷ ❺
④ ⟷ ❹
⑤ ⟷ ❸
⑥ ⟷ ❷
⑦ ⟷ ❶
Be careful when swapping the places of the four higher-order bits L_i and four lower-order bits R_i (where i = 0, 1, 2).

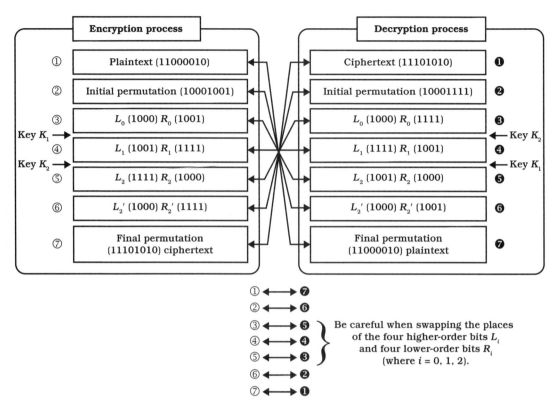

Figure 2-11: Relationship between the encryption and decryption processes

GENERATING DES KEYS

Now that we have seen how encryption and decryption are performed using reduced DES, let's discuss how keys are generated from the key schedule. Reduced DES requires an input of an 8-bit key K_0, and the key given by the user generates two 8-bit keys, which are then used in the encryption and decryption process.

$$K_0 = (10011001)_2$$

The key schedule, which is the procedure for generating the keys K_1 and K_2, is shown in Figure 2-12.

Symmetric private key K_0
Permuted choice PC–1
K_0'
4 bits
4 bits
C_0
D_0
Circular shift 1 bit to the left
Circular shift 1 bit to the right
4 bits
4 bits
Round 1
C_1
D_1
6 bits
Key K_1
Permuted choice PC–2
Circular shift 2 bits to the left
Circular shift 2 bits to the right
4 bits
4 bits
Round 2
C_2
D_2
6 bits
Key K_2
Permuted choice PC–2

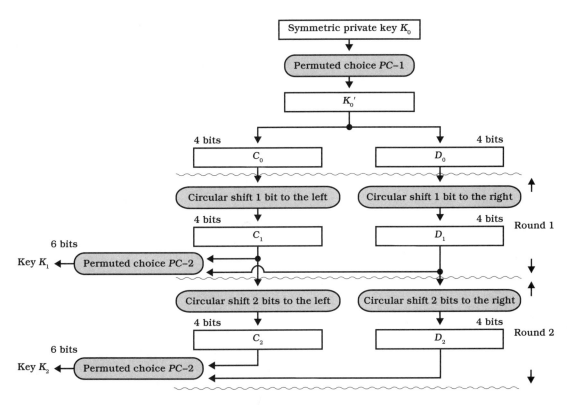

Figure 2-12: Generating encryption keys and decryption keys

PERFORM PERMUTED CHOICE PC–1

The symmetric key K_0 is permuted according to PC–1.

$$K_0' = (00110101)_2$$

The bits are transposed, as shown in Table 2-7.

TABLE 2-7: PERMUTED CHOICE *PC*–1

	4 higher-order bits				**4 lower-order bits**			
Input bits (original position)	b_1	b_2	b_3	b_4	b_5	b_6	b_7	b_8
Output bits (using original input positions)	b_3	b_6	b_4	b_8	b_7	b_5	b_2	b_1

When the transposition in Table 2-7 is applied to K_0, we acquire K_0', as shown in Figure 2-13.

Initial key K_0
1 0 0 1 1 0 0 1
Permuted choice PC–1
K_0'
0 0 1 1
0 1 0 1
C_0
D_0

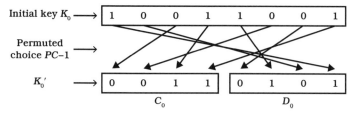

Figure 2-13: Permuted choice PC–1

Here, K_0' is divided into C_0, which is made up of the four higher-order bits, and D_0, the key's four lower-order bits, and is expressed as follows:

$$C_0 = (0011)_2$$
$$D_0 = (0101)_2$$

ROTATE THE BITS

C_0 and D_0 are each rotated one bit to the left, as Figure 2-14 shows, and the results are expressed as C_1 and D_1. During round 1, bits are all shifted by one position.

$$C_1 = (0110)_2$$
$$D_1 = (1010)_2$$

The bits in C_0 and D_0 are rotated independently to produce C_1 and D_1, as shown in Figure 2-14.

C_0
D_0
0 0 1 1
0 1 0 1
Rotate 1 bit to the left
0 1 1 0
1 0 1 0
C_1
D_1

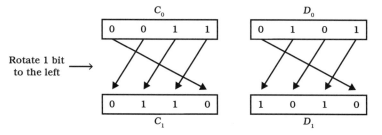

Figure 2-14: Rotating C_0 *and* D_0 *one bit to the left*

PERFORM PERMUTED CHOICE PC-2

Based on permuted choice PC–2, C_1 and D_1 are compressed from 8 bits to 6 bits, yielding the key K_1, which is used in round 1 of encryption.

$$K_1 = (110001)_2$$

Permuted choice *PC*–2 is shown in Table 2-8.

TABLE 2-8: PERMUTED CHOICE *PC*–2

Position of input bits	b_1	b_2	b_3	b_4	b_5	b_6	b_7	b_8
Output labeled with original input bits	b_7	b_5	b_1	b_8	b_6	b_2		

Figure 2-15 shows the results of applying permuted choice *PC*–2 from Table 2-8 to C_1 and D_1.

C1
D1
0 1 1 0
1 0 1 0
Permuted choice PC–2
Key K1
1 1 0 0 0 1

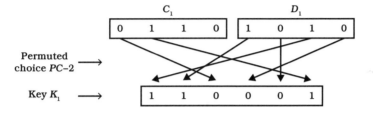

Figure 2-15: Permuted choice PC–2

Repeating the key schedule steps will yield new keys to use for reduced DES.

ROTATE THE BITS AGAIN

Now we are going to generate K_2. Each bit of C_1 and D_1 is rotated to the left by two bits, as shown in Figure 2-16.

C1
D1
0 1 1 0
1 0 1 0
Rotate 2 bits to the left
1 0 0 1
1 0 1 0
C2
D2

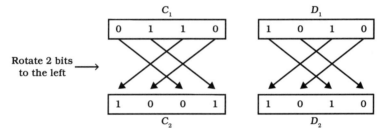

Figure 2-16: Rotating C_1 *and* D_1 *two bits to the left*

This results in C_2 and D_2:

$$C_2 = (1001)_2$$
$$D_2 = (1010)_2$$

COMPRESS THE BITS

Based on permuted choice *PC*–2 in Table 2-8, C_2 and D_2 are compressed from a total of 8 bits to 6 bits. This yields key K_2, which is used in the second round of encryption:

$$K_2 = (111000)_2$$

Figure 2-17 shows how permuted choice *PC*–2 compresses the bits of C_2 and D_2.

C_2
D_2
1 0 0 1
1 0 1 0
Permuted choice *PC*–2
Key K_2
1 1 1 0 0 0

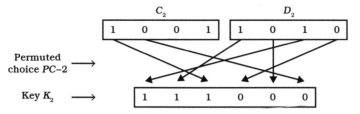

Figure 2-17: Using permuted choice PC–2 *to produce* K_2

HOW REDUCED DES DIFFERS FROM REAL DES

We've learned how reduced DES works. As mentioned at the beginning of this chapter, real DES used in practice is more complex.

DES (and its reduced version) is no longer secure and should not be used in any practical implementations.

Reduced DES is a modified DES that encrypts and decrypts only 8-bit messages using an 8-bit key, while real DES encrypts and decrypts 64-bit messages with a 56-bit key. This means that all of the procedures done in real DES use a different expansion function, *f* function, and S-box to accommodate for the size of the inputs. In addition, real DES performs 16 rounds rather than the 2 rounds of the Feistel network. The key schedule is also different, because real DES generates 16 keys and performs only one circular bit shift rather than two.

Although we didn't cover real DES, this section should still give you an idea of just how involved, exhaustive, and particular the steps in modern-day encryption schemes are.

3

PUBLIC-KEY
ENCRYPTION

THE BASICS OF PUBLIC-KEY ENCRYPTION

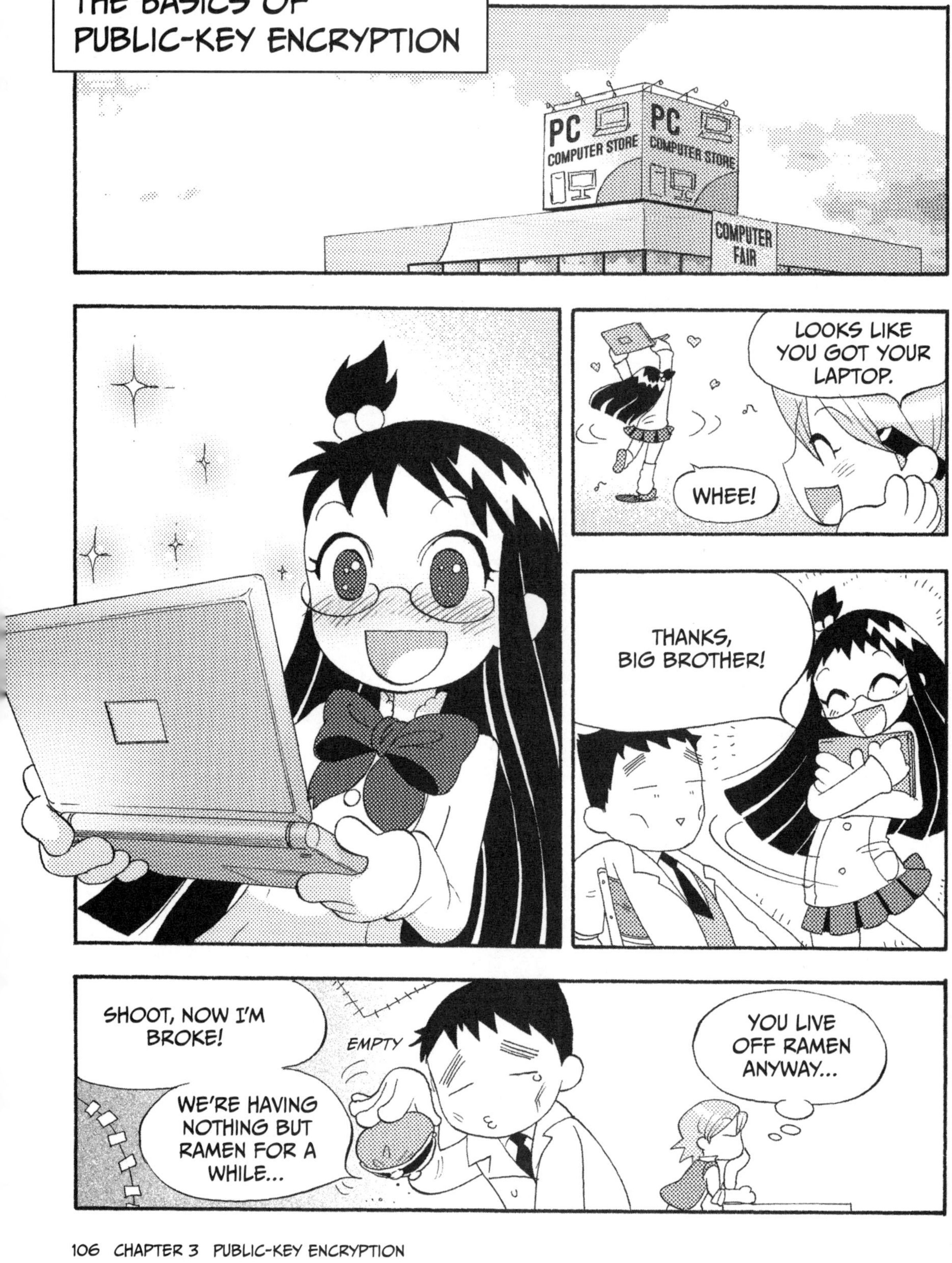
PC
COMPUTER STORE
PC
COMPUTER STORE
COMPUTER FAIR
LOOKS LIKE YOU GOT YOUR LAPTOP.
WHEE!
THANKS, BIG BROTHER!
SHOOT, NOW I'M BROKE!
EMPTY
WE'RE HAVING NOTHING BUT RAMEN FOR A WHILE...
YOU LIVE OFF RAMEN ANYWAY...

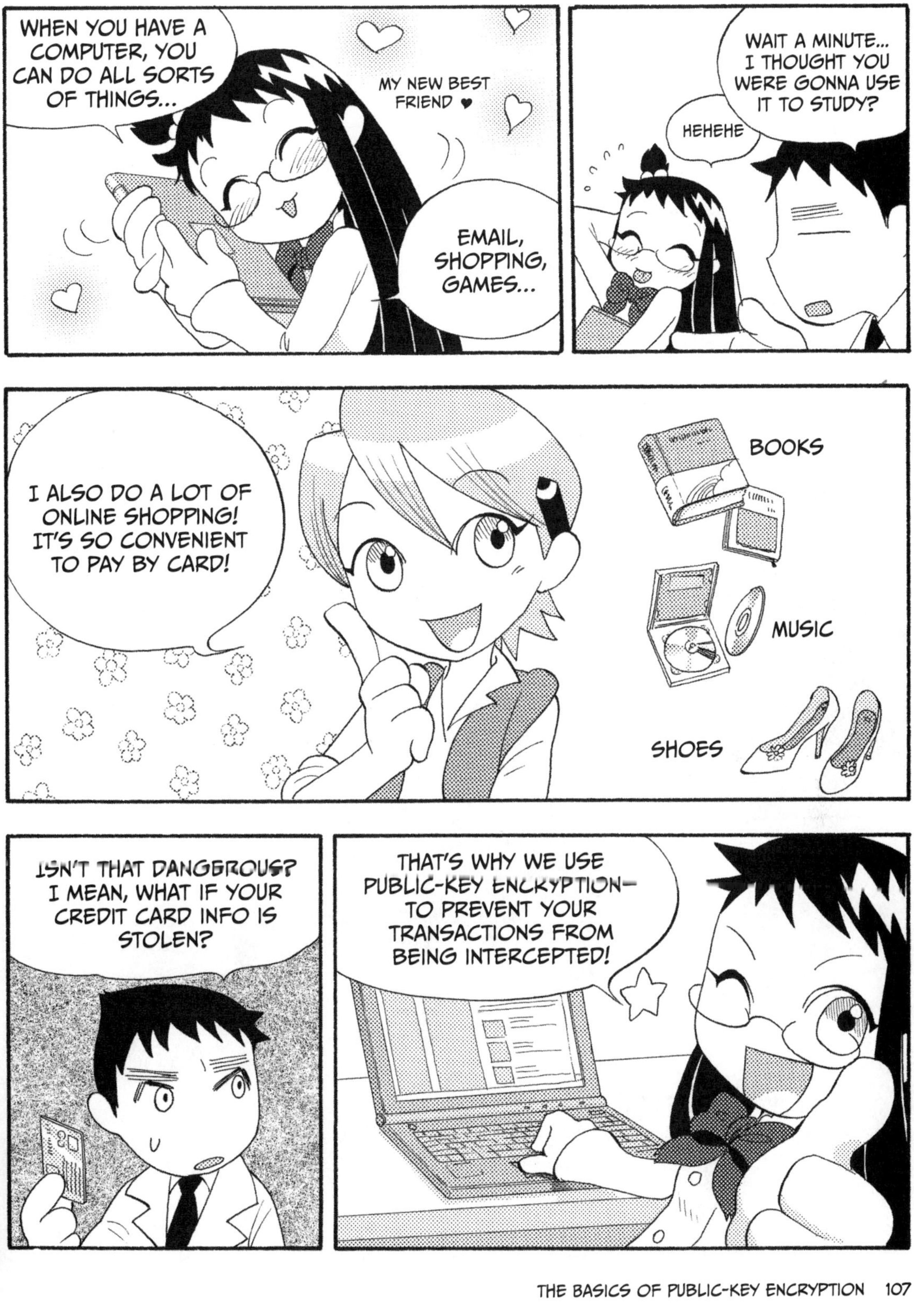
WHEN YOU HAVE A COMPUTER, YOU CAN DO ALL SORTS OF THINGS...
MY NEW BEST FRIEND ♥
EMAIL, SHOPPING, GAMES...
WAIT A MINUTE... I THOUGHT YOU WERE GONNA USE IT TO STUDY?
HEHEHE
I ALSO DO A LOT OF ONLINE SHOPPING! IT'S SO CONVENIENT TO PAY BY CARD!
BOOKS
MUSIC
SHOES
ISN'T THAT DANGEROUS? I MEAN, WHAT IF YOUR CREDIT CARD INFO IS STOLEN?
THAT'S WHY WE USE PUBLIC-KEY ENCRYPTION—TO PREVENT YOUR TRANSACTIONS FROM BEING INTERCEPTED!

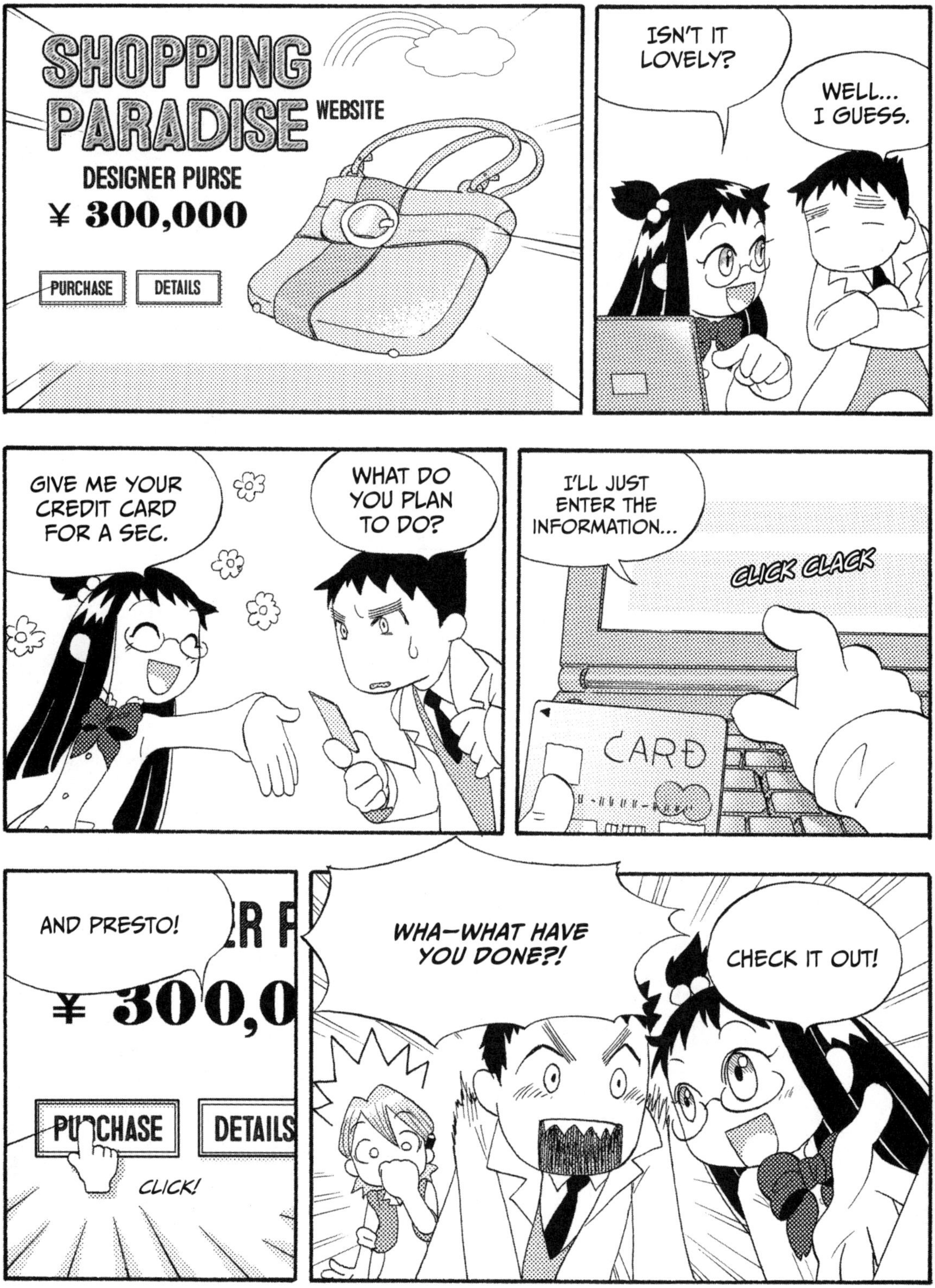
SHOPPING PARADISE WEBSITE
DESIGNER PURSE
¥ 300,000
PURCHASE
DETAILS
ISN'T IT LOVELY?
WELL... I GUESS.
GIVE ME YOUR CREDIT CARD FOR A SEC.
WHAT DO YOU PLAN TO DO?
I'LL JUST ENTER THE INFORMATION...
CLICK CLACK
CARD
AND PRESTO!
¥ 300,0
PURCHASE
DETAILS
CLICK!
WHA–WHAT HAVE YOU DONE?!
CHECK IT OUT!

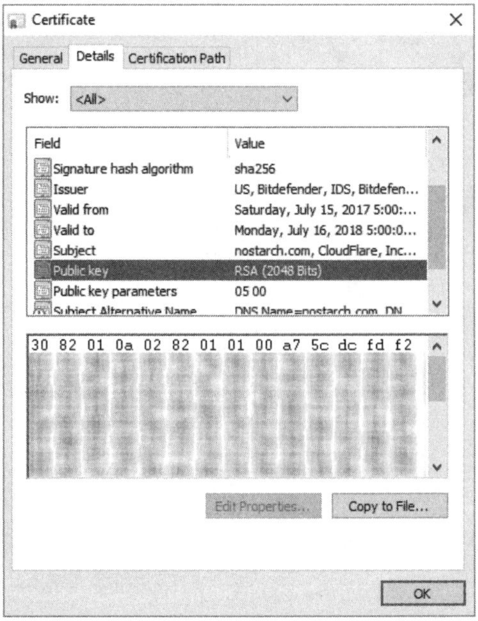
Certificate
General
Details
Certification Path
Show: <All>
Field
Value
Signature hash algorithm
sha256
Issuer
US, Bitdefender, IDS, Bitdefen...
Valid from
Saturday, July 15, 2017 5:00:...
Valid to
Monday, July 16, 2018 5:00:0...
Subject
nostarch.com, CloudFlare, Inc...
Public key
RSA (2048 Bits)
Public key parameters
05 00
30 82 01 0a 02 82 01 01 00 a7 5c dc fd f2
Edit Properties...
Copy to File...
OK

You can view the public key used for encrypting messages to a website you are currently communicating with in your web browser. If you're using Google Chrome, click the lock symbol in the address bar, and then click the **Valid** option under the Certificate heading. Switch to the **Details** tab and select **Public key**. You would also click the lock symbol in Firefox and Safari to view your SSL certificate.

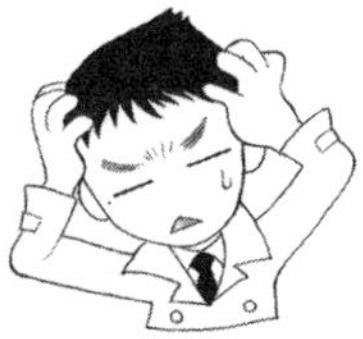

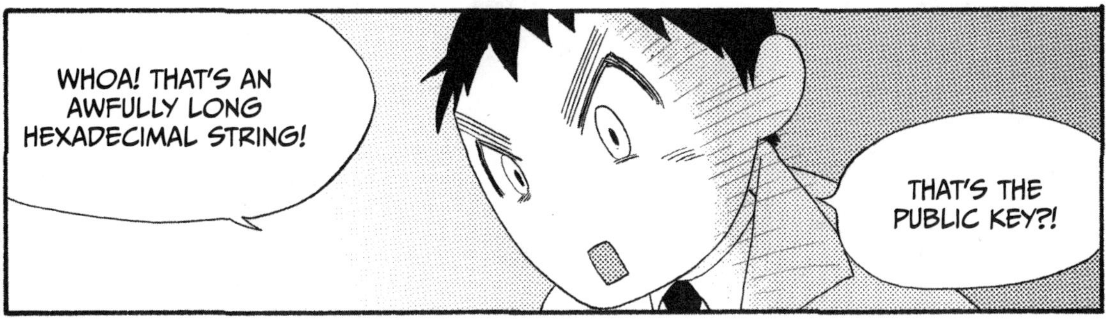
WHOA! THAT'S AN AWFULLY LONG HEXADECIMAL STRING!
THAT'S THE PUBLIC KEY?!

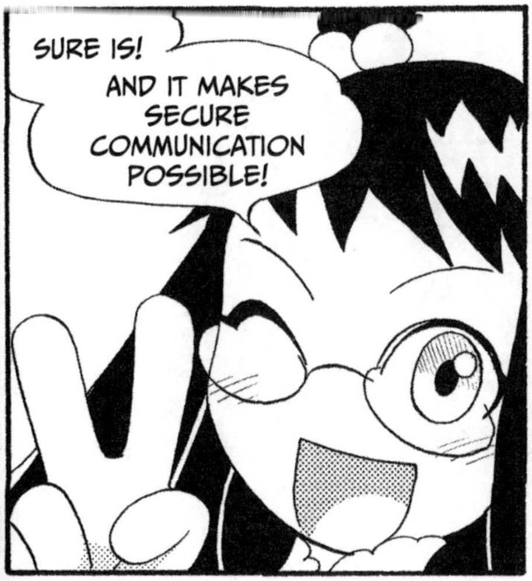
SURE IS!
AND IT MAKES SECURE COMMUNICATION POSSIBLE!

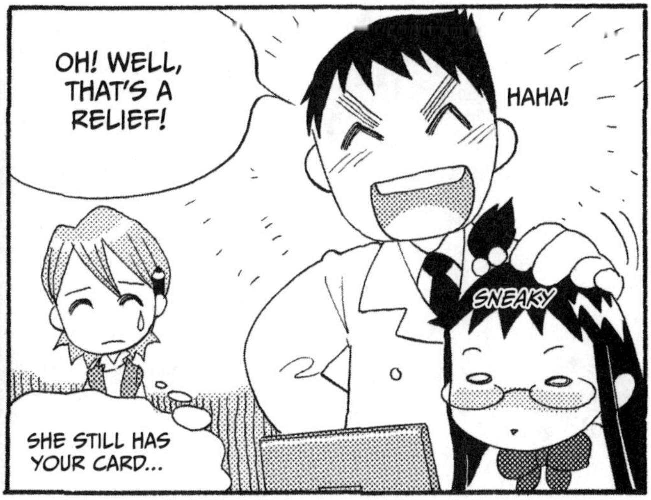
OH! WELL, THAT'S A RELIEF!
HAHA!
SNEAKY
SHE STILL HAS YOUR CARD...

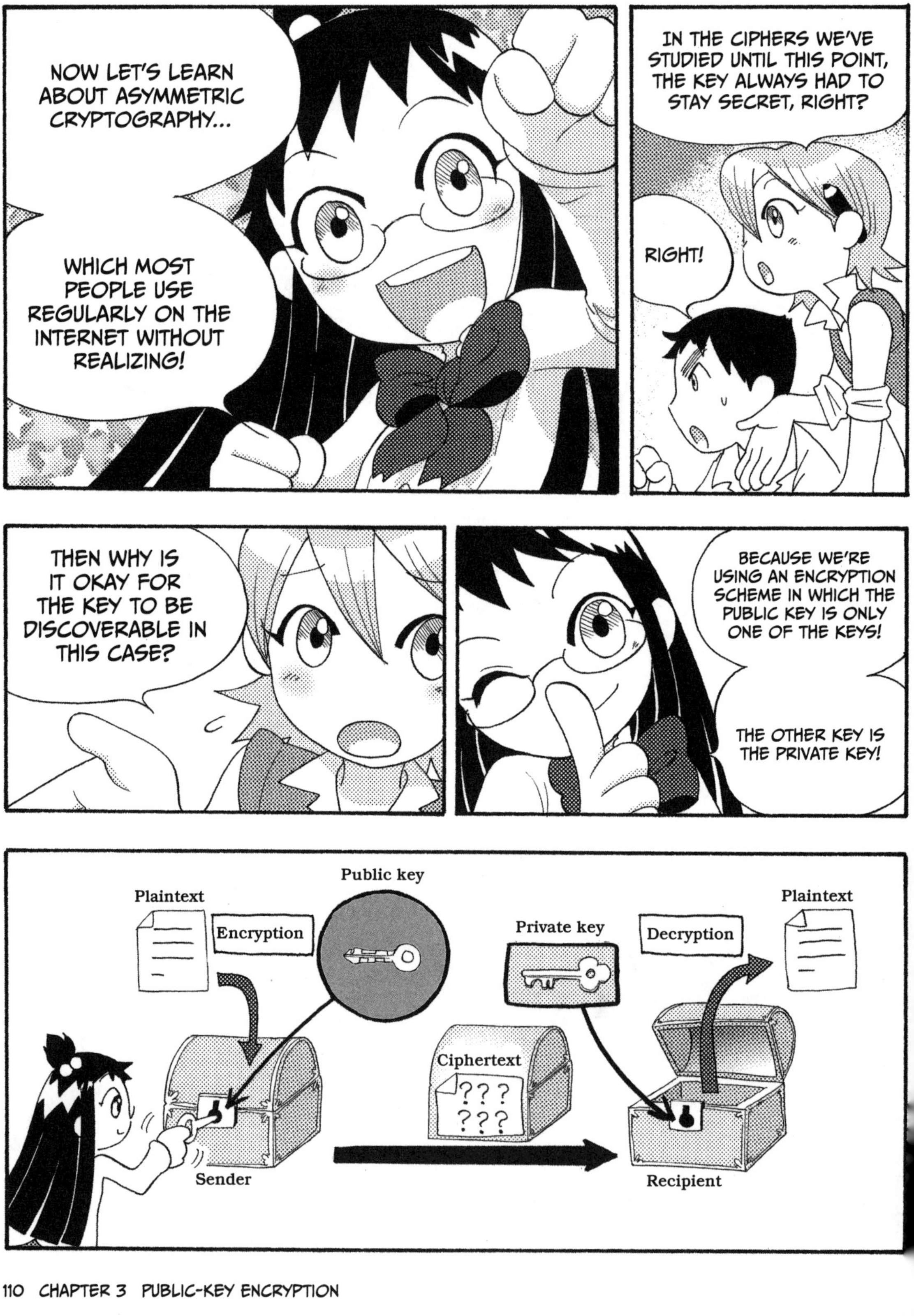
NOW LET'S LEARN ABOUT ASYMMETRIC CRYPTOGRAPHY...
WHICH MOST PEOPLE USE REGULARLY ON THE INTERNET WITHOUT REALIZING!
IN THE CIPHERS WE'VE STUDIED UNTIL THIS POINT, THE KEY ALWAYS HAD TO STAY SECRET, RIGHT?
RIGHT!
THEN WHY IS IT OKAY FOR THE KEY TO BE DISCOVERABLE IN THIS CASE?
BECAUSE WE'RE USING AN ENCRYPTION SCHEME IN WHICH THE PUBLIC KEY IS ONLY ONE OF THE KEYS!
THE OTHER KEY IS THE PRIVATE KEY!
Plaintext
Encryption
Public key
Private key
Decryption
Plaintext
Ciphertext
??? ???
Sender
Recipient

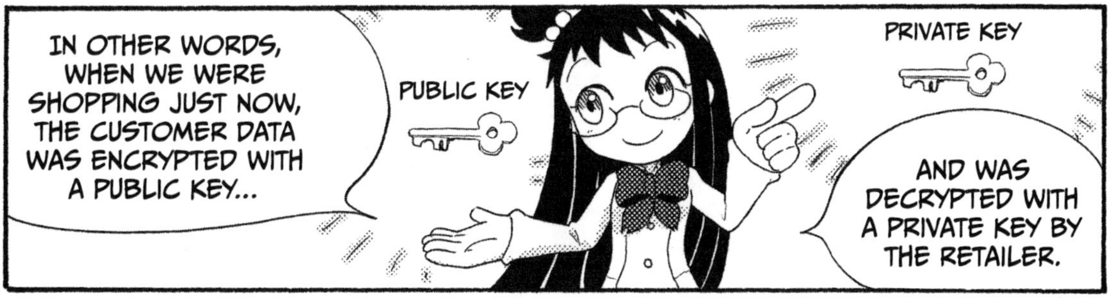
IN OTHER WORDS, WHEN WE WERE SHOPPING JUST NOW, THE CUSTOMER DATA WAS ENCRYPTED WITH A PUBLIC KEY...
PUBLIC KEY
PRIVATE KEY
AND WAS DECRYPTED WITH A PRIVATE KEY BY THE RETAILER.

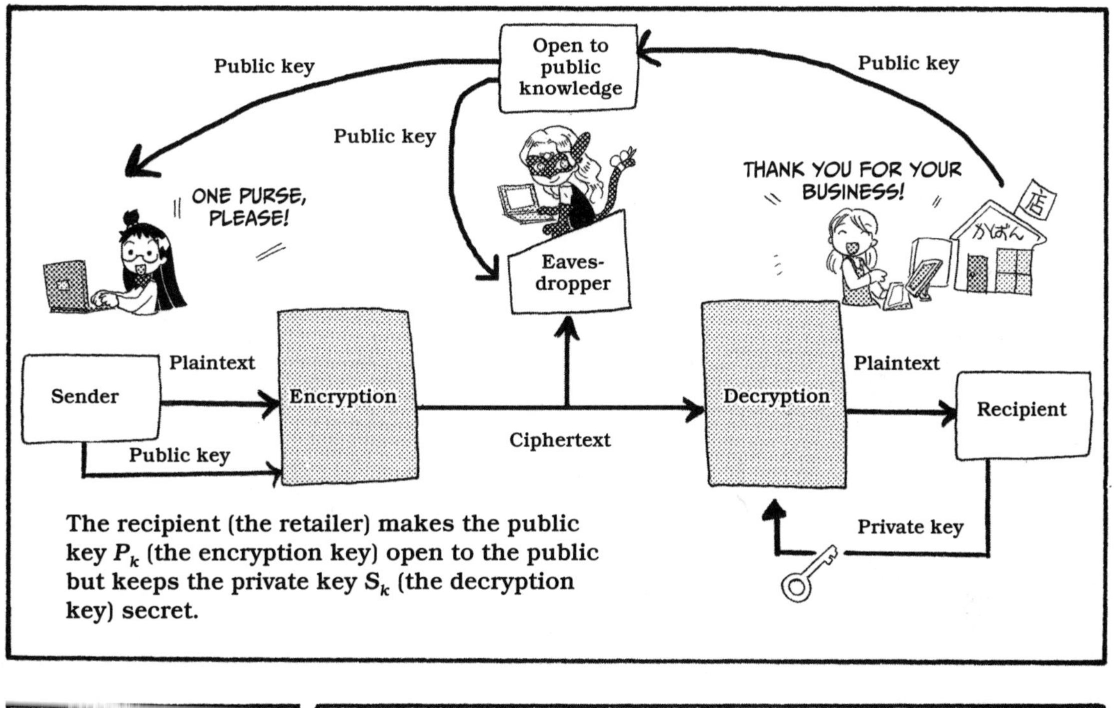
Open to public knowledge
Public key
Public key
Public key
ONE PURSE, PLEASE!
THANK YOU FOR YOUR BUSINESS!
店
かばん
Eaves-dropper
Sender
Plaintext
Public key
Encryption
Ciphertext
Decryption
Plaintext
Recipient
Private key

The recipient (the retailer) makes the public key P_k (the encryption key) open to the public but keeps the private key S_k (the decryption key) secret.

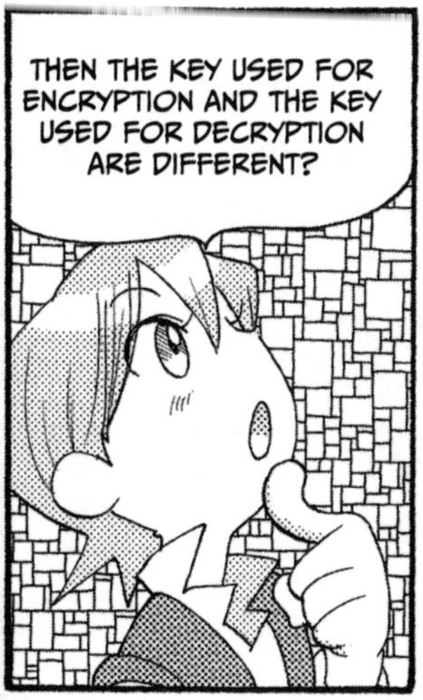
THEN THE KEY USED FOR ENCRYPTION AND THE KEY USED FOR DECRYPTION ARE DIFFERENT?

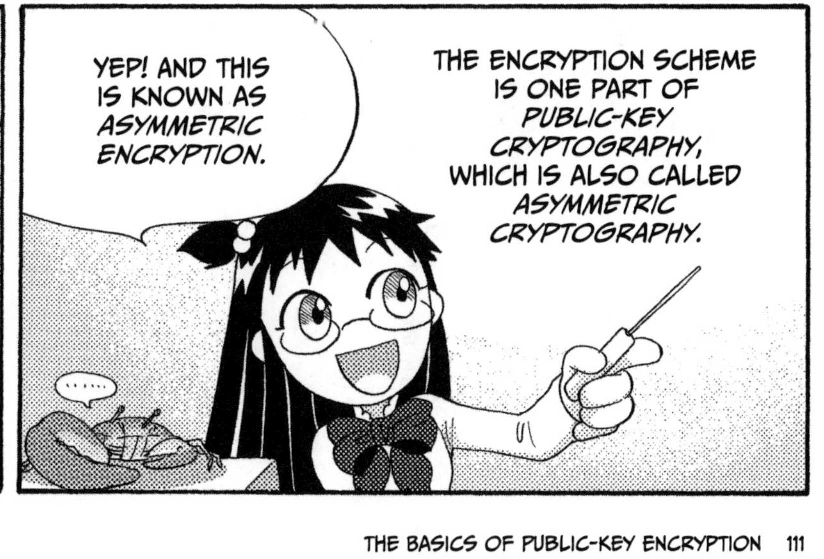
YEP! AND THIS IS KNOWN AS *ASYMMETRIC ENCRYPTION*.
THE ENCRYPTION SCHEME IS ONE PART OF *PUBLIC-KEY CRYPTOGRAPHY*, WHICH IS ALSO CALLED *ASYMMETRIC CRYPTOGRAPHY*.
......

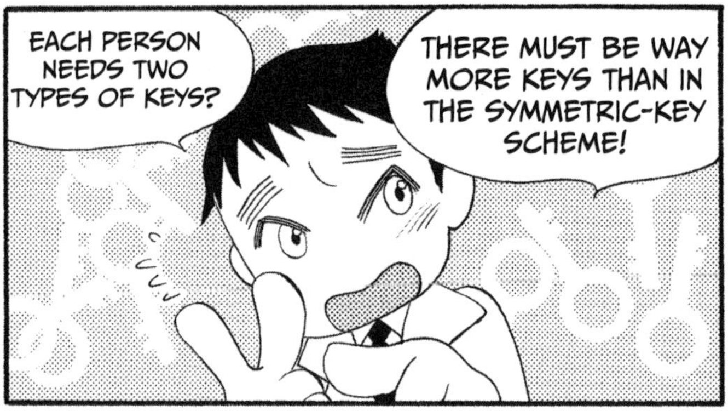
EACH PERSON NEEDS TWO TYPES OF KEYS?
THERE MUST BE WAY MORE KEYS THAN IN THE SYMMETRIC-KEY SCHEME!
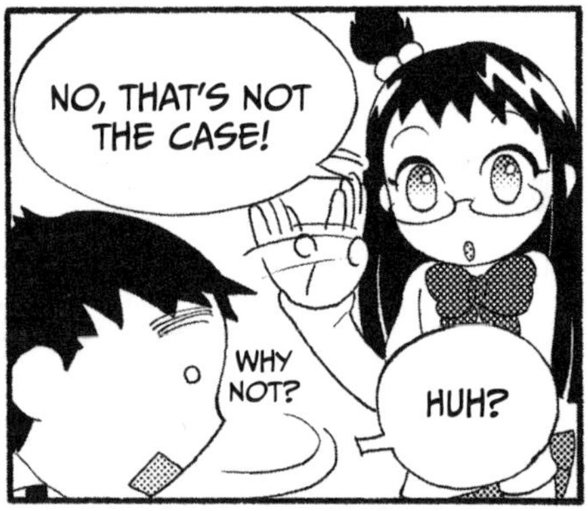
NO, THAT'S NOT THE CASE!
WHY NOT?
HUH?
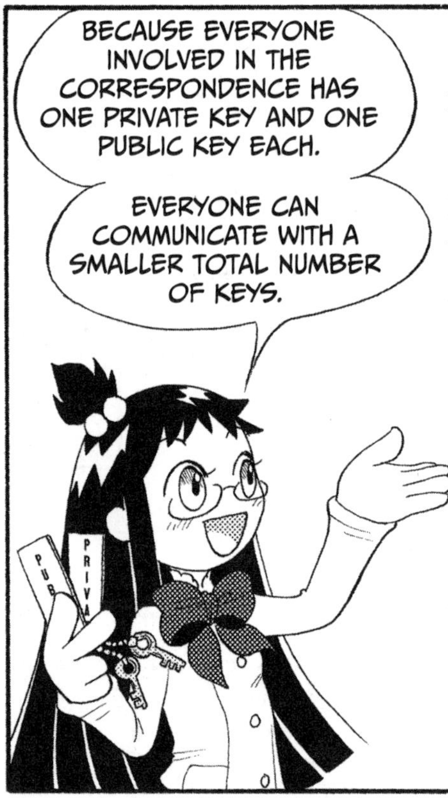
BECAUSE EVERYONE INVOLVED IN THE CORRESPONDENCE HAS ONE PRIVATE KEY AND ONE PUBLIC KEY EACH.
EVERYONE CAN COMMUNICATE WITH A SMALLER TOTAL NUMBER OF KEYS.

In the public-key encryption scheme, even if n users were communicating with encryption, the total number of keys involved is only $2n$. That's because each user's public key from their key pair is what others will use to encrypt a message to that person. When there are 1,000 users in a symmetric-key scheme, the number of keys is calculated as follows (using the equation on page 61):

$$_{1,000}C_2 = \frac{1,000 \times (1,000 - 1)}{2}$$

This means that you need 499,500 keys for a symmetric-key scheme. But for public-key encryption, the key calculation is just 2 × 1,000, which means you need only 2,000 keys.

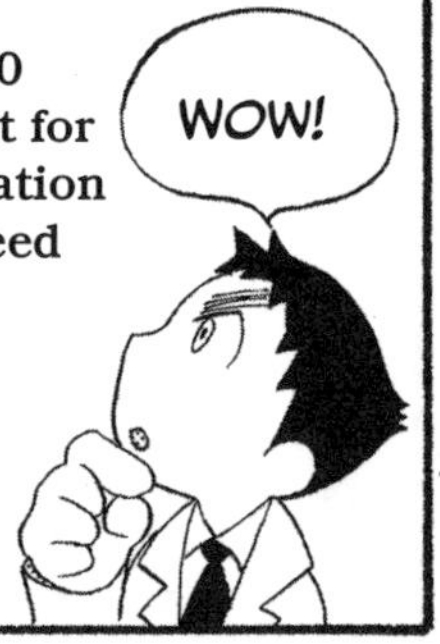
WOW!
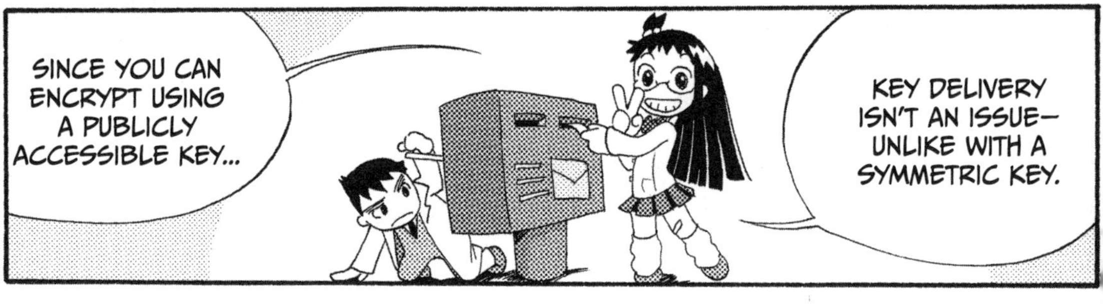
SINCE YOU CAN ENCRYPT USING A PUBLICLY ACCESSIBLE KEY...
KEY DELIVERY ISN'T AN ISSUE—UNLIKE WITH A SYMMETRIC KEY.

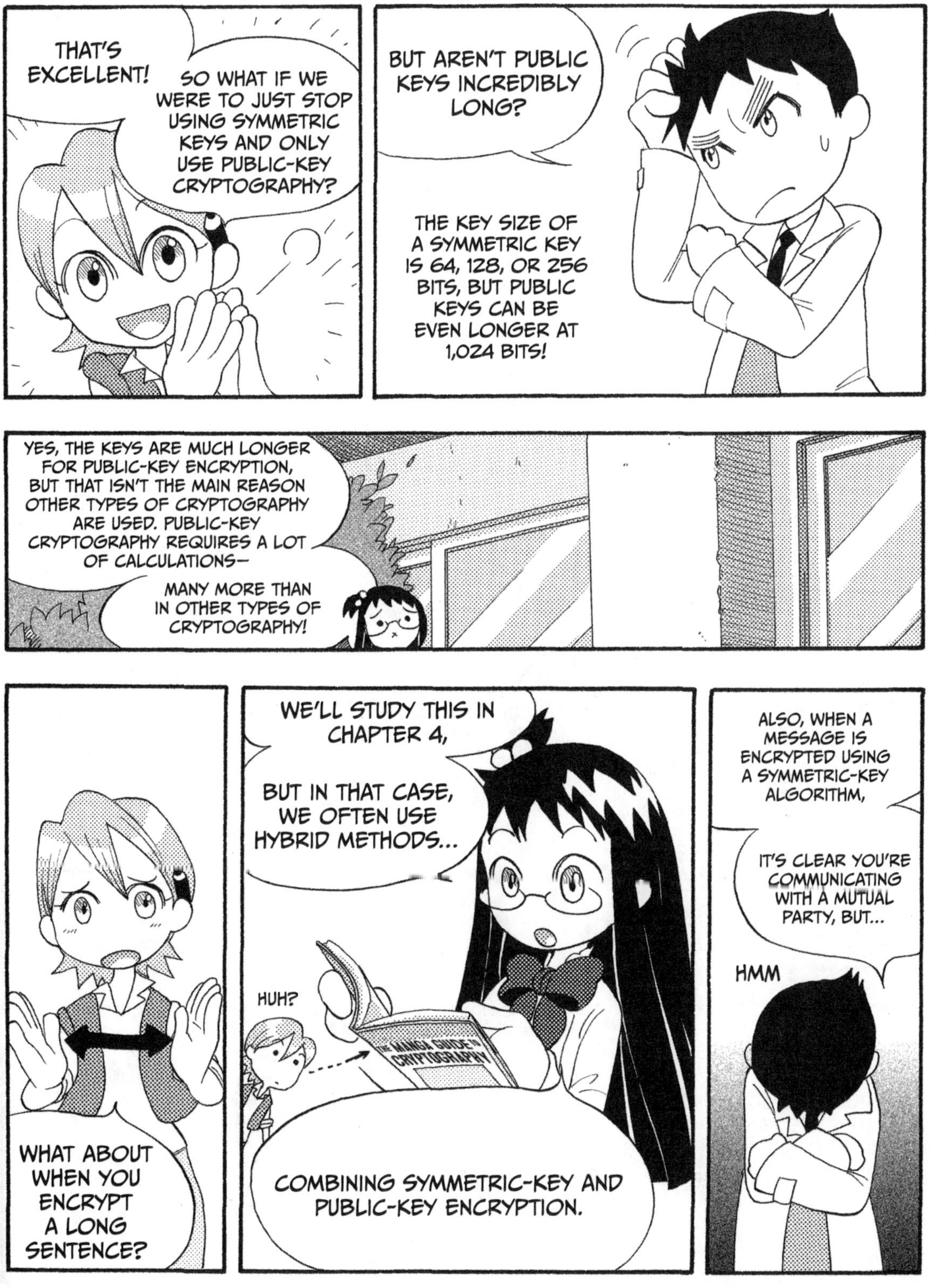
THAT'S EXCELLENT!
SO WHAT IF WE WERE TO JUST STOP USING SYMMETRIC KEYS AND ONLY USE PUBLIC-KEY CRYPTOGRAPHY?
BUT AREN'T PUBLIC KEYS INCREDIBLY LONG?
THE KEY SIZE OF A SYMMETRIC KEY IS 64, 128, OR 256 BITS, BUT PUBLIC KEYS CAN BE EVEN LONGER AT 1,024 BITS!
YES, THE KEYS ARE MUCH LONGER FOR PUBLIC-KEY ENCRYPTION, BUT THAT ISN'T THE MAIN REASON OTHER TYPES OF CRYPTOGRAPHY ARE USED. PUBLIC-KEY CRYPTOGRAPHY REQUIRES A LOT OF CALCULATIONS—
MANY MORE THAN IN OTHER TYPES OF CRYPTOGRAPHY!
WHAT ABOUT WHEN YOU ENCRYPT A LONG SENTENCE?
WE'LL STUDY THIS IN CHAPTER 4,
BUT IN THAT CASE, WE OFTEN USE HYBRID METHODS...
HUH?
THE MANGA GUIDE TO CRYPTOGRAPHY
COMBINING SYMMETRIC-KEY AND PUBLIC-KEY ENCRYPTION.
ALSO, WHEN A MESSAGE IS ENCRYPTED USING A SYMMETRIC-KEY ALGORITHM,
IT'S CLEAR YOU'RE COMMUNICATING WITH A MUTUAL PARTY, BUT...
HMM

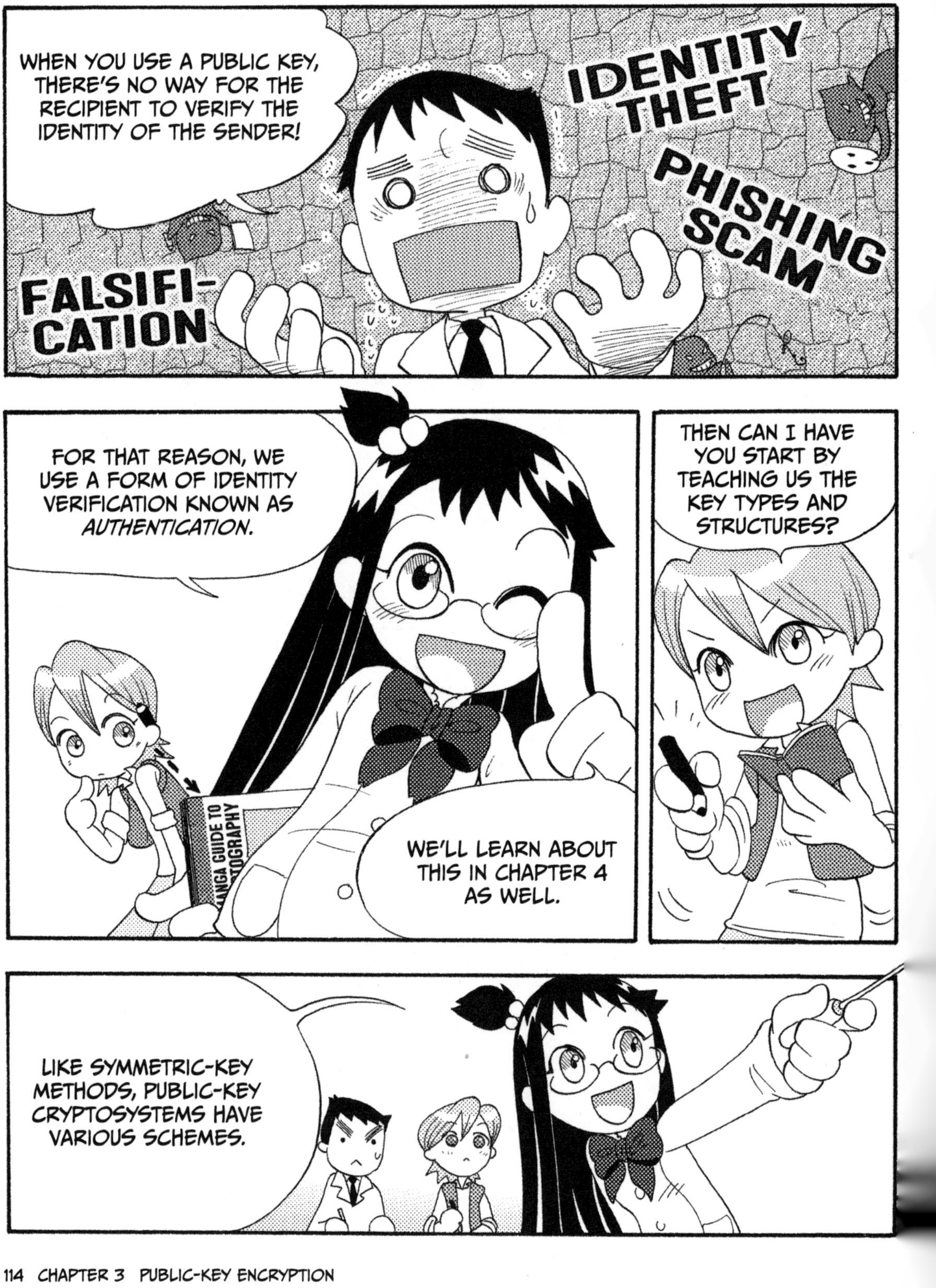
WHEN YOU USE A PUBLIC KEY, THERE'S NO WAY FOR THE RECIPIENT TO VERIFY THE IDENTITY OF THE SENDER!
IDENTITY THEFT
PHISHING SCAM
FALSIFI-CATION
FOR THAT REASON, WE USE A FORM OF IDENTITY VERIFICATION KNOWN AS *AUTHENTICATION*.
WE'LL LEARN ABOUT THIS IN CHAPTER 4 AS WELL.
THEN CAN I HAVE YOU START BY TEACHING US THE KEY TYPES AND STRUCTURES?
LIKE SYMMETRIC-KEY METHODS, PUBLIC-KEY CRYPTOSYSTEMS HAVE VARIOUS SCHEMES.

MATHEMATICAL DEPENDENCIES OF PUBLIC-KEY ENCRYPTION

PUBLIC-KEY ENCRYPTION SCHEMES RELY ON TWO TYPES
OF MATHEMATICAL PROBLEMS:

THE INTEGER FACTORIZATION PROBLEM IS USED BY RSA ENCRYPTION, RABIN ENCRYPTION, AND OTHER SCHEMES.

THE DISCRETE LOGARITHM PROBLEM IS USED BY ELGAMAL ENCRYPTION, DSA AUTHENTICATION, AND SO ON.

I NEED TO KNOW MATH?!

THE INTEGER FACTORIZATION PROBLEM? THE DISCRETE LOGARITHM PROBLEM?

WHAT IS ALL THIS?!

DON'T WORRY! I'LL TEACH YOU THE MATH BEHIND ENCRYPTION STARTING FROM THE BASICS.

YOU CAN THINK OF ENCRYPTION AS A HARD-TO-SOLVE MATH PROBLEM WHERE SECURITY INCREASES WITH THE DIFFICULTY OF THE PROBLEM. THE MORE TIME NEEDED TO SOLVE A PROBLEM, THE HARDER THE PROBLEM IS.

GAAAAH

WHY DO WE HAVE TO LEARN SUCH DIFFICULT MATH?

YOU CAN'T MAKE ME!

TO UNDERSTAND THE STRUCTURE OF A CRYPTOSYSTEM, YOU NEED TO KNOW THE MATH BEHIND IT!

FIRST I'LL EXPLAIN ONE-WAY FUNCTIONS,

WHICH ARE NEEDED TO GUARANTEE THE SECURITY OF PUBLIC-KEY ENCRYPTION.

ONE-WAY FUNCTIONS

A *one-way function* is a function F for which it is easy to compute $F(x)$ for a given input x but not easy to find the input x given the calculation of $F(x)$. Let's look at an example of a one-way function.

INTEGER FACTORIZATION PROBLEM

Multiplying two large prime numbers and finding the resulting composite number is simple. On the other hand, attempting to find the original two primes is exceedingly difficult when you are given only the composite number. The process of deriving the original primes based on the composite number is known as the integer factorization problem (explained later in "Prime Numbers and Integer Factorization" on page 120).

DISCRETE LOGARITHM PROBLEM

Consider the following equation, which uses modular arithmetic:

$$a^x = y \pmod{p}$$

When you know a and x, finding y is comparatively simple. But if you know a and y, finding x, the logarithm of y, is extraordinarily difficult. This is the discrete logarithm problem.

THAT'S A LOT OF COMPLEX TERMINOLOGY,

BUT YOU'LL COME TO UNDERSTAND IT LITTLE BY LITTLE.

YOU REALLY MEAN THAT, RIGHT?!

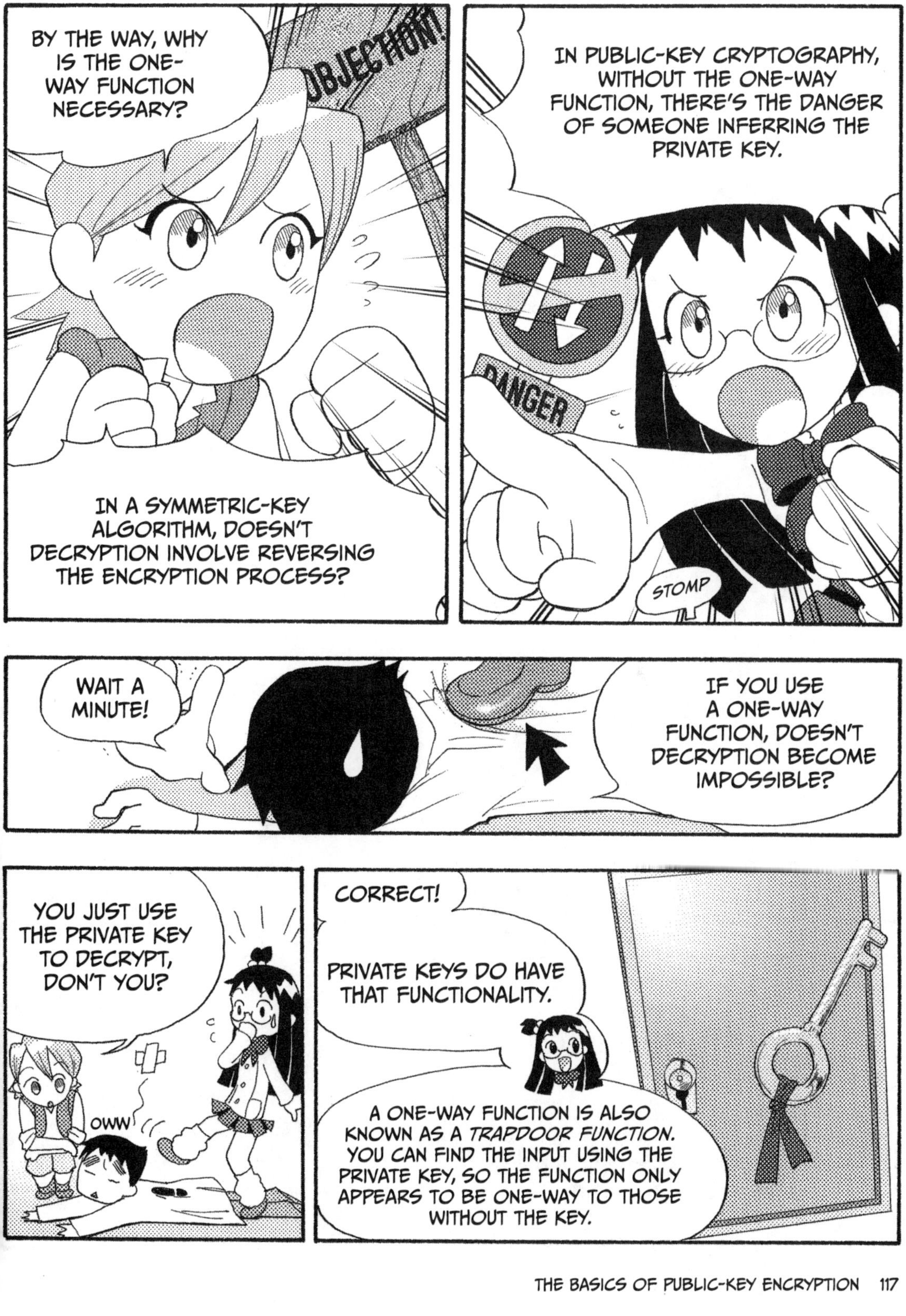
BY THE WAY, WHY IS THE ONE-WAY FUNCTION NECESSARY?
OBJECTION!
IN A SYMMETRIC-KEY ALGORITHM, DOESN'T DECRYPTION INVOLVE REVERSING THE ENCRYPTION PROCESS?
IN PUBLIC-KEY CRYPTOGRAPHY, WITHOUT THE ONE-WAY FUNCTION, THERE'S THE DANGER OF SOMEONE INFERRING THE PRIVATE KEY.
DANGER
STOMP
WAIT A MINUTE!
IF YOU USE A ONE-WAY FUNCTION, DOESN'T DECRYPTION BECOME IMPOSSIBLE?
YOU JUST USE THE PRIVATE KEY TO DECRYPT, DON'T YOU?
OWW
CORRECT!
PRIVATE KEYS DO HAVE THAT FUNCTIONALITY.
A ONE-WAY FUNCTION IS ALSO KNOWN AS A *TRAPDOOR FUNCTION*. YOU CAN FIND THE INPUT USING THE PRIVATE KEY, SO THE FUNCTION ONLY APPEARS TO BE ONE-WAY TO THOSE WITHOUT THE KEY.

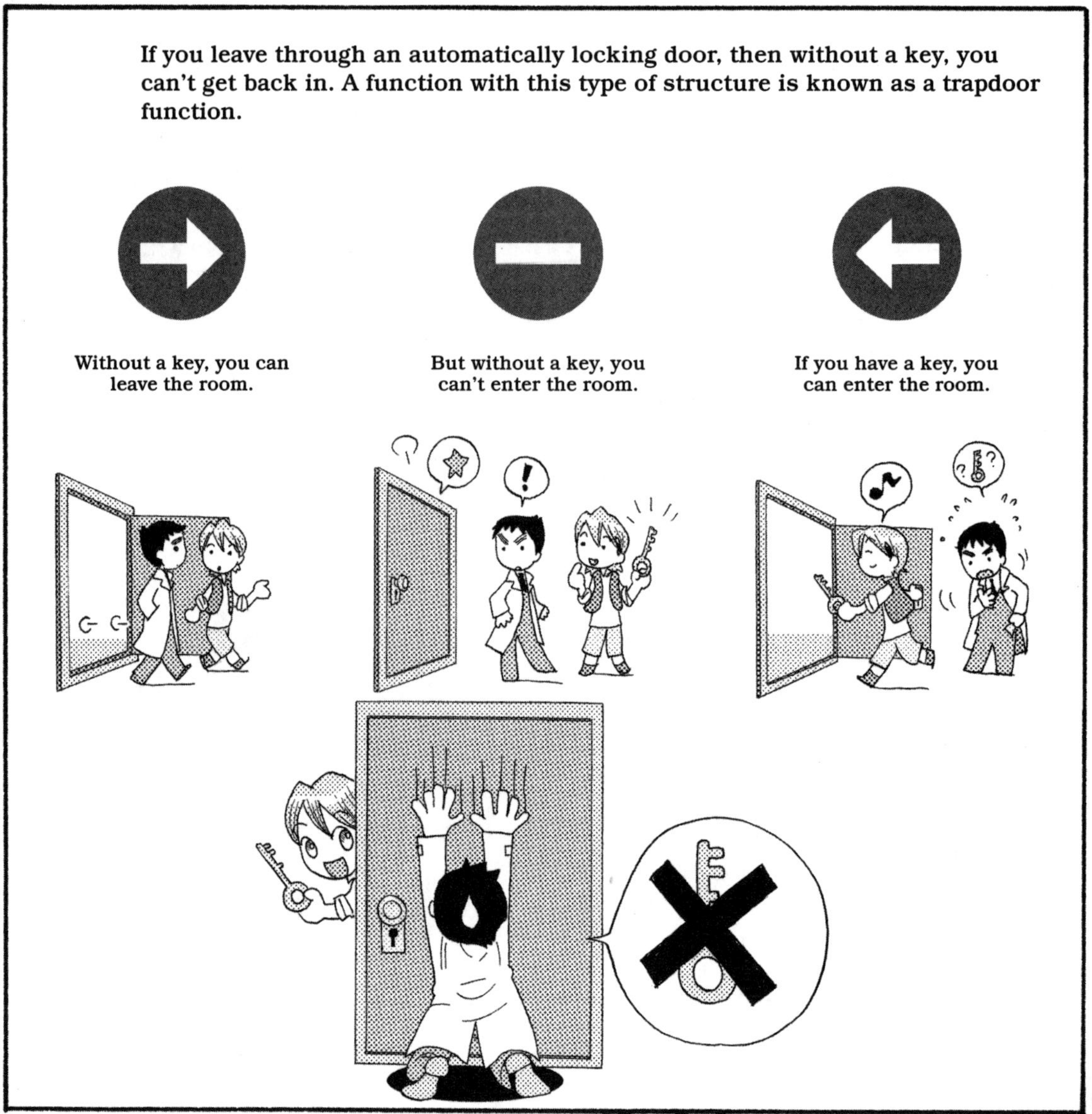
If you leave through an automatically locking door, then without a key, you can't get back in. A function with this type of structure is known as a trapdoor function.
Without a key, you can leave the room.
But without a key, you can't enter the room.
If you have a key, you can enter the room.

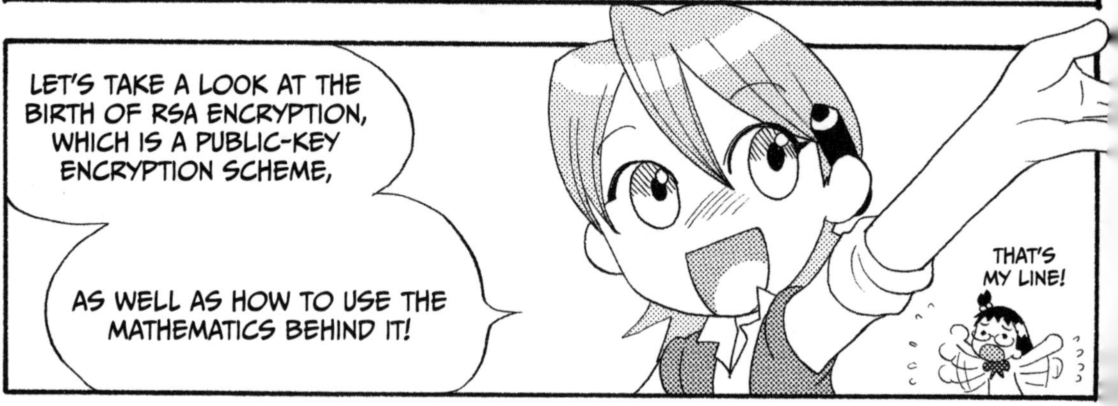
LET'S TAKE A LOOK AT THE BIRTH OF RSA ENCRYPTION, WHICH IS A PUBLIC-KEY ENCRYPTION SCHEME,
AS WELL AS HOW TO USE THE MATHEMATICS BEHIND IT!
THAT'S MY LINE!

THE BIRTH OF RSA ENCRYPTION

RSA was introduced in 1977 as the world's first public-key encryption system. Its name derives from the initials of the three American researchers who developed it: Rivest, Shamir, and Adleman.

RSA's strength lies in the difficulty of solving the integer factorization problem developers published in a science magazine in 1977. The problem involves applying integer factorization to a given number to decipher a message.

Here is the 129-digit natural number they presented:

> 11438162575788886766923577997614661201021829672124
> 236256256184293570693524573389783059712356395870
> 50589890751475992900268795435415

Not until 1994 was the number's integer factorization calculated and the message deciphered. Doing so took some 1,600 computers. It may seem as though 17 years is a long time to find the factors of a number, but one of the RSA developers, Rivest, had anticipated that it would take a thousand years, so the creators were actually surprised the cipher was cracked when it was. Incidentally, the decoded message was "THE MAGIC WORDS ARE SQUEAMISH OSSIFRAGE."

The numbers currently used in RSA encryption are more than 300 digits long in base 10 and, even with computers, would take an astronomical amount of time to perform integer factorization on.

PRIME NUMBERS AND INTEGER FACTORIZATION

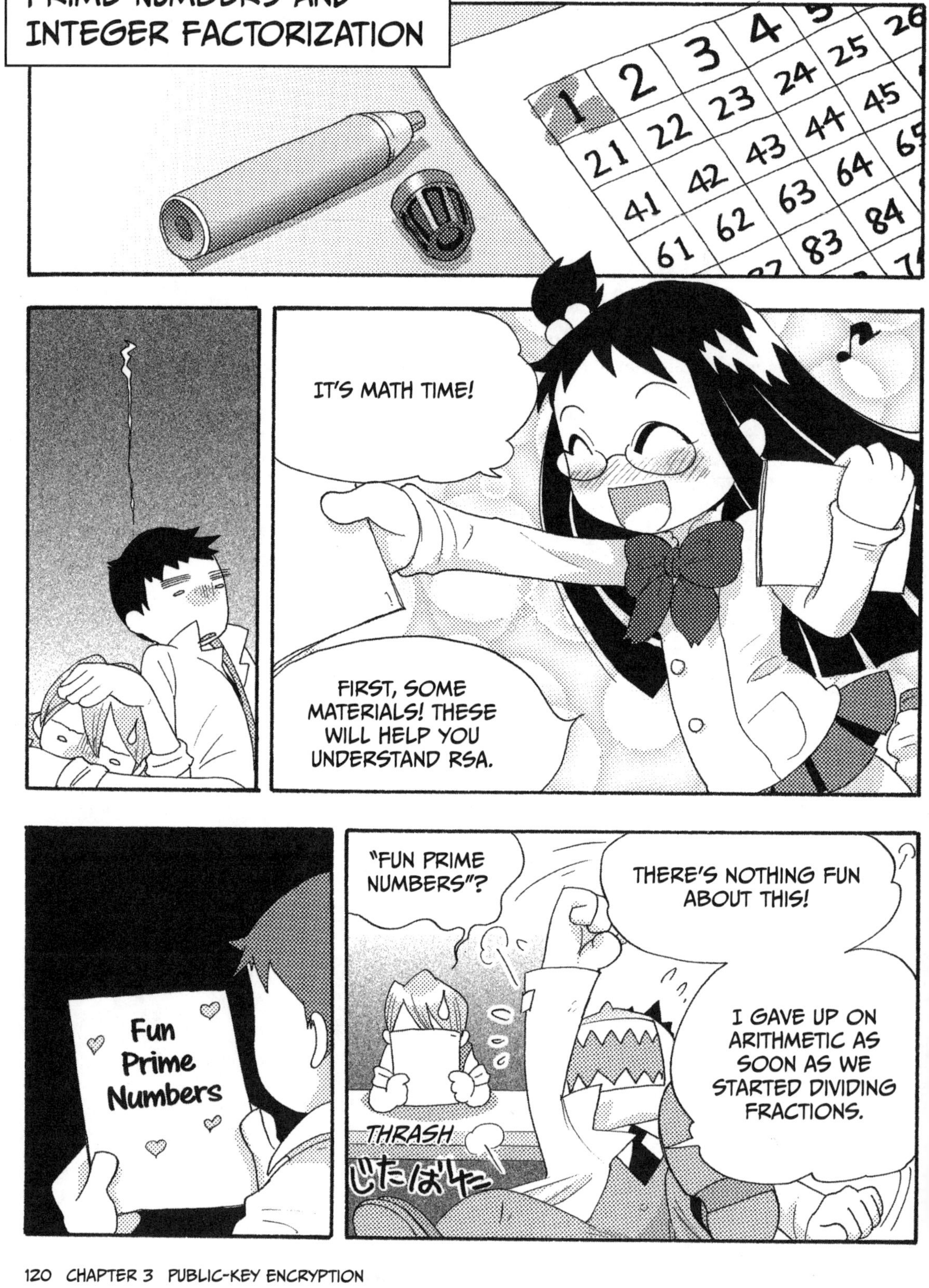

IT'S MATH TIME!
FIRST, SOME MATERIALS! THESE WILL HELP YOU UNDERSTAND RSA.
Fun Prime Numbers
"FUN PRIME NUMBERS"?
THERE'S NOTHING FUN ABOUT THIS!
I GAVE UP ON ARITHMETIC AS SOON AS WE STARTED DIVIDING FRACTIONS.
THRASH
じたばた

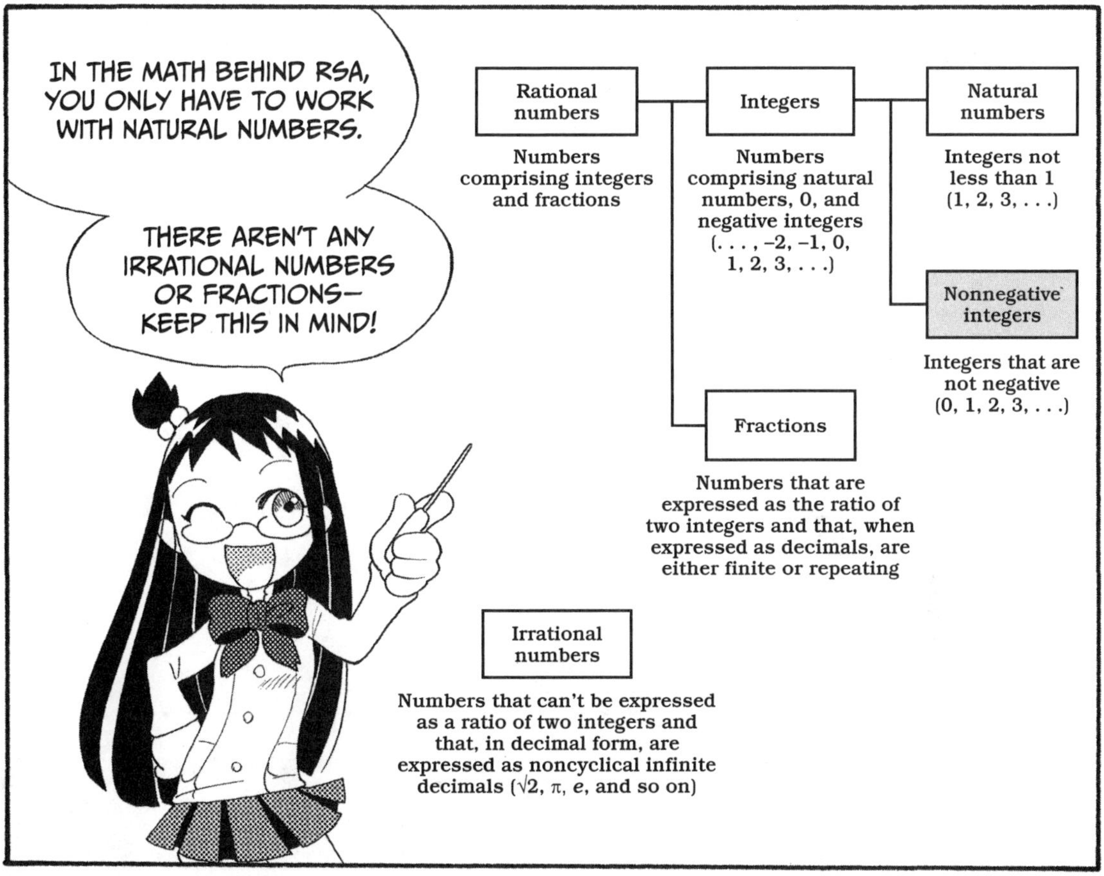
IN THE MATH BEHIND RSA, YOU ONLY HAVE TO WORK WITH NATURAL NUMBERS.
THERE AREN'T ANY IRRATIONAL NUMBERS OR FRACTIONS— KEEP THIS IN MIND!
Rational numbers
Numbers comprising integers and fractions
Integers
Numbers comprising natural numbers, 0, and negative integers (. . . , –2, –1, 0, 1, 2, 3, . . .)
Natural numbers
Integers not less than 1 (1, 2, 3, . . .)
Nonnegative integers
Integers that are not negative (0, 1, 2, 3, . . .)
Fractions
Numbers that are expressed as the ratio of two integers and that, when expressed as decimals, are either finite or repeating
Irrational numbers
Numbers that can't be expressed as a ratio of two integers and that, in decimal form, are expressed as noncyclical infinite decimals (√2, π, e, and so on)

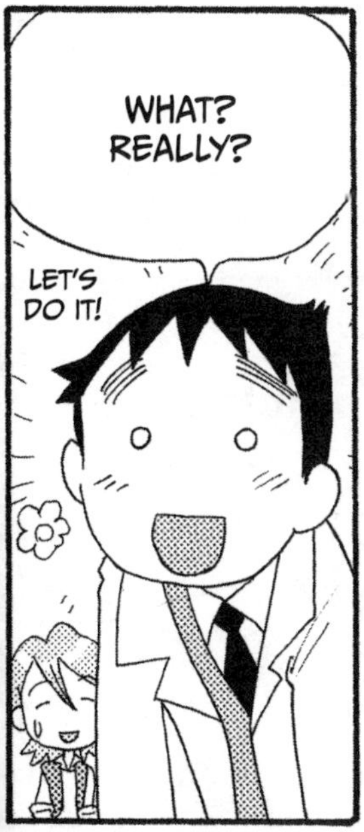
WHAT? REALLY?
LET'S DO IT!

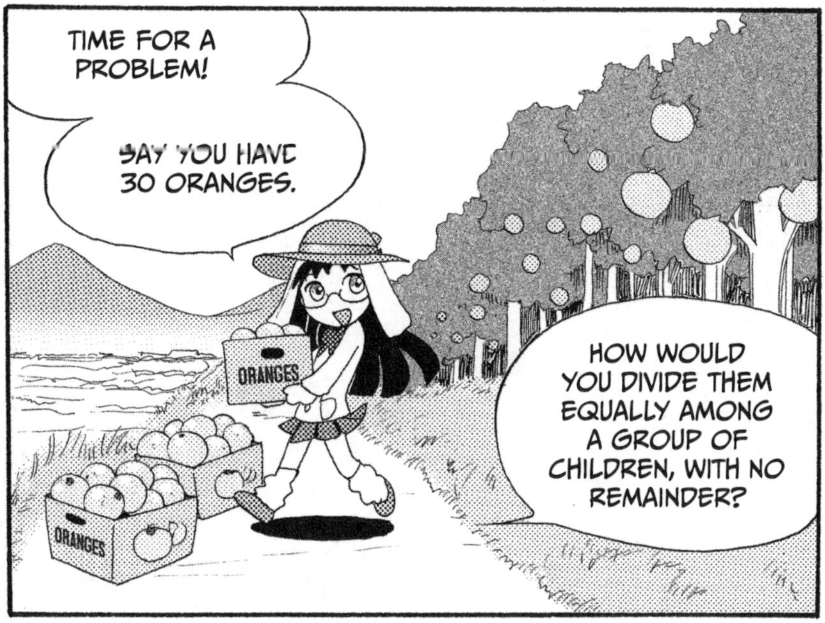
TIME FOR A PROBLEM!
SAY YOU HAVE 30 ORANGES.
ORANGES
ORANGES
HOW WOULD YOU DIVIDE THEM EQUALLY AMONG A GROUP OF CHILDREN, WITH NO REMAINDER?

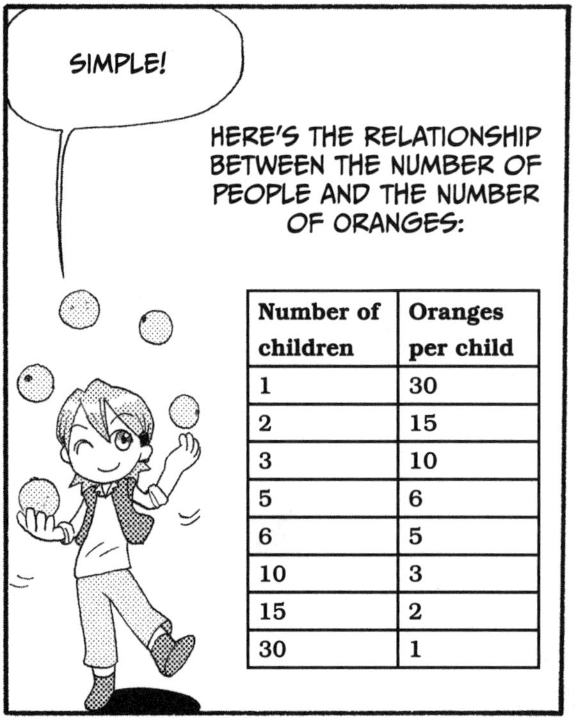
SIMPLE!
HERE'S THE RELATIONSHIP BETWEEN THE NUMBER OF PEOPLE AND THE NUMBER OF ORANGES:

Number of children	Oranges per child
1	30
2	15
3	10
5	6
6	5
10	3
15	2
30	1

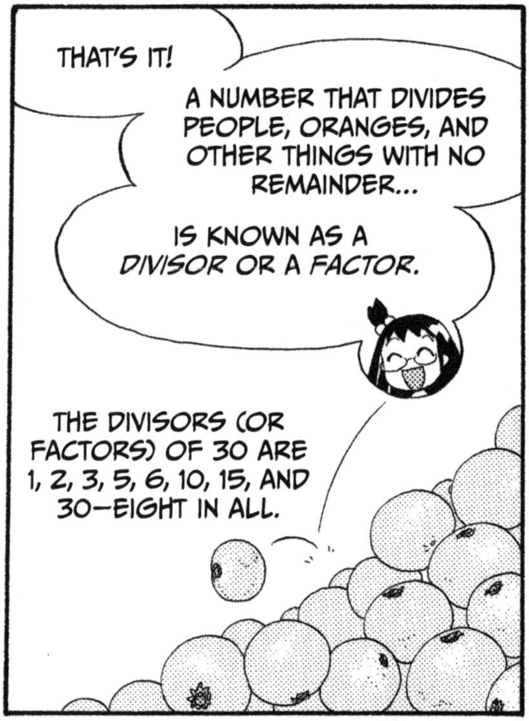
THAT'S IT!
A NUMBER THAT DIVIDES PEOPLE, ORANGES, AND OTHER THINGS WITH NO REMAINDER...
IS KNOWN AS A *DIVISOR* OR A *FACTOR*.
THE DIVISORS (OR FACTORS) OF 30 ARE 1, 2, 3, 5, 6, 10, 15, AND 30—EIGHT IN ALL.

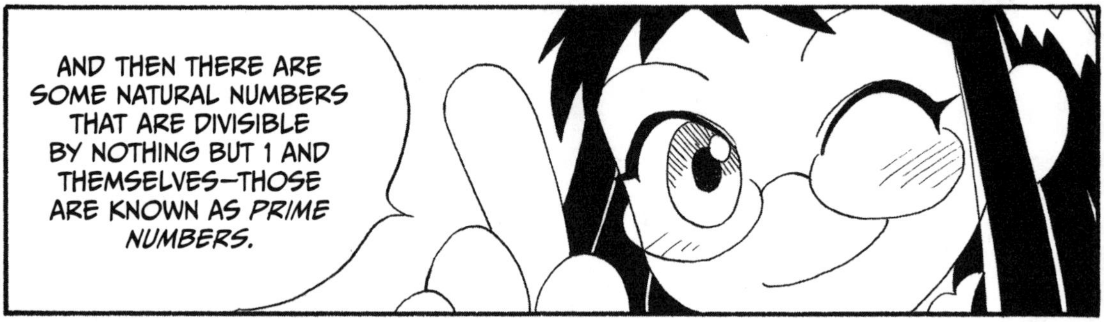
AND THEN THERE ARE SOME NATURAL NUMBERS THAT ARE DIVISIBLE BY NOTHING BUT 1 AND THEMSELVES—THOSE ARE KNOWN AS *PRIME NUMBERS*.

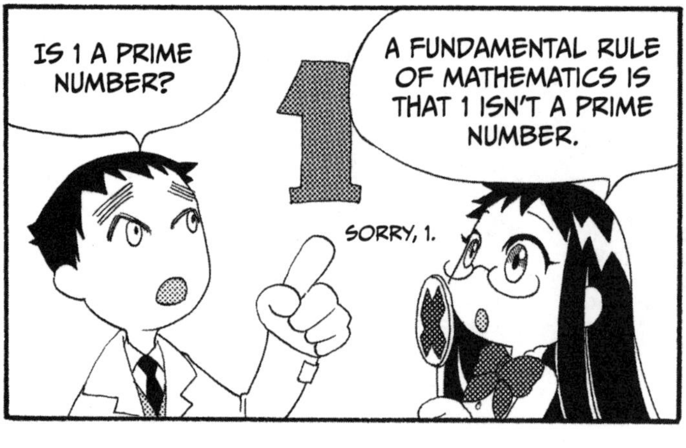
IS 1 A PRIME NUMBER?
1
A FUNDAMENTAL RULE OF MATHEMATICS IS THAT 1 ISN'T A PRIME NUMBER.
SORRY, 1.

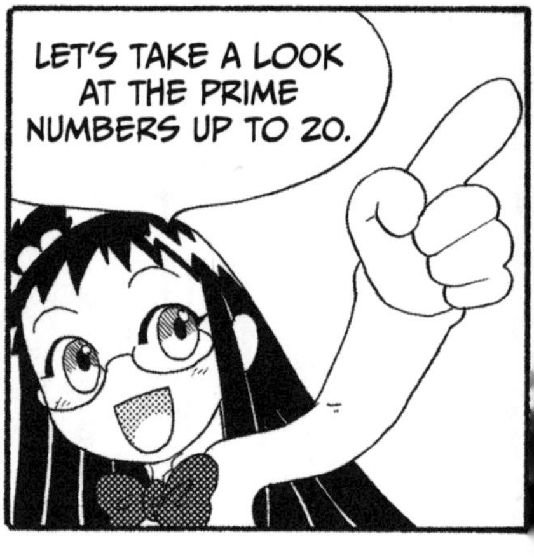
LET'S TAKE A LOOK AT THE PRIME NUMBERS UP TO 20.

2	Divisible only by itself (2) and 1	Prime number
3	Divisible only by itself (3) and 1	Prime number
4	Divisible by 2	Not prime
5	Divisible only by itself (5) and 1	Prime number
6	Divisible by 2 and 3	Not prime
7	Divisible only by itself (7) and 1	Prime number
8	Divisible by 2 and 4	Not prime
9	Divisible by 3	Not prime
10	Divisible by 2 and 5	Not prime
11	Divisible only by itself (11) and 1	Prime number
12	Divisible by 2, 3, 4, and 6	Not prime
13	Divisible only by itself (13) and 1	Prime number
14	Divisible by 2 and 7	Not prime
15	Divisible by 3 and 5	Not prime
16	Divisible by 2, 4, and 8	Not prime
17	Divisible only by itself (17) and 1	Prime number
18	Divisible by 2, 3, 6, and 9	Not prime
19	Divisible only by itself (19) and 1	Prime number
20	Divisible by 2, 4, 5, and 10	Not prime

NONPRIME NUMBERS ARE CALLED COMPOSITE NUMBERS, AND THEY CAN BE EXPRESSED AS THE PRODUCT OF ONE OR MORE PRIMES.

THIS IS CALLED INTEGER FACTORIZATION.

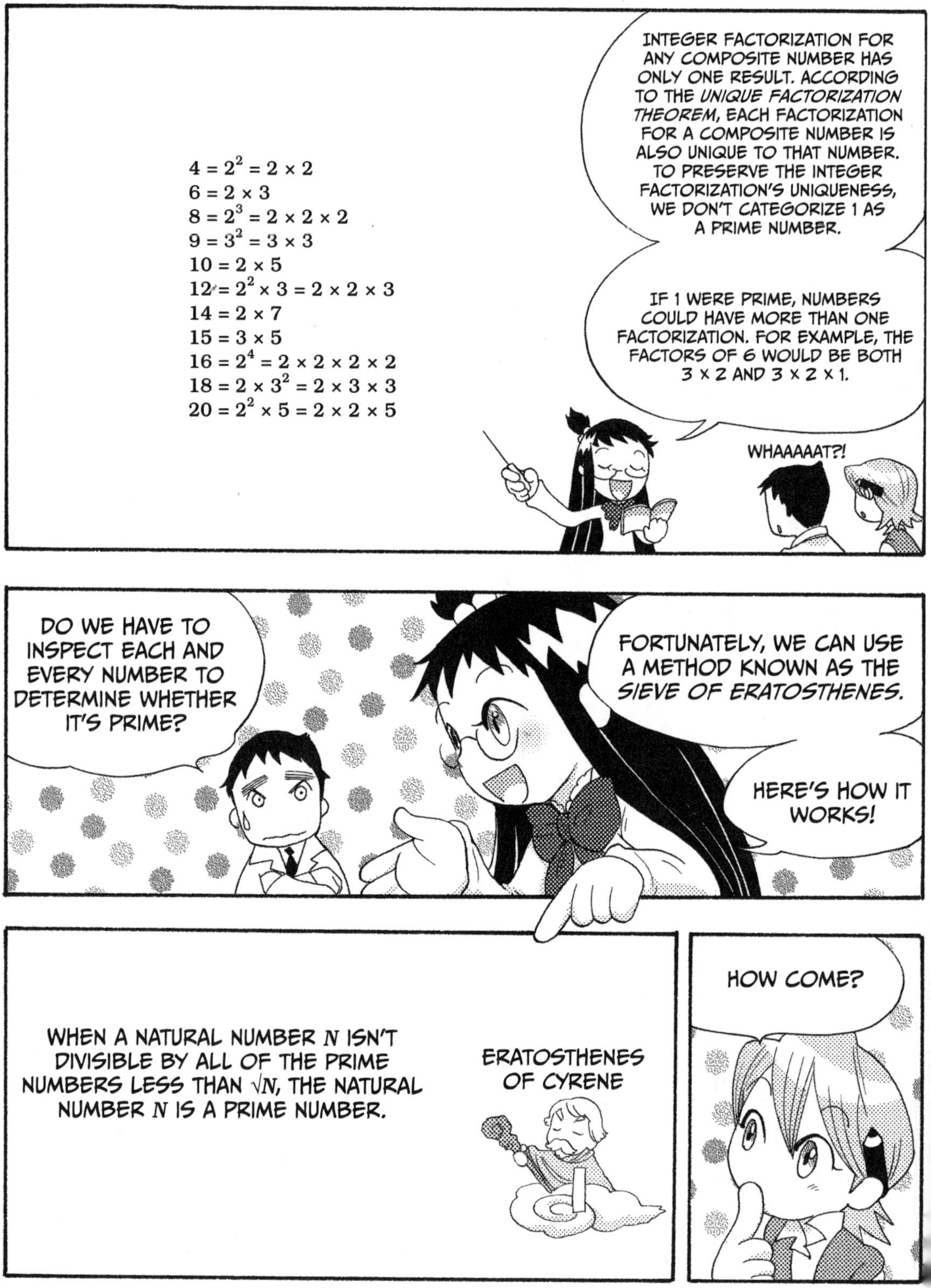
$4 = 2^2 = 2 \times 2$
$6 = 2 \times 3$
$8 = 2^3 = 2 \times 2 \times 2$
$9 = 3^2 = 3 \times 3$
$10 = 2 \times 5$
$12 = 2^2 \times 3 = 2 \times 2 \times 3$
$14 = 2 \times 7$
$15 = 3 \times 5$
$16 = 2^4 = 2 \times 2 \times 2 \times 2$
$18 = 2 \times 3^2 = 2 \times 3 \times 3$
$20 = 2^2 \times 5 = 2 \times 2 \times 5$
INTEGER FACTORIZATION FOR ANY COMPOSITE NUMBER HAS ONLY ONE RESULT. ACCORDING TO THE *UNIQUE FACTORIZATION THEOREM*, EACH FACTORIZATION FOR A COMPOSITE NUMBER IS ALSO UNIQUE TO THAT NUMBER. TO PRESERVE THE INTEGER FACTORIZATION'S UNIQUENESS, WE DON'T CATEGORIZE 1 AS A PRIME NUMBER.
IF 1 WERE PRIME, NUMBERS COULD HAVE MORE THAN ONE FACTORIZATION. FOR EXAMPLE, THE FACTORS OF 6 WOULD BE BOTH 3×2 AND $3 \times 2 \times 1$.
WHAAAAAT?!
DO WE HAVE TO INSPECT EACH AND EVERY NUMBER TO DETERMINE WHETHER IT'S PRIME?
FORTUNATELY, WE CAN USE A METHOD KNOWN AS THE *SIEVE OF ERATOSTHENES*.
HERE'S HOW IT WORKS!
WHEN A NATURAL NUMBER N ISN'T DIVISIBLE BY ALL OF THE PRIME NUMBERS LESS THAN $\sqrt{N}$, THE NATURAL NUMBER N IS A PRIME NUMBER.
ERATOSTHENES OF CYRENE
HOW COME?

THINK OF N AS BEING EQUAL TO pq.

$$p \leq \sqrt{N} \quad \text{OR} \quad q \leq \sqrt{N}$$

IF N CAN BE EXPRESSED AS THE PRODUCT OF THE TWO PRIME NUMBERS pq, AT LEAST p OR q MUST BE LESS THAN $\sqrt{N}$.

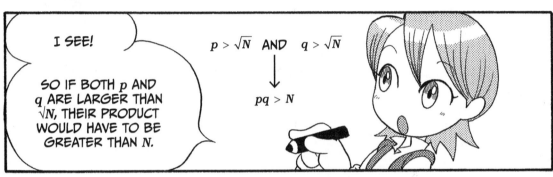

I SEE!

SO IF BOTH p AND q ARE LARGER THAN $\sqrt{N}$, THEIR PRODUCT WOULD HAVE TO BE GREATER THAN N.

$$p > \sqrt{N} \quad \text{AND} \quad q > \sqrt{N}$$
$$\downarrow$$
$$pq > N$$

SO WHAT'S ERA... WHATEVER IT IS YOU SAID?

I'M AN ANCIENT GREEK SCHOLAR!

I WAS THE FIRST PERSON TO CALCULATE THE SIZE OF EARTH!

THE SIEVE OF ERATOSTHENES AN EFFICIENT METHOD OF DETERMINING WHETHER A NUMBER IS PRIME.

LOOK AT THIS PRINTOUT.

POM!

THESE BOXES CONTAIN THE NUMBERS FROM 1 TO 400.

1	2	3	4	5	6	7	8	9	10	11	12	13	14	15	16	17	18	19	20
21	22	23	24	25	26	27	28	29	30	31	32	33	34	35	36	37	38	39	40
41	42	43	44	45	46	47	48	49	50	51	52	53	54	55	56	57	58	59	60
61	62	63	64	65	66	67	68	69	70	71	72	73	74	75	76	77	78	79	80
81	82	83	84	85	86	87	88	89	90	91	92	93	94	95	96	97	98	99	100
101	102	103	104	105	106	107	108	109	110	111	112	113	114	115	116	117	118	119	120
121	122	123	124	125	126	127	128	129	130	131	132	133	134	135	136	137	138	139	140
141	142	143	144	145	146	147	148	149	150	151	152	153	154	155	156	157	158	159	160
161	162	163	164	165	166	167	168	169	170	171	172	173	174	175	176	177	178	179	180
181	182	183	184	185	186	187	188	189	190	191	192	193	194	195	196	197	198	199	200
201	202	203	204	205	206	207	208	209	210	211	212	213	214	215	216	217	218	219	220
221	222	223	224	225	226	227	228	229	230	231	232	233	234	235	236	237	238	239	240
241	242	243	244	245	246	247	248	249	250	251	252	253	254	255	256	257	258	259	260
261	262	263	264	265	266	267	268	269	270	271	272	273	274	275	276	277	278	279	280
281	282	283	284	285	286	287	288	289	290	291	292	293	294	295	296	297	298	299	300
301	302	303	304	305	306	307	308	309	310	311	312	313	314	315	316	317	318	319	320
321	322	323	324	325	326	327	328	329	330	331	332	333	334	335	336	337	338	339	340
341	342	343	344	345	346	347	348	349	350	351	352	353	354	355	356	357	358	359	360
361	362	363	364	365	366	367	368	369	370	371	372	373	374	375	376	377	378	379	380
381	382	383	384	385	386	387	388	389	390	391	392	393	394	395	396	397	398	399	400

SINCE $\sqrt{400} = 20$, THE PRIME NUMBERS LESS THAN 400 CAN'T BE DIVIDED BY PRIME NUMBERS GREATER THAN 20.

THE SET {2, 3, 5, 7, 11, 13, 17, 19} COMPRISES ALL OF THE PRIME NUMBERS LESS THAN 20.

FIRST, SINCE 2 IS A PRIME NUMBER, LEAVE IT ALONE.

THEN BLOT OUT ALL MULTIPLES OF 2!

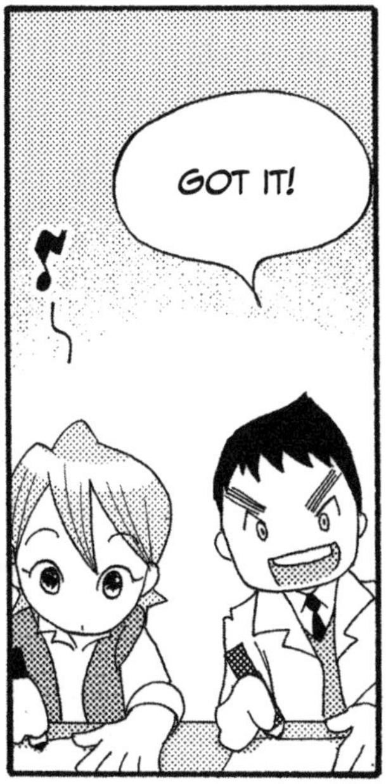
GOT IT!

	2	3	4	5	6	7	8	9	10	11	12	13	14	15	16	17	18	19	20
21	22	23	24	25	26	27	28	29	30	31	32	33	34	35	36	37	38	39	40
41	42	43	44	45	46	47	48	49	50	51	52	53	54	55	56	57	58	59	60
61	62	63	64	65	66	67	68	69	70	71	72	73	74	75	76	77	78	79	80
81	82	83	84	85	86	87	88	89	90	91	92	93	94	95	96	97	98	99	100
101	102	103	104	105	106	107	108	109	110	111	112	113	114	115	116	117	118	119	120
121	122	123	124	125	126	127	128	129	130	131	132	133	134	135	136	137	138	139	140
141	142	143	144	145	146	147	148	149	150	151	152	153	154	155	156	157	158	159	160
161	162	163	164	165	166	167	168	169	170	171	172	173	174	175	176	177	178	179	180
181	182	183	184	185	186	187	188	189	190	191	192	193	194	195	196	197	198	199	200
201	202	203	204	205	206	207	208	209	210	211	212	213	214	215	216	217	218	219	220
221	222	223	224	225	226	227	228	229	230	231	232	233	234	235	236	237	238	239	240
241	242	243	244	245	246	247	248	249	250	251	252	253	254	255	256	257	258	259	260
261	262	263	264	265	266	267	268	269	270	271	272	273	274	275	276	277	278	279	280
281	282	283	284	285	286	287	288	289	290	291	292	293	294	295	296	297	298	299	300
301	302	303	304	305	306	307	308	309	310	311	312	313	314	315	316	317	318	319	320
321	322	323	324	325	326	327	328	329	330	331	332	333	334	335	336	337	338	339	340
341	342	343	344	345	346	347	348	349	350	351	352	353	354	355	356	357	358	359	360
361	362	363	364	365	366	367	368	369	370	371	372	373	374	375	376	377	378	379	380
381	382	383	384	385	386	387	388	389	390	391	392	393	394	395	396	397	398	399	400

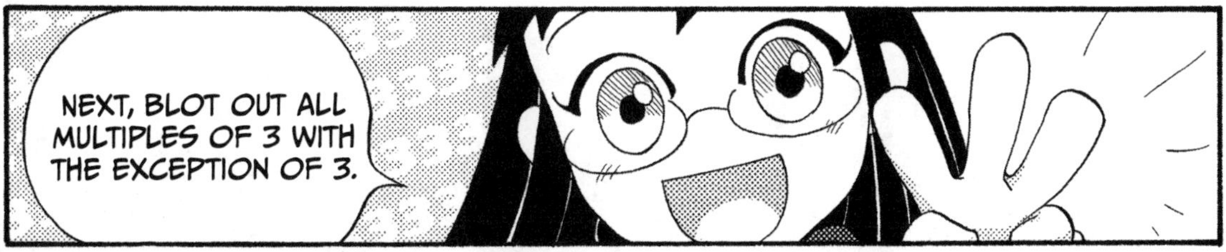
NEXT, BLOT OUT ALL MULTIPLES OF 3 WITH THE EXCEPTION OF 3.

	2	3		5		7		9		11		13		15		17		19	
21		23		25		27		29		31		33		35		37		39	
41		43		45		47		49		51		53		55		57		59	
61		63		65		67		69		71		73		75		77		79	
81		83		85		87		89		91		93		95		97		99	
101		103		105		107		109		111		113		115		117		119	
121		123		125		127		129		131		133		135		137		139	
141		143		145		147		149		151		153		155		157		159	
161		163		165		167		169		171		173		175		177		179	
181		183		185		187		189		191		193		195		197		199	
201		203		205		207		209		211		213		215		217		219	
221		223		225		227		229		231		233		235		237		239	
241		243		245		247		249		251		253		255		257		259	
261		263		265		267		269		271		273		275		277		279	
281		283		285		287		289		291		293		295		297		299	
301		303		305		307		309		311		313		315		317		319	
321		323		325		327		329		331		333		335		337		339	
341		343		345		347		349		351		353		355		357		359	
361		363		365		367		369		371		373		375		377		379	
381		383		385		387		389		391		393		395		397		399	

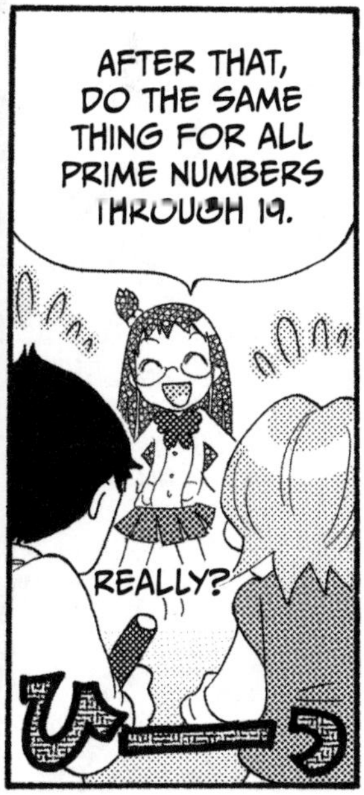
AFTER THAT, DO THE SAME THING FOR ALL PRIME NUMBERS THROUGH 19.
REALLY?

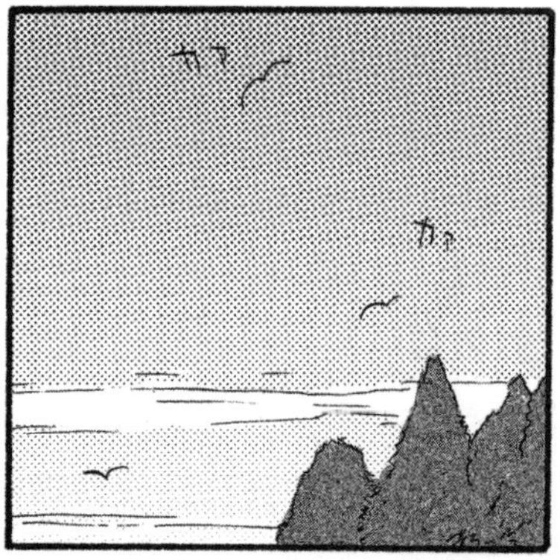

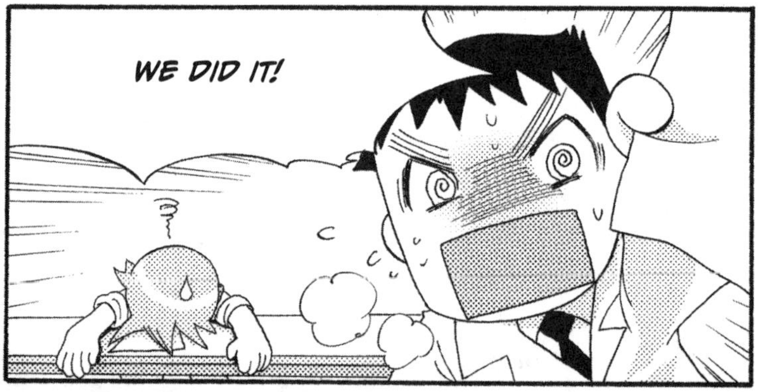

WE DID IT!

	2	3		5		7				11		13				17		19	
		23						29		31						37			
41		43				47						53						59	
61						67				71		73						79	
		83						89								97			
101		103				107		109				113							
						127				131						137		139	
								149		151						157			
		163				167						173						179	
181										191		193				197		199	
										211									
		223				227		229				233						239	
241										251						257			
		263						269		271						277			
281		283										293							
						307				311		313				317			
										331						337			
						347		349				353						359	
						367						373						379	
		383						389								397			

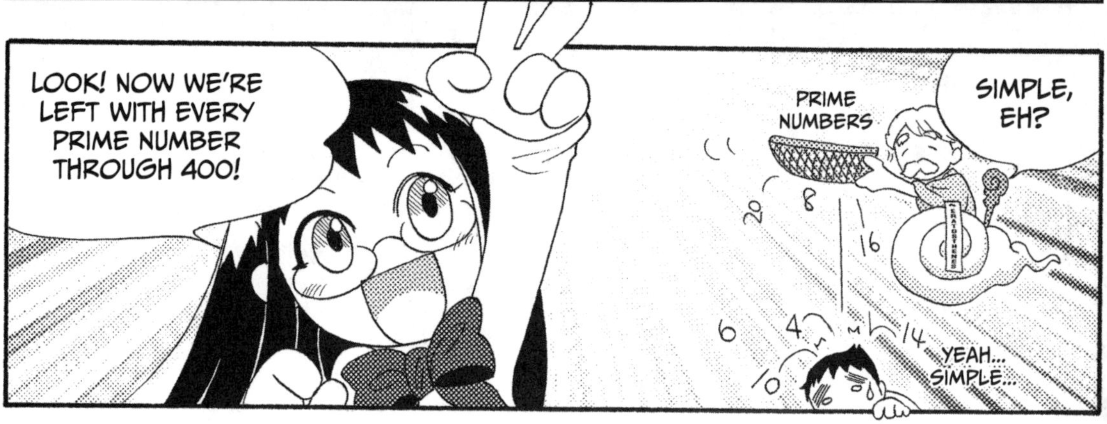

LOOK! NOW WE'RE LEFT WITH EVERY PRIME NUMBER THROUGH 400!
PRIME NUMBERS
SIMPLE, EH?
YEAH... SIMPLE...

THIS MIGHT HAVE BEEN EASY USING A COMPUTER...

BUT FINDING LARGER PRIMES WOULD BE TOUGH EITHER WAY!

AND AREN'T THE PRIME NUMBERS USED IN RSA REALLY, REALLY LARGE?

SWAT

SWAT

LET'S SAY WE'VE FOUND A LARGE NUMBER THAT APPEARS TO BE PRIME.

WE HAVE A METHOD TO DETERMINE WHETHER OR NOT IT IS TRULY PRIME.

TYPES OF PRIMALITY TESTS

The sieve of Eratosthenes is a reliable method for finding prime numbers. When determining whether a very large number is prime, however, using this method takes a great deal of time. Instead, we can use Fermat's method. It isn't completely reliable because it determines prime numbers probabilistically, but it is faster. We'll cover Fermat's method in depth later, but for now, you just need to know that this method has a small chance of misidentifying a nonprime number n (a composite number) as prime.

We could also use the Miller-Rabin method, which improves upon Fermat's method. In a given test, the probability of misidentifying a composite number as prime is less than with the Fermat method. In fact, this method can determine prime numbers with near certainty.

NUMBERS THAT ARE PROBABLE PRIMES ARE KNOWN AS PSEUDOPRIMES.

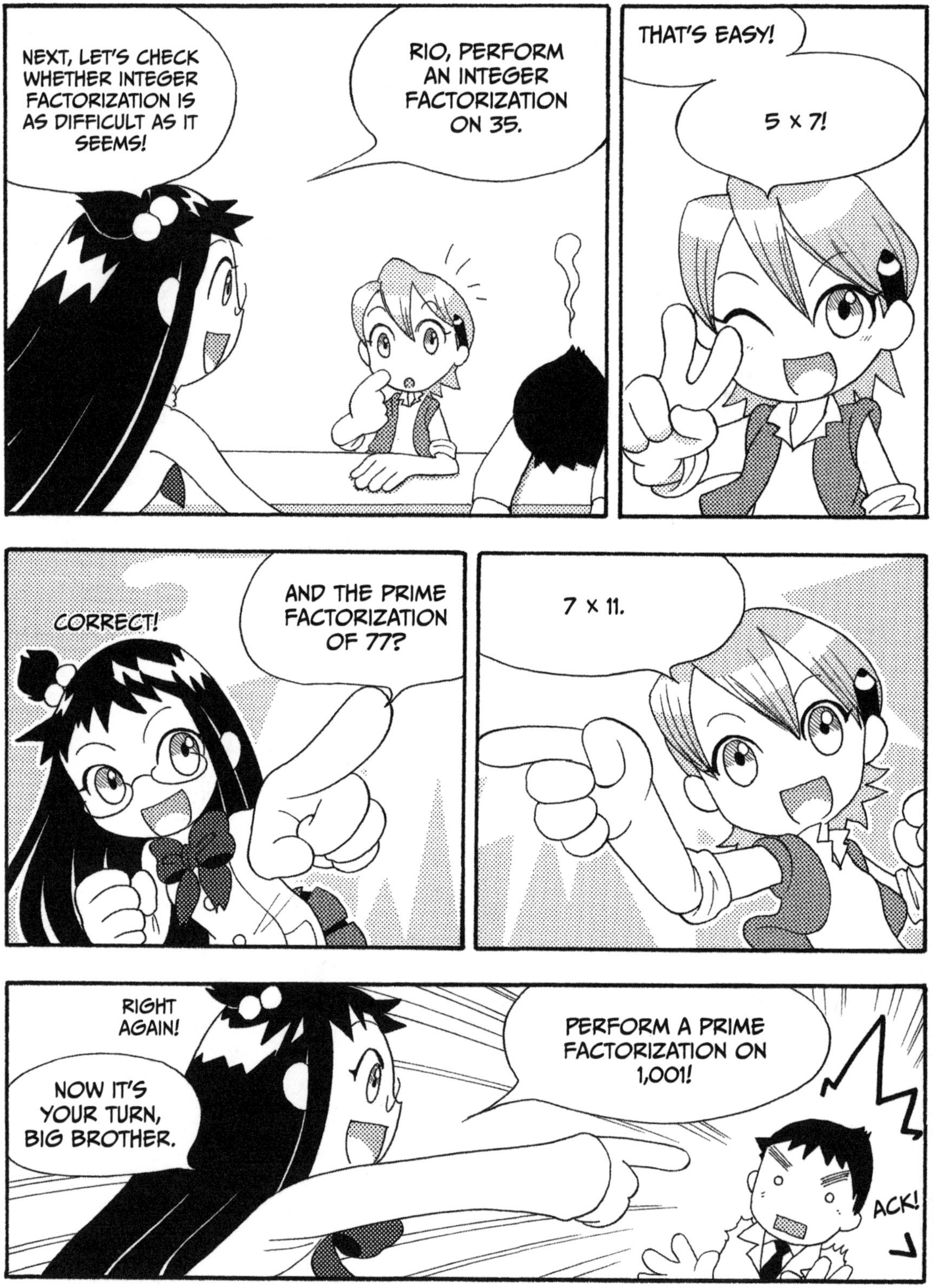
NEXT, LET'S CHECK WHETHER INTEGER FACTORIZATION IS AS DIFFICULT AS IT SEEMS!
RIO, PERFORM AN INTEGER FACTORIZATION ON 35.
THAT'S EASY!
5 × 7!
CORRECT!
AND THE PRIME FACTORIZATION OF 77?
7 × 11.
RIGHT AGAIN!
NOW IT'S YOUR TURN, BIG BROTHER.
PERFORM A PRIME FACTORIZATION ON 1,001!
ACK!

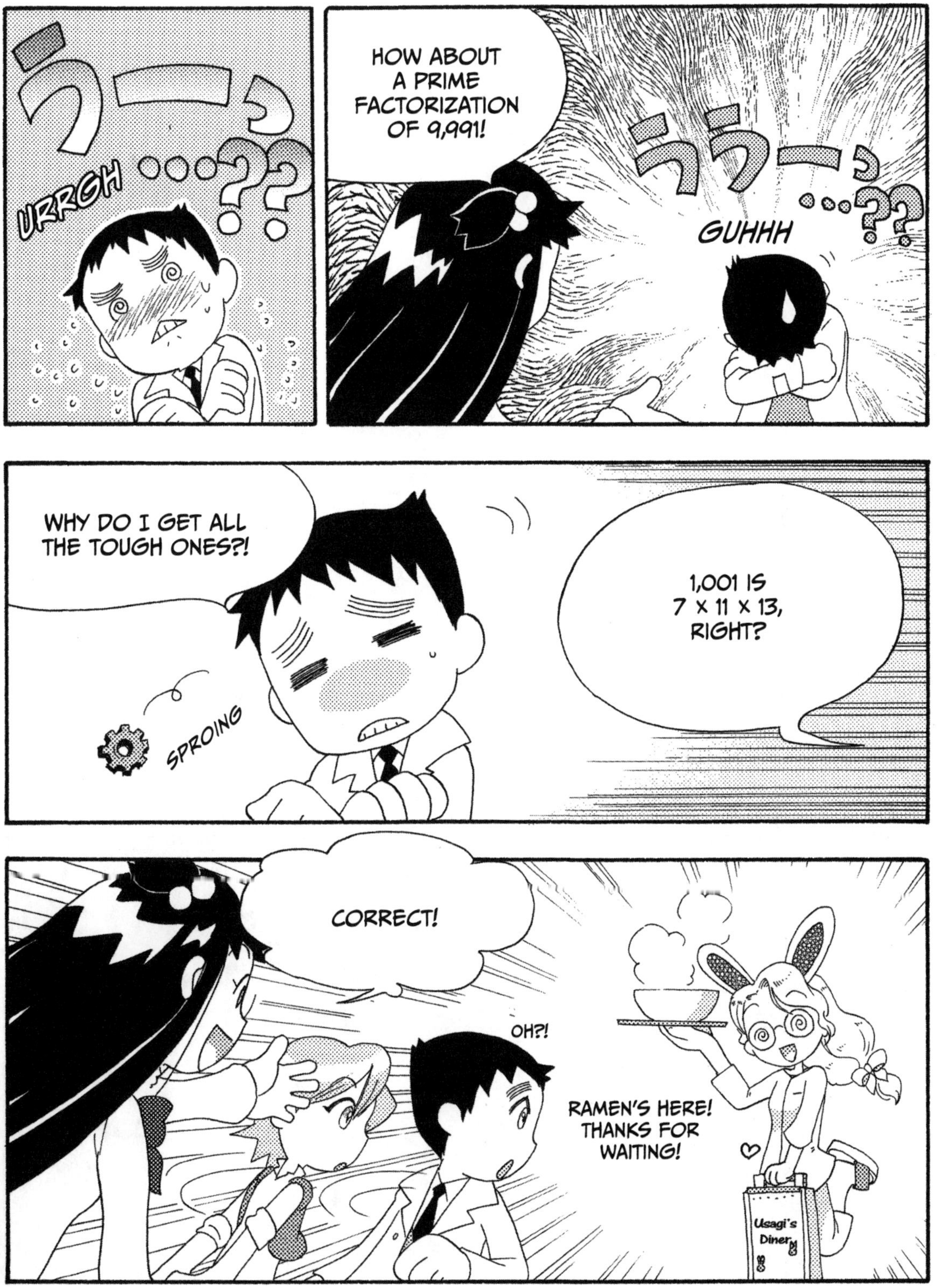
うーっ
URRGH ...??
HOW ABOUT A PRIME FACTORIZATION OF 9,991!
ううーっ
GUHHH ...??
WHY DO I GET ALL THE TOUGH ONES?!
SPROING
1,001 IS 7 × 11 × 13, RIGHT?
CORRECT!
OH?!
RAMEN'S HERE! THANKS FOR WAITING!
Usagi's Diner

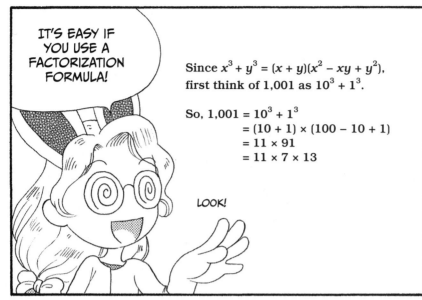

IT'S EASY IF YOU USE A FACTORIZATION FORMULA!

Since $x^3 + y^3 = (x + y)(x^2 - xy + y^2)$, first think of 1,001 as $10^3 + 1^3$.

So,
$$\begin{aligned} 1,001 &= 10^3 + 1^3 \\ &= (10 + 1) \times (100 - 10 + 1) \\ &= 11 \times 91 \\ &= 11 \times 7 \times 13 \end{aligned}$$

LOOK!

OH, I SEE!

DO YOU REALLY?

9,991 IS 103 × 97!

$$x^2 - y^2 = (x + y)(x - y),$$
$$\begin{aligned} \text{so } 9,991 &= 100^2 - 3^2 \\ &= (100 + 3) \times (100 - 3) \\ &= 103 \times 97 \end{aligned}$$

OOOOH!

DID YOU SEE THAT?

YOU DIDN'T SOLVE IT...

WELL DONE!

SO 10,001 WOULD BE?

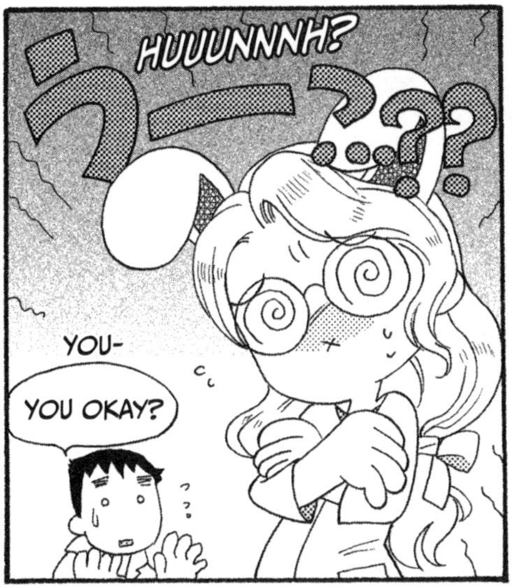
HUUUNNNH?
うー
YOU-
YOU OKAY?

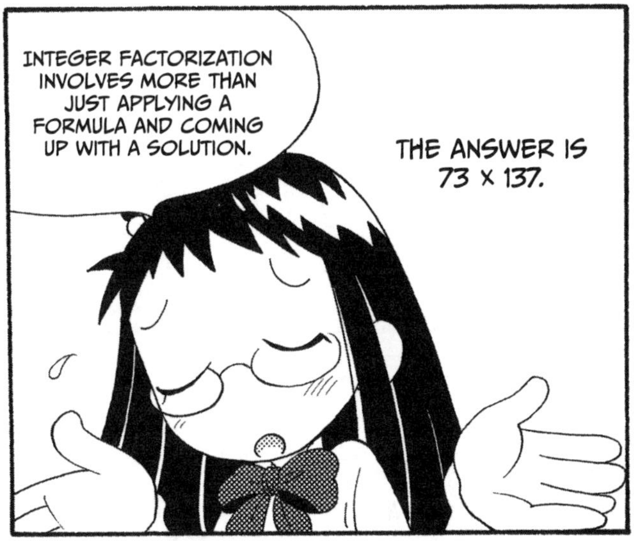
INTEGER FACTORIZATION INVOLVES MORE THAN JUST APPLYING A FORMULA AND COMING UP WITH A SOLUTION.
THE ANSWER IS 73 × 137.

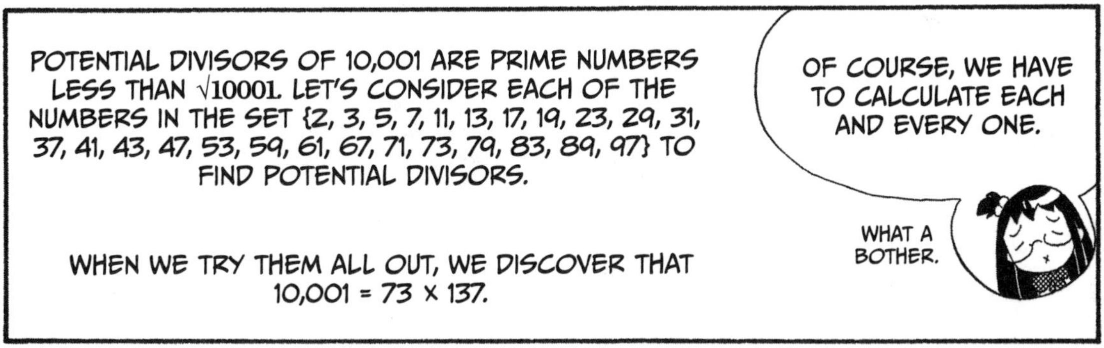
POTENTIAL DIVISORS OF 10,001 ARE PRIME NUMBERS LESS THAN √10001. LET'S CONSIDER EACH OF THE NUMBERS IN THE SET {2, 3, 5, 7, 11, 13, 17, 19, 23, 29, 31, 37, 41, 43, 47, 53, 59, 61, 67, 71, 73, 79, 83, 89, 97} TO FIND POTENTIAL DIVISORS.
WHEN WE TRY THEM ALL OUT, WE DISCOVER THAT 10,001 = 73 × 137.
OF COURSE, WE HAVE TO CALCULATE EACH AND EVERY ONE.
WHAT A BOTHER.

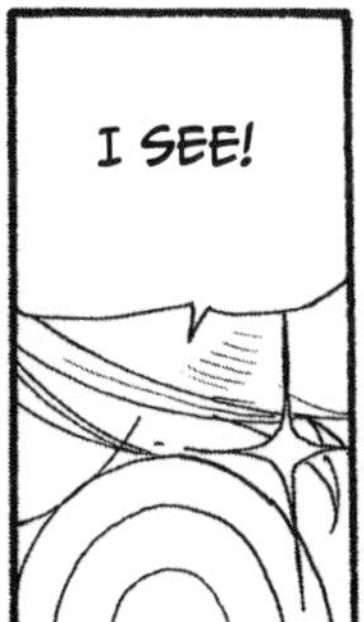
I SEE!

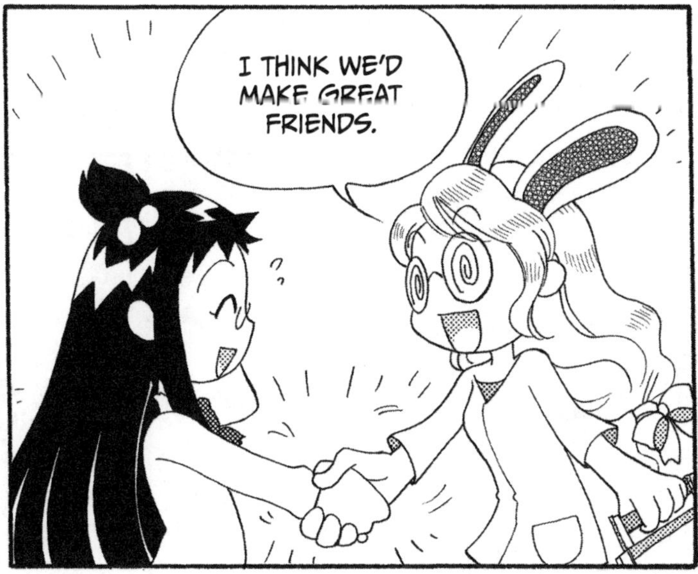
I THINK WE'D MAKE GREAT FRIENDS.

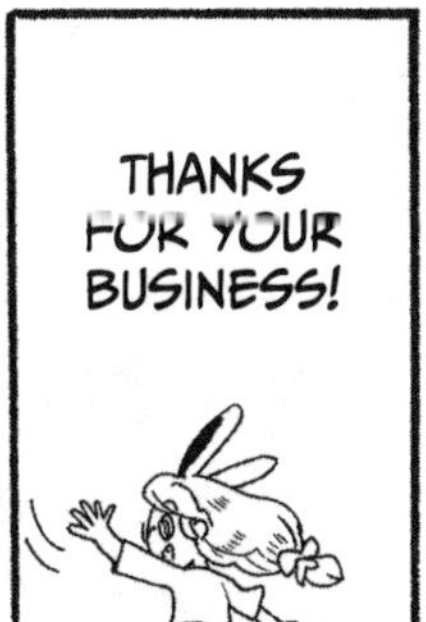
THANKS FOR YOUR BUSINESS!

MODULO OPERATIONS

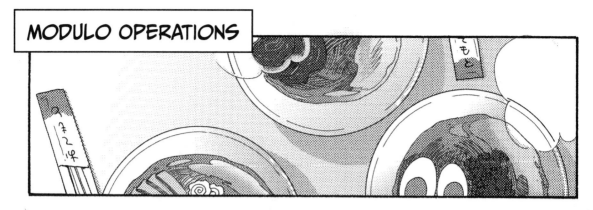

NEXT, LET'S TAKE A LOOK AT THE REMAINDER OF INTEGER DIVISION.

YOU NEED TO BECOME FAMILIAR WITH MODULO OPERATIONS TO UNDERSTAND RSA ENCRYPTION.

YOU MEAN LIKE THE REMAINDER DIVISION YOU LEARN IN ELEMENTARY SCHOOL?

$15 \div 7 = 2$
WITH A REMAINDER OF 1

SLUUUUURP

IN MODULAR ARITHMETIC, WE WOULD EXPRESS THE SAME EQUATION LIKE THIS.

$15 = 1 \pmod 7$

THE EQUATION REPRESENTS THE REMAINDER WHEN YOU DIVIDE 15 BY 7.

WHAT DOES MOD MEAN?

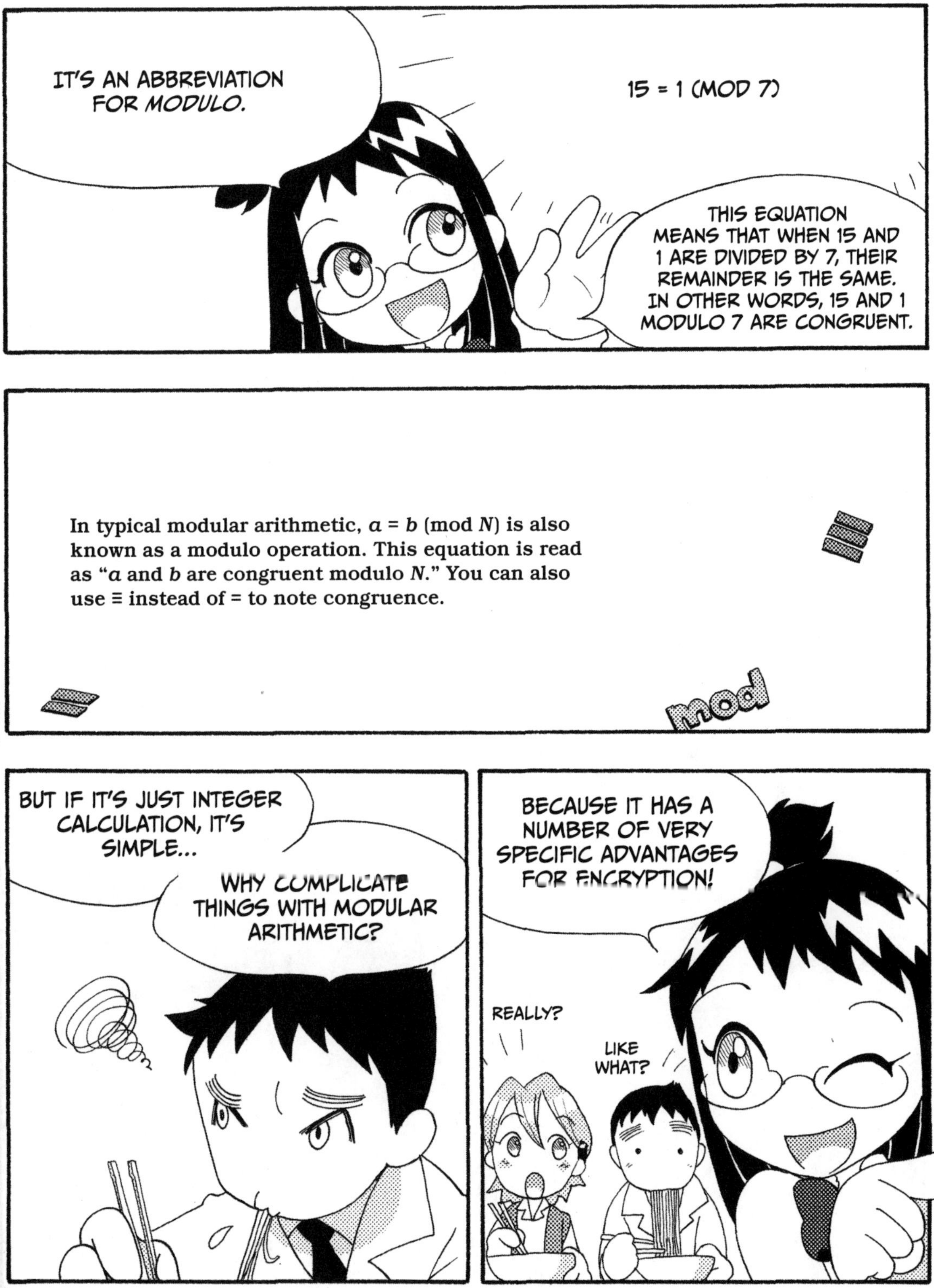

IT'S AN ABBREVIATION FOR *MODULO*.
15 = 1 (MOD 7)
THIS EQUATION MEANS THAT WHEN 15 AND 1 ARE DIVIDED BY 7, THEIR REMAINDER IS THE SAME. IN OTHER WORDS, 15 AND 1 MODULO 7 ARE CONGRUENT.
In typical modular arithmetic, $a = b$ (mod N) is also known as a modulo operation. This equation is read as "a and b are congruent modulo N." You can also use ≡ instead of = to note congruence.
mod
BUT IF IT'S JUST INTEGER CALCULATION, IT'S SIMPLE...
WHY COMPLICATE THINGS WITH MODULAR ARITHMETIC?
BECAUSE IT HAS A NUMBER OF VERY SPECIFIC ADVANTAGES FOR ENCRYPTION!
REALLY?
LIKE WHAT?

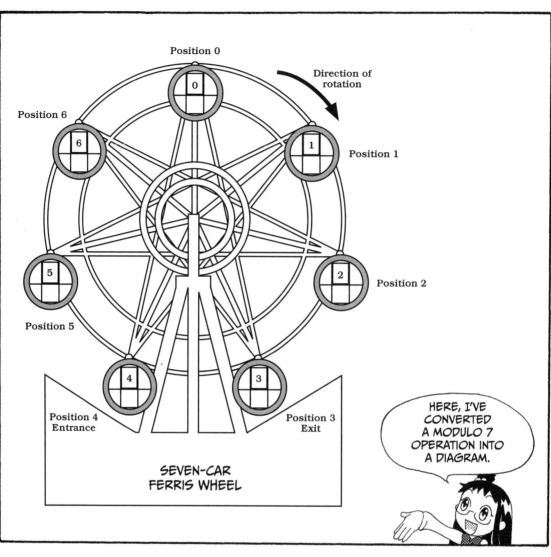

Position 0

Direction of rotation

Position 6

Position 1

Position 2

Position 5

Position 4
Entrance

Position 3
Exit

SEVEN-CAR
FERRIS WHEEL

HERE, I'VE CONVERTED A MODULO 7 OPERATION INTO A DIAGRAM.

SINCE THE PROBLEM INVOLVES FINDING THE REMAINDER AFTER WE DIVIDE BY 7, WE'RE ONLY WORKING WITH THE NUMBERS 0 THROUGH 6.

THAT'S THE FIRST ADVANTAGE!

THE SURPLUS (REMAINDER) WILL ALWAYS BE SMALLER THAN THE DIVISOR N (MODULO N OR MOD N).

SO OUR RESULTING VALUE IS LIMITED TO A SPECIFIC RANGE.

DOES THIS FERRIS WHEEL MOVE?
IT MOVES CLOCKWISE FOR ADDITION AND COUNTERCLOCKWISE FOR SUBTRACTION.
ADDITION
SUBTRACTION

ADDITION AND SUBTRACTION IN MODULO OPERATIONS

Let's use the Ferris wheel to model a modulo operation. Each of the seven cars is labeled with a number from 0 to 6. The cars correspond with numbered positions: we start with 0 at the top, and the positions are numbered 1 to 6 clockwise. Position 3 is the exit, and position 4 is the entrance.

Initially, car 0 is in position 0, car 1 is in position 1, and so forth. When we perform addition, the cars are rotated clockwise.

First, take a look at car 0. After moving 1/7 of a rotation, car 0 moves from position 0 to position 1. This is defined as +1 (the addition of 1). When the wheel makes 2/7 of a rotation, car 0 moves from position 0 to position 2. This is +2 (the addition of 2). When the wheel has made 7/7 of a rotation—in other words, one full rotation—car 0 returns once again to position 0. This is +7, which is the equivalent of 0—in other words, it is the same as if the wheel had not moved at all.

1/7 rotation = +1
2/7 rotation = +2
7/7 rotation = +7 = 0
0
1
2
3
4
5
6

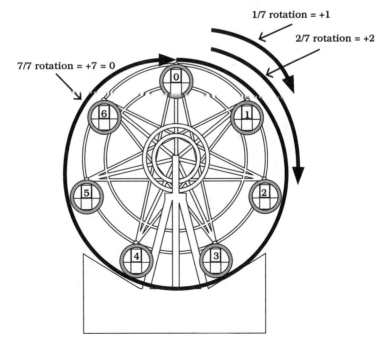

This Ferris wheel model can be used to explain modulo addition. For example, consider 5 + 6. In the initial state, the 5 in 5 + 6 corresponds to car 5. When this car moves by 6/7 of a rotation, where do you think it will end up?

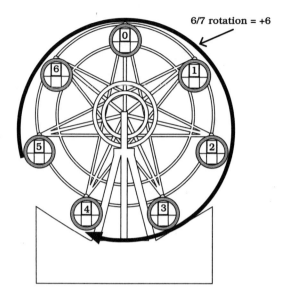

6/7 rotation = +6

If we move the car six positions clockwise, we find that it ends up in position 4. In other words, we end up with the following equation:

$$5 + 6 = 4 \pmod 7$$

When a is the car in its initial state (the car's initial position) and is moved $b/7$ of a rotation, its final position is the solution to the addition problem. We can review all of the different additions here.

$a + b$ MODULO 7

a / b	0	1	2	3	4	5	6
0	0	1	2	3	4	5	6
1	1	2	3	4	5	6	0
2	2	3	4	5	6	0	1
3	3	4	5	6	0	1	2
4	4	5	6	0	1	2	3
5	5	6	0	1	2	3	4
6	6	0	1	2	3	4	5

Next, let's use the Ferris wheel to explore subtraction.

First, take a look at car 0 in the left Ferris wheel as we put it through its paces. After moving counterclockwise by 1/7 of a rotation, car 0 moves from position 0 to position 6. This is defined as –1 (a subtraction of 1). After moving counterclockwise by 2/7 of a rotation, car 0 moves from position 0 to position 5. This is –2 (a subtraction of 2). If it moves a full rotation counterclockwise, car 0 returns to position 0. This is –7, which is also the equivalent of the car having not moved at all.

This Ferris wheel model can be used to explain all instances of subtraction. For example, let's consider the problem 3 – 4 using the Ferris wheel on the right.

In its initial state, the 3 in the expression 3 – 4 is car 3. After car 3 moves 4/7 of a rotation counterclockwise, it arrives at position 6.

1/7 rotation = –1
7/7 rotation = –7 = 0
2/7 rotation = –2
0
1
2
3
4
5
6
4/7 rotation = –4
0
1
2
3
4
5
6

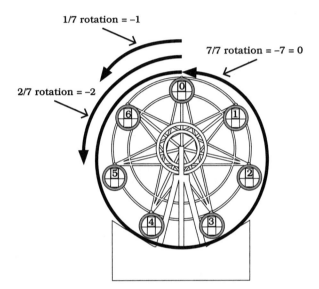

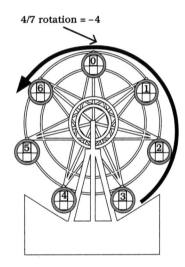

In other words, this is the equivalent of the following equation:

$$3 - 4 = 6 \pmod 7$$

When a is the car in its initial state (the car's initial position) and is moved counterclockwise b/7 of a rotation, its final position is the solution to our subtraction problem. The different combinations of subtracting a and b are shown in the table.

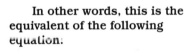

a – *b* MODULO 7

b \ a	0	1	2	3	4	5	6
0	0	6	5	4	3	2	1
1	1	0	6	5	4	3	2
2	2	1	0	6	5	4	3
3	3	2	1	0	6	5	4
4	4	3	2	1	0	6	5
5	5	4	3	2	1	0	6
6	6	5	4	3	2	1	0

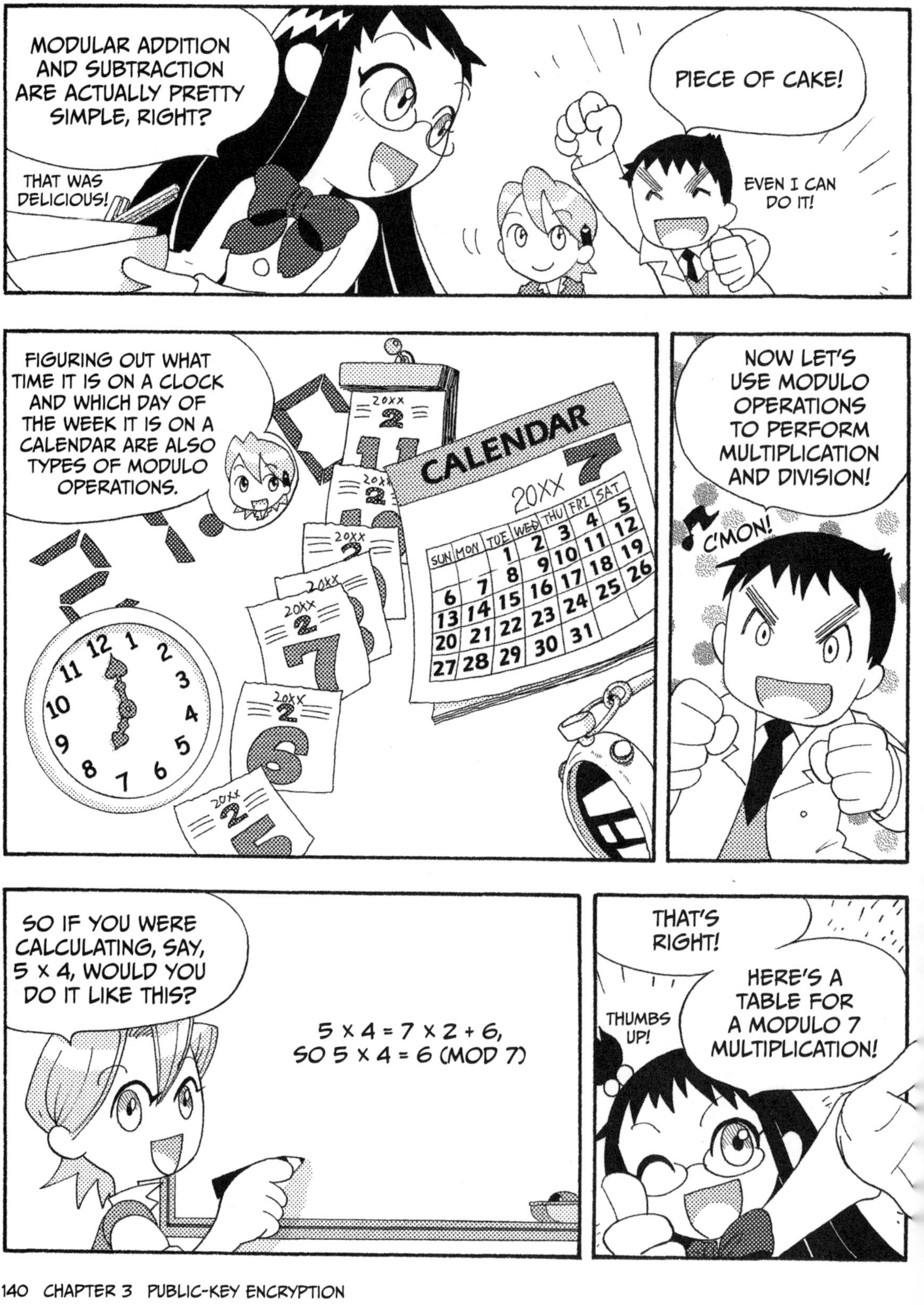
MODULAR ADDITION AND SUBTRACTION ARE ACTUALLY PRETTY SIMPLE, RIGHT?
THAT WAS DELICIOUS!
PIECE OF CAKE!
EVEN I CAN DO IT!
FIGURING OUT WHAT TIME IT IS ON A CLOCK AND WHICH DAY OF THE WEEK IT IS ON A CALENDAR ARE ALSO TYPES OF MODULO OPERATIONS.
CALENDAR
20XX
NOW LET'S USE MODULO OPERATIONS TO PERFORM MULTIPLICATION AND DIVISION!
C'MON!
SO IF YOU WERE CALCULATING, SAY, 5 × 4, WOULD YOU DO IT LIKE THIS?
5 × 4 = 7 × 2 + 6,
SO 5 × 4 = 6 (MOD 7)
THAT'S RIGHT!
THUMBS UP!
HERE'S A TABLE FOR A MODULO 7 MULTIPLICATION!

$a \times b$ MODULO 7

b \ a	0	1	2	3	4	5	6
0	0	0	0	0	0	0	0
1	0	1	2	3	4	5	6
2	0	2	4	6	1	3	5
3	0	3	6	2	5	1	4
4	0	4	1	5	2	6	3
5	0	5	3	1	6	4	2
6	0	6	5	4	3	2	1

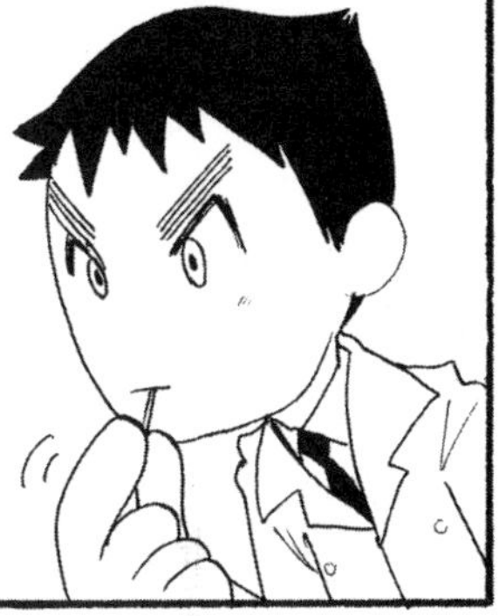
THE NUMBERS IN THIS TABLE SEEM PRETTY CHAOTIC, THOUGH...

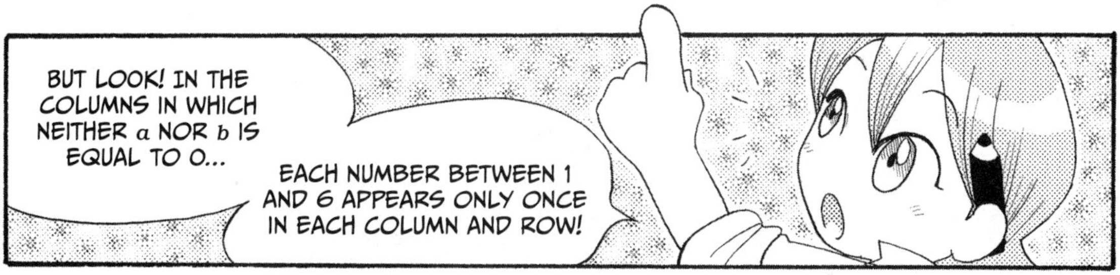
BUT LOOK! IN THE COLUMNS IN WHICH NEITHER a NOR b IS EQUAL TO 0...
EACH NUMBER BETWEEN 1 AND 6 APPEARS ONLY ONCE IN EACH COLUMN AND ROW!

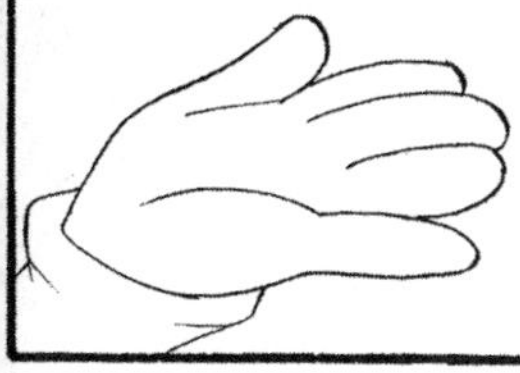
GREAT POINT!
HERE'S HOW MODULO 8 MULTIPLICATION WORKS.

$a \times b$ MODULO 8

b \ a	0	1	2	3	4	5	6	7
0	0	0	0	0	0	0	0	0
1	0	1	2	3	4	5	6	7
2	0	2	4	6	0	2	4	6
3	0	3	6	1	4	7	2	5
4	0	4	0	4	0	4	0	4
5	0	5	2	7	4	1	6	3
6	0	6	4	2	0	6	4	2
7	0	7	6	5	4	3	2	1

WHEN NEITHER a NOR b IS 0, COLUMNS 1, 3, 5, AND 7 INCLUDE ALL OF THE NUMBERS BETWEEN 1 AND 7...

BUT THIS DOESN'T APPLY TO ROWS 2, 4, AND 6...

AND THERE ARE RANDOM ZEROS?!

FOR MULTIPLICATION TO YIELD ZERO WHEN ZERO ISN'T PART OF THE EQUATION—THAT SEEMS WEIRD, RIGHT?

IN THIS CASE, THE RULE THAT "WHEN $a \times b = 0$, EITHER a OR b HAS TO EQUAL 0" NO LONGER HOLDS TRUE.

WHY DOES THIS HAPPEN?

WELL... IT HAPPENS IN SITUATIONS WHEN MODULO 8 AND EITHER a OR b AREN'T COPRIME.

JUMP ON IN, THE WATER'S COPRIME...

HIDDEN SPRING

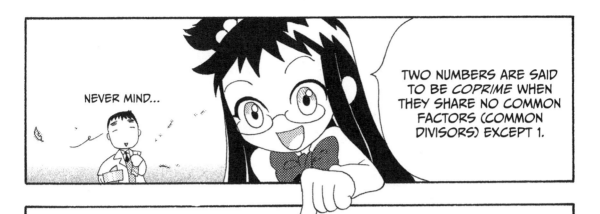

NEVER MIND...
TWO NUMBERS ARE SAID TO BE *COPRIME* WHEN THEY SHARE NO COMMON FACTORS (COMMON DIVISORS) EXCEPT 1.

For example, in addition to 1, the numbers 8 and 2 share the common factor (common divisor) 2, so they aren't coprime. The numbers 4 and 6 in the modulo 8 multiplication table likewise share the common divisor 2 with 8, so they aren't coprime.

On the other hand, 1, 3, 5, and 7 are coprime to 8. You can determine whether two integers are coprime by confirming that the greatest common divisor of both is 1.

Thus, all prime numbers are coprime to integers that are not multiples of themselves. This property allows us to uncover prime numbers when using the sieve of Eratosthenes method.

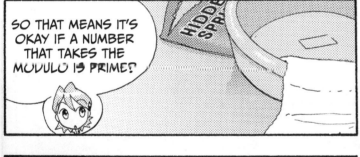

SO THAT MEANS IT'S OKAY IF A NUMBER THAT TAKES THE MODULO IS PRIME?

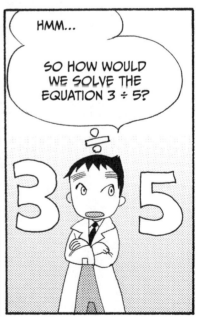

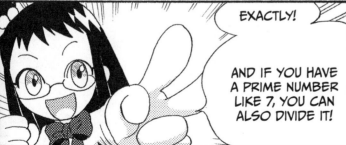

EXACTLY!
AND IF YOU HAVE A PRIME NUMBER LIKE 7, YOU CAN ALSO DIVIDE IT!

HMM...
SO HOW WOULD WE SOLVE THE EQUATION 3 ÷ 5?
3
÷
5

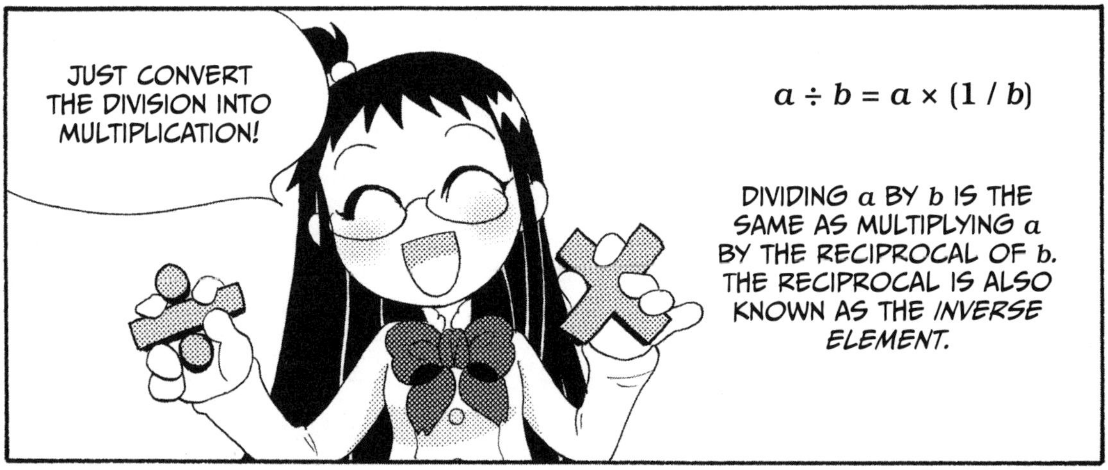
JUST CONVERT THE DIVISION INTO MULTIPLICATION!
$a \div b = a \times (1 / b)$
DIVIDING *a* BY *b* IS THE SAME AS MULTIPLYING *a* BY THE RECIPROCAL OF *b*. THE RECIPROCAL IS ALSO KNOWN AS THE *INVERSE ELEMENT*.

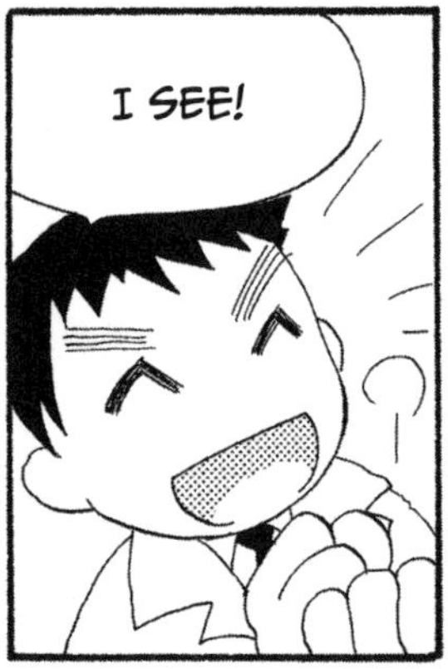
I SEE!

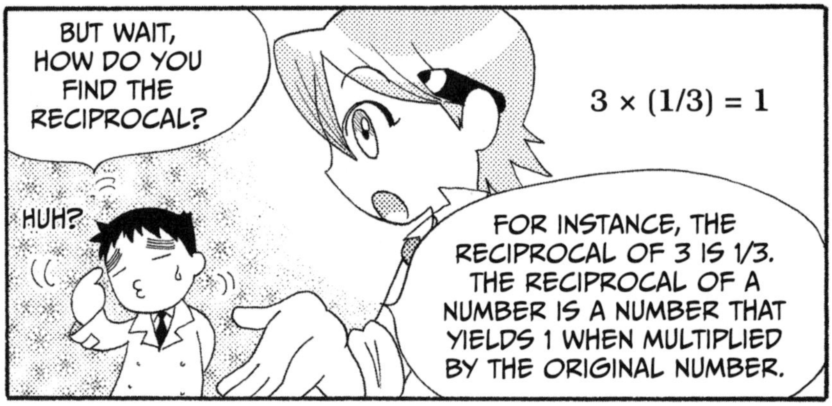
BUT WAIT, HOW DO YOU FIND THE RECIPROCAL?
HUH?
$3 \times (1/3) = 1$
FOR INSTANCE, THE RECIPROCAL OF 3 IS 1/3. THE RECIPROCAL OF A NUMBER IS A NUMBER THAT YIELDS 1 WHEN MULTIPLIED BY THE ORIGINAL NUMBER.

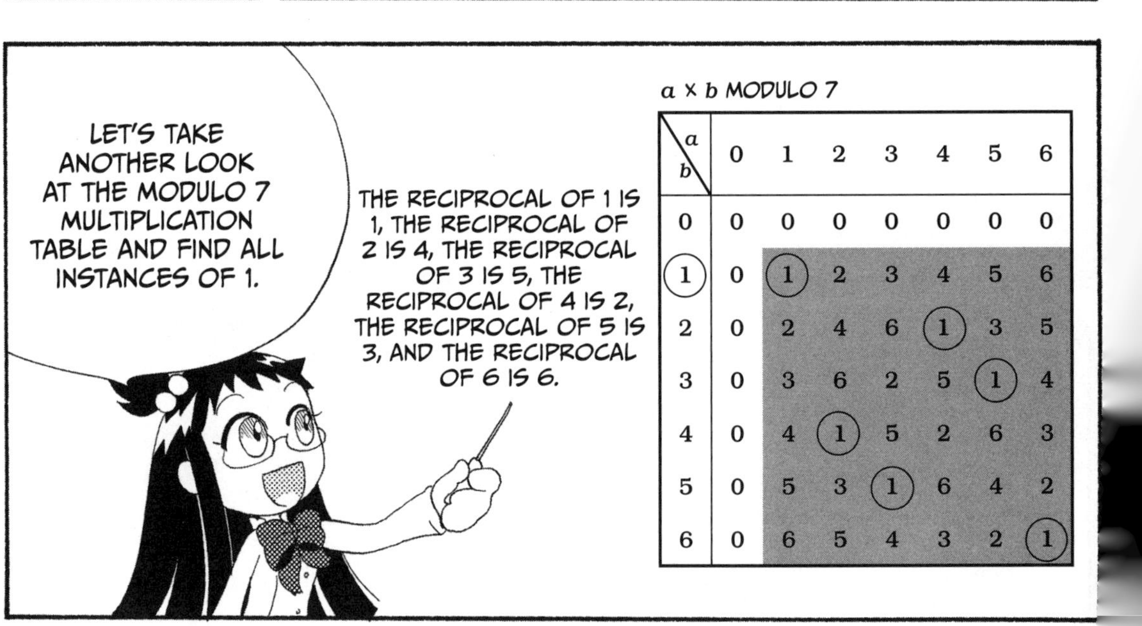
LET'S TAKE ANOTHER LOOK AT THE MODULO 7 MULTIPLICATION TABLE AND FIND ALL INSTANCES OF 1.
THE RECIPROCAL OF 1 IS 1, THE RECIPROCAL OF 2 IS 4, THE RECIPROCAL OF 3 IS 5, THE RECIPROCAL OF 4 IS 2, THE RECIPROCAL OF 5 IS 3, AND THE RECIPROCAL OF 6 IS 6.

a × *b* MODULO 7

b \ *a*	0	1	2	3	4	5	6
0	0	0	0	0	0	0	0
1	0	1	2	3	4	5	6
2	0	2	4	6	1	3	5
3	0	3	6	2	5	1	4
4	0	4	1	5	2	6	3
5	0	5	3	1	6	4	2
6	0	6	5	4	3	2	1

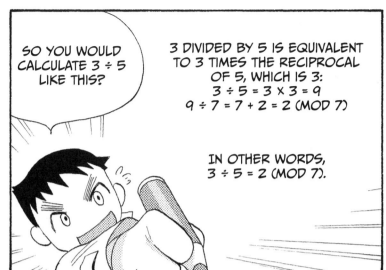

SO YOU WOULD CALCULATE $3 \div 5$ LIKE THIS?

3 DIVIDED BY 5 IS EQUIVALENT TO 3 TIMES THE RECIPROCAL OF 5, WHICH IS 3:
$$3 \div 5 = 3 \times 3 = 9$$
$$9 \div 7 = 7 + 2 = 2 \ (\text{MOD } 7)$$

IN OTHER WORDS, $3 \div 5 = 2 \ (\text{MOD } 7)$.

GREAT JOB!

YEAH! GREAT!

THERE'S A DIVISION TABLE, TOO.

$a \div b$ MODULO 7

a / b	0	1	2	3	4	5	6
0	—	0	0	0	0	0	0
1	—	1	4	5	2	3	6
2	—	2	1	3	4	6	5
3	—	3	5	1	6	2	4
4	—	4	2	6	1	5	3
5	—	5	0	4	0	1	2
6	—	6	3	2	5	4	1

WE CAN ALSO USE THE FERRIS WHEEL MODEL TO EXPLAIN MULTIPLICATION AND DIVISION!

MULTIPLICATION AND DIVISION OF MODULO OPERATIONS

Let's start by explaining multiplication using the seven-car Ferris wheel model. It's best to think of multiplication in terms of rotational speed.

In the initial state, car 0 is in position 0, car 1 is in position 1, and so on—all of the car numbers and position numbers match.

If in 1 minute, a car moves 1/7 of a rotation (in other words, in 7 minutes, it moves one full rotation), car 0's position after 3 minutes would be as follows:

1 (speed) × 3 (minutes) = 3 (position after rotation)

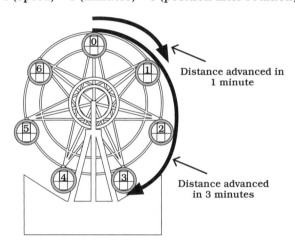

Distance advanced in 1 minute

Distance advanced in 3 minutes

When the car moves at a rate of 5/7 of a rotation per minute, what position would it be in after 6 minutes?

$$5 \times 6 = 30$$
$$30 = 7 \times 4 + 2 \ (30 \div 7 = 4 \text{ with a remainder of 2})$$

Therefore, 5 × 6 = 2 (mod 7).

In other words, after the value of 30 is divided by 7, we have 4 rotations with a remainder of 2. In this case, 4 rotations is equivalent to 0 rotations when dealing with modulo, so you only have to pay attention to the remainder of 2.

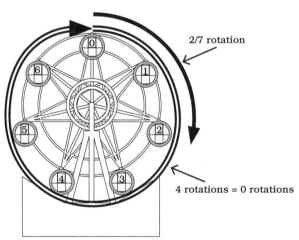

2/7 rotation

4 rotations = 0 rotations

Think of division as the opposite of multiplication. Given the final position and the rotational speed, we determine the time the car was in motion using an inverse operation.

With a speed of 1/7 of a rotation per minute, car 0 begins at position 1 and finally ends up in position 5. Let's determine how many minutes the car was in motion.

$$5 \text{ (final position)} \div 1 \text{ (speed)} = 5 \text{ (minutes)}$$

So, it was in motion for 5 minutes. Were it to move for 12 minutes, or 19 minutes, it would end up in the same position, since each of these rotations is equal to 5 added to a multiple of 7 $(5 + 7n)$. However, because the times in our mod 7 calculation range only from 0 to 6 minutes, we can't visually represent the passage of 12 or 19 minutes. They would appear identical to 5 minutes. (See the Ferris wheel at the bottom left.)

At a rate of 2/7 of a rotation per minute (in other words, two full rotations per 7 minutes), car 0 begins at position 0 and finally arrives at position 5. Using the division table, we can determine the number of minutes it was in motion as follows:

$$5 \text{ (final position)} \div 2 \text{ (speed)} = 6 \text{ (minutes)}$$

The answer is that it rotated for 6 minutes, but what's the best way to explain this?

Consider this: the final position was 5, but there was actually one surplus rotation. In other words, in reality the final position was $2 \times 6 = 12$, which in mod 7 is expressed as 5.

Therefore, since $12 \div 2 = 6$, the answer is that the car rotated for 6 minutes. (See the Ferris wheel at the right.)

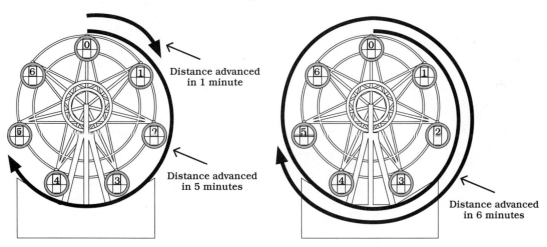

Distance advanced
in 1 minute

Distance advanced
in 5 minutes

Distance advanced
in 6 minutes

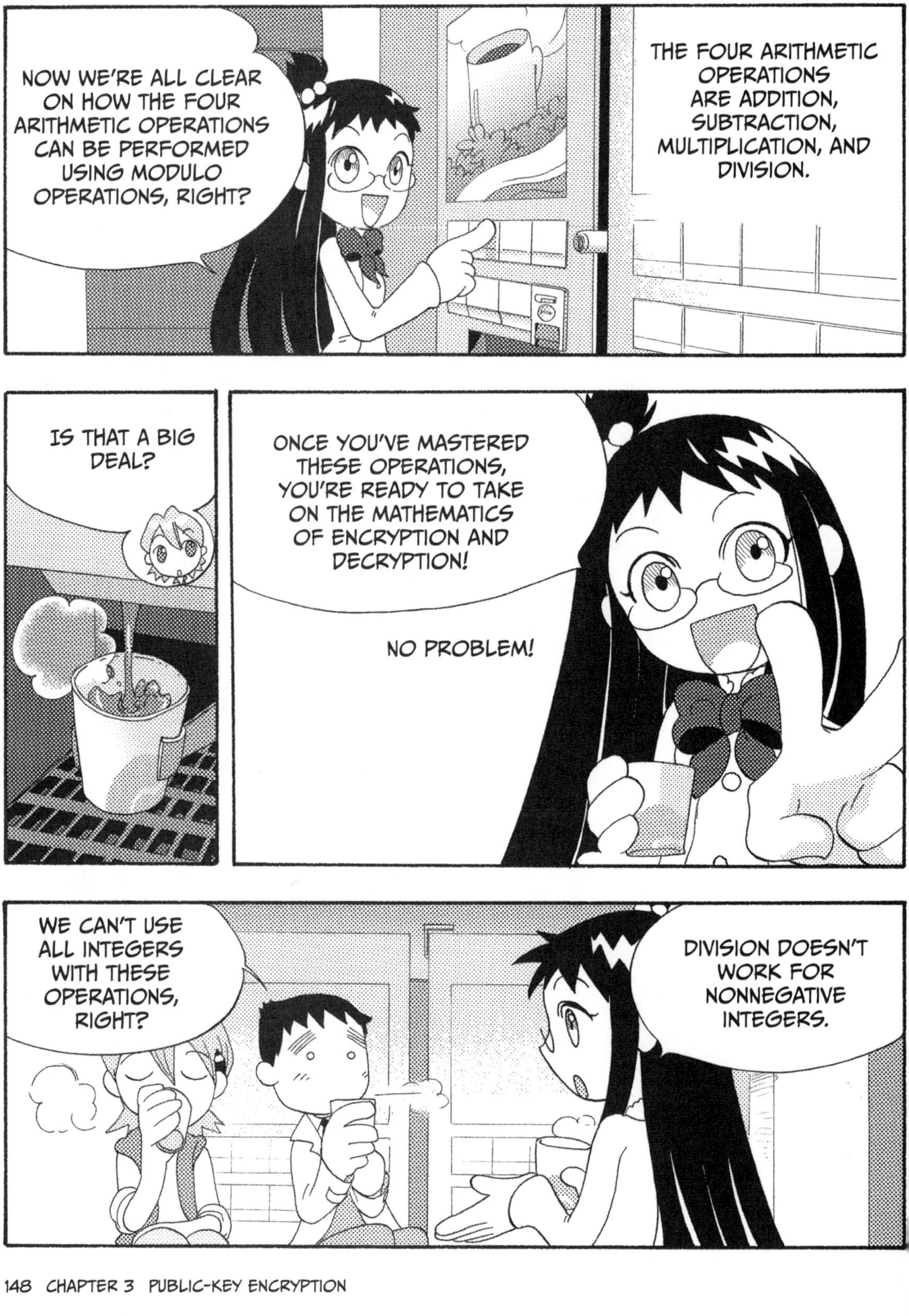
NOW WE'RE ALL CLEAR ON HOW THE FOUR ARITHMETIC OPERATIONS CAN BE PERFORMED USING MODULO OPERATIONS, RIGHT?
THE FOUR ARITHMETIC OPERATIONS ARE ADDITION, SUBTRACTION, MULTIPLICATION, AND DIVISION.
IS THAT A BIG DEAL?
ONCE YOU'VE MASTERED THESE OPERATIONS, YOU'RE READY TO TAKE ON THE MATHEMATICS OF ENCRYPTION AND DECRYPTION!
NO PROBLEM!
WE CAN'T USE ALL INTEGERS WITH THESE OPERATIONS, RIGHT?
DIVISION DOESN'T WORK FOR NONNEGATIVE INTEGERS.

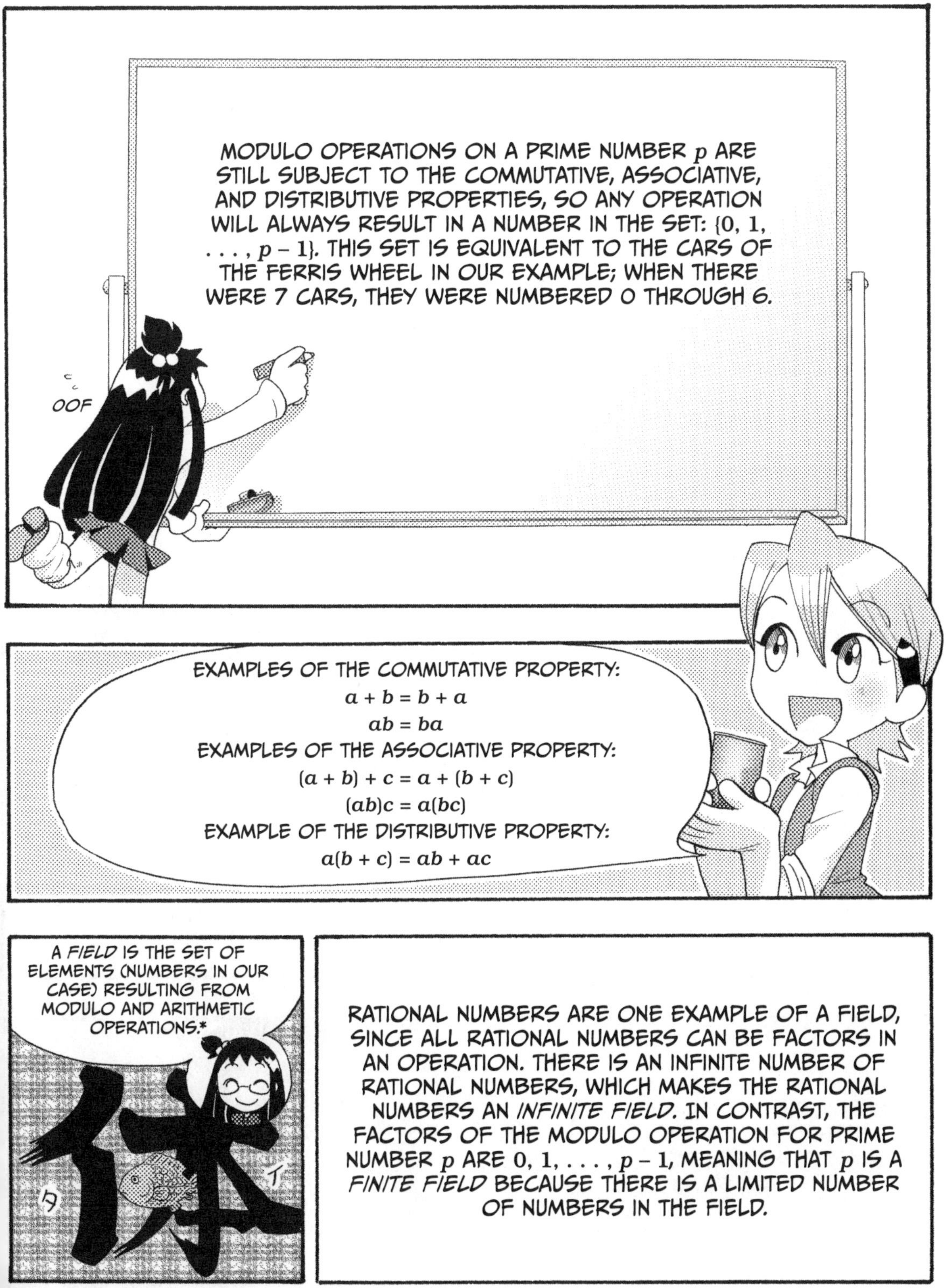
MODULO OPERATIONS ON A PRIME NUMBER p ARE STILL SUBJECT TO THE COMMUTATIVE, ASSOCIATIVE, AND DISTRIBUTIVE PROPERTIES, SO ANY OPERATION WILL ALWAYS RESULT IN A NUMBER IN THE SET: $\{0, 1, \ldots, p - 1\}$. THIS SET IS EQUIVALENT TO THE CARS OF THE FERRIS WHEEL IN OUR EXAMPLE; WHEN THERE WERE 7 CARS, THEY WERE NUMBERED 0 THROUGH 6.
OOF
EXAMPLES OF THE COMMUTATIVE PROPERTY:
$a + b = b + a$
$ab = ba$
EXAMPLES OF THE ASSOCIATIVE PROPERTY:
$(a + b) + c = a + (b + c)$
$(ab)c = a(bc)$
EXAMPLE OF THE DISTRIBUTIVE PROPERTY:
$a(b + c) = ab + ac$
A *FIELD* IS THE SET OF ELEMENTS (NUMBERS IN OUR CASE) RESULTING FROM MODULO AND ARITHMETIC OPERATIONS.*
体
タ
イ
RATIONAL NUMBERS ARE ONE EXAMPLE OF A FIELD, SINCE ALL RATIONAL NUMBERS CAN BE FACTORS IN AN OPERATION. THERE IS AN INFINITE NUMBER OF RATIONAL NUMBERS, WHICH MAKES THE RATIONAL NUMBERS AN *INFINITE FIELD*. IN CONTRAST, THE FACTORS OF THE MODULO OPERATION FOR PRIME NUMBER p ARE $0, 1, \ldots, p - 1$, MEANING THAT p IS A *FINITE FIELD* BECAUSE THERE IS A LIMITED NUMBER OF NUMBERS IN THE FIELD.

* THE JAPANESE WORD FOR *FIELD* SOUNDS SIMILAR TO THE WORD FOR A TYPE OF FISH.

GREAT! NOW WE'RE FINISHED WITH MODULO OPERATIONS, RIGHT?

PAPER CUPS ONLY

THERE'S ONE LAST THING!

MORE?

KEEP AT IT!

HERE'S A POWER TABLE.

a^b MODULO 7

b \ a	1	2	3	4	5	6
1	1	1	1	1	1	1
2	2	4	1	2	4	1
3	3	2	6	4	5	1
4	4	2	1	4	2	1
5	5	4	6	2	3	1
6	6	1	6	1	6	1

TO CALCULATE THE VALUES IN THE TABLE, TAKE THE NUMBER a^b AND DIVIDE IT BY 7 TO GET THE REMAINDER. FOR EXAMPLE, TAKING ANY VALUE OF a BETWEEN 1 AND 6 TO THE 6TH POWER AND THEN DIVIDING THE RESULT BY 7 WILL ALWAYS RESULT IN A REMAINDER OF 1, WHICH IS REPRESENTED IN THE LAST COLUMN OF THE TABLE.

$$1^6 = 1 = 0 \times 7 + 1$$
$$2^6 = 64 = 9 \times 7 + 1$$
$$3^6 = 729 = 104 \times 7 + 1$$
$$4^6 = 4,096 = 585 \times 7 + 1$$
$$5^6 = 15,625 = 2,232 \times 7 + 1$$
$$6^6 = 46,656 = 6,665 \times 7 + 1$$

THIS MODULO OPERATION RESULTS IN VALUES THAT ARE PRETTY SPREAD OUT...

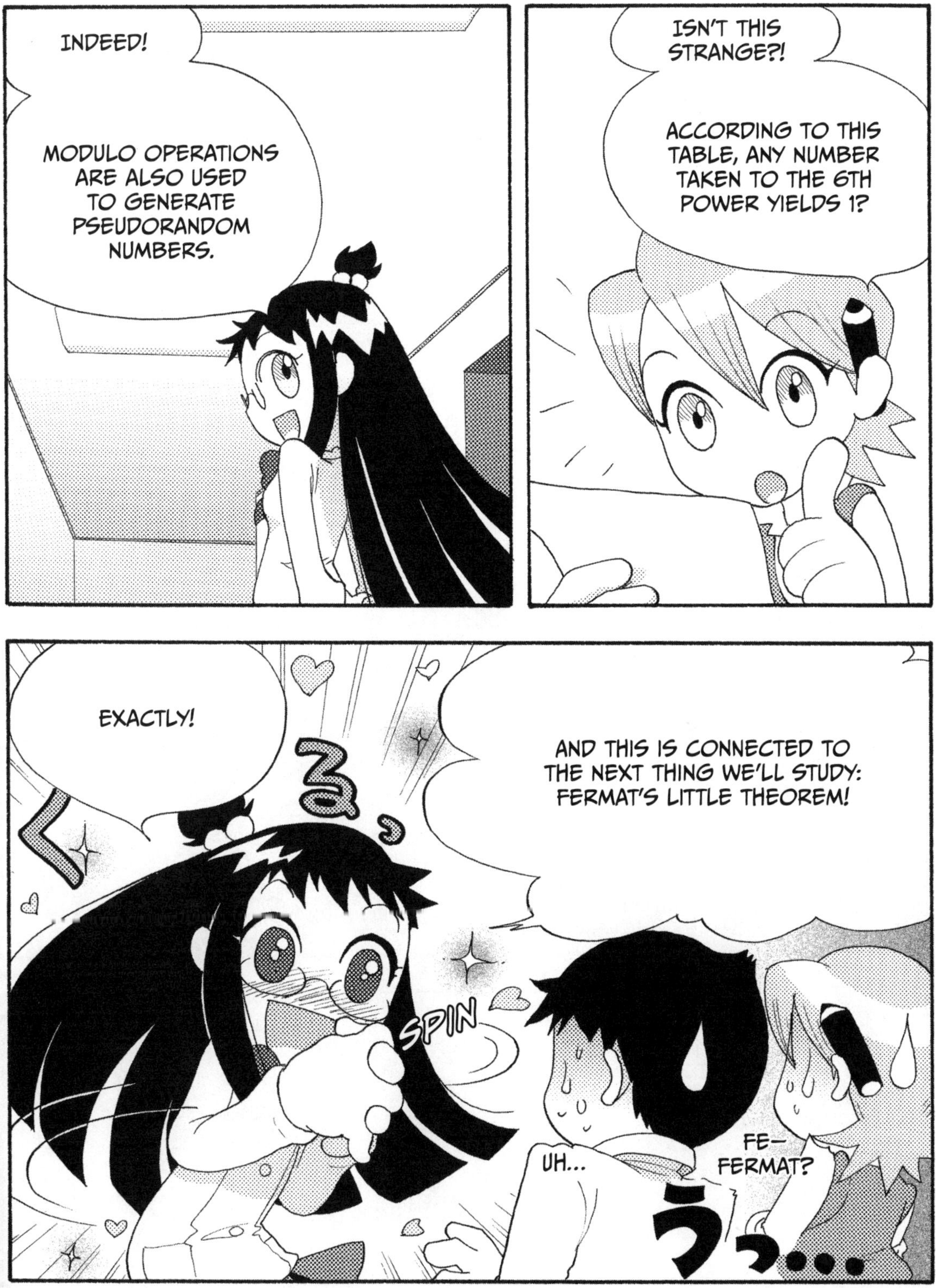
INDEED!
MODULO OPERATIONS ARE ALSO USED TO GENERATE PSEUDORANDOM NUMBERS.
ISN'T THIS STRANGE?!
ACCORDING TO THIS TABLE, ANY NUMBER TAKEN TO THE 6TH POWER YIELDS 1?
EXACTLY!
くるっ
AND THIS IS CONNECTED TO THE NEXT THING WE'LL STUDY: FERMAT'S LITTLE THEOREM!
SPIN
UH...
FE- FERMAT?
うっ...

FERMAT'S LITTLE THEOREM AND EULER'S THEOREM

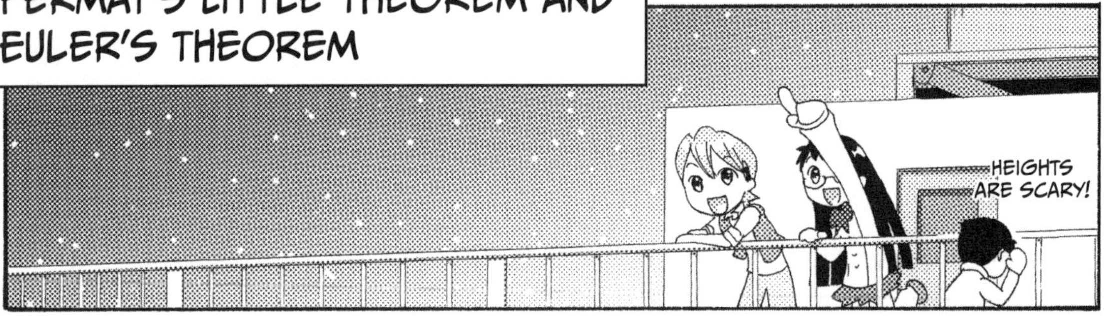
HEIGHTS ARE SCARY!

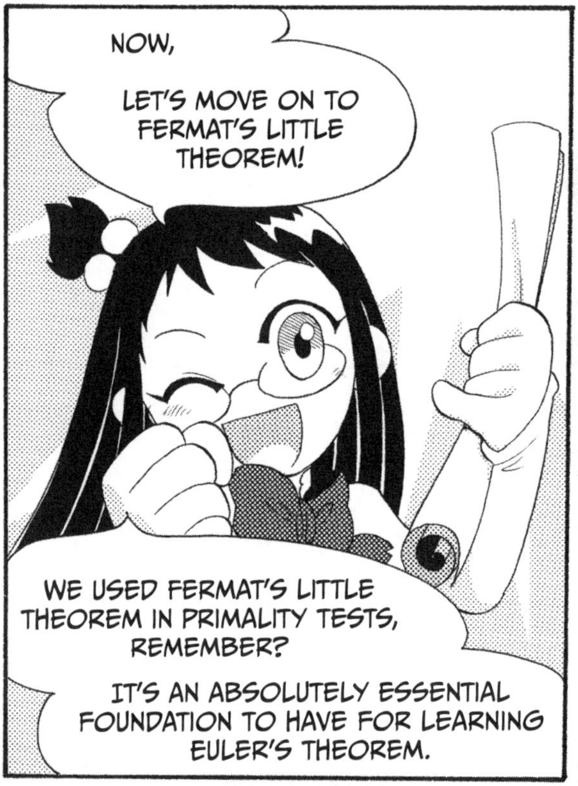
NOW,
LET'S MOVE ON TO FERMAT'S LITTLE THEOREM!
WE USED FERMAT'S LITTLE THEOREM IN PRIMALITY TESTS, REMEMBER?
IT'S AN ABSOLUTELY ESSENTIAL FOUNDATION TO HAVE FOR LEARNING EULER'S THEOREM.

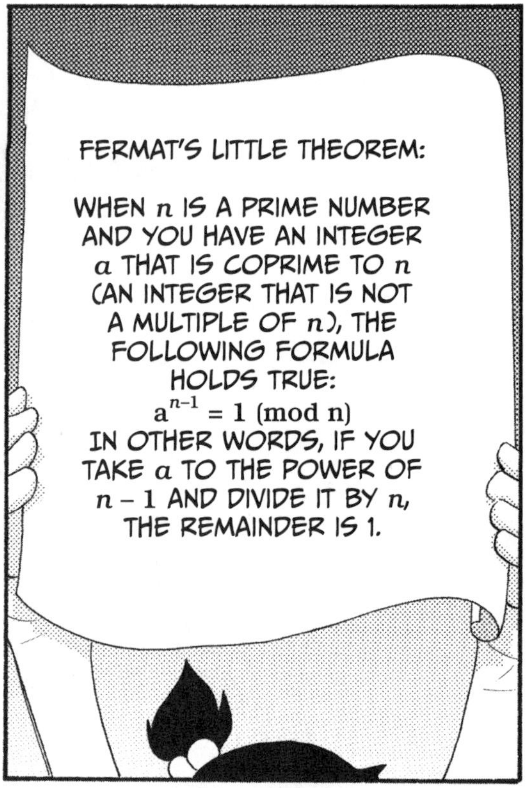
FERMAT'S LITTLE THEOREM:
WHEN n IS A PRIME NUMBER AND YOU HAVE AN INTEGER a THAT IS COPRIME TO n (AN INTEGER THAT IS NOT A MULTIPLE OF n), THE FOLLOWING FORMULA HOLDS TRUE:
$a^{n-1} = 1 \pmod{n}$
IN OTHER WORDS, IF YOU TAKE a TO THE POWER OF $n - 1$ AND DIVIDE IT BY n, THE REMAINDER IS 1.

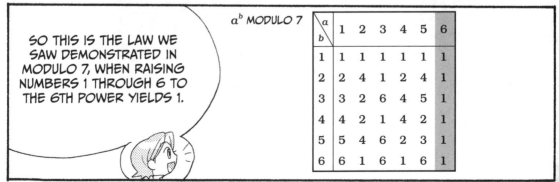

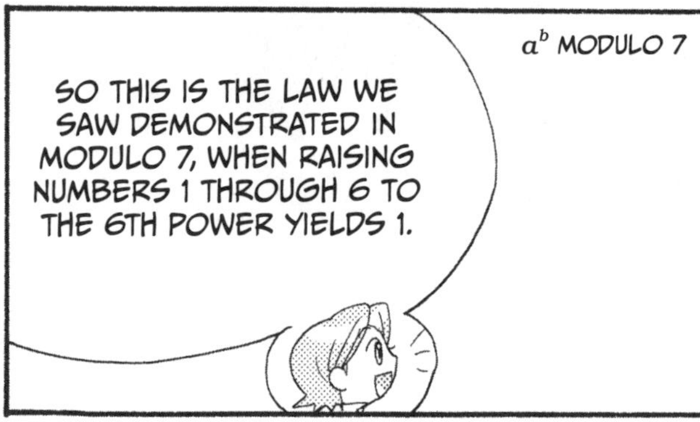
SO THIS IS THE LAW WE SAW DEMONSTRATED IN MODULO 7, WHEN RAISING NUMBERS 1 THROUGH 6 TO THE 6TH POWER YIELDS 1.

a^b MODULO 7

b \ a	1	2	3	4	5	6
1	1	1	1	1	1	1
2	2	4	1	2	4	1
3	3	2	6	4	5	1
4	4	2	1	4	2	1
5	5	4	6	2	3	1
6	6	1	6	1	6	1

WHO WAS THIS FERMAT GUY?

FERMAT: THE FATHER OF NUMBER THEORY

Pierre de Fermat (1601–1665) was a 17th-century French lawyer and prominent mathematician. He made great contributions to the field of number theory, including but not limited to creating the modulo operation.

He created not only Fermat's little theorem but also what is known as Fermat's big theorem (or last theorem).

Fermat's big theorem states that given a natural number n whose value is 3 or more, no three natural numbers (x, y, z) can solve the equation $x^n + y^n = z^n$. Interestingly, Fermat himself left no proof of this theorem.

At first glance, the contents of the theorem look so simple that it seems like a middle schooler could solve it. I'm sure you're familiar with the Pythagorean theorem, which states that if the lengths of the sides of a right triangle are a, b, and c, then $a^2 + b^2 = c^2$. Fermat's theorem concerns an equation for when the 2 in $a^2 + b^2 = c^2$ is replaced by a value of 3 or more.

Proof of the big theorem came 330 years after Fermat's death, in 1995, thanks to British mathematician Andrew Wiles (1953–).

FERMAT HAD APPARENTLY WRITTEN THIS IN HIS NOTEBOOK·

I THOUGHT I WOULD WRITE A PROOF OF MY BIG THEOREM HERE, BUT THERE ISN'T ENOUGH SPACE IN THE MARGIN!

THERE, THERE.

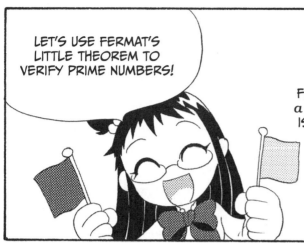

LET'S USE FERMAT'S LITTLE THEOREM TO VERIFY PRIME NUMBERS!

TAKE THE CONTRAPOSITION OF FERMAT'S LITTLE THEOREM. IF n AND a ARE COPRIME AND $a^{(n-1)} \neq 1 \pmod{n}$ IS TRUE, THEN WE CAN SAY THAT n IS NOT A PRIME NUMBER.

WHAT'S CONTRAPOSITION?

COBRA POSITION?

A *CONTRAPOSITION* CONTRASTS WITH A *PROPOSITION*. FOR EXAMPLE, IF WE HAD THE PROPOSITION "IF A, THEN B," THE CONTRAPOSITION WOULD BE "IF NOT B, THEN NOT A."

IF A, THEN B

IF NOT B, THEN NOT A

THE CONTRAPOSITION OF A CORRECT PROPOSITION IS ALWAYS TRUE.

I SEE... WAIT, THIS ISN'T A MANGA.

QUIVER QUIVER

Fun Prime Numbers

IF THE PROPOSITION "ALL MANGA ARE FUN" IS TRUE, THEN THE CONTRAPOSITION "IF IT IS NOT FUN, IT IS NOT A MANGA" IS ALSO TRUE.

USING THIS AS A METHOD OF DETERMINING PRIME NUMBERS...

IS KNOWN AS *FERMAT'S METHOD!*

NO MORE...

OH DEAR.

FERMAT'S METHOD AND PSEUDOPRIME NUMBERS

To perform a primality test using Fermat's method, use this equation:

$$a^{n-1} \neq 1 \pmod{n},$$

where n, the number you are performing the primality test on, and a are coprime.

Although Fermat's method is very efficient at testing for primality, even if the number n passes the primality test for several of its coprimes, that doesn't necessarily prove n is a prime number.

With Fermat's method, there are situations in which a number may be probabilistically determined to be prime even when it really isn't prime. We call such values *pseudoprime numbers*.

For example, when $n = 3,215,031,751$, it passes the primality test for the coprimes 2, 3, 5, and 7:

$$2^{3215031750} = 1 \pmod{3,215,031,751}$$
$$3^{3215031750} = 1 \pmod{3,215,031,751}$$
$$5^{3215031750} = 1 \pmod{3,215,031,751}$$
$$7^{3215031750} = 1 \pmod{3,215,031,751}$$

However, 3,215,031,751 is not actually a prime number. You can see this when you perform integer factorization:

$$3,215,031,751 = 151 \times 751 \times 28,351$$

However, out of the numbers n less than 250 billion, 3,215,031,751 is the only nonprime that passes the Fermat method's primality test for the four prime numbers 2, 3, 5, and 7.

NEXT UP IS EULER'S THEOREM.

IT'S THE MATHEMATICAL FOUNDATION OF ENCRYPTION. ONCE YOU LEARN EULER'S THEOREM, YOU'LL HAVE THE BASICS TO UNDERSTAND RSA!

EULER'S THEOREM

Given a natural number n and a coprime integer a, we present the following equation:

$$a^{\phi(n)} = 1 \ (\text{mod } n)$$

The $\phi(n)$ is known as *Euler's totient function*. Euler's totient function gives the number of integers between 1 and n that are coprime to n.

In addition, if we multiply $a^{\phi(n)}$ by a, we get $a^{\phi(n)+1}$, and from this we can extrapolate the following equation:

$$a^{\phi(n)+1} = a \ (\text{mod } n)$$

When k is an integer, $a^{k\phi(n)} \ (\text{mod } n)$ will result in 1, as we saw in this equation:

$$a^{\phi(n)} = 1 \ (\text{mod } n)$$

This might not be apparent at first sight, but for example, when $k = 1$,

$$a^{k\phi(n)} = a^{1 \times \phi(n)} = a^{\phi(n)}$$

We can express an even number as $k\phi(n) + 1$, since adding 1 to any odd number will result in an even number. Because we know that multiplying both sides of Euler's theorem equation by a results in

$$a^{\phi(n)+1} = a \ (\text{mod } n),$$

that means modding $ak^{\phi(n)+1}$ by n will also result in a. You should get the following formulas:

$$ak^{\phi(n)} = 1 \ (\text{mod } n)$$
$$ak^{\phi(n)+1} = a \ (\text{mod } n)$$

This means that when a is any integer between 1 and $(n - 1)$, the following formula will apply:

$$a^{k\phi(n)+1} = a \ (\text{mod } n)$$

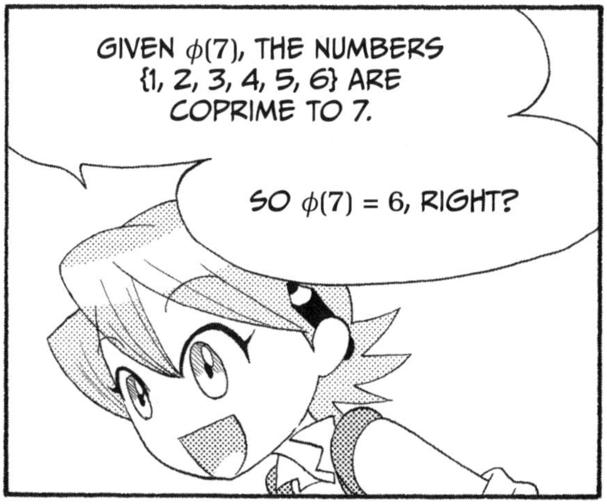
GIVEN $\phi(7)$, THE NUMBERS {1, 2, 3, 4, 5, 6} ARE COPRIME TO 7.
SO $\phi(7) = 6$, RIGHT?

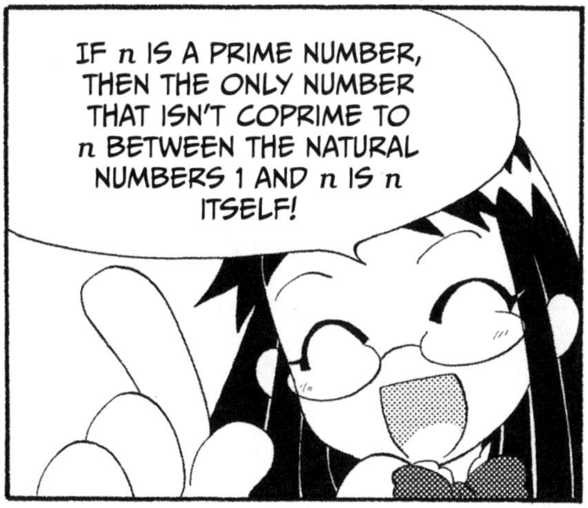
IF n IS A PRIME NUMBER, THEN THE ONLY NUMBER THAT ISN'T COPRIME TO n BETWEEN THE NATURAL NUMBERS 1 AND n IS n ITSELF!

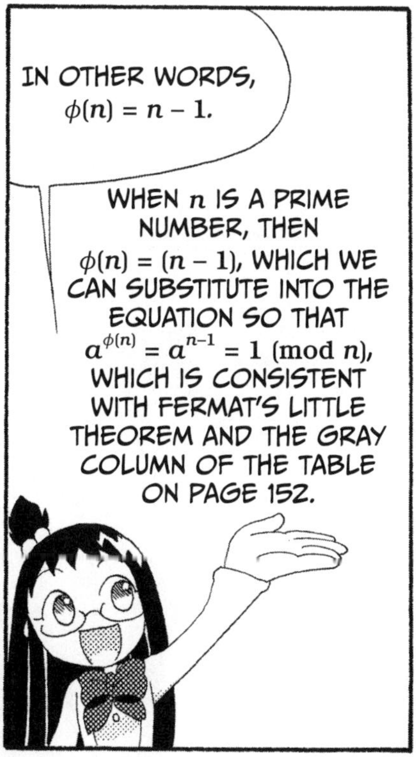
IN OTHER WORDS, $\phi(n) = n - 1$.
WHEN n IS A PRIME NUMBER, THEN $\phi(n) = (n - 1)$, WHICH WE CAN SUBSTITUTE INTO THE EQUATION SO THAT $a^{\phi(n)} = a^{n-1} = 1 \pmod{n}$, WHICH IS CONSISTENT WITH FERMAT'S LITTLE THEOREM AND THE GRAY COLUMN OF THE TABLE ON PAGE 152.

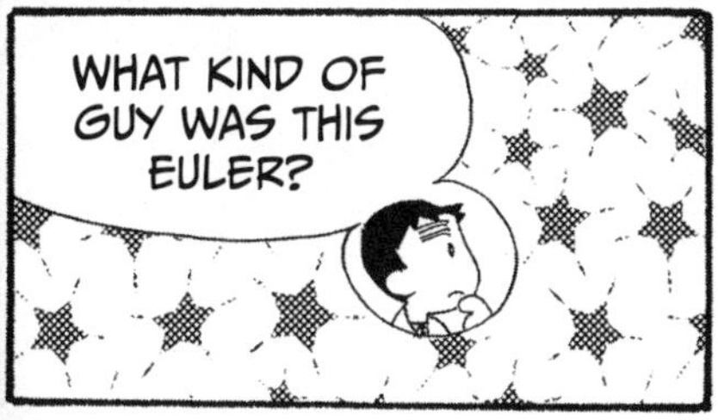
WHAT KIND OF GUY WAS THIS EULER?

THE MATHEMATICIAN EULER

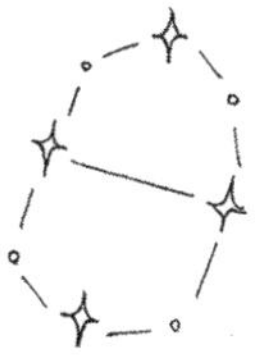

Leonhard Euler (1707–1783) was a prominent Swiss mathematician of the 18th century.

He not only made huge contributions to the broad field of mathematics but also contributed to the fields of physics and astronomy. His most well-known contribution to mathematics is known as *Euler's formula*:

$$ei^{\theta} = \cos\theta + i(\sin\theta)$$

We won't cover it in detail, but this formula demonstrates the relationship between the complex exponential function ei^{θ} and the trigonometric functions $\cos\theta$ and $\sin\theta$ through the imaginary number $i = \sqrt{-1}$.

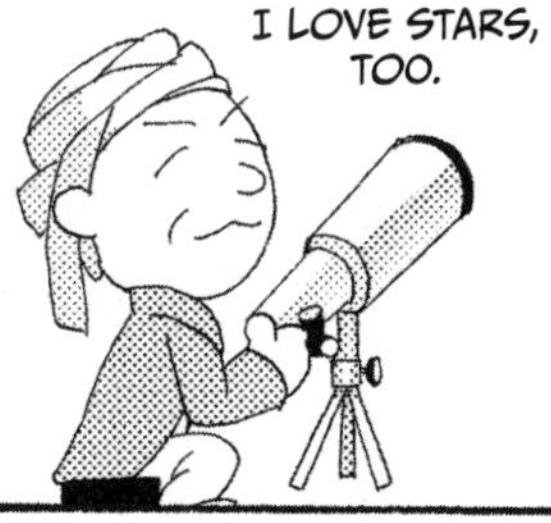
I LOVE STARS, TOO.

LET'S LOOK AT AN EULER FUNCTION IN WHICH A NONPRIME NUMBER N IS EXPRESSED AS THE PRODUCT OF TWO PRIME NUMBERS p AND q.

EULER FUNCTION ON THE PRODUCT OF TWO PRIME NUMBERS

N is the product of two prime numbers p and q. Here, in order to derive the Euler function of N using p and q, we need to first count the integers that are not coprime to N. Since p and q are prime numbers, we know that multiples of p and multiples of q make up all the numbers that are not coprime to N.

1. Because the multiples of p between 1 and qp are p, $2p$, $3p$, . . . , up to qp, there are q number of multiples of p.

2. Because the multiples of q between 1 and qp are q, $2q$, $3q$, . . . , up to pq, there are p number of multiples of q.

3. Of the multiples of q and p, only qp and pq are shared by both p and q, but because qp and pq are both equal to N, they are the same number.

For a prime number n, $\phi(n) = n - 1$, but because N isn't prime and the multiples of the prime numbers q and p are not coprime with it, we need to subtract the number of multiples of p and q from N instead. Through our analysis from steps 1 and 2, we found that there are $q + p$ number of integers not coprime with N. In other words,

$$\phi(N) = N - p - q + 1$$

Since $N = pq$, we can substitute it into the equation to get this:

$$\phi(N) = pq - p - q + 1 = (p - 1)(q - 1)$$

This means that $\phi(pq) = \phi(p)\phi(q)$. If we apply Euler's theorem to p and q individually, we would get these equations:

$$a^{p-1} = 1 \ (\text{mod } p)$$
$$a^{q-1} = 1 \ (\text{mod } q)$$

We can combine these equations to derive another equation. The smallest multiple $(p - 1)$ and $(q - 1)$ share is known as their *lowest common multiple*, which we'll represent as L. This means that when $(p - 1)$ is multiplied by some integer m, it equals L, and when $(q - 1)$ is multiplied by some integer n, it also equals L. Therefore, $L = m(p - 1) = n(q - 1)$.

With $a^{p-1} = 1 \ (\text{mod } p)$, if we raise both sides by m, we get

$$a^{(p-1)m} = 1^m \ (\text{mod } p)$$
$$a^L = 1 \ (\text{mod } p)$$

If we do the same with $a^{q-1} = 1$ (mod q), we get the same result:

$$a^{(q-1)n} = 1^n \ (\text{mod } q)$$

$$a^L = 1 \ (\text{mod } q)$$

We can combine these two equations to get $a^L = 1$ (mod p, mod q). Because N is equal to pq, we would get the following equation:

$$a^L = 1 \ (\text{mod } N)$$

In other words, L functions identically to Euler's theorem $\phi(N)$. In addition, because the product of two arbitrary positive integers is equal to the product of the lowest common multiple and the greatest common divisor (which we'll call G), we would get the equation $(p-1)(q-1) = LG$, and we can derive the following:

$$L = \frac{(p-1)(q-1)}{G}$$

For example, let's say $p = 3$ and $q = 5$, so $N = pq$ is 15. Therefore, $(p-1)$ is 2, $(q-1)$ is 4, and $\phi(N) = (p-1)(q-1)$ is 8. The lowest common multiple L of 2 and 4 is 4, and the greatest common divisor G is 2. In this case, for any natural number a that is coprime to 15 and for any k that is a nonnegative integer, the following formula applies:

$$a^{4k} = 1 \ (\text{mod } 15)$$

In other words, until we take a to the $\phi(N)$th power, the greatest common divisor $G = 1$ sometimes appears periodically for every L numbers. According to the Euler's theorem equation, for all of the integers a between 1 and $(N-1)$, this applies:

$$a^{kL+1} = a \ (\text{mod } N)$$

You can see this in the gray columns of this table.

PRODUCT OF TWO PRIME NUMBERS WHEN a^b ($N = 3 \times 5$, $\phi(15) = 8$, $L = 4$, $G = 2$)

a \\ b	1	2	3	4	5	6	7	8
1	1	1	1	1	1	1	1	1
2	2	4	8	1	2	4	8	1
3	3	9	12	6	3	9	12	6
4	4	1	4	1	4	1	4	1
5	5	10	5	10	5	10	5	10
6	6	6	6	6	6	6	6	6
7	7	4	13	1	7	4	13	1
8	8	4	2	1	8	4	2	1
9	9	6	9	6	9	6	9	6
10	10	10	10	10	10	10	10	10
11	11	1	11	1	11	1	11	1
12	12	9	3	6	12	9	3	6
13	13	4	7	1	13	4	7	1
14	14	1	14	1	14	1	14	1

1 cycle   1 cycle

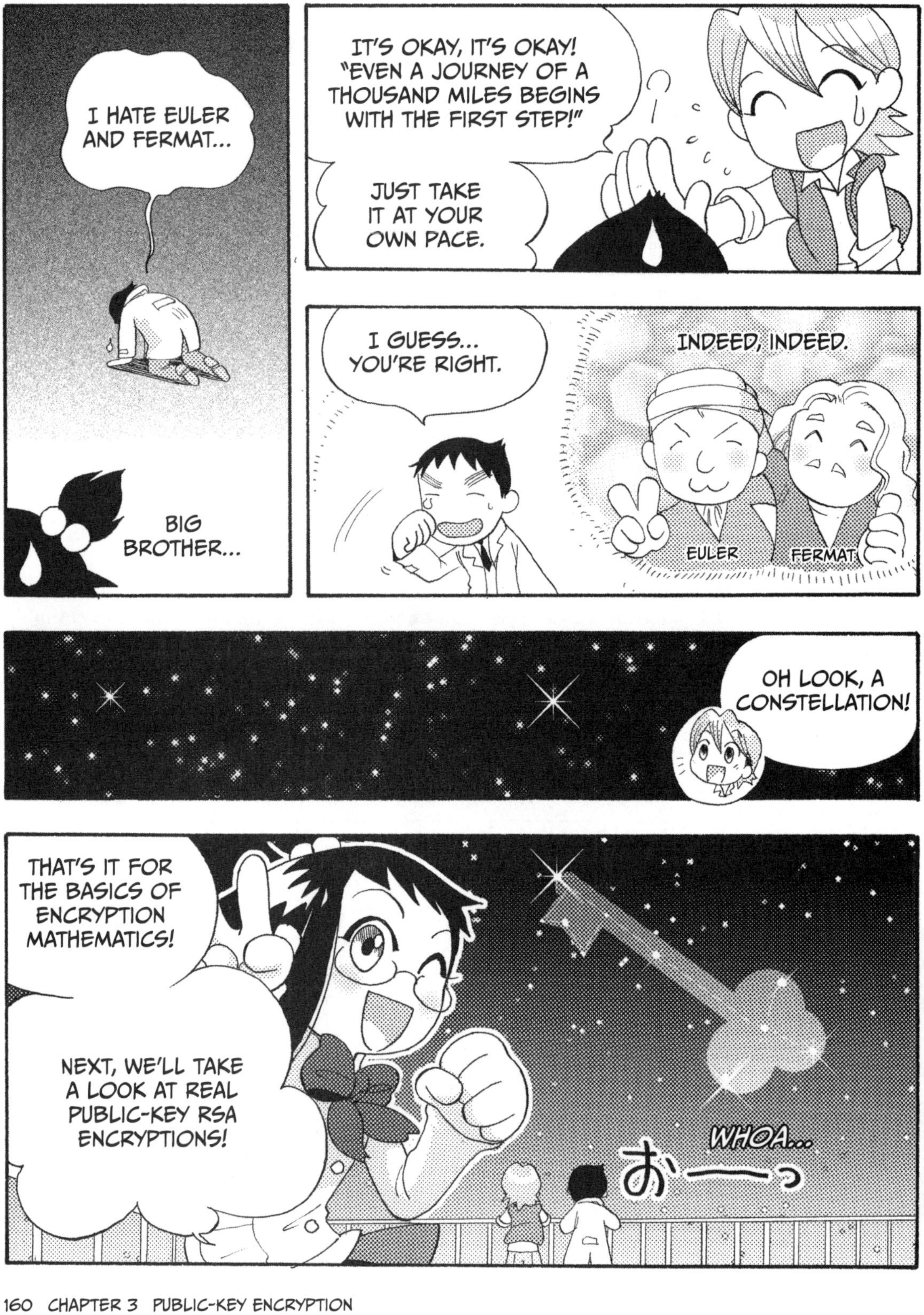
I HATE EULER AND FERMAT...
BIG BROTHER...
IT'S OKAY, IT'S OKAY! "EVEN A JOURNEY OF A THOUSAND MILES BEGINS WITH THE FIRST STEP!"
JUST TAKE IT AT YOUR OWN PACE.
I GUESS... YOU'RE RIGHT.
INDEED, INDEED.
EULER
FERMAT
OH LOOK, A CONSTELLATION!
THAT'S IT FOR THE BASICS OF ENCRYPTION MATHEMATICS!
NEXT, WE'LL TAKE A LOOK AT REAL PUBLIC-KEY RSA ENCRYPTIONS!
WHOA...
おーーっ

THE STRUCTURE OF RSA ENCRYPTION

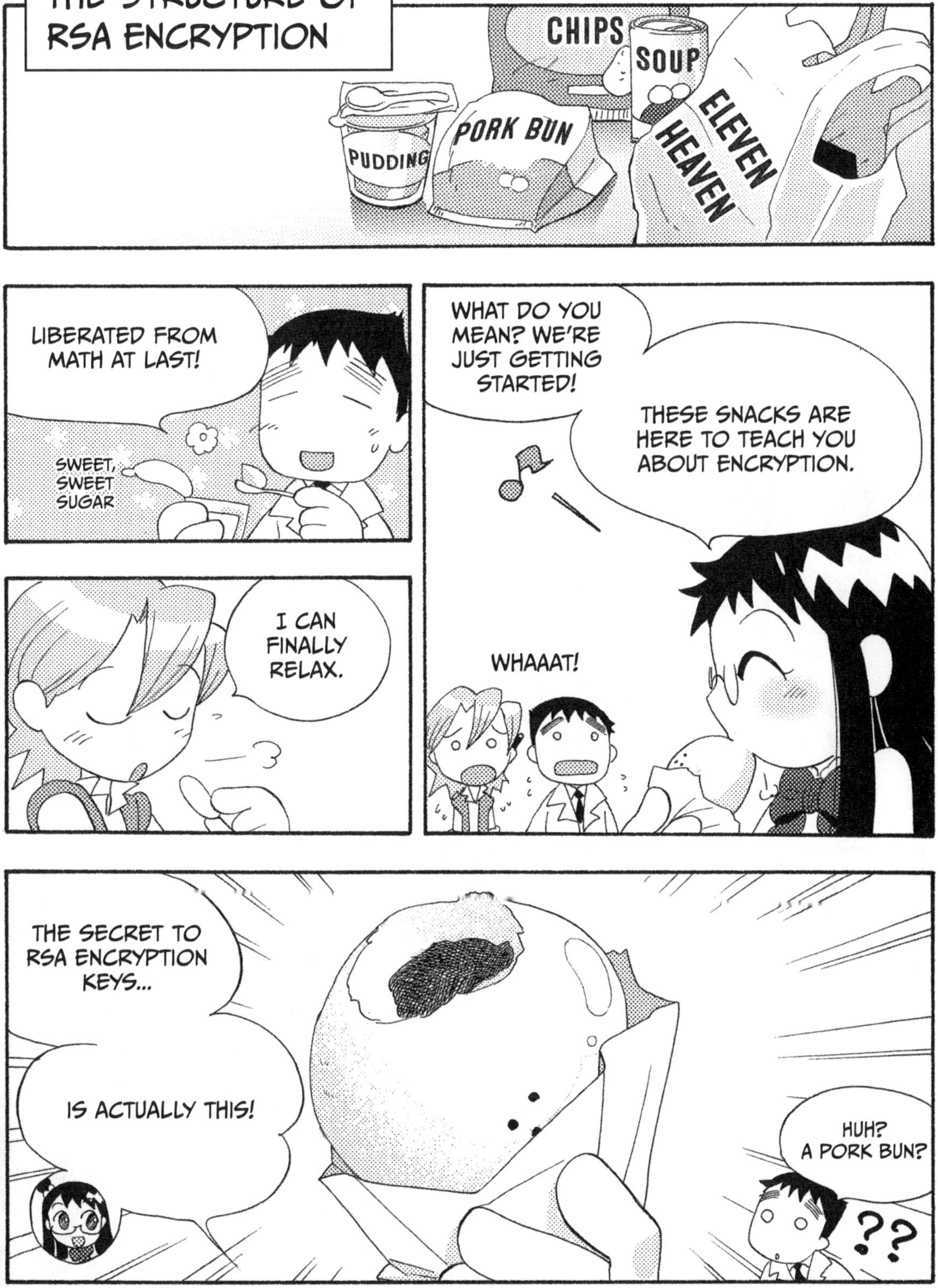
CHIPS
SOUP
PUDDING
PORK BUN
ELEVEN HEAVEN
LIBERATED FROM MATH AT LAST!
SWEET, SWEET SUGAR
I CAN FINALLY RELAX.
WHAT DO YOU MEAN? WE'RE JUST GETTING STARTED!
THESE SNACKS ARE HERE TO TEACH YOU ABOUT ENCRYPTION.
WHAAAT!
THE SECRET TO RSA ENCRYPTION KEYS...
IS ACTUALLY THIS!
HUH? A PORK BUN?
??

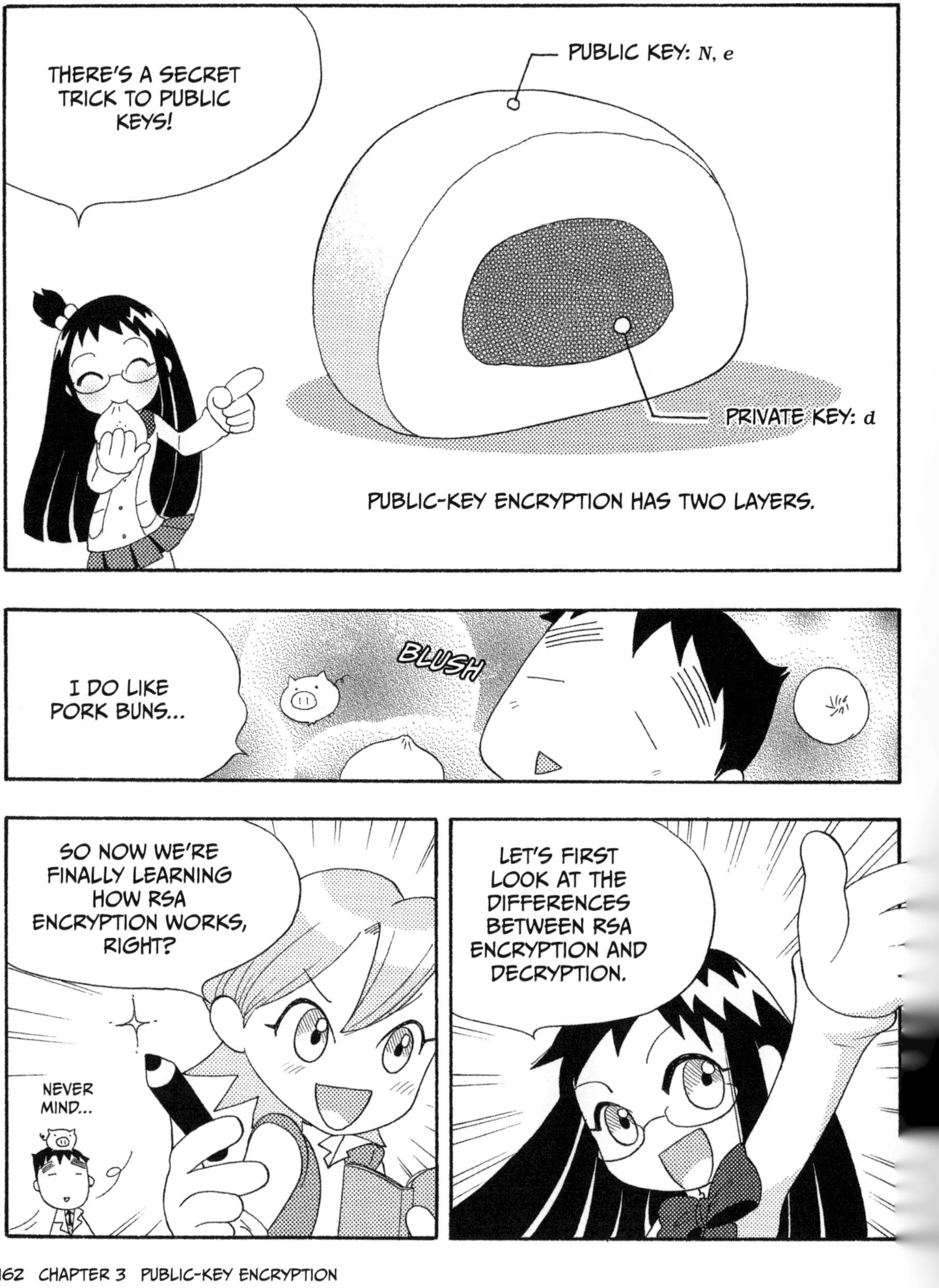
THERE'S A SECRET TRICK TO PUBLIC KEYS!
PUBLIC KEY: N, e
PRIVATE KEY: d
PUBLIC-KEY ENCRYPTION HAS TWO LAYERS.
I DO LIKE PORK BUNS...
BLUSH
SO NOW WE'RE FINALLY LEARNING HOW RSA ENCRYPTION WORKS, RIGHT?
NEVER MIND...
LET'S FIRST LOOK AT THE DIFFERENCES BETWEEN RSA ENCRYPTION AND DECRYPTION.

RSA ENCRYPTION: ENCRYPTION AND DECRYPTION

With a plaintext message m and ciphertext C, encryption is expressed as follows:

$$C = m^e \ (\text{mod } N)$$

In other words, if we raise m (the plaintext) to the power of e (a public key) and divide it by N (another public key), we're left with C (the ciphertext).

Decryption is expressed as follows:

$$m = C^d \ (\text{mod } N)$$

In other words, in decryption, C raised to the power of d (the private key) divided by N yields m. Here, N is made up of two different and large prime numbers p and q.

DO YOU KNOW WHY WE CAN'T DECODE THE FIRST EQUATION, EVEN THOUGH THE PUBLIC KEYS e AND N AND THE CIPHERTEXT c ARE KNOWN?

IF YOU THINK OF m IN TERMS OF AN UNKNOWN VALUE x IN AN EQUATION...

I DON'T WANNA HEAR IT!

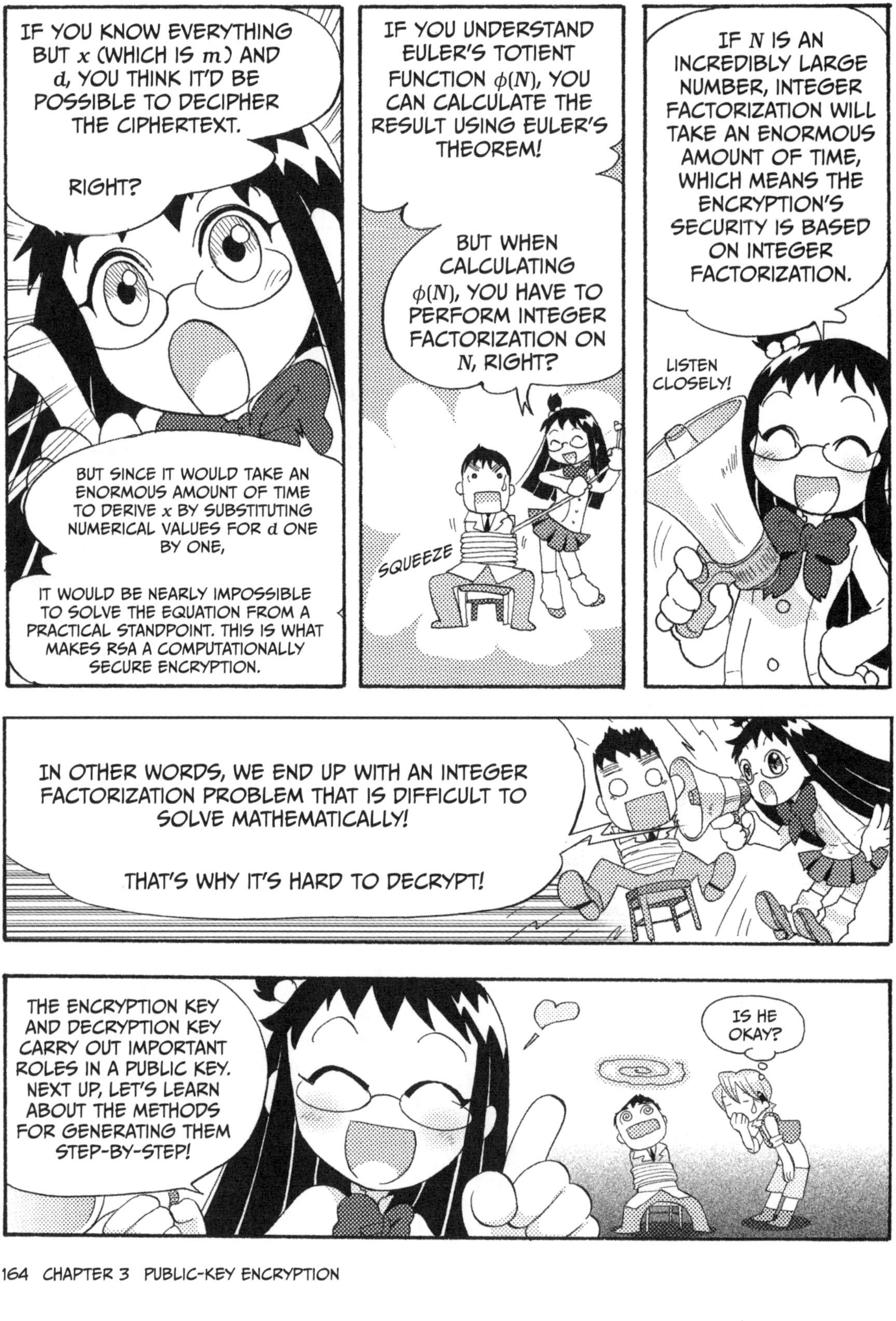

IF YOU KNOW EVERYTHING BUT x (WHICH IS m) AND d, YOU THINK IT'D BE POSSIBLE TO DECIPHER THE CIPHERTEXT.
RIGHT?
BUT SINCE IT WOULD TAKE AN ENORMOUS AMOUNT OF TIME TO DERIVE x BY SUBSTITUTING NUMERICAL VALUES FOR d ONE BY ONE,
IT WOULD BE NEARLY IMPOSSIBLE TO SOLVE THE EQUATION FROM A PRACTICAL STANDPOINT. THIS IS WHAT MAKES RSA A COMPUTATIONALLY SECURE ENCRYPTION.
IF YOU UNDERSTAND EULER'S TOTIENT FUNCTION $\phi(N)$, YOU CAN CALCULATE THE RESULT USING EULER'S THEOREM!
BUT WHEN CALCULATING $\phi(N)$, YOU HAVE TO PERFORM INTEGER FACTORIZATION ON N, RIGHT?
SQUEEZE
IF N IS AN INCREDIBLY LARGE NUMBER, INTEGER FACTORIZATION WILL TAKE AN ENORMOUS AMOUNT OF TIME, WHICH MEANS THE ENCRYPTION'S SECURITY IS BASED ON INTEGER FACTORIZATION.
LISTEN CLOSELY!
IN OTHER WORDS, WE END UP WITH AN INTEGER FACTORIZATION PROBLEM THAT IS DIFFICULT TO SOLVE MATHEMATICALLY!
THAT'S WHY IT'S HARD TO DECRYPT!
THE ENCRYPTION KEY AND DECRYPTION KEY CARRY OUT IMPORTANT ROLES IN A PUBLIC KEY. NEXT UP, LET'S LEARN ABOUT THE METHODS FOR GENERATING THEM STEP-BY-STEP!
IS HE OKAY?

GENERATING AN RSA ENCRYPTION KEY

We'll first generate the public key, and then we'll generate the private key.

PUBLIC-KEY GENERATION

Public-key generation involves several steps.

1. Select two different, large prime numbers, p and q, at random and calculate $N = pq$.

2. Solve Euler's function $\phi(N) = \phi(pq) = \phi(p)\phi(q) = (p - 1)(q - 1)$.

After you solve Euler's function, p and q become unnecessary! You should discard them so that other parties don't find them. This is crucial because if an adversary finds p and q, it is trivial to then calculate d and break RSA encryption.

3. Select a random positive integer e such that e is coprime with N: $1 < e < \phi(n)$

However, select e such that $m^e > N$! If $m^e \leq N$, we wouldn't be able to use the modulo operation since we would get $m^e = C$, where C is the ciphertext. We wouldn't be able to mod by N to scramble the equation. Because we don't know what messages we'll be encrypting, it is best to choose a reasonably large e (in the past, 65,537 has commonly been used as a value for e).

PRIVATE-KEY GENERATION

Find a positive integer d that satisfies the following equations:

$$d = e{-}1 \ (\text{mod } \phi(N))$$
$$ed = 1 \ (\text{mod } \phi(N)),$$

where d is less than $\phi(N)$ but larger than both p and q.
Now the public key is the pair (n, e), and the private key is d.

d IS EQUIVALENT TO THE RECIPROCAL (INVERSE ELEMENT) OF *e* IN MULTIPLICATION WHEN MODDING BY $\phi(N)$.

IN OTHER WORDS, YOU NEED TO SOLVE FOR THE DECRYPTION KEY *d* AND THE ENCRYPTION KEY *e* AS A PAIR!

VERIFYING THAT THE PUBLIC KEY E AND PRIVATE KEY D WORK IN RSA ENCRYPTION

Since we know that $ed = 1 \pmod{\phi(n)}$, we can subtract 1 from each side of the equation to get $ed - 1 = 0 \pmod{\phi(n)}$. In other words, $ed - 1$ leaves no remainder when modded by $\phi(n)$, meaning that it is a multiple of $\phi(n)$. So, you get

$$ed - 1 = k\,\phi(n),$$

where k is a nonnegative integer. In addition, we can manipulate the equation to be this:

$$ed = k\,\phi(n) + 1$$

Therefore, if we take the earlier equation $a^{kL+1} = a \pmod{N}$ (see page 159), we can express all of the natural numbers of m (the plaintext) from 1 to $(N - 1)$ in the following equation:

$$m^{kL+1} = m \pmod{N}$$

Because $ed = k\phi(n) + 1$, we can substitute the exponent, so when the ciphertext is raised to the private key, we get the following:

$$m^{ed} = m^{k\phi(n)+1} = m \pmod{N}$$

Since the ciphertext $C = m^e$, $m^{ed} = Ce$, it becomes clear that d allows us to decrypt plaintext m.

PRIVATE KEY *d* AND PUBLIC KEY *e* CANCEL EACH OTHER TO REVEAL THE PLAINTEXT!

LET'S PRACTICE CREATING PUBLIC AND PRIVATE KEYS!

HOW TO MAKE PUBLIC KEYS AND PRIVATE KEYS

Now, given two prime numbers $p = 5$ and $q = 11$, let's solve for public key N and private key d.

STEP 1

The product of p and q is N.

$$N = pq = 5 \times 11 = 55$$

STEP 2

Solve the Euler function of N, $\phi(N)$.

$$\phi(55) = (5 - 1) \times (11 - 1) = 4 \times 10 = 40$$

STEP 3

Choose a random integer e such that e is coprime to N and $1 < e < \phi(N)$. The list of candidates that fulfill these requirements for our current example is {1, 3, 7, 9, 11, 13, 17, 19}. We'll use $e = 17$, so the public key is (55, 17).

STEP 4

Solve for the private key d. We know that $e = 17$, and we are using modulo $\phi(N)$(40). The equation we need to solve is

$$d = e - 1 \ (\text{mod } \phi(N))$$

$$ed = 1 \ (\text{mod } \phi(N))$$

$$17d = 1 \ (\text{mod } 40)$$

We can see that d multiplied by 17 modulo 40 must equal 1. From the extended Euclidean algorithm, which we'll see later, we get that $d = 33$.
For now, let's verify that:

$$17d = 1 \ (\text{mod } 40)$$

$$17 \times 33 = 1 \ (\text{mod } 40)$$

$$561 = 1 \ (\text{mod } 40)$$

where

$$561 = 1 + 40k$$

$$561 = 1 + (40 \times 14) \text{ for } k = 14$$

$$561 = 1 + 560$$

This shows that $d = 33$ is valid; thus the private key is $d = 33$.

STEP 5

Solve for the decryption key d, which is the inverse of encryption key e. We know that $e = 17$ and are modding by 40 ($\phi(55) = 40$).

$$ed = k\phi(n) + 1 \pmod{40}, \text{ so } 17d = 40k + 1$$

When you rearrange this equation, you get

$$\frac{40k + 1}{17}$$

Because we know d must be an integer, the right side of the equation can't leave a remainder. So we can search for solutions in which $40k + 1$ is a multiple of 17 and find that one solution is $k = 11$.

Furthermore, you can calculate what d is in relation to each e acquired in step 4 by solving the same formula, $ed = 40k + 1$. You would get the following d and e pairs:

$$(e = 3, d = 27), (e = 7, d = 23), (e = 9, d = 9),$$
$$(e = 11, d = 11), (e = 17, d = 33), (e = 19, d = 19)$$

In general, the encryption key and decryption key should be different integers ($e \neq d$), and larger integers are preferred for encryption key e; $e = 17$ and $d = 33$ are just examples we will use here.

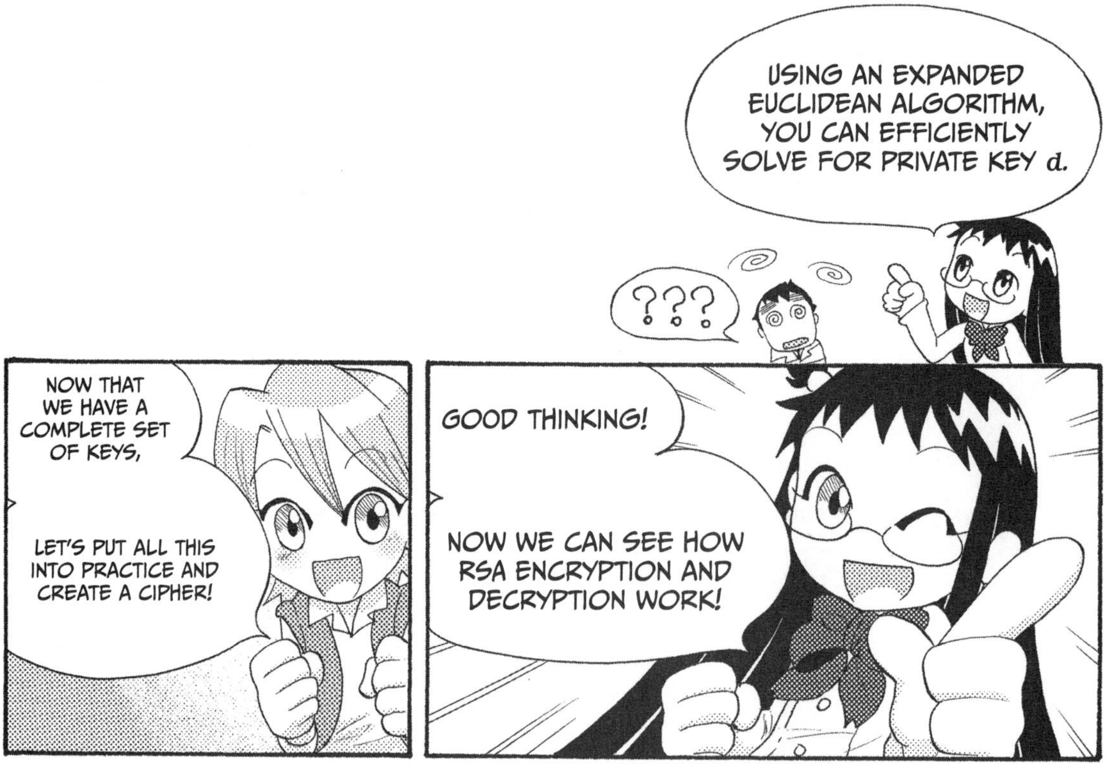
USING AN EXPANDED EUCLIDEAN ALGORITHM, YOU CAN EFFICIENTLY SOLVE FOR PRIVATE KEY d.
???
NOW THAT WE HAVE A COMPLETE SET OF KEYS,
LET'S PUT ALL THIS INTO PRACTICE AND CREATE A CIPHER!
GOOD THINKING!
NOW WE CAN SEE HOW RSA ENCRYPTION AND DECRYPTION WORK!

GENERATING A CIPHERTEXT USING RSA

To begin, we'll look at the procedure for using a public key to generate a ciphertext.

To make this a concrete example, we'll encrypt the four-letter plaintext GOLF using the encryption key $e = 17$ that we calculated earlier.

STEP 1

First, use the table at the right to encode the characters as integers. This is non-standard character encoding, but it is convenient for this exercise.

```
G        O        L        F
↓        ↓        ↓        ↓
32       40       37       31
```

STEP 2

Convert the integers to 6-bit binary.

```
32       40       37       31
↓        ↓        ↓        ↓
100000   101000   100101   011111
```

STEP 3

Express the binary data as a nonnegative integer less than $(N - 1)$. In this example, since $N = 55$ and $N - 1 = 55 - 1 = 54$, the data is divided into 5-bit units. In other words, the greatest value that can be expressed in 5 bits is 31, which is below 54 and fulfills the conditions. Of course, we could use 3- or 4-bit sections instead, but using larger-bit sections is more efficient.

CHARACTER ENCODING

Character	Code	Character	Code
a	0	K	36
b	1	L	37
c	2	M	38
...	...	N	39
w	22	O	40
x	23	P	41
y	24	Q	42
z	25	R	43
A	26	S	44
B	27	T	45
C	28	U	46
D	29	V	47
E	30	W	48
F	31	X	49
G	32	Y	50
H	33	Z	51
I	34	...	...
J	35	Space	63

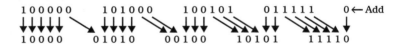

```
1 0 0 0 0 0   1 0 1 0 0 0   1 0 0 1 0 1   0 1 1 1 1 1   0 ← Add
1 0 0 0 0     0 1 0 1 0     0 0 1 0 0     1 0 1 0 1     1 1 1 1 0
```

We append the final 0 to pad the last section because there is an insufficient number of bits to make the section a complete 5-bit unit. Here, we're using 0, but other padding digits could be used instead, depending on the encryption scheme.

STEP 4

Convert the binary data into decimal notation.

```
10000    01010    00100    10101    11110
↓        ↓        ↓        ↓        ↓
16       10       4        21       30
```

Using the encryption keys ($N = 55$, $e = 17$), perform the encryption. In concrete terms, this involves raising the data in decimal notation to the 17th power, dividing by 55, and searching for the remainder. By performing these calculations for each integer as follows . . .

$$16^{17} \text{ (mod 55)}, \ 10^{17} \text{ (mod 55)}, \ 4^{17} \text{ (mod 55)}, \ 21^{17} \text{ (mod 55)}, \ 30^{17} \text{ (mod 55)}$$

. . . we obtain the encrypted data. For example, we can calculate this for 16 by finding the solution to 16^{17} (mod 55). We can reduce 16^{17} by expanding the exponent as follows:

$$16^{17} = 16^2 \times 16^2 \times 16^2 \times 16^2 \times 16^2 \times 16^2 \times 16^2 \times 16^2 \times 16 \text{ (mod 55)}$$

Because $16^2 = 256 = 36$ (mod 55), we can replace each 16^2 with 36:

$$= 36 \times 36 \times 36 \times 36 \times 36 \times 36 \times 36 \times 36 \times 16 \text{ (mod 55)}$$

which is equal to

$$= 36^2 \times 36^2 \times 36^2 \times 36^2 \times 16 \text{ (mod 55)}$$

And since $36^2 = 1{,}296 = 31$ (mod 55), we can further reduce the equation:

$$= 31 \times 31 \times 31 \times 31 \times 16 \text{ (mod 55)}$$
$$= 31^2 \times 31^2 \times 16 \text{ (mod 55)}$$

Then because $31^2 = 961 = 26$ (mod 55), we get

$$= 26 \times 26 \times 16 \text{ (mod 55)}$$
$$= 26^2 \times 16 \text{ (mod 55)}$$

And finally, because $26^2 = 676 = 16$ (mod 55), we get

$$= 16 \times 16 \text{ (mod 55)}$$
$$= 36 \text{ (mod 55)}$$

The remaining encryption is performed in the same way, and we record the results as follows:

$$10^{17} \text{ (mod 55)} = 10$$
$$4^{17} \text{ (mod 55)} = 49$$
$$21^{17} \text{ (mod 55)} = 21$$
$$30^{17} \text{ (mod 55)} = 35$$

Thus, the ciphertext expressed in decimal notation is as follows:

$$36 \quad 10 \quad 49 \quad 21 \quad 35$$

Then we can encode the decimal notation into letters:

36	10	49	21	35
↓	↓	↓	↓	↓
K	k	X	v	J

So the ciphertext is KkXvJ.

DECRYPTING A CIPHERTEXT USING RSA

Now let's go over the process of using the private key to decrypt a ciphertext into plaintext. We'll use the private encryption key $d = 33$ in our concrete example.

STEP 1

Using decryption key $d = 33$, calculate C^d (mod N). This involves raising each number in the decimal-form ciphertext (36   10   49   21   35) to the 33rd power, dividing by 55, and seeking out the remainder to obtain the plaintext data as follows:

$$36^{33} \text{ (mod 55)}, 10^{33} \text{ (mod 55)}, 49^{33} \text{ (mod 55)}, 21^{33} \text{ (mod 55)}, 35^{33} \text{ (mod 55)}$$

To calculate this for the first decimal digit 36, adopt the same technique used in step 5 of generating the ciphertext, as follows:

$$36^{33} = 36^3 \times 36^3 \times 36^3 \times 36^3 \times 36^3 \times 36^3 \times 36^3 \times 36^3 \times 36^3 \times 36^3 \times 36^3 \text{ (mod 55)}$$

$$= 46{,}656 \times 46{,}656 \times 46{,}656 \times 46{,}656 \times 46{,}656 \times 46{,}656 \times 46{,}656 \times 46{,}656 \times$$
$$46{,}656 \times 46{,}656 \times 46{,}656 \text{ (mod 55)}$$

$$= 16 \times 16 \times 16 \times 16 \times 16 \times 16 \times 16 \times 16 \times 16 \times 16 \times 16 \text{ (mod 55)}$$

$$= 16^2 \times 16^2 \times 16^2 \times 16^2 \times 16^2 \times 16 \text{ (mod 55)}$$

$$= 36 \times 36 \times 36 \times 36 \times 36 \times 16 \text{ (mod 55)}$$

$$= 967{,}458{,}816 \text{ (mod 55)}$$

$$= 16 \text{ (mod 55)}$$

The remaining encrypted data {10, 49, 21, 35} is calculated in the same way, and we record the results as follows:

$$10^{33} \text{ (mod 55)} = 10$$
$$49^{33} \text{ (mod 55)} = 4$$
$$21^{33} \text{ (mod 55)} = 21$$
$$35^{33} \text{ (mod 55)} = 30$$

Thus, we would get the plaintext data represented in decimal notation as follows:

$$16 \quad 10 \quad 4 \quad 21 \quad 30$$

STEP 2

Next, convert the decimal numbers you have obtained into 5-bit binary data:

16	10	4	21	30
↓	↓	↓	↓	↓
10000	01010	00100	10101	11110

STEP 3

To make the bits correspond with the character encoding in the table on page 169, divide the binary data into 6-bit units:

Because the last 0 was used as padding, it won't fit into a 6-bit unit. You can eliminate it.

STEP 4

Convert each 6-bit binary unit into an integer:

100000	101000	100101	011111
↓	↓	↓	↓
32	40	37	31

STEP 5

Using the table on page 169, encode the integer data into characters:

32	40	37	31
↓	↓	↓	↓
G	O	L	F

Now you've completed the decryption process.

WHY ENCRYPT THE WORD GOLF?

IT'S THE AUTHOR'S HOBBY... PROBABLY.

PUBLIC-KEY ENCRYPTION AND DISCRETE LOGARITHM PROBLEMS

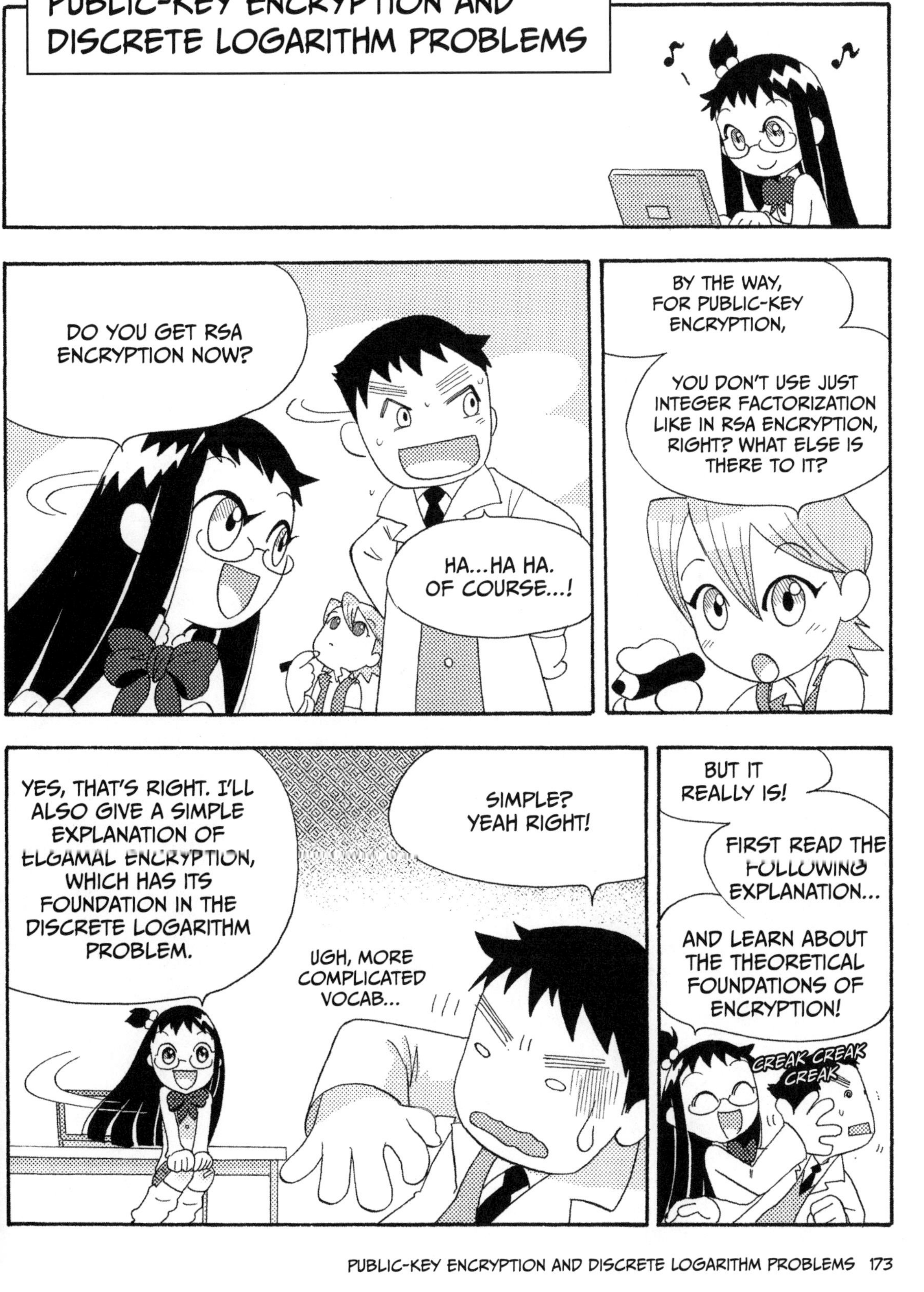
DO YOU GET RSA ENCRYPTION NOW?
HA...HA HA. OF COURSE...!
BY THE WAY, FOR PUBLIC-KEY ENCRYPTION,
YOU DON'T USE JUST INTEGER FACTORIZATION LIKE IN RSA ENCRYPTION, RIGHT? WHAT ELSE IS THERE TO IT?
YES, THAT'S RIGHT. I'LL ALSO GIVE A SIMPLE EXPLANATION OF ELGAMAL ENCRYPTION, WHICH HAS ITS FOUNDATION IN THE DISCRETE LOGARITHM PROBLEM.
SIMPLE? YEAH RIGHT!
UGH, MORE COMPLICATED VOCAB...
BUT IT REALLY IS!
FIRST READ THE FOLLOWING EXPLANATION...
AND LEARN ABOUT THE THEORETICAL FOUNDATIONS OF ENCRYPTION!
CREAK CREAK CREAK

DISCRETE LOGARITHM PROBLEMS

Take another look at the modulo 7 power table. This table contains all the powers between 1 and 6 and shows the results of modding them by 7. We can express the possible results of a modulo 7 operation as a finite field comprising these members:

$$\{0, 1, 2, 3, 4, 5, 6\}$$

We'll represent this finite field in group notation. When we have a number n and a field of numbers related to n, we can represent the whole group as $Z_n{}^*$. In this case, n is 7, so we get $Z_7{}^* = \{0, 1, 2, 3, 4, 5, 6\}$. You'll notice that every number in this set is coprime to 7 except 0. We'll represent the group of coprimes in $Z_n{}^*$ as Z_i.

You'll notice in the table to the right that in the row showing the power of 3 mod 7, the values from 1 to 6 each appear in the row only once. This means $Z_7{}^*$ with the exception of 0 is expressed in the power of 3 modulo 7. When we have a number n, if the power of a modulo n contains every coprime of n in $Z_n{}^*$, then a is called n's *primitive root*.

a^b MODULO 7

a / b	1	2	3	4	5	6
1	1	1	1	1	1	1
2	2	4	1	2	4	1
3	3	2	6	4	5	1
4	4	2	1	4	2	1
5	5	4	6	2	3	1
6	6	1	6	1	6	1

Every prime number p has primitive roots, and the number of primitive roots is $\phi(p - 1)$. For modulo 7, the result of this equation would be

$$\phi(7 - 1) = \phi(6) = \phi(2 \times 3) = (2 - 1) \times (3 - 1) = 2$$

This means that modulo 7 has two primitive roots. Thus, aside from 3, there must be one other numerical value that is a primitive root, and, if we look at the a^b modulo 7 table, we can ascertain that it is 5. Where p is a prime number, α represents a primitive root modulo p, and k is a nonnegative integer but also fulfills the equation $k \leq p - 1$, we can express any member of Z_i as a modulo operation like so:

$$\alpha^k = Z_i \; (\text{mod } p)$$

With some rearrangement of this equation, the exponent k of primitive root α can also be expressed as the following equation:

$$k = \log_\alpha Z_i \; (\text{mod } p)$$

When this is the case, k is known as a *discrete logarithm* with base α.

Let's quickly go over log notation. For example, the equation $2^3 = 8$ is the same as

$$3 = 3 \log_2 2 = \log_2 2^3 = \log_2 8$$

This is similar to rephrasing the expression "2 to the power of 3 is 8" to be "to get 8, you must multiply 2 by itself 3 times."

As is also explained on page 116, when you have the equation

$$\alpha^k = Z_i \pmod{p},$$

it isn't difficult to find Z_i when α, k, and p are known, but finding the discrete logarithm k is incredibly difficult even if you know α, Z_i, and p. This is the *discrete logarithm problem*.

y = logα AND
x = αy!

DID YOU UNDERSTAND THE EXPLANATION?
HA...HA HA...
WELL, NEXT I'LL EXPLAIN ELGAMAL ENCRYPTION, AN ALGORITHM THAT USES THE DISCRETE LOGARITHM PROBLEM.
HANG IN THERE.
SOB

ENCRYPTION AND DECRYPTION IN ELGAMAL ENCRYPTION

In this cipher, the sender is Ruka, and the recipient is Ran.

1. **Recipient Ran prepares a large prime number q and the primitive root α.**

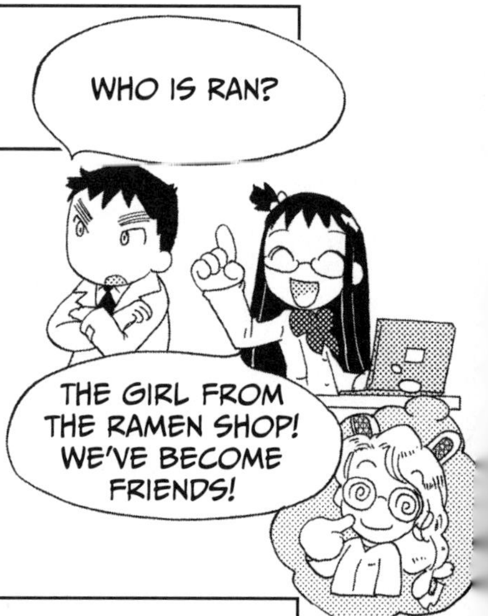
WHO IS RAN?
THE GIRL FROM THE RAMEN SHOP! WE'VE BECOME FRIENDS!

2. **Recipient Ran randomly chooses a private key d, performs the following calculation, and makes the public keys g, α, and q available to others.**

$$g = \alpha d \pmod{q}$$

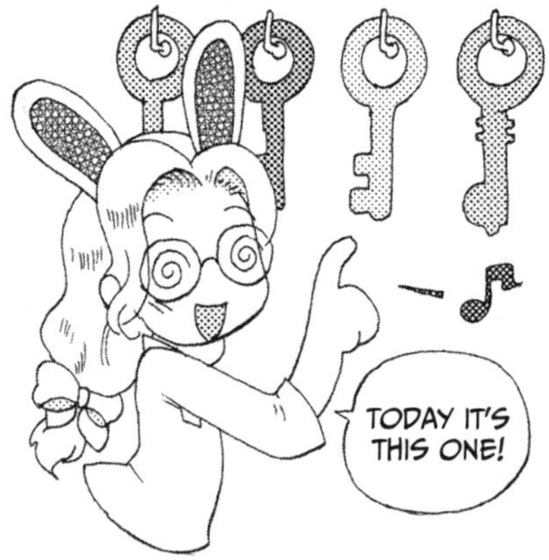
TODAY IT'S THIS ONE!

3. **Sender Ruka selects a random number r and calculates $C_1 = \alpha r$ (mod q).**

   In addition, she calculates $C_2 = m \times gr$ (mod q) for the plaintext message m.

4. Sender Ruka sends C_1 and C_2 to Ran.

Private key d

Public keys g, α, and q

USAGI'S DINER

C_1, C_2

5. The recipient Ran uses private key d to calculate the following equation and decrypt the message:

$$m = \frac{C_2}{C_1^{\,d}} \, (\text{mod } q)$$

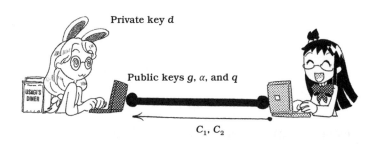

WE HAVE

$$C_1^{\,d} = \left(\alpha^r\right)^d = \left(\alpha^d\right)^r = \alpha^{rd} = g^r$$

SO

$$\frac{C_2}{C_1^{\,d}} = \frac{m \times g^r}{g^r} = m$$

IS THE DECRYPTION OF m.

WOW! WE'VE DECRYPTED THE PLAINTEXT m!

AMAZING!

SHARING A KEY IN ELGAMAL ENCRYPTION IS SIMILAR TO SHARING A KEY WITH THE DIFFIE-HELLMAN METHOD.

PINCH

PAY ATTENTION!

1. Ruka and Ran share the large primary number p and the primitive root α, neither of which is private.

2. Ruka selects a secret random number c and then sends αc (mod p) to Ran. On the other end, Ran selects a private random number d and then sends αd (mod p) to Ruka.

3. The shared key is αcd. Ruka obtains the shared key by calculating $(\alpha d)c = \alpha cd$ (mod p) from private key c, and Ran obtains the shared key by calculating $(\alpha c)d = \alpha cd$ (mod p) from private key d.

The two of them are able to share a key.

OHHH, THAT'S EASY TO UNDERSTAND!

ON TOP OF THAT, ELGAMAL ENCRYPTION IS REALLY STRONG!

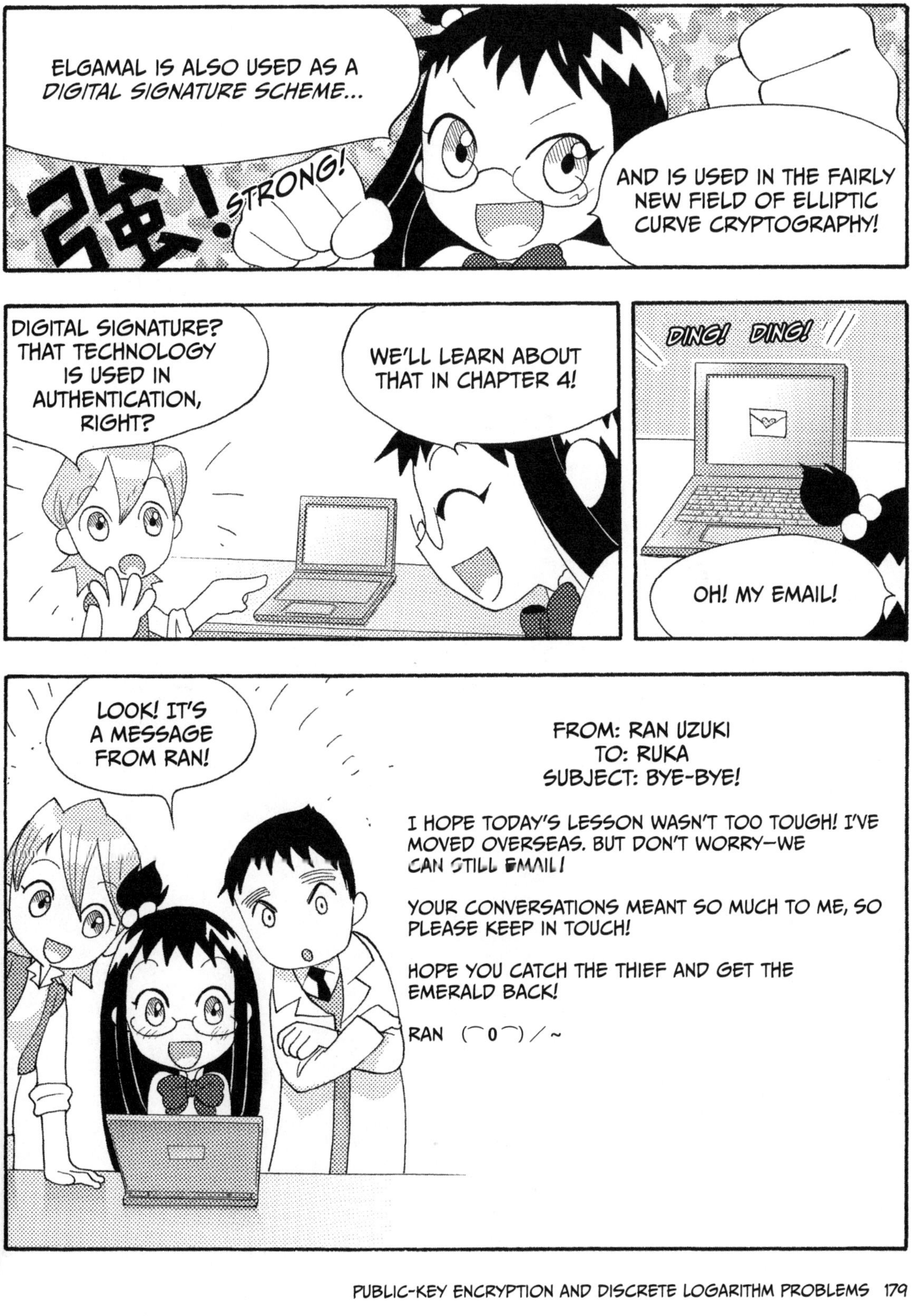
ELGAMAL IS ALSO USED AS A DIGITAL SIGNATURE SCHEME...
強! STRONG!
AND IS USED IN THE FAIRLY NEW FIELD OF ELLIPTIC CURVE CRYPTOGRAPHY!
DIGITAL SIGNATURE? THAT TECHNOLOGY IS USED IN AUTHENTICATION, RIGHT?
WE'LL LEARN ABOUT THAT IN CHAPTER 4!
DING! DING!
OH! MY EMAIL!
LOOK! IT'S A MESSAGE FROM RAN!
FROM: RAN UZUKI
TO: RUKA
SUBJECT: BYE-BYE!
I HOPE TODAY'S LESSON WASN'T TOO TOUGH! I'VE MOVED OVERSEAS. BUT DON'T WORRY—WE CAN STILL EMAIL!
YOUR CONVERSATIONS MEANT SO MUCH TO ME, SO PLEASE KEEP IN TOUCH!
HOPE YOU CATCH THE THIEF AND GET THE EMERALD BACK!
RAN (¯0¯)/~

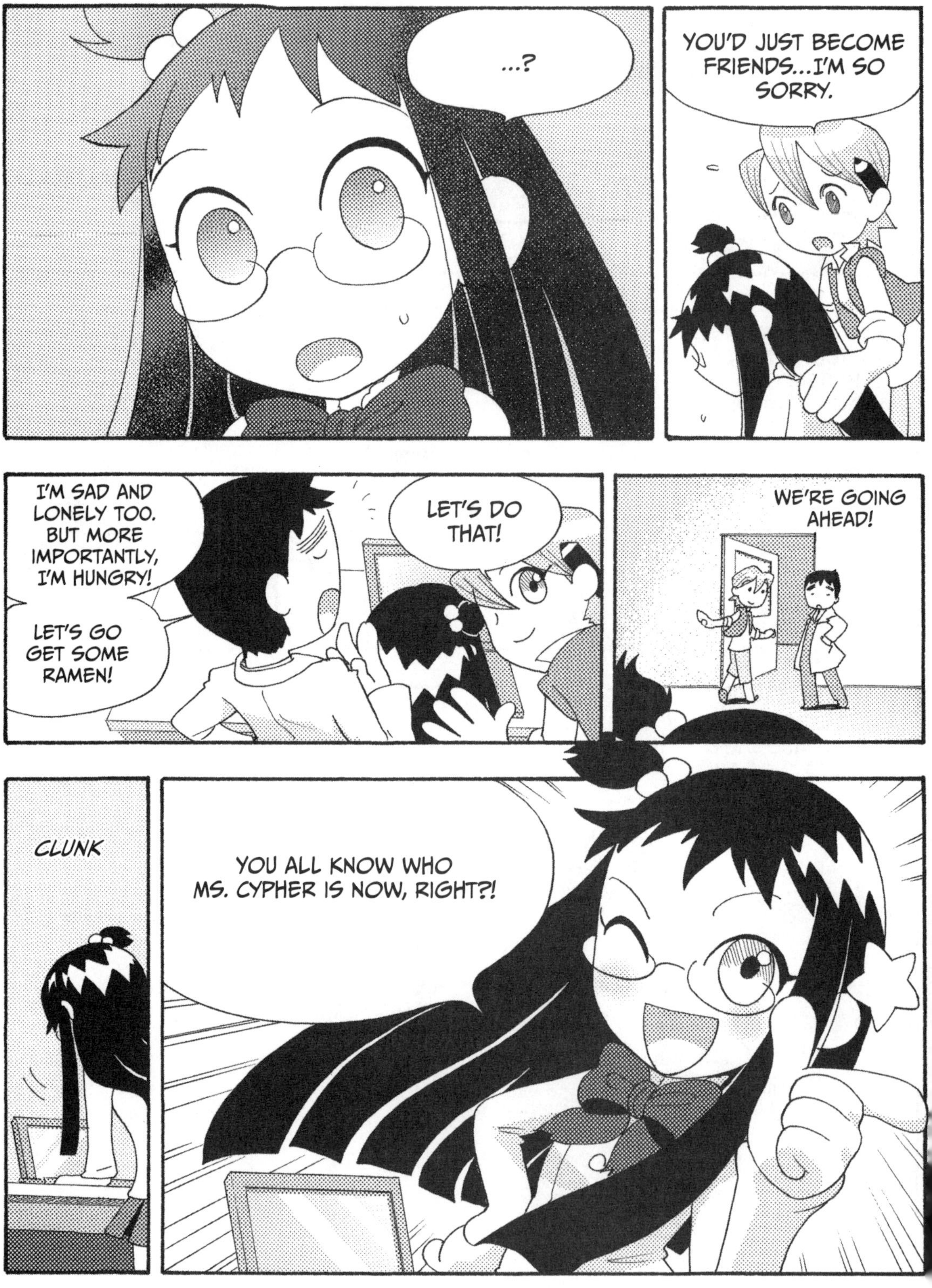
...?
YOU'D JUST BECOME FRIENDS...I'M SO SORRY.
I'M SAD AND LONELY TOO. BUT MORE IMPORTANTLY, I'M HUNGRY!
LET'S GO GET SOME RAMEN!
LET'S DO THAT!
WE'RE GOING AHEAD!
CLUNK
YOU ALL KNOW WHO MS. CYPHER IS NOW, RIGHT?!

THE EXTENDED EUCLIDEAN ALGORITHM

The *Euclidean algorithm* derives the greatest common divisor of two natural numbers more efficiently than does base factorization. The procedure for identifying the greatest common divisor of two natural numbers a and b (where $a > b$) using the Euclidean algorithm is as follows:

1. Divide a by b to find the remainder r.

2. When $r = 0$, the greatest common divisor is b, and the process is finished.

3. When $r \neq 0$, replace a and b with b and r, and perform the first step again.

In other words, repeat steps 1–3, and when you arrive at a remainder of 0, the divided number is the greatest common divisor.

For example, let's solve for the greatest common divisor of 1,365 and 77. Although the Euclidean algorithm deals with remainders, its proof is conventionally written without using modular arithmetic, so we'll do the same:

$$1{,}365 = 17 \times 77 + 56 \qquad 1{,}365 \div 77 = 17 \text{ with a remainder of } 56$$
$$77 = 1 \times 56 + 21 \qquad 77 \div 56 = 1 \text{ with a remainder of } 21$$
$$56 = 2 \times 21 + 14 \qquad 56 \div 21 = 2 \text{ with a remainder of } 14$$
$$21 = 1 \times 14 + ⑦ \qquad 21 \div 14 = 1 \text{ with a remainder of } 7$$
$$14 = 2 \times ⑦ + 0 \qquad 14 \div 7 = 2 \text{ with a remainder of } 0$$

So, the greatest common divisor is 7.

Next, we'll locate the greatest common divisor for the coprimes 20 and 17.

$$20 = 1 \times 17 + 3$$
$$17 = 5 \times 3 + 2$$
$$3 = 1 \times 2 + 1$$
$$2 = 2 \times 1 + 0$$

Of course, since the greatest common divisor is 1 for coprimes, the Euclidean algorithm seems unnecessary. However, the extended Euclidean algorithm is very useful to us.

The extended Euclidean algorithm is used to solve for the modular multiplicative inverse, which is one of the calculations required in RSA. It aims to solve for the coefficients of Bezout's identity, which is the following equation,

$$ax + by = d,$$

where d is the greatest common divisor of a and b (x and y are the coefficients we aim to solve for). To solve for x and y, we must perform a few more steps after Euclid's algorithm (hence the name extended Euclidean algorithm).

First, we'll transpose the first three equations into the following equations:

$$20 - 1 \times 17 = 3$$
$$17 - 5 \times 3 = 2$$
$$3 - 1 \times 2 = 1$$

Since 2 is equal to $(17 - 5 \times 3)$, as seen in the earlier equations, we'll take the last equation we created and substitute it for 2.

$$3 - 1 \times 2 = 1$$
$$3 - 1 \times (17 - 5 \times 3) = 1$$

Then manipulate the equation by distributing and combining like terms. The goal of these substitutions is to express everything on the left side in terms of $ax + by$ where $a = 20$ and $b = 17$.

$$3 - 1 \times (17 - 5 \times 3) = 1$$
$$3 + (-1 \times 17) + [-1(-5 \times 3)] = 1$$
$$(-1 \times 17) + 3 + (5 \times 3) = 1$$
$$(-1 \times 17) + (6 \times 3) = 1$$

Next, we'll substitute $(20 - 1 \times 17)$ for 3:

$$(-1 \times 17) + 6 \times (20 - 1 \times 17) = 1$$
$$(-1 \times 17) + (6 \times 20) + (-6 \times 17) = 1$$
$$(6 \times 20) + (-7 \times 17) = 1$$

The result of this series of procedures is rewritten as follows:

$$20(6) + 17(-7) = 1$$

This is exactly what we were looking for. The value $d = 1$ because a and b are coprimes, $a = 20$ and $b = 17$ as expected, and we now have the values of x and y.

The solution to the extended Euclidean algorithm here is $x = 6$, $y = -7$.

CALCULATING THE PRIVATE KEY IN RSA KEY GENERATION

Here we'll show how we got $d = 33$ in our key generation example, which requires calculating inverse elements in a modulo operation.

In our example, we were trying to solve for the private key d and had this equation:

$$17d = 1 \ (\text{mod } 40)$$

To solve this, you can rearrange the equation into Bezoat's identity ($ax + by = 1$) and use the extended Euclidean algorithm. We'll arrange the equation so that $a = 17$, $b = 40$, and $x = d$ to get

$$17x + 40y = 1$$

Now, to solve for x, let's first perform Euclid's algorithm:

$$40 = (2 \times 17) + 6$$
$$17 = (2 \times 6) + 5$$
$$6 = (1 \times 5) + 1$$
$$5 = (5 \times 1) + 0$$

Now we'll perform the extended Euclidean algorithm. Let's start with the second-to-last equation from our calculations for Euclid's algorithm:

$$6 - 1 \times 5 = 1$$

Now substitute the third-to-last equation into the second-to-last equation:

$$6 - 1 \times (17 - 2 \times 6) = 1$$

Now substitute in the first equation as well:

$$(40 - 2 \times 17) - 1 \times (17 - 2 \times (40 - 2 \times 17)) = 1$$

Group the numbers into similar terms. In this case, group them into 17s and 40s:

$$-7 \times 17 + 3 \times 40 = 1$$

Given that we had $17x + 40y = 1$ and were solving for x, we can see that our private key $d = x = -7 = 33 \pmod{40}$ became $-7 + 40 = 33$.

Now that you've completed this hands-on example, you should have the confidence to solve for other private keys for RSA key generation!

4

PRACTICAL
APPLICATIONS OF
ENCRYPTION

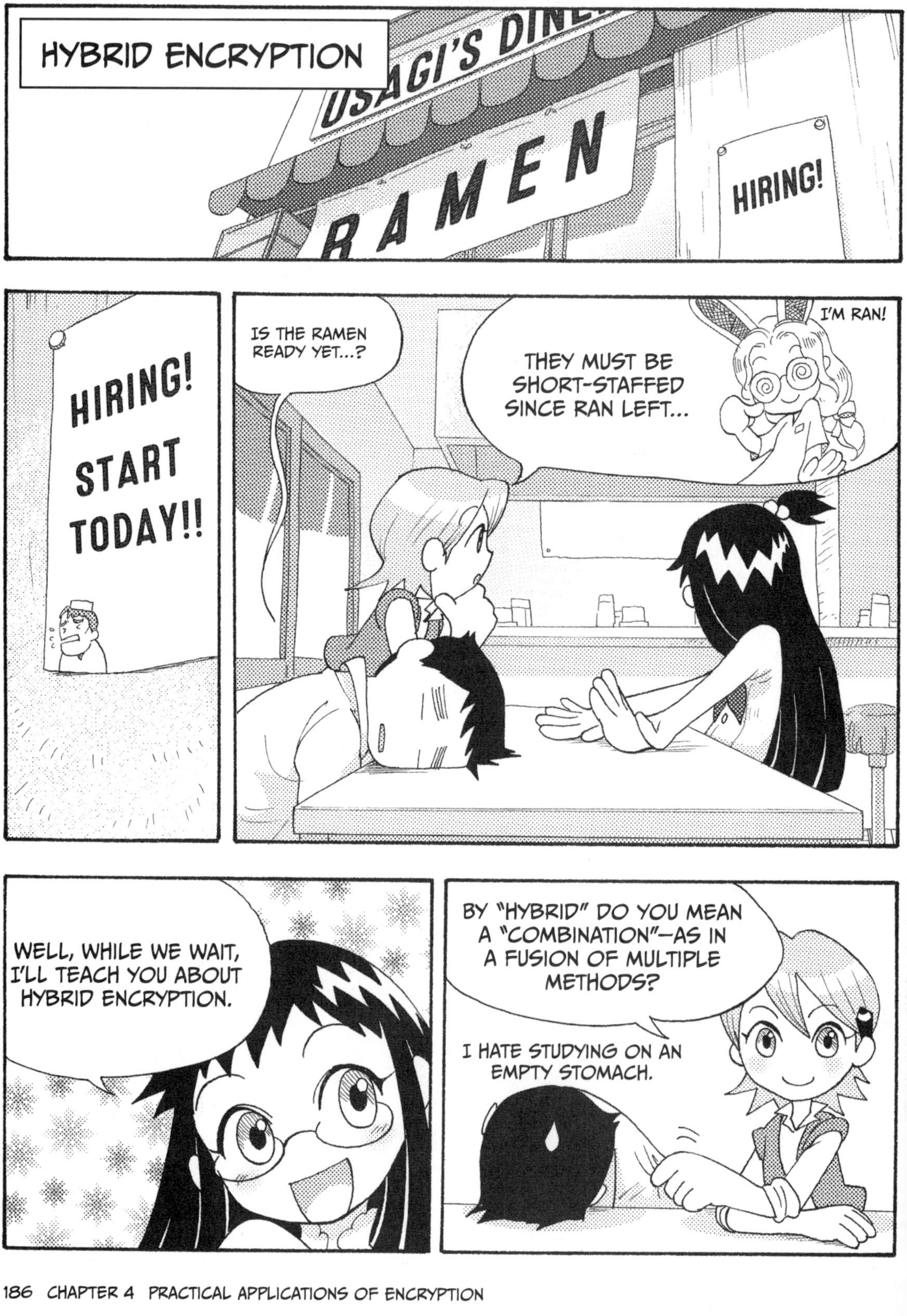
HYBRID ENCRYPTION
RAMEN
HIRING!
HIRING! START TODAY!!
IS THE RAMEN READY YET...?
THEY MUST BE SHORT-STAFFED SINCE RAN LEFT...
I'M RAN!
WELL, WHILE WE WAIT, I'LL TEACH YOU ABOUT HYBRID ENCRYPTION.
BY "HYBRID" DO YOU MEAN A "COMBINATION"—AS IN A FUSION OF MULTIPLE METHODS?
I HATE STUDYING ON AN EMPTY STOMACH.

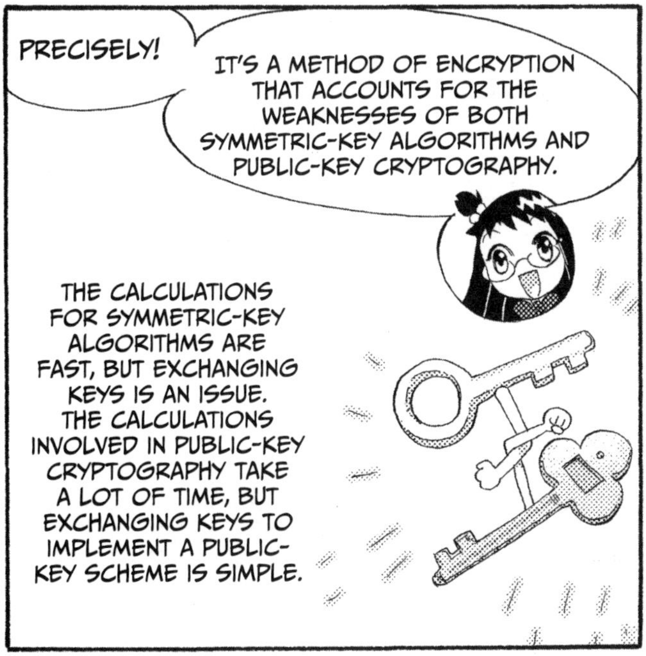
PRECISELY!
IT'S A METHOD OF ENCRYPTION THAT ACCOUNTS FOR THE WEAKNESSES OF BOTH SYMMETRIC-KEY ALGORITHMS AND PUBLIC-KEY CRYPTOGRAPHY.
THE CALCULATIONS FOR SYMMETRIC-KEY ALGORITHMS ARE FAST, BUT EXCHANGING KEYS IS AN ISSUE. THE CALCULATIONS INVOLVED IN PUBLIC-KEY CRYPTOGRAPHY TAKE A LOT OF TIME, BUT EXCHANGING KEYS TO IMPLEMENT A PUBLIC-KEY SCHEME IS SIMPLE.

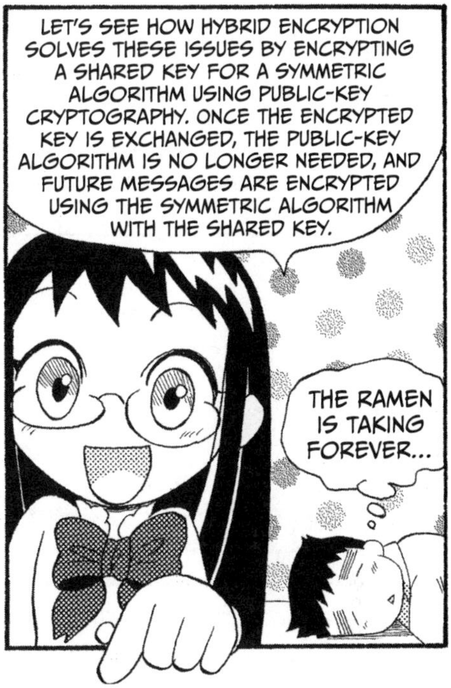
LET'S SEE HOW HYBRID ENCRYPTION SOLVES THESE ISSUES BY ENCRYPTING A SHARED KEY FOR A SYMMETRIC ALGORITHM USING PUBLIC-KEY CRYPTOGRAPHY. ONCE THE ENCRYPTED KEY IS EXCHANGED, THE PUBLIC-KEY ALGORITHM IS NO LONGER NEEDED, AND FUTURE MESSAGES ARE ENCRYPTED USING THE SYMMETRIC ALGORITHM WITH THE SHARED KEY.
THE RAMEN IS TAKING FOREVER...

Symmetric algorithm

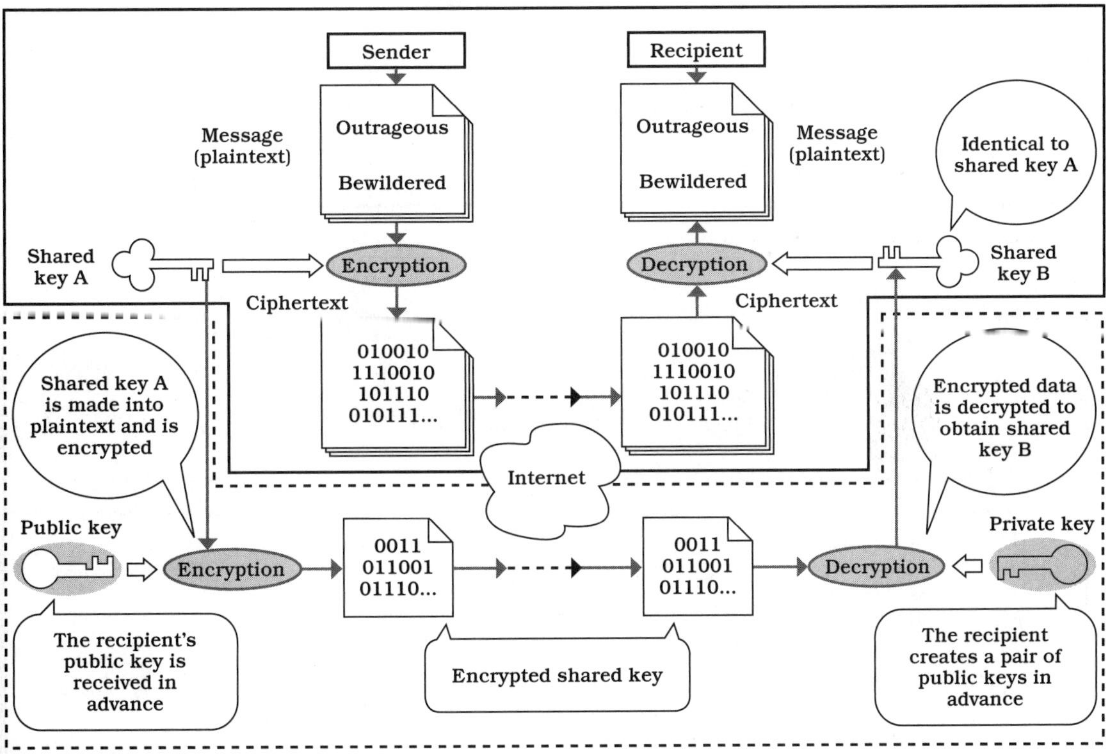
Sender
Message (plaintext)
Outraggeous
Bewildered
Shared key A
Encryption
Ciphertext
010010 1110010 101110 010111...
Recipient
Outrageous
Bewildered
Message (plaintext)
Identical to shared key A
Decryption
Shared key B
Ciphertext
010010 1110010 101110 010111...
Internet
Shared key A is made into plaintext and is encrypted
Public key
Encryption
0011 011001 01110...
0011 011001 01110...
Decryption
Private key
Encrypted data is decrypted to obtain shared key B
The recipient's public key is received in advance
Encrypted shared key
The recipient creates a pair of public keys in advance

Public-key encryption process

As demonstrated in the previous figure, public-key encryption is used only to encrypt and decrypt the shared key so that the symmetric-key algorithm can be used to encrypt and decrypt the actual messages that are exchanged. Since the shared key is encrypted using a public key, the greatest weakness of a shared key—the delivery of the key—is avoided.

So, now let's look at a real-life example of encryption using ramen orders.

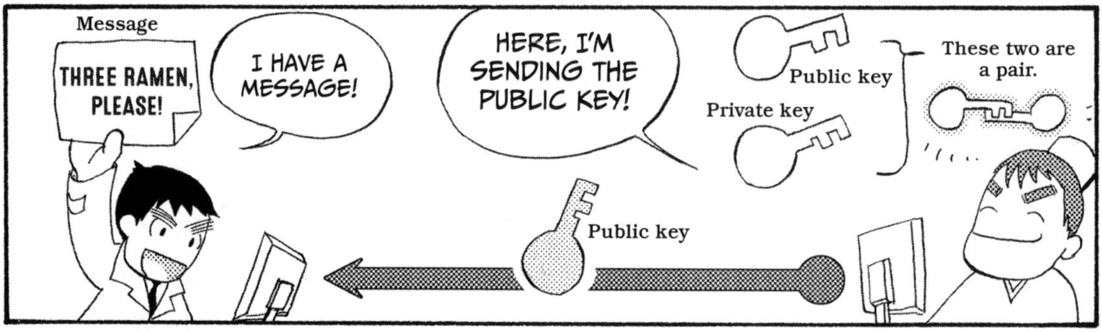
Message
THREE RAMEN, PLEASE!
I HAVE A MESSAGE!
HERE, I'M SENDING THE PUBLIC KEY!
Public key
Private key
These two are a pair.
Public key

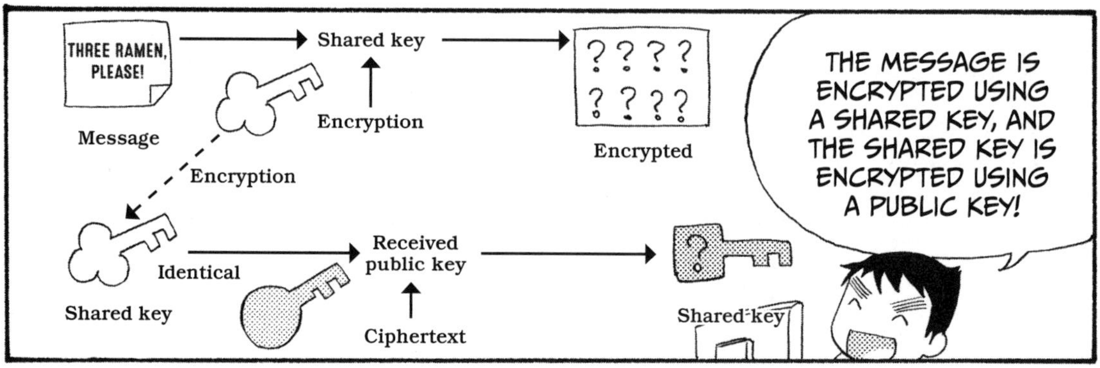
THREE RAMEN, PLEASE!
Message
Shared key
Encryption
Encrypted
Encryption
Shared key
Identical
Received public key
Ciphertext
Shared key
THE MESSAGE IS ENCRYPTED USING A SHARED KEY, AND THE SHARED KEY IS ENCRYPTED USING A PUBLIC KEY!

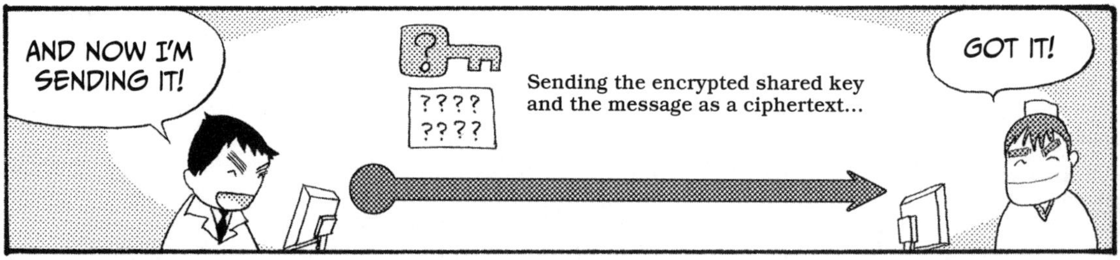
AND NOW I'M SENDING IT!
Sending the encrypted shared key and the message as a ciphertext...
GOT IT!

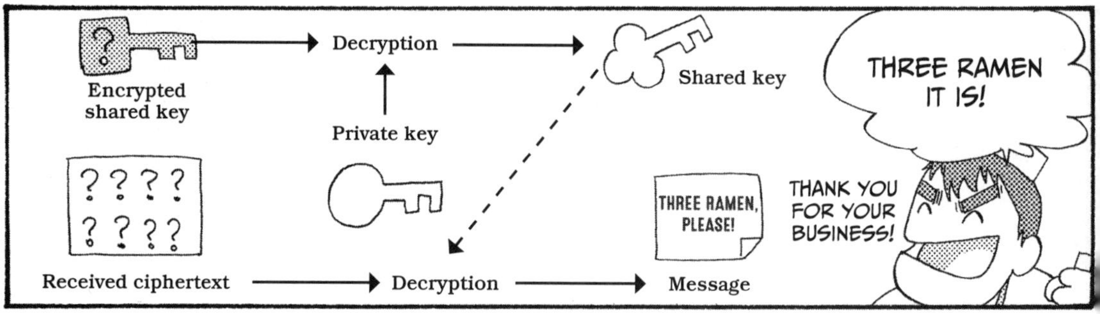
Encrypted shared key
Decryption
Private key
Shared key
Received ciphertext
Decryption
THREE RAMEN, PLEASE!
Message
THREE RAMEN IT IS!
THANK YOU FOR YOUR BUSINESS!

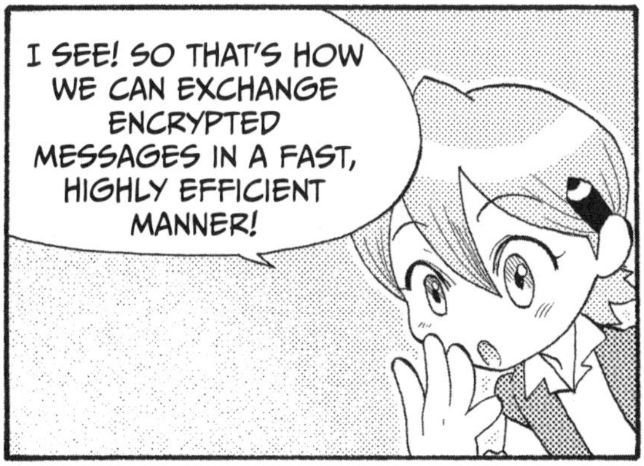
I SEE! SO THAT'S HOW WE CAN EXCHANGE ENCRYPTED MESSAGES IN A FAST, HIGHLY EFFICIENT MANNER!

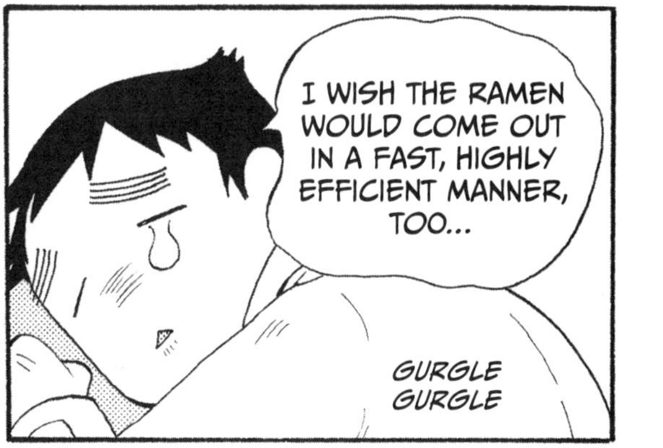
I WISH THE RAMEN WOULD COME OUT IN A FAST, HIGHLY EFFICIENT MANNER, TOO...
GURGLE GURGLE

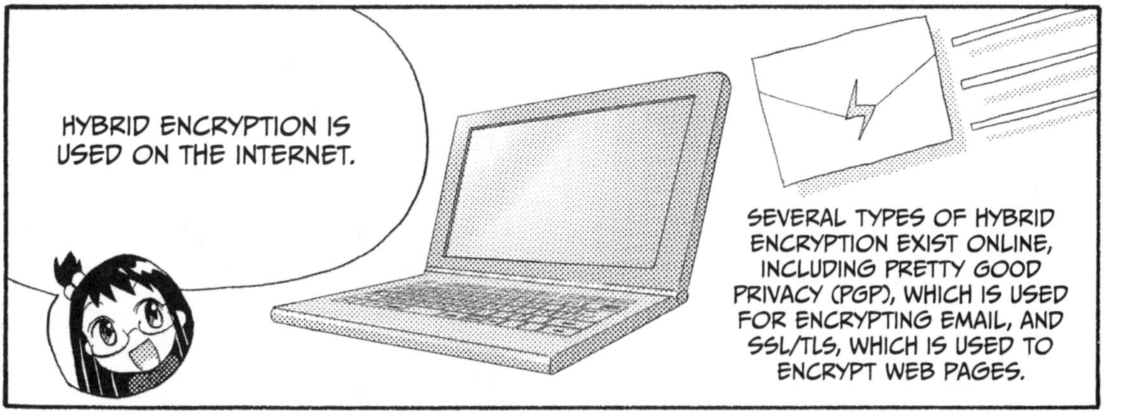
HYBRID ENCRYPTION IS USED ON THE INTERNET.
SEVERAL TYPES OF HYBRID ENCRYPTION EXIST ONLINE, INCLUDING PRETTY GOOD PRIVACY (PGP), WHICH IS USED FOR ENCRYPTING EMAIL, AND SSL/TLS, WHICH IS USED TO ENCRYPT WEB PAGES.

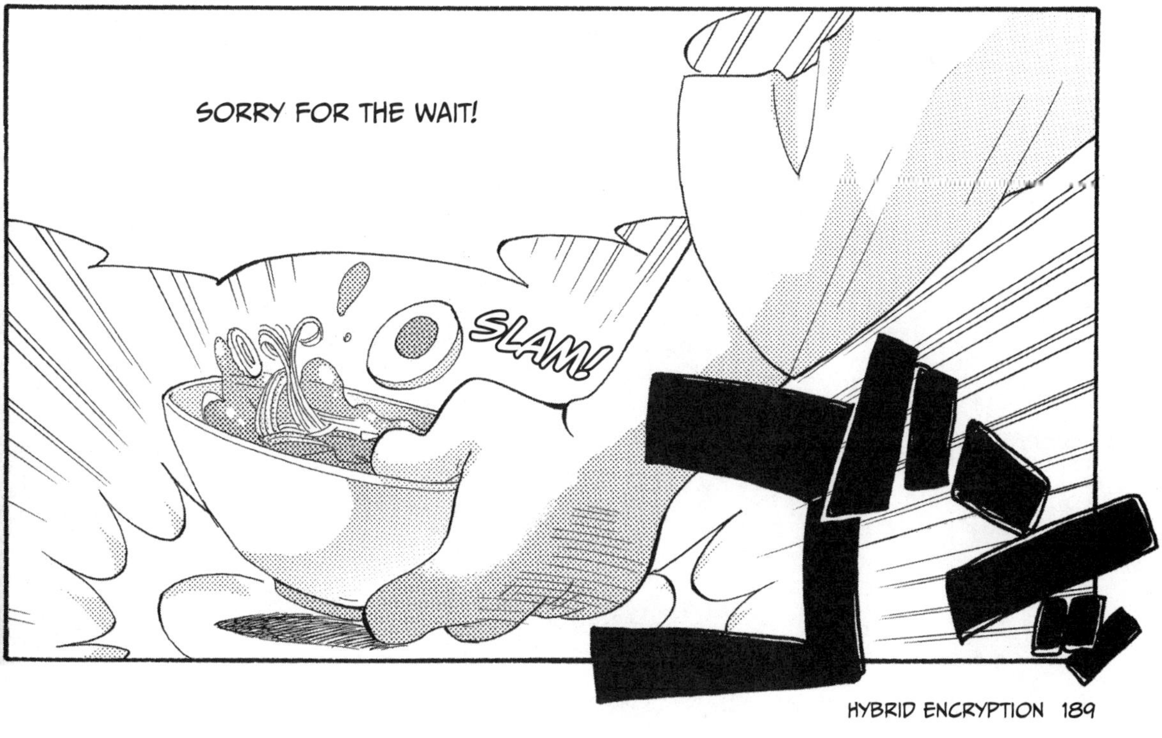
SORRY FOR THE WAIT!
SLAM!

HASH FUNCTIONS AND MESSAGE AUTHENTICATION CODES

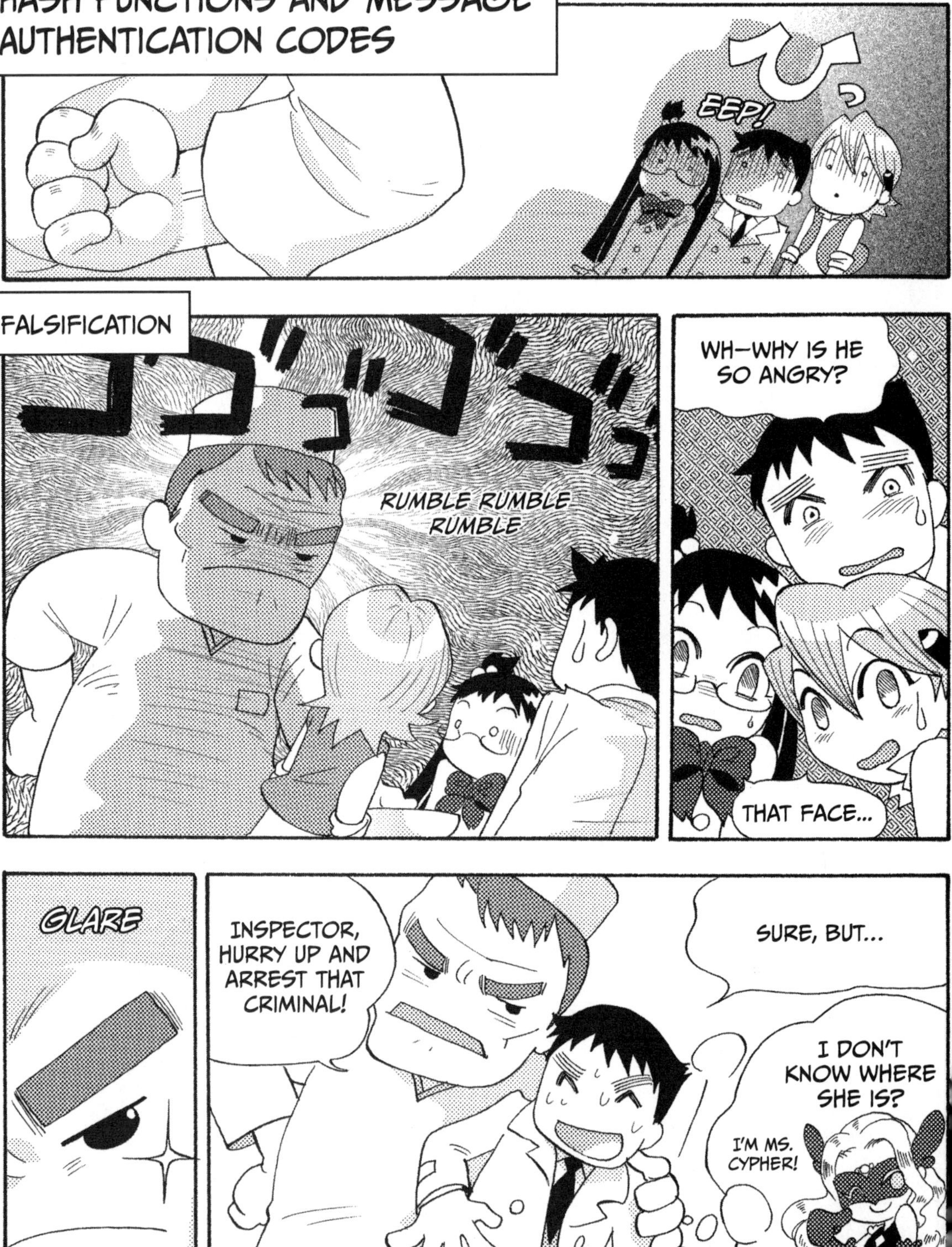

ひっ
EEP!
FALSIFICATION
ゴゴゴゴ
RUMBLE RUMBLE RUMBLE
WH—WHY IS HE SO ANGRY?
THAT FACE...
GLARE
INSPECTOR, HURRY UP AND ARREST THAT CRIMINAL!
SURE, BUT...
I DON'T KNOW WHERE SHE IS?
I'M MS. CYPHER!

WE LOST 29 BOWLS OF RAMEN THE OTHER DAY!

RAMEN?!

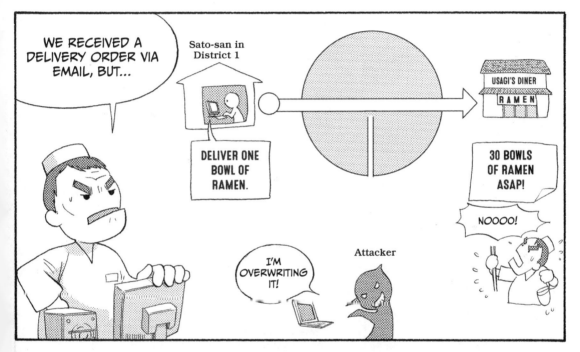

WE RECEIVED A DELIVERY ORDER VIA EMAIL, BUT...

Sato-san in District 1

DELIVER ONE BOWL OF RAMEN.

USAGI'S DINER

R A M E N

30 BOWLS OF RAMEN ASAP!

NOOOO!

I'M OVERWRITING IT!

Attacker

THE MESSAGE WAS TAMPERED WITH!

ARRGGHHH!

SCARY...

CAN'T YOU PREVENT MESSAGE TAMPERING USING ENCRYPTION?

OH DEAR...

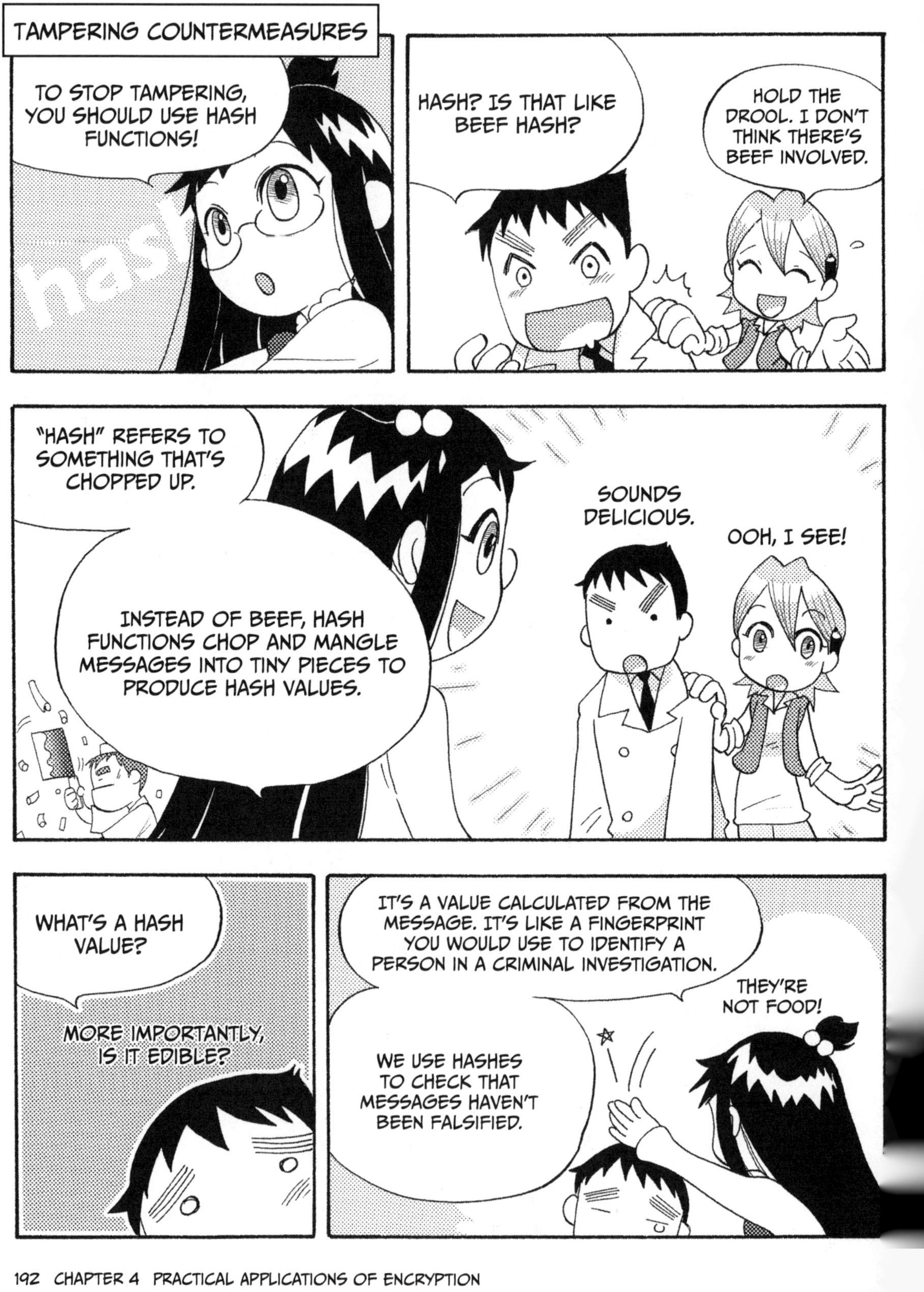
TAMPERING COUNTERMEASURES
TO STOP TAMPERING, YOU SHOULD USE HASH FUNCTIONS!
HASH? IS THAT LIKE BEEF HASH?
HOLD THE DROOL. I DON'T THINK THERE'S BEEF INVOLVED.
"HASH" REFERS TO SOMETHING THAT'S CHOPPED UP.
INSTEAD OF BEEF, HASH FUNCTIONS CHOP AND MANGLE MESSAGES INTO TINY PIECES TO PRODUCE HASH VALUES.
SOUNDS DELICIOUS.
OOH, I SEE!
WHAT'S A HASH VALUE?
MORE IMPORTANTLY, IS IT EDIBLE?
IT'S A VALUE CALCULATED FROM THE MESSAGE. IT'S LIKE A FINGERPRINT YOU WOULD USE TO IDENTIFY A PERSON IN A CRIMINAL INVESTIGATION.
WE USE HASHES TO CHECK THAT MESSAGES HAVEN'T BEEN FALSIFIED.
THEY'RE NOT FOOD!

HASH FUNCTIONS

A hash value identifies a message, like a fingerprint. The hash value is a small, fixed size, whereas the input is often larger than the hash. A hash function is used to calculate a hash value from a message.

The sender transmits a hash value with a message to guarantee the message's integrity. A message has *integrity* when the recipient is assured that the message hasn't been falsified. The recipient recalculates the hash using the same hash function as the sender and then compares that calculated hash to the hash attached to the message. If the values are the same, the message hasn't been falsified. This process, shown in the following figure, is called performing a *checksum*.

Sender
Buddha and all of creation
Hash function (fingerprint extraction)
Message (plaintext)
Fingerprint extraction
Buddha and all of creation
Message (plaintext)
0101 001101 111011
Hash value (fingerprint)
Internet
Hash function
0101 001101 111011
Tampering has occurred
Hashes are different
Results
Compare
Hashes are the same
Tampering has not occurred
Buddha and all of creation
Message (plaintext)
+
0101 001101 111011
Hash value (fingerprint)
Buddha and all of creation
Message (plaintext)
Recipient

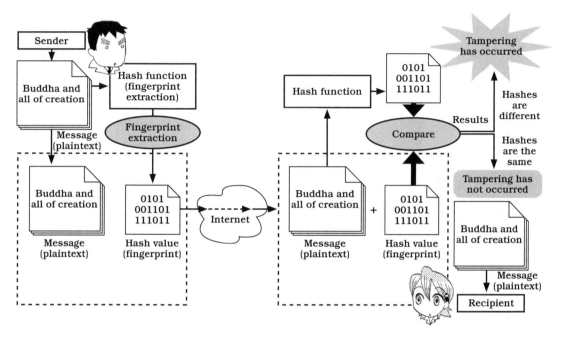

A hash function is a one-way function. The original message can't be derived from the hash value. This property is referred to as *irreversibility*.

Hash functions need to be resistant to *collision attacks*, which guess the hashes for messages. Because a hash needs to be unique to a message, the hash function can't produce the same hash for different messages. When a hash function fulfills this requirement, it has *strong collision resistance*. In addition to being resistant to hash collisions, a hash function shouldn't produce similar values for similar messages. For example, if we were to give the input 01001 to a hash function, it should output a different value than if we used 01000 as the input, which differs by only 1 bit. Real-life hash functions have a larger input than output, which means collisions are unavoidable. Therefore, they don't have strong collision resistance. However, hash functions can be developed to make finding an input that matches an output as difficult as possible. This is accomplished by using a large output and sets of calculations that are thought to be resistant to reverse engineering. Some hash functions developed with these requirements in mind are MD5, SHA-1, SHA-256, and SHA-512, but these functions are not foolproof. For example, researchers discovered that MD5 and SHA-1 are vulnerable to collision, so they are no longer safe to use.

IDENTITY FRAUD

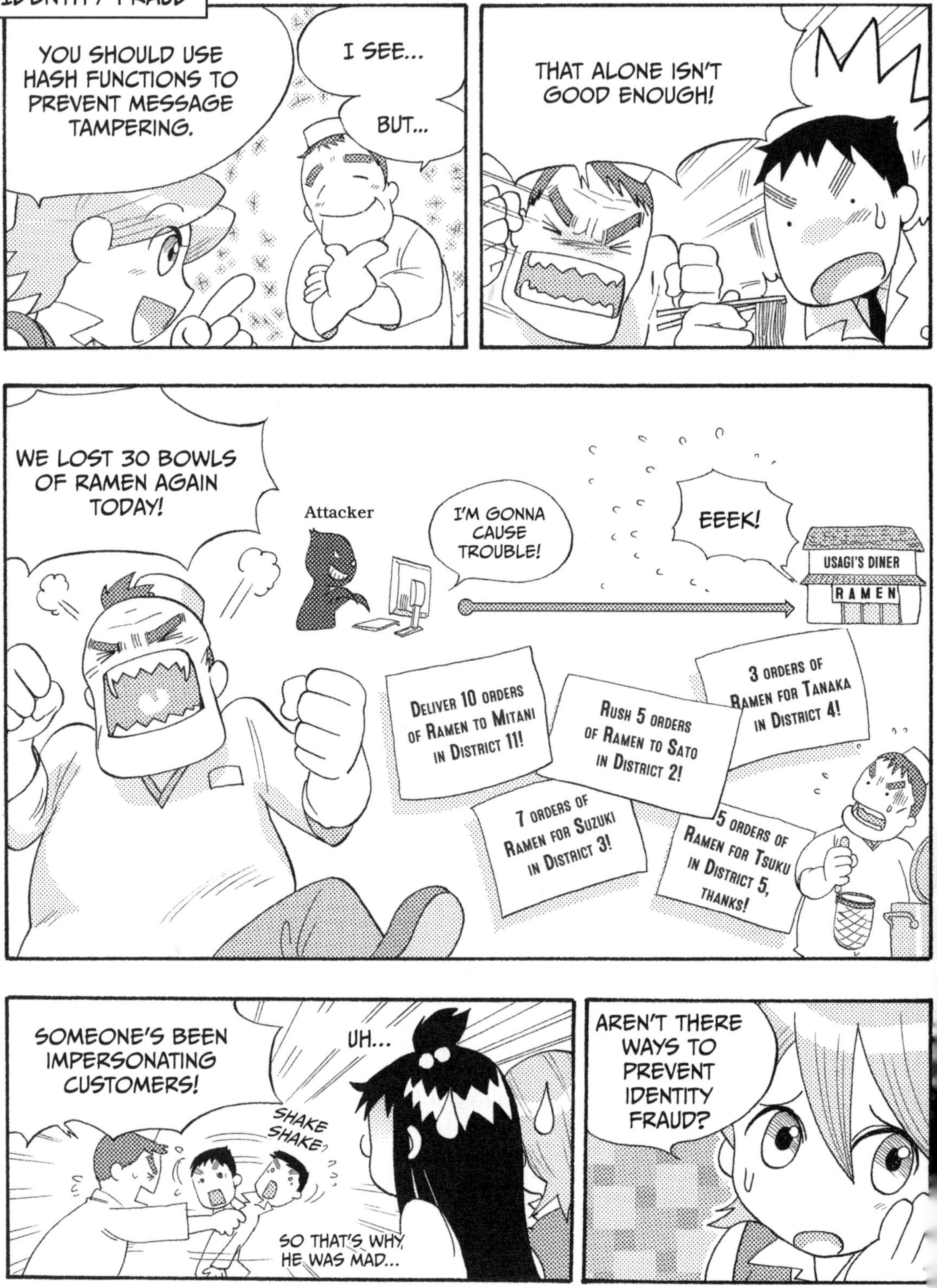
YOU SHOULD USE HASH FUNCTIONS TO PREVENT MESSAGE TAMPERING.
I SEE...
BUT...
THAT ALONE ISN'T GOOD ENOUGH!
WE LOST 30 BOWLS OF RAMEN AGAIN TODAY!
Attacker
I'M GONNA CAUSE TROUBLE!
EEEK!
USAGI'S DINER
RAMEN
DELIVER 10 ORDERS OF RAMEN TO MITANI IN DISTRICT 11!
RUSH 5 ORDERS OF RAMEN TO SATO IN DISTRICT 2!
3 ORDERS OF RAMEN FOR TANAKA IN DISTRICT 4!
7 ORDERS OF RAMEN FOR SUZUKI IN DISTRICT 3!
5 ORDERS OF RAMEN FOR TSUKU IN DISTRICT 5, THANKS!
SOMEONE'S BEEN IMPERSONATING CUSTOMERS!
UH...
SHAKE SHAKE
SO THAT'S WHY HE WAS MAD...
AREN'T THERE WAYS TO PREVENT IDENTITY FRAUD?

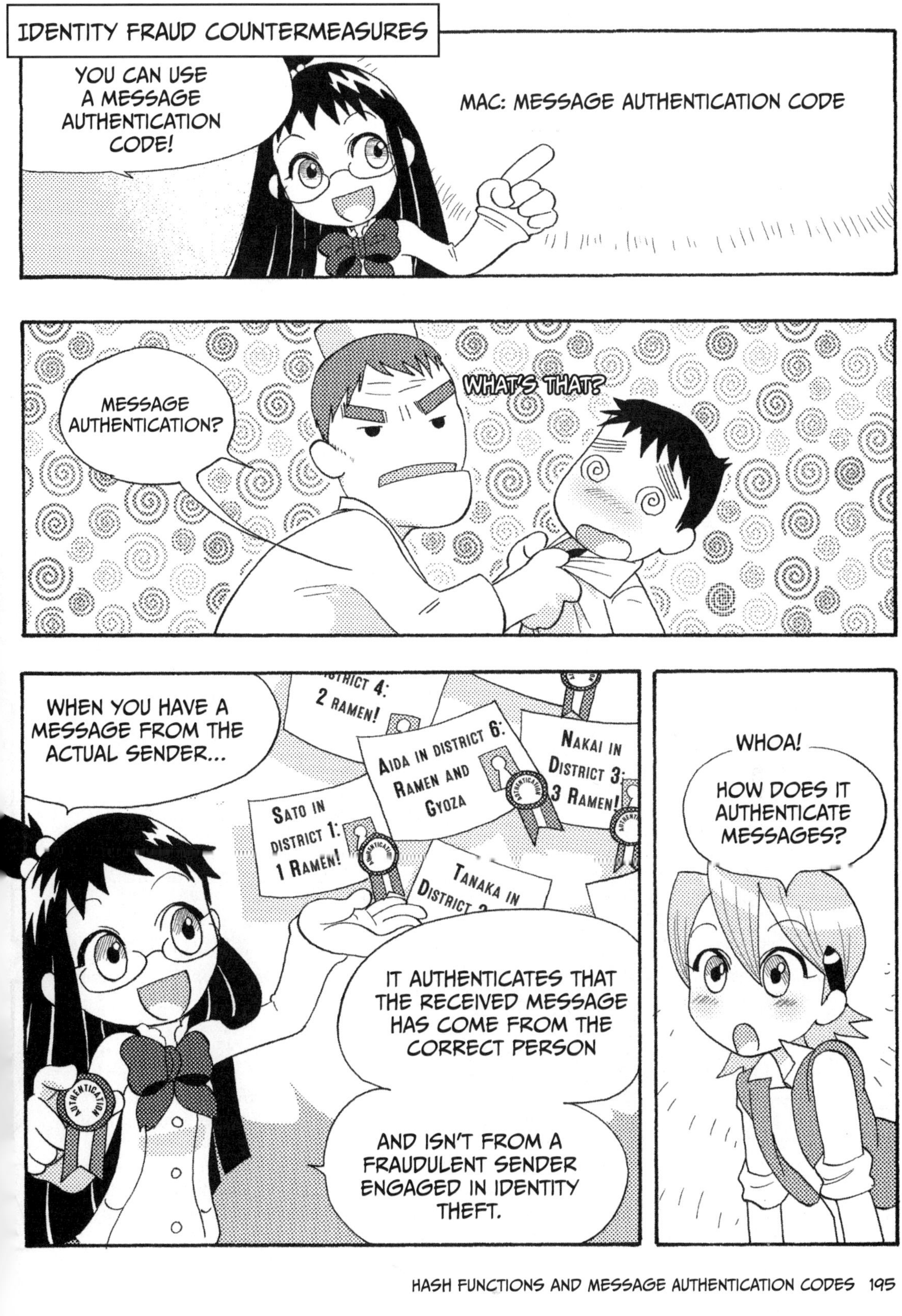
IDENTITY FRAUD COUNTERMEASURES
YOU CAN USE A MESSAGE AUTHENTICATION CODE!
MAC: MESSAGE AUTHENTICATION CODE
MESSAGE AUTHENTICATION?
WHAT'S THAT?
WHEN YOU HAVE A MESSAGE FROM THE ACTUAL SENDER...
2 RAMEN!
AIDA IN DISTRICT 6: RAMEN AND GYOZA
NAKAI IN DISTRICT 3: 3 RAMEN!
SATO IN DISTRICT 1: 1 RAMEN!
TANAKA IN
AUTHENTICATION
IT AUTHENTICATES THAT THE RECEIVED MESSAGE HAS COME FROM THE CORRECT PERSON
AND ISN'T FROM A FRAUDULENT SENDER ENGAGED IN IDENTITY THEFT.
WHOA!
HOW DOES IT AUTHENTICATE MESSAGES?

STRUCTURE OF MESSAGE AUTHENTICATION CODES

A message authentication code is a procedure that confirms a message's authenticity and certifies a message. Let's look at the following figure to learn how a message authentication code can be produced.

The sender transmits a message and the MAC value (also called a tag) derived from their message. The MAC value is used to perform a checksum in the same way as with a hash value.

Sender
Shared key
The shared key is exchanged between the sender and recipient prior to the message authentication protocol
Generation of a message authentication code (a one-way hash function dependent on a key)
Pass the buck
Grim prospects
Message (plaintext)
MAC value is generated
Pass the buck
Grim prospects
+
0111
011101
110010...
Message (plaintext)
MAC value
Internet
Shared key
MAC value is generated
0111
011101
110010...
Recipient
Message (plaintext)
Pass the buck
Grim prospects
No falsification
Same
Compare
Results
Different
Pass the buck
Grim prospects
+
0111
011101
110010...
Message (plaintext)
MAC value
Falsified message!

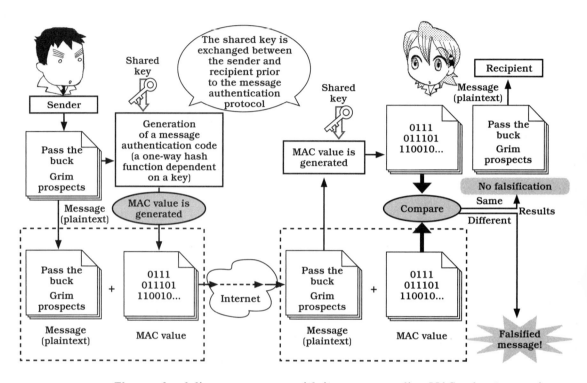

The sender delivers a message with its corresponding MAC value to a recipient. The recipient calculates a MAC value from the message they received and compares their MAC with the original MAC value from the sender. If the two MAC values match, the recipient is assured that the integrity of the message is intact and that the message is from the sender.

NOTE: *The recipient knows that the message is from the sender because it is assumed that only the sender and recipient have the key. If the recipient didn't create the tag (the MAC value), then it must be from the sender.*

Think of a message authentication code as a one-way hash function that is associated with the shared key. MAC values are similar to hash functions because they possess the same mechanisms and confirm the authenticity of a message by calculating and comparing values on the sender's and recipient's ends.

When the two parties calculate the MAC value, they use a key that is shared only between themselves. By calculating the MAC value from the message, the receiving party can be assured that the sender of the message is in fact the person who has the same shared key.

MAC values provide integrity for a message. When the two MAC values are identical, the message has not been tampered with en route from the sender. When the two MAC values differ, the message has potentially been falsified, and the sender may not be the one who shared the key.

A message authentication code works in this way, but as with public-key encryption, there are issues with the security of the shared key.

Message authentication codes are also used for SSL/TLS, which is used by international banks for money transfers and in online shopping.

REPUDIATION

MISTER, NOW YOU CAN REST EASY!

NOW LET'S HAVE SOME RAMEN!

NO—WAIT!

IS THERE STILL AN ISSUE?

WHAT WOULD YOU DO IN THIS SITUATION?

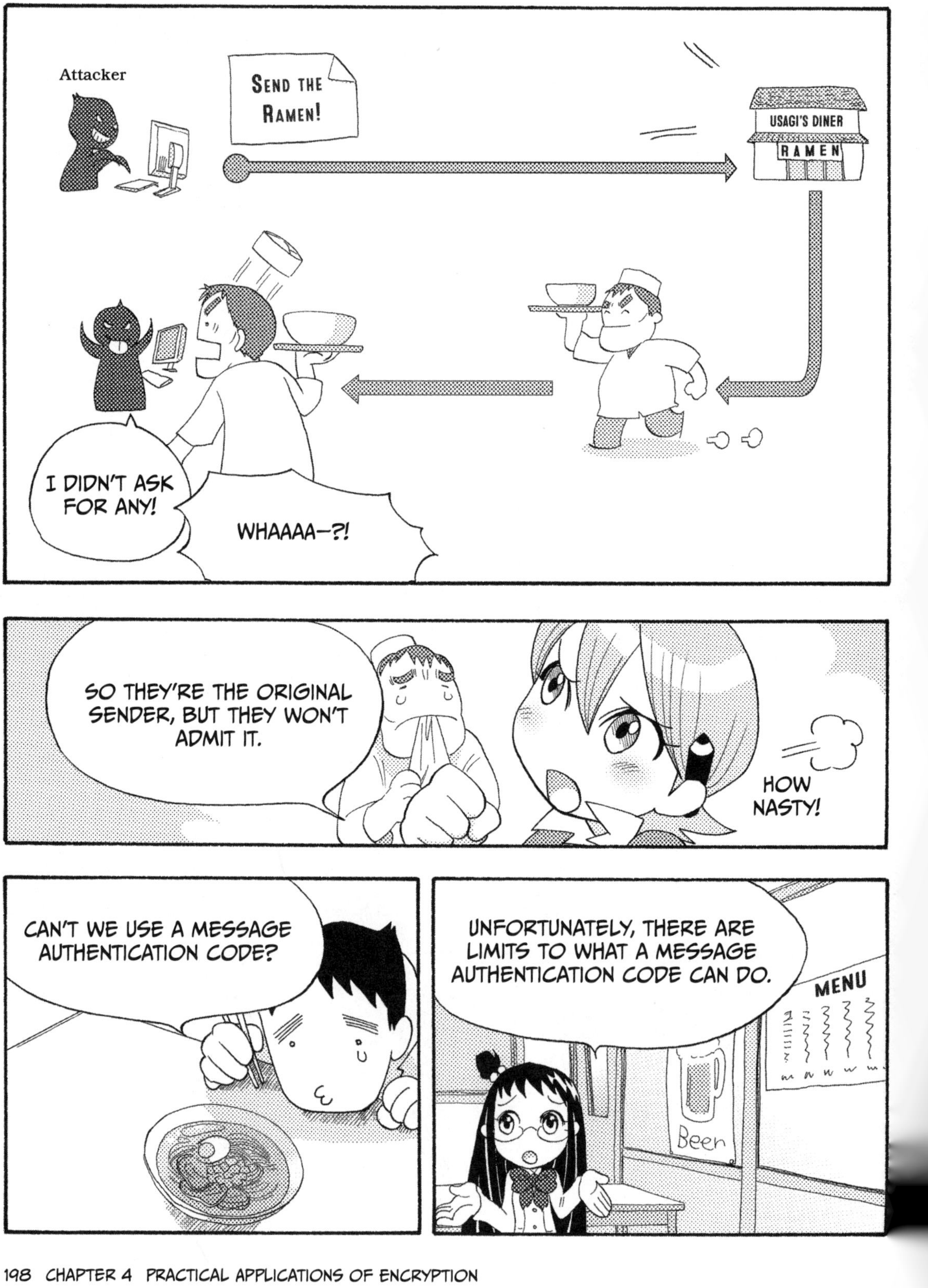
Attacker
SEND THE RAMEN!
USAGI'S DINER
RAMEN
I DIDN'T ASK FOR ANY!
WHAAAA–?!
SO THEY'RE THE ORIGINAL SENDER, BUT THEY WON'T ADMIT IT.
HOW NASTY!
CAN'T WE USE A MESSAGE AUTHENTICATION CODE?
UNFORTUNATELY, THERE ARE LIMITS TO WHAT A MESSAGE AUTHENTICATION CODE CAN DO.
MENU
Beer

DRAWBACKS OF MESSAGE AUTHENTICATION CODES

Repudiation is the ability to deny being the sender of a message. For example, a message and MAC value are sent from A to B, and afterward A claims, "I didn't send this message to B. B made this up." There's no way to disprove A's statement, and even if B enlisted the help of a third party to find out the truth, this third party wouldn't have a way to determine whether the message and MAC value were generated by A or by B.

When a message is sent from A to B, B can't verify to a third party C that the message was sent from A. This is because the message and MAC value can be generated by either A or B. In other words, C is unable to determine whether the MAC value was generated by A or B.

WHAT SHOULD I DO?!

ギュー

SQUEEZE

ECCCK!

THERE'S A GOOD WAY TO DEFEND AGAINST REPUDIATION!

DIGITAL SIGNATURES

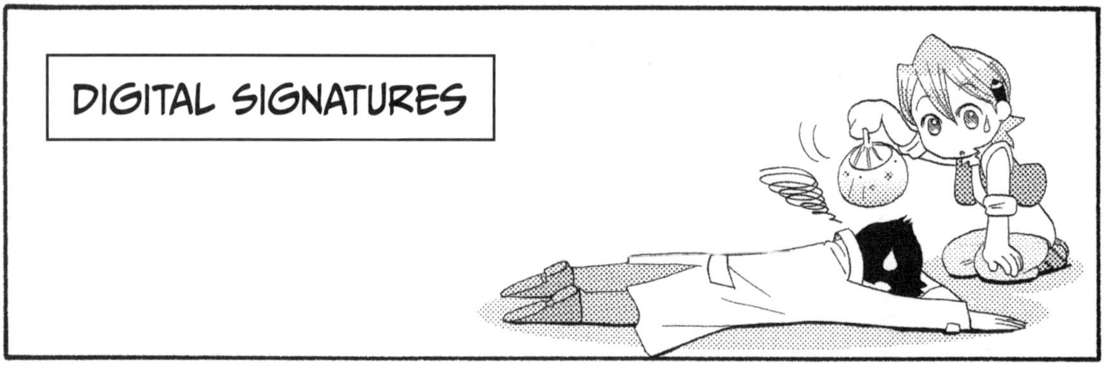

REPUDIATION MEASURES

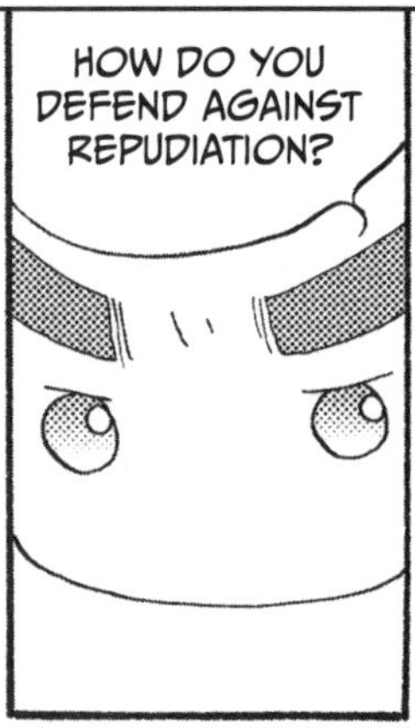
HOW DO YOU DEFEND AGAINST REPUDIATION?

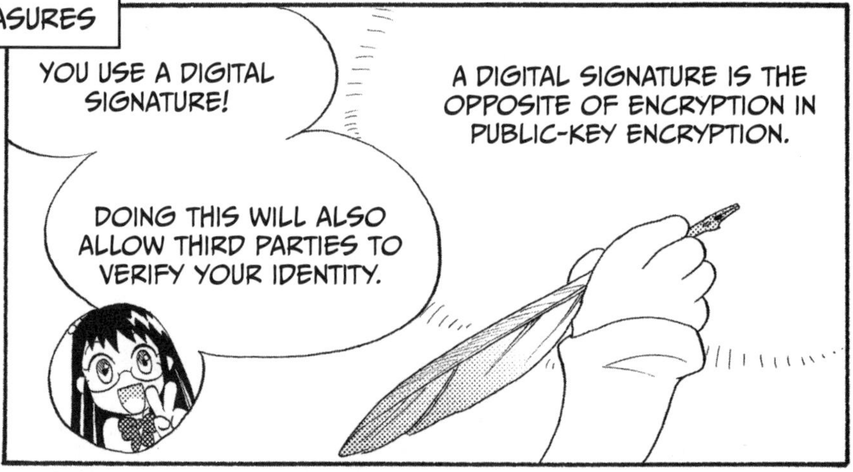
YOU USE A DIGITAL SIGNATURE!
DOING THIS WILL ALSO ALLOW THIRD PARTIES TO VERIFY YOUR IDENTITY.
A DIGITAL SIGNATURE IS THE OPPOSITE OF ENCRYPTION IN PUBLIC-KEY ENCRYPTION.

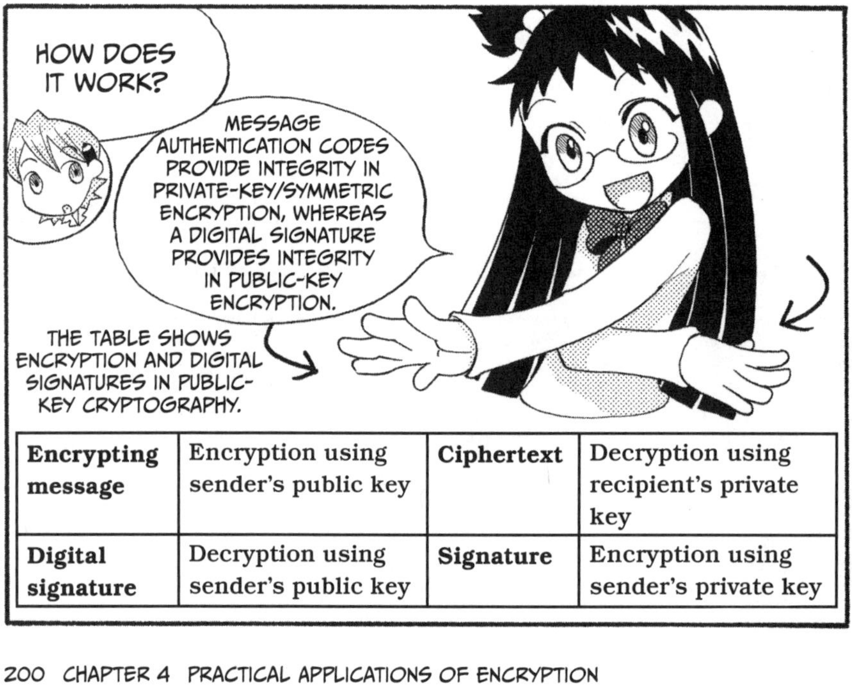
HOW DOES IT WORK?
MESSAGE AUTHENTICATION CODES PROVIDE INTEGRITY IN PRIVATE-KEY/SYMMETRIC ENCRYPTION, WHEREAS A DIGITAL SIGNATURE PROVIDES INTEGRITY IN PUBLIC-KEY ENCRYPTION.
THE TABLE SHOWS ENCRYPTION AND DIGITAL SIGNATURES IN PUBLIC-KEY CRYPTOGRAPHY.

Encrypting message	Encryption using sender's public key	**Ciphertext**	Decryption using recipient's private key
Digital signature	Decryption using sender's public key	**Signature**	Encryption using sender's private key

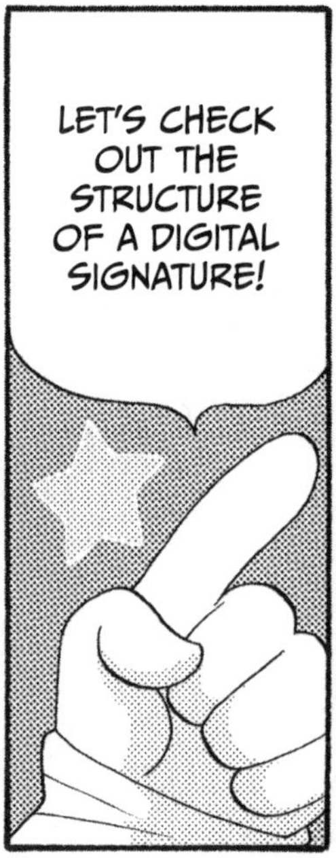
LET'S CHECK OUT THE STRUCTURE OF A DIGITAL SIGNATURE!

THE WORKINGS OF A DIGITAL SIGNATURE

When using a digital signature, the sender signs a message that has been encrypted using their own private key. This signature is sent to the recipient along with the message.

The recipient decrypts the signature using the sender's public key to obtain the message. Then the recipient compares the decrypted message to the sent message.

If the two are the same, the message is verified as authentic, and the sender is thought to be legitimate. Because the sender's public key is used for decryption, a third party can also verify the signature. When a third party is able to verify that a message came from a specific sender, we have nonrepudiation—the sender can't deny they sent a message.

Let's look at some examples of how a digital signature works. The following figure has been simplified to make the general concept of a digital signature easier to understand.

Sender
Private key
Public-key encryption and decryption
Public key
Recipient
Received message
A warrior worth 1,000 warriors Let the brush follow the mind
Encryption
Decryption
No problems with authentication
Message (plaintext)
Compare
Same
Different
Result
010010 101100 010011 010011...
Internet
Signature (ciphertext)
Problem with authentication!

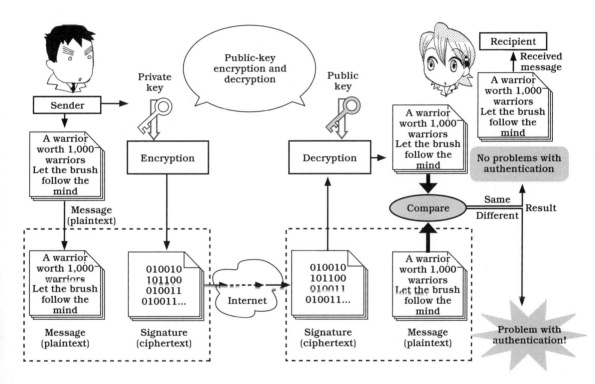

In this figure, the message shown is immediately encrypted and signed. In reality, it takes time to sign an entire message with public-key cryptography.

It is common to first use a hash function to turn the message into a hash value and then convert the hash into a signature, as shown in the following figure.

Sender
Scenic beauty
Castle in the sky
Hash function
011010
111100
Hash value
Private key
Encryption
Scenic beauty
Castle in the sky
Message (plaintext)
xxxx
xxxx
xxxx
Signature (hash-value ciphertext)
Internet
xxxx
xxxx
xxxx
Signature (hash-function ciphertext)
Scenic beauty
Castle in the sky
Message (plaintext)
Public key
Decryption
Hash value obtained from encrypted data
011010
111100
Compare
Different
Problem with authentication!
Same
011010
111100
Hash value obtained from received message
Hash function
No problems with authentication
Scenic beauty
Castle in the sky
Message (plaintext)
Recipient

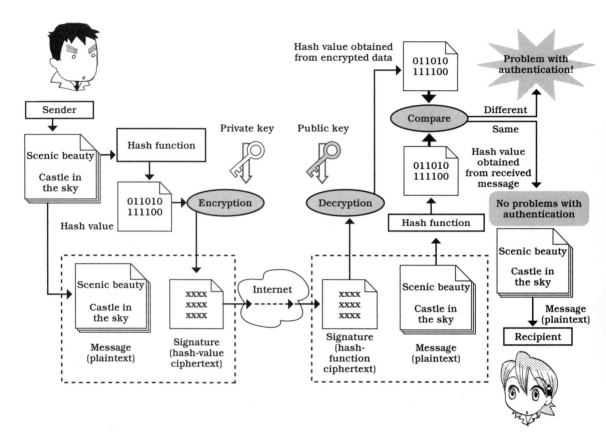

A digital signature is also used to generate a server certificate that authenticates the legitimacy of an SSL/TLS server. A certificate is something that appends a digital signature to a public key (in this case, the server's public key). Certificates also append digital signatures to software downloads to protect software from being falsified.

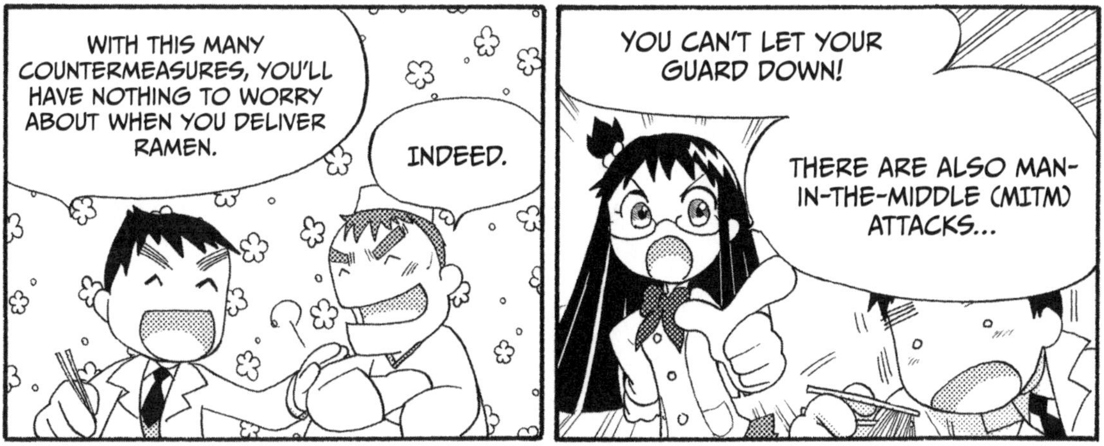
WITH THIS MANY COUNTERMEASURES, YOU'LL HAVE NOTHING TO WORRY ABOUT WHEN YOU DELIVER RAMEN.
INDEED.
YOU CAN'T LET YOUR GUARD DOWN!
THERE ARE ALSO MAN-IN-THE-MIDDLE (MITM) ATTACKS...

MAN-IN-THE-MIDDLE ATTACK

Let's say we have a sender A and a receiver B. We'll have Mr. Sato of District 1 be A and Usagi's Diner be B. Sender A corresponds with B using encryption, but first he has to receive B's public key. A person in the middle, an attacker, intercepts the public key as it is transmitted from B to A and then sends their own public key to A instead.

Since the encrypted message sent by A has been encrypted using the attacker's public key, the attacker can decode the message using their own private key. The attacker alters the contents of the message, encrypts it using B's public key, and sends it. Once the attacker is done, B has no idea that the message was tampered with and has no way to check for falsification. Let's see what this looks like.

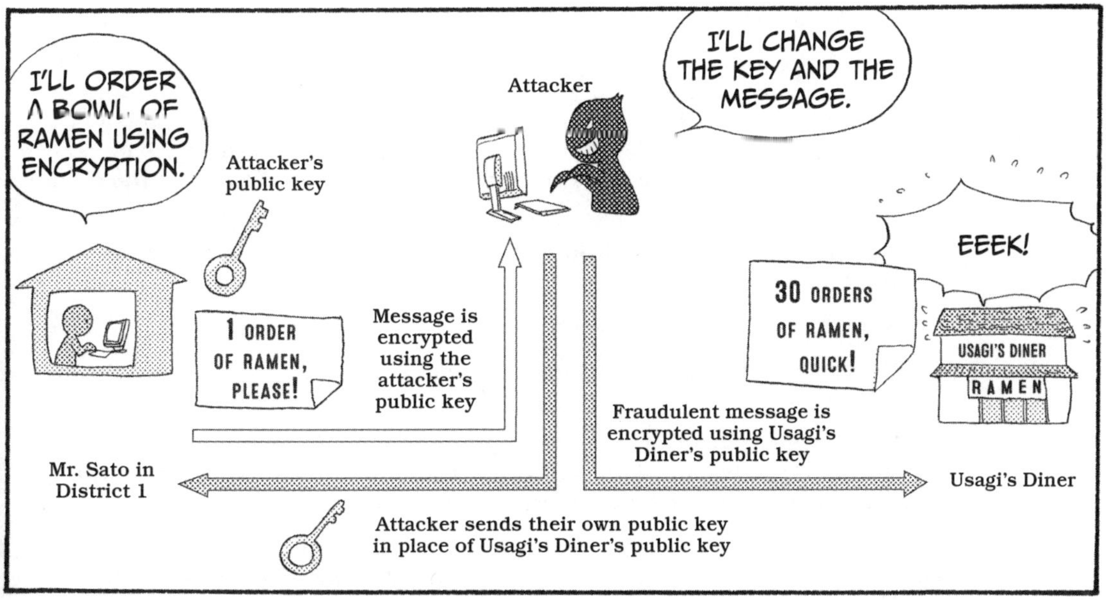
I'LL ORDER A BOWL OF RAMEN USING ENCRYPTION.
Attacker's public key
Attacker
I'LL CHANGE THE KEY AND THE MESSAGE.
EEEK!
1 ORDER OF RAMEN, PLEASE!
Message is encrypted using the attacker's public key
30 ORDERS OF RAMEN, QUICK!
USAGI'S DINER
RAMEN
Fraudulent message is encrypted using Usagi's Diner's public key
Mr. Sato in District 1
Usagi's Diner
Attacker sends their own public key in place of Usagi's Diner's public key

HMM...
BUT IF YOU KNOW WHOSE KEY WAS USED TO ENCRYPT THE MESSAGE, THAT TAKES CARE OF THE PROBLEM!
THAT'S RIGHT!
IF YOU HAVE A TRUSTED THIRD PARTY (A CERTIFICATE AUTHORITY) WHO CAN ACCURATELY VERIFY WHOSE KEY IT IS, YOU'RE GOOD!

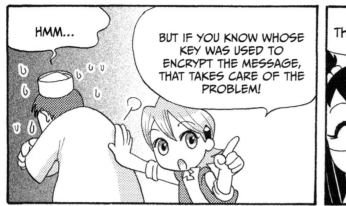

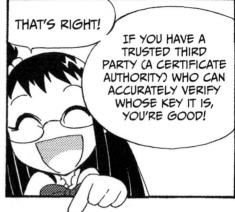

USING CERTIFICATES TO PROTECT AGAINST MAN-IN-THE-MIDDLE ATTACKS

A *certificate* attaches the digital signature of a public key and that key to an identity. A certificate is published by a *certificate authority*. When someone wants to make a public key available, they register their public key using a certificate authority and simultaneously request publication of the certificate.

Based on this request, the certificate authority verifies the authenticity of the user, and, if the public key meets the certificate authority's standards, the certificate authority generates a certificate for the public-key and digital-signature set. Sometimes the user creates the public- and private-key set, while other times the certificate authority generates these during registration.

The process of verifying the certificate guarantees that the public key indeed belongs to a specific user. The certificate authority, a trusted third party, verifies that the public key is correct on behalf of the user. Now let's look at the procedure shown in the next figure and outlined in these six steps.

1. User A requests that the certificate authority publish the user's public key.
2. After the certificate authority confirms the identity of User A, the certificate authority produces a digital signature for User A's public key, and the certificate is published. The published certificate affixes a digital signature to User A's public key by means of the certificate authority. The certificate is usually made up of the public key of User A (PKA) and the digital signature of PKA.
3. The certificate authority stores the certificate in a *repository* (a data storehouse).
4. User B downloads User A's certificate from the repository.
5. User B decrypts the digital signature using the certificate authority's public key.
6. The decrypted key is compared with the public key attached to the certificate. If the two keys are the same, the public key included with the certificate is verified as belonging to User A.

By means of the certificate-issuing procedure, User B can obtain User A's verified public key. By using User A's secured public key, User B can verify that the message was encrypted with User A's private key and affixed with a digital signature.

The validated message will simultaneously meet the following three conditions:

1. The message has not been falsified.
2. The message has not been generated by a third party posing as User A.
3. User A can't repudiate the message. In other words, User A can't deny they generated the message.

As long as the legitimacy of a public key is verified, any message affixed with the public key's digital signature is assured to meet these three conditions. Let's finish up by discussing the mechanisms behind public-key infrastructure (PKI).

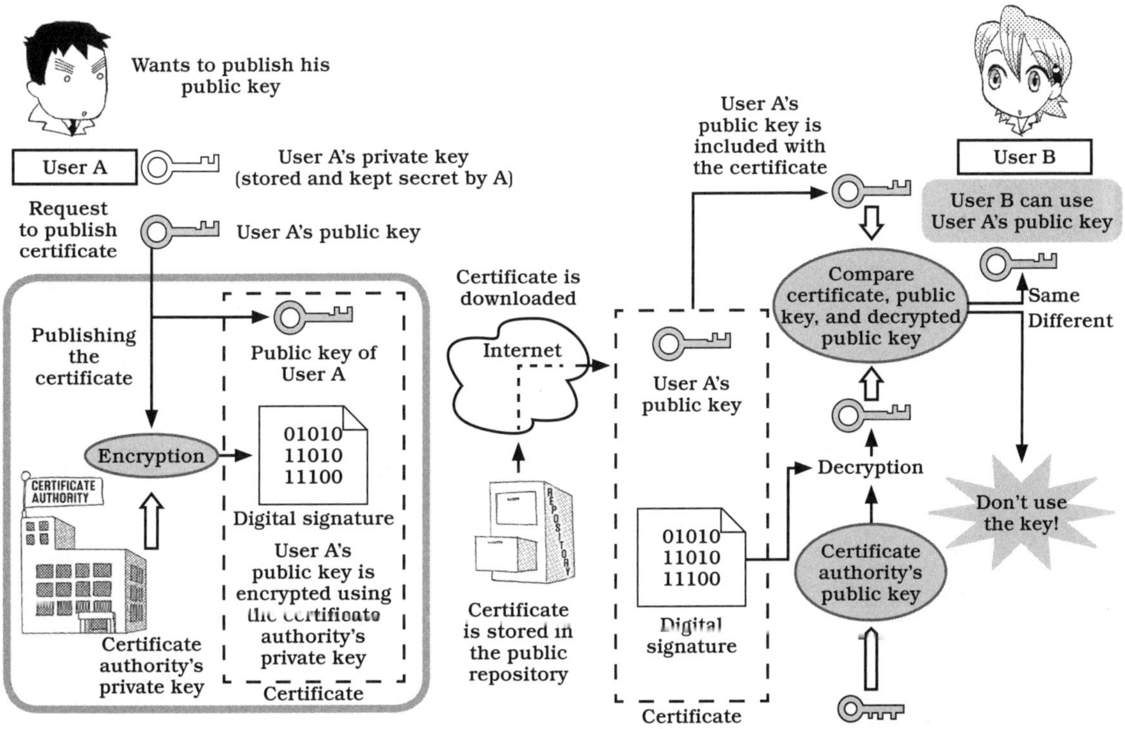

Wants to publish his public key
User A
User A's private key (stored and kept secret by A)
Request to publish certificate
User A's public key
Publishing the certificate
Public key of User A
Encryption
01010
11010
11100
Digital signature
User A's public key is encrypted using the certificate authority's private key
CERTIFICATE AUTHORITY
Certificate authority's private key
Certificate
Certificate is downloaded
Internet
REPOSITORY
Certificate is stored in the public repository
User A's public key is included with the certificate
User A's public key
01010
11010
11100
Digital signature
Certificate
User B
User B can use User A's public key
Compare certificate, public key, and decrypted public key
Same
Different
Decryption
Certificate authority's public key
Don't use the key!

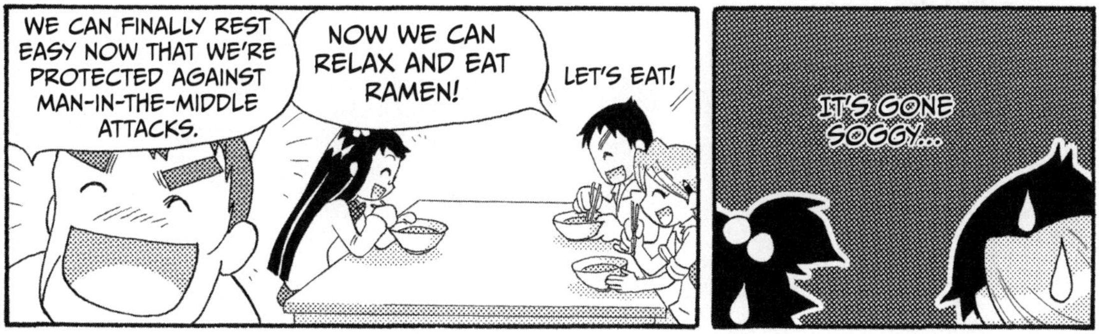

WE CAN FINALLY REST EASY NOW THAT WE'RE PROTECTED AGAINST MAN-IN-THE-MIDDLE ATTACKS.
NOW WE CAN RELAX AND EAT RAMEN!
LET'S EAT!
IT'S GONE SOGGY...

PUBLIC-KEY INFRASTRUCTURE

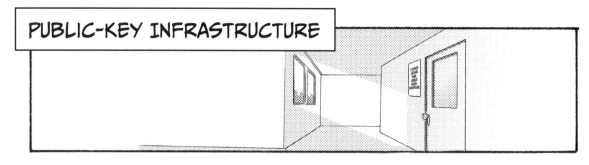

WE'RE ALMOST DONE STUDYING ENCRYPTION!

BUT CAN WE REALLY RELY ON THOSE CERTIFICATES?

HOW CAN WE KNOW A CERTIFICATE ACTUALLY WAS PUBLISHED BY A CERTIFICATE AUTHORITY?

CAN WE REALLY TRUST THE CERTIFICATE AUTHORITY?

I STILL HAVE SOME DOUBTS.

HOW DO WE KNOW INFORMATION IS AUTHENTIC?

FOR EXAMPLE... LET'S THINK ABOUT IT IN TERMS OF CURRENCY.

TA-DA!

OOOOH, A ¥10,000 NOTE!

RUKA'S LOADED!

IN REALITY, THIS IS JUST A SLIP OF PAPER.

IF THE VALUE OF MONEY INFLATES...

HUH? THE ¥10,000 NOTE THAT WAS IN MY WALLET IS GONE...

IF MONEY LOSES VALUE, IT REALLY WILL BE JUST A SLIP OF PAPER.

STRAWBERRY SHORTCAKE ¥1,000,000

BUT NOTES ARE ISSUED BY THE BANK OF JAPAN, WHICH WE CAN TRUST, RIGHT?

SO IT WAS MINE! WHEN DID YOU EVEN...?

HERE, I'LL GIVE IT BACK TO YOU.

HERE!

CURRENCY

BANK OF JAPAN

THAT'S NOT ALL!

THE BANK IS CRUCIAL TO MAINTAINING THE STABILITY OF PAPER MONEY'S VALUE SO CITIZENS CAN FEEL SECURE USING CURRENCY.

IN OTHER WORDS, CURRENCY HAS VALUE BECAUSE OF SOCIAL INFRASTRUCTURE.

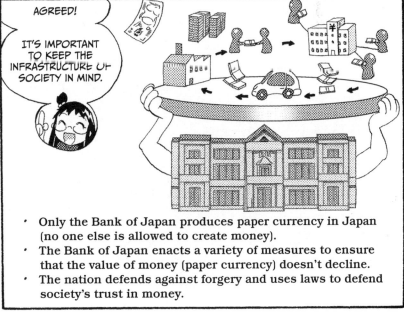

AGREED!

IT'S IMPORTANT TO KEEP THE INFRASTRUCTURE OF SOCIETY IN MIND.

- Only the Bank of Japan produces paper currency in Japan (no one else is allowed to create money).
- The Bank of Japan enacts a variety of measures to ensure that the value of money (paper currency) doesn't decline.
- The nation defends against forgery and uses laws to defend society's trust in money.

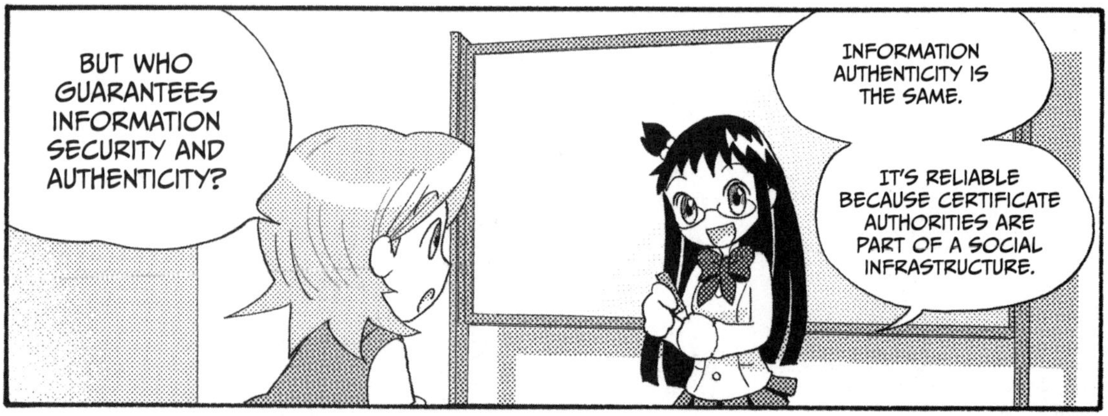
BUT WHO GUARANTEES INFORMATION SECURITY AND AUTHENTICITY?
INFORMATION AUTHENTICITY IS THE SAME.
IT'S RELIABLE BECAUSE CERTIFICATE AUTHORITIES ARE PART OF A SOCIAL INFRASTRUCTURE.

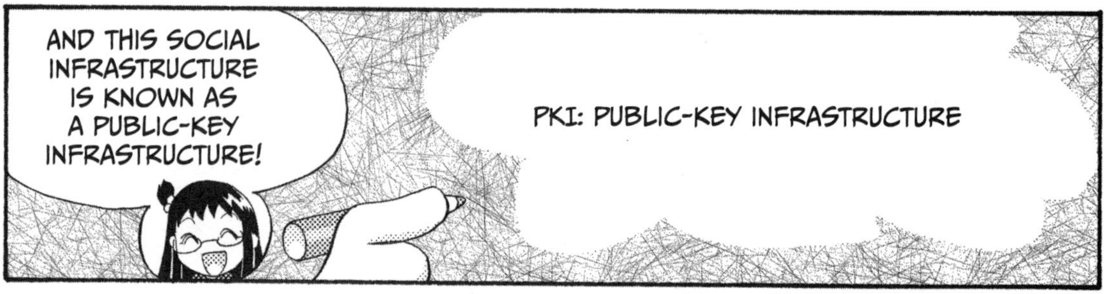
AND THIS SOCIAL INFRASTRUCTURE IS KNOWN AS A PUBLIC-KEY INFRASTRUCTURE!
PKI: PUBLIC-KEY INFRASTRUCTURE

Just as social infrastructure maintains the security and authenticity of money, *public-key infrastructure (PKI)* guarantees information security and authenticity for public-key encryption.

In other words, because of PKI, we can use public-key encryption to exchange emails, do business over the internet, and perform other actions with peace of mind.

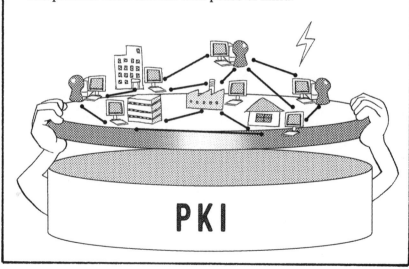

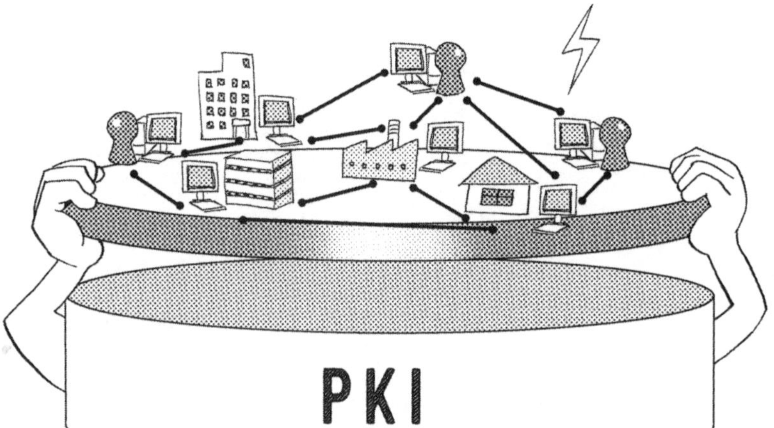
PKI

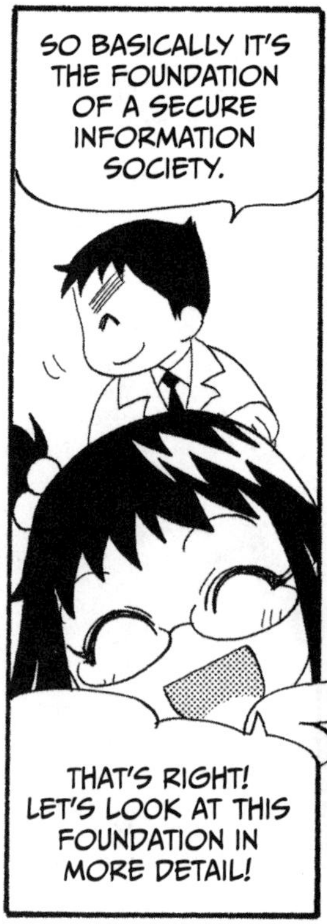
SO BASICALLY IT'S THE FOUNDATION OF A SECURE INFORMATION SOCIETY.
THAT'S RIGHT! LET'S LOOK AT THIS FOUNDATION IN MORE DETAIL!

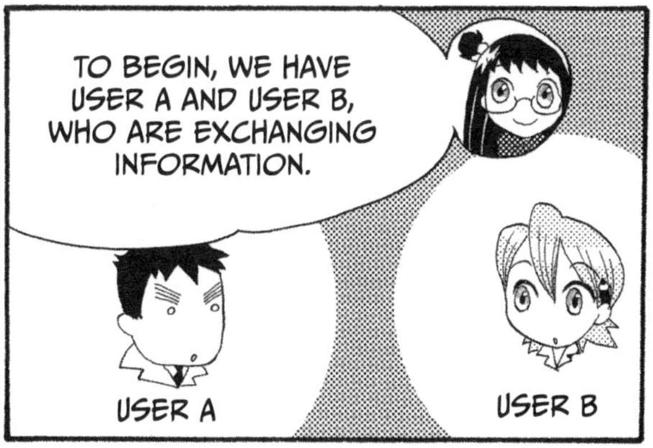
TO BEGIN, WE HAVE USER A AND USER B, WHO ARE EXCHANGING INFORMATION.
USER A
USER B
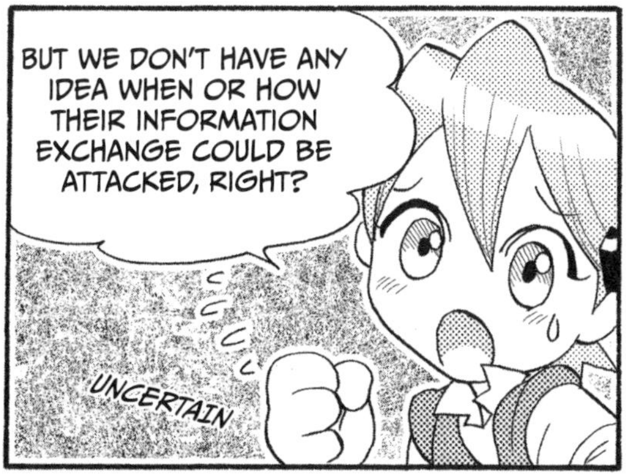
BUT WE DON'T HAVE ANY IDEA WHEN OR HOW THEIR INFORMATION EXCHANGE COULD BE ATTACKED, RIGHT?
UNCERTAIN
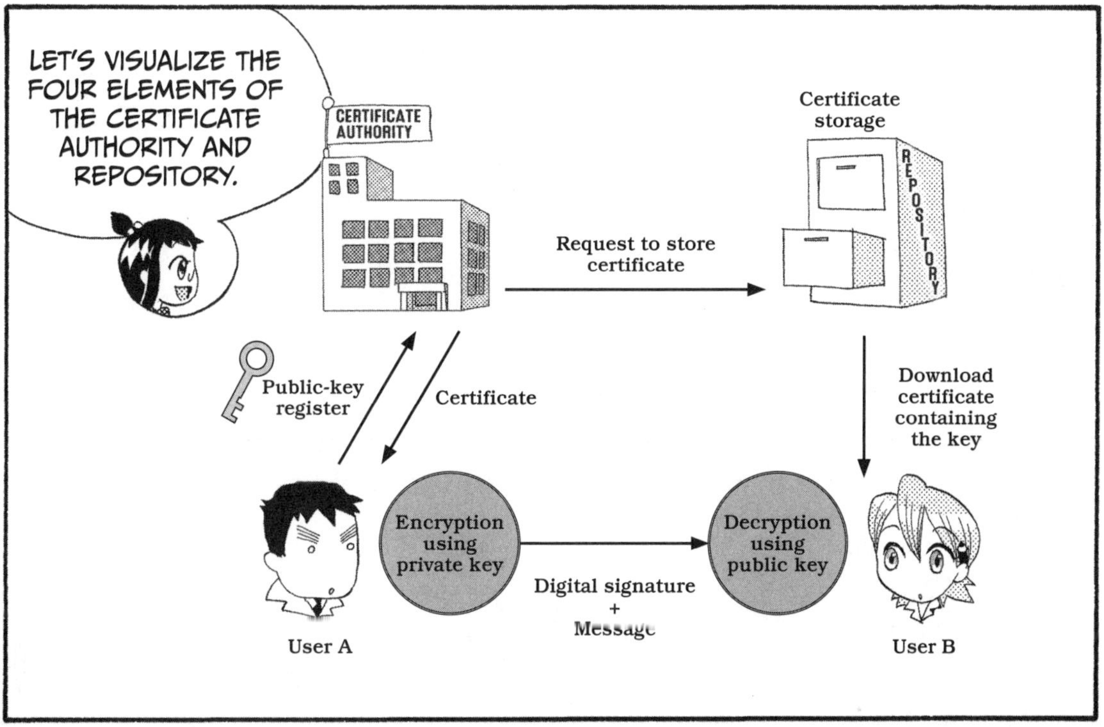
LET'S VISUALIZE THE FOUR ELEMENTS OF THE CERTIFICATE AUTHORITY AND REPOSITORY.
CERTIFICATE AUTHORITY
Certificate storage
REPOSITORY
Request to store certificate
Public-key register
Certificate
Download certificate containing the key
Encryption using private key
Decryption using public key
Digital signature + Message
User A
User B
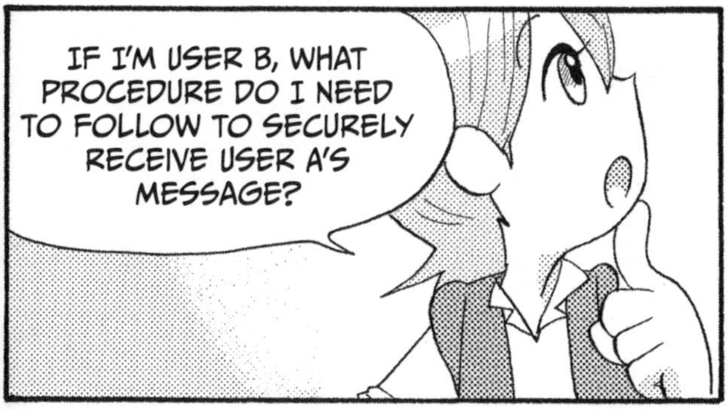
IF I'M USER B, WHAT PROCEDURE DO I NEED TO FOLLOW TO SECURELY RECEIVE USER A'S MESSAGE?
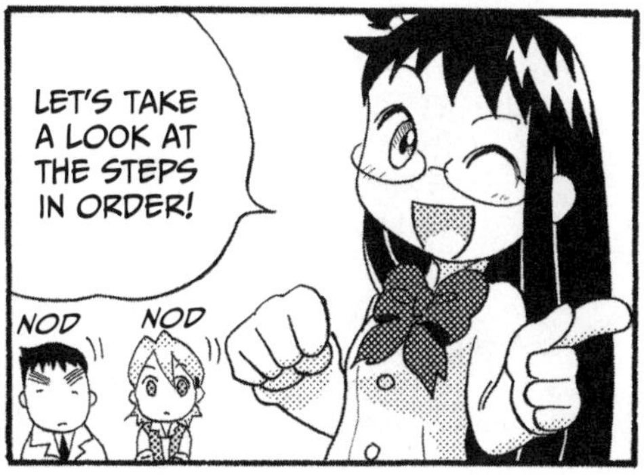
LET'S TAKE A LOOK AT THE STEPS IN ORDER!
NOD
NOD

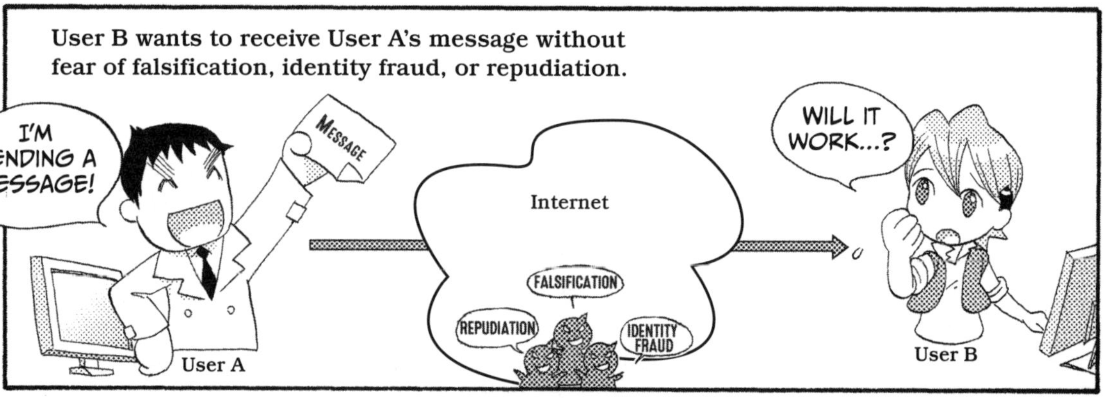
User B wants to receive User A's message without fear of falsification, identity fraud, or repudiation.
I'M SENDING A MESSAGE!
MESSAGE
User A
Internet
FALSIFICATION
REPUDIATION
IDENTITY FRAUD
WILL IT WORK...?
User B

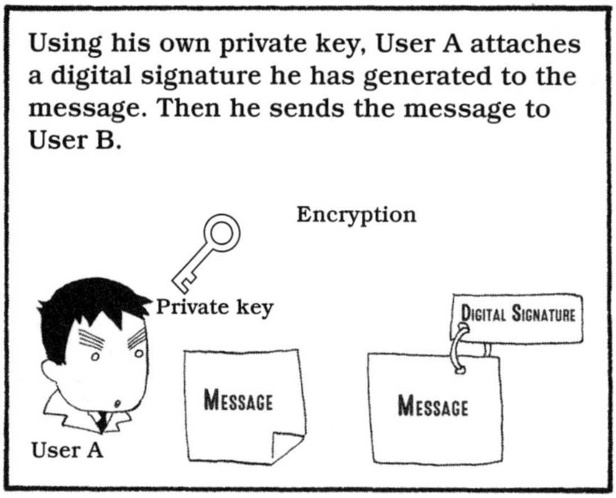
Using his own private key, User A attaches a digital signature he has generated to the message. Then he sends the message to User B.
Encryption
Private key
User A
MESSAGE
DIGITAL SIGNATURE
MESSAGE

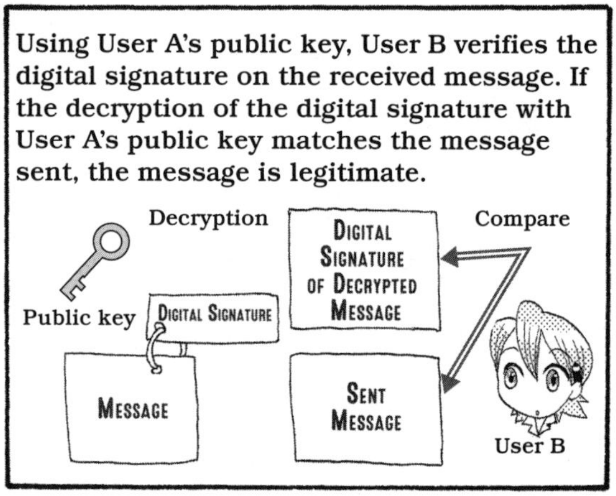
Using User A's public key, User B verifies the digital signature on the received message. If the decryption of the digital signature with User A's public key matches the message sent, the message is legitimate.
Decryption
DIGITAL SIGNATURE OF DECRYPTED MESSAGE
Compare
Public key
DIGITAL SIGNATURE
MESSAGE
SENT MESSAGE
User B

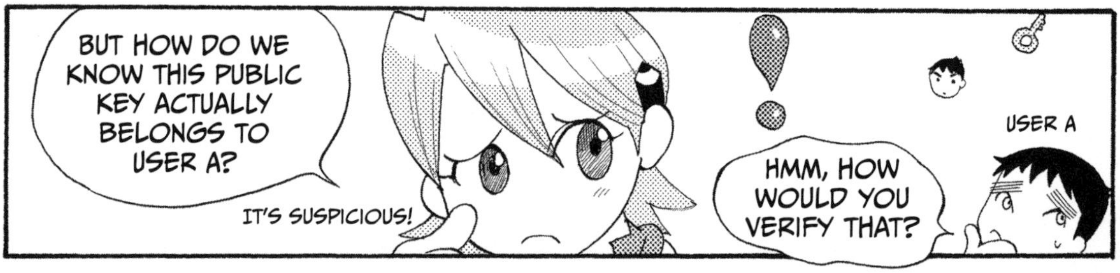
BUT HOW DO WE KNOW THIS PUBLIC KEY ACTUALLY BELONGS TO USER A?
IT'S SUSPICIOUS!
USER A
HMM, HOW WOULD YOU VERIFY THAT?

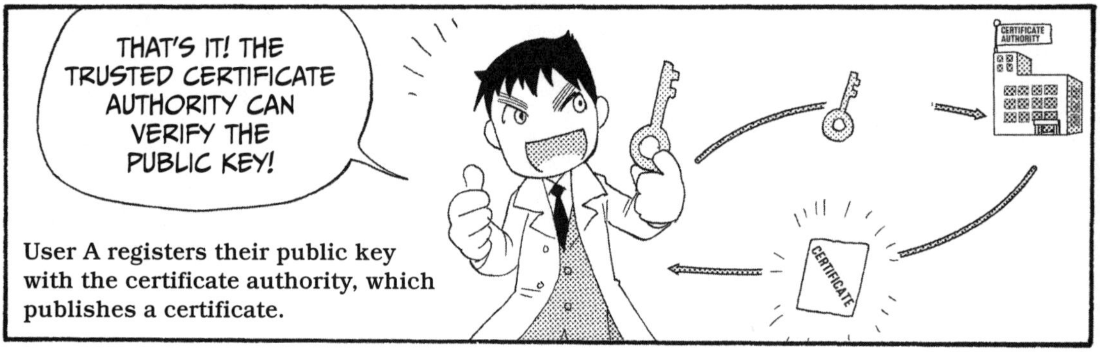
THAT'S IT! THE TRUSTED CERTIFICATE AUTHORITY CAN VERIFY THE PUBLIC KEY!
CERTIFICATE AUTHORITY
CERTIFICATE
User A registers their public key with the certificate authority, which publishes a certificate.

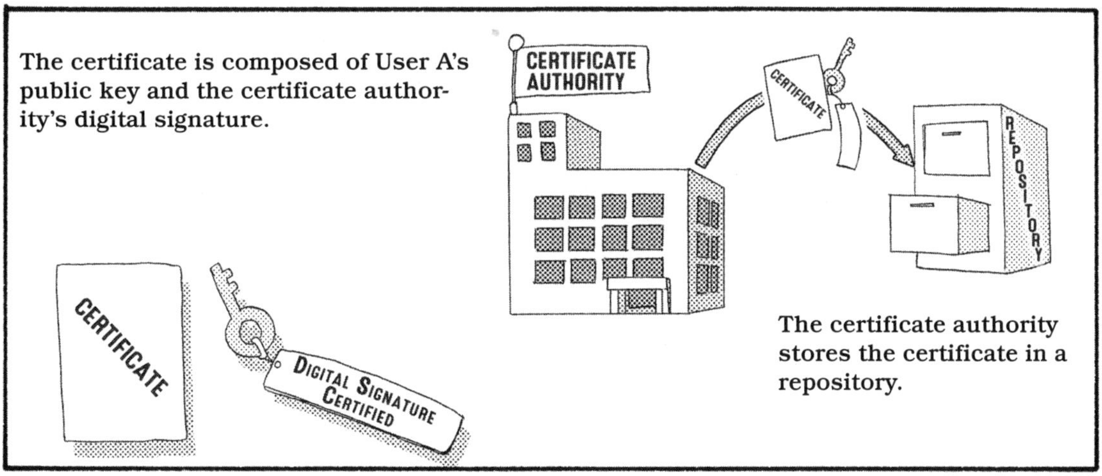
The certificate is composed of User A's public key and the certificate authority's digital signature.
CERTIFICATE AUTHORITY
CERTIFICATE
REPOSITORY
CERTIFICATE
DIGITAL SIGNATURE CERTIFIED
The certificate authority stores the certificate in a repository.

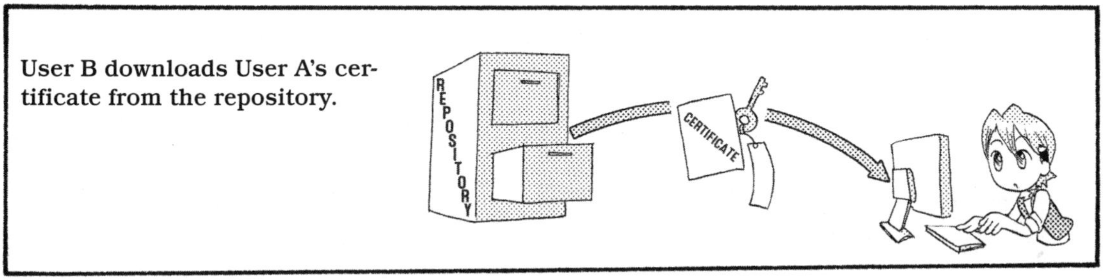
User B downloads User A's certificate from the repository.
REPOSITORY
CERTIFICATE

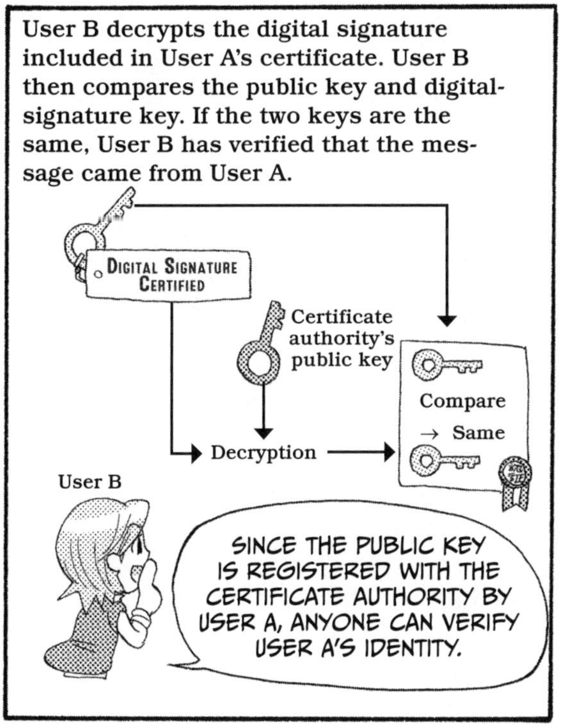
User B decrypts the digital signature included in User A's certificate. User B then compares the public key and digital-signature key. If the two keys are the same, User B has verified that the message came from User A.
DIGITAL SIGNATURE CERTIFIED
Certificate authority's public key
Compare
→ Same
Decryption
User B
SINCE THE PUBLIC KEY IS REGISTERED WITH THE CERTIFICATE AUTHORITY BY USER A, ANYONE CAN VERIFY USER A'S IDENTITY.

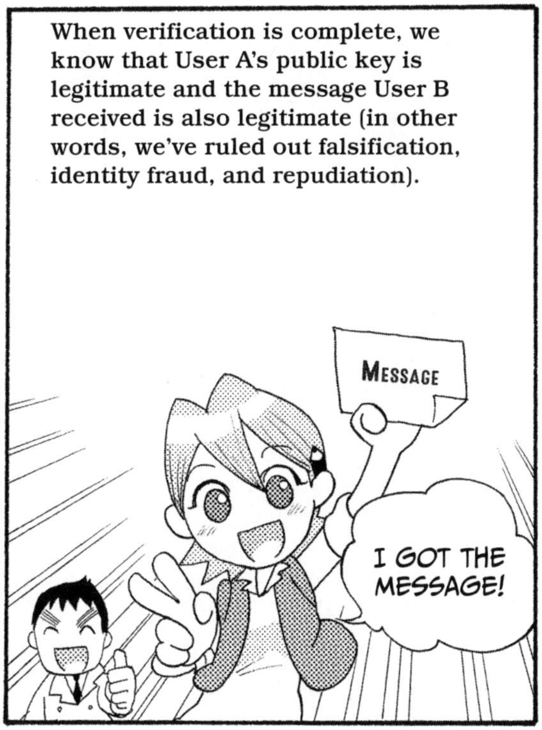
When verification is complete, we know that User A's public key is legitimate and the message User B received is also legitimate (in other words, we've ruled out falsification, identity fraud, and repudiation).
MESSAGE
I GOT THE MESSAGE!

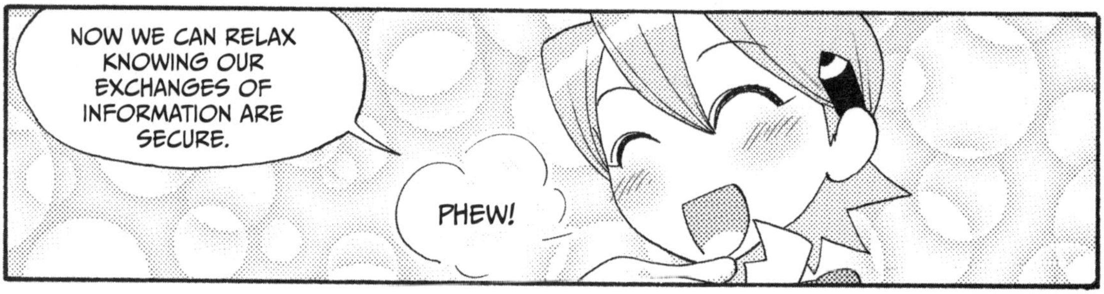
NOW WE CAN RELAX KNOWING OUR EXCHANGES OF INFORMATION ARE SECURE.
PHEW!

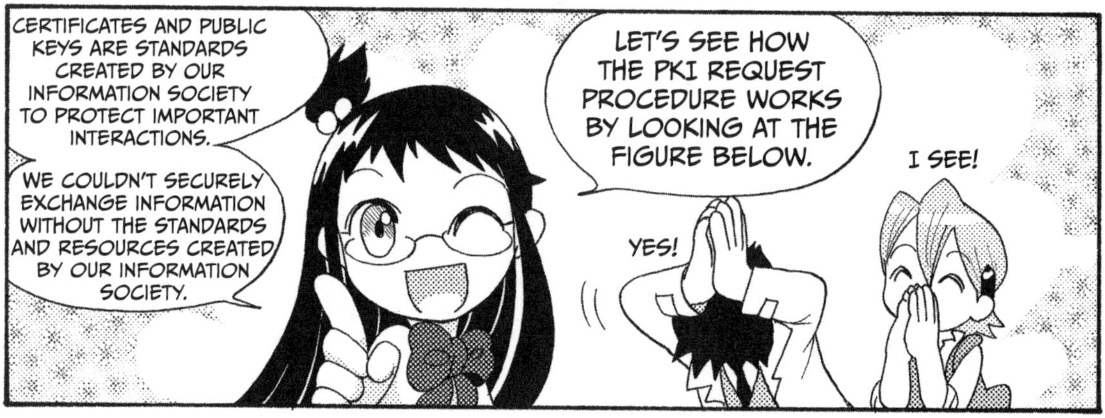
CERTIFICATES AND PUBLIC KEYS ARE STANDARDS CREATED BY OUR INFORMATION SOCIETY TO PROTECT IMPORTANT INTERACTIONS.
WE COULDN'T SECURELY EXCHANGE INFORMATION WITHOUT THE STANDARDS AND RESOURCES CREATED BY OUR INFORMATION SOCIETY.
LET'S SEE HOW THE PKI REQUEST PROCEDURE WORKS BY LOOKING AT THE FIGURE BELOW.
YES!
I SEE!

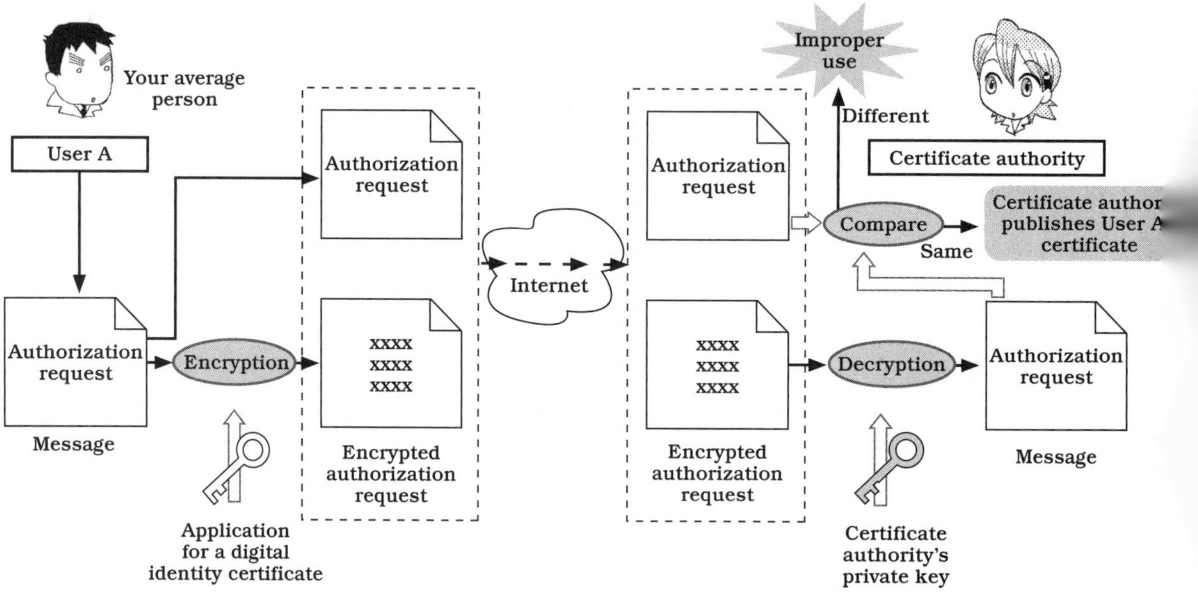
Your average person
User A
Authorization request
Message
Encryption
Application for a digital identity certificate
Authorization request
xxxx
xxxx
xxxx
Encrypted authorization request
Internet
Authorization request
xxxx
xxxx
xxxx
Encrypted authorization request
Improper use
Different
Certificate authority
Compare
Same
Certificate author
publishes User A
certificate
Decryption
Certificate authority's private key
Authorization request
Message

When the decryption of the received application and the public key are verified, the certificate authority will grant User A the certificate.

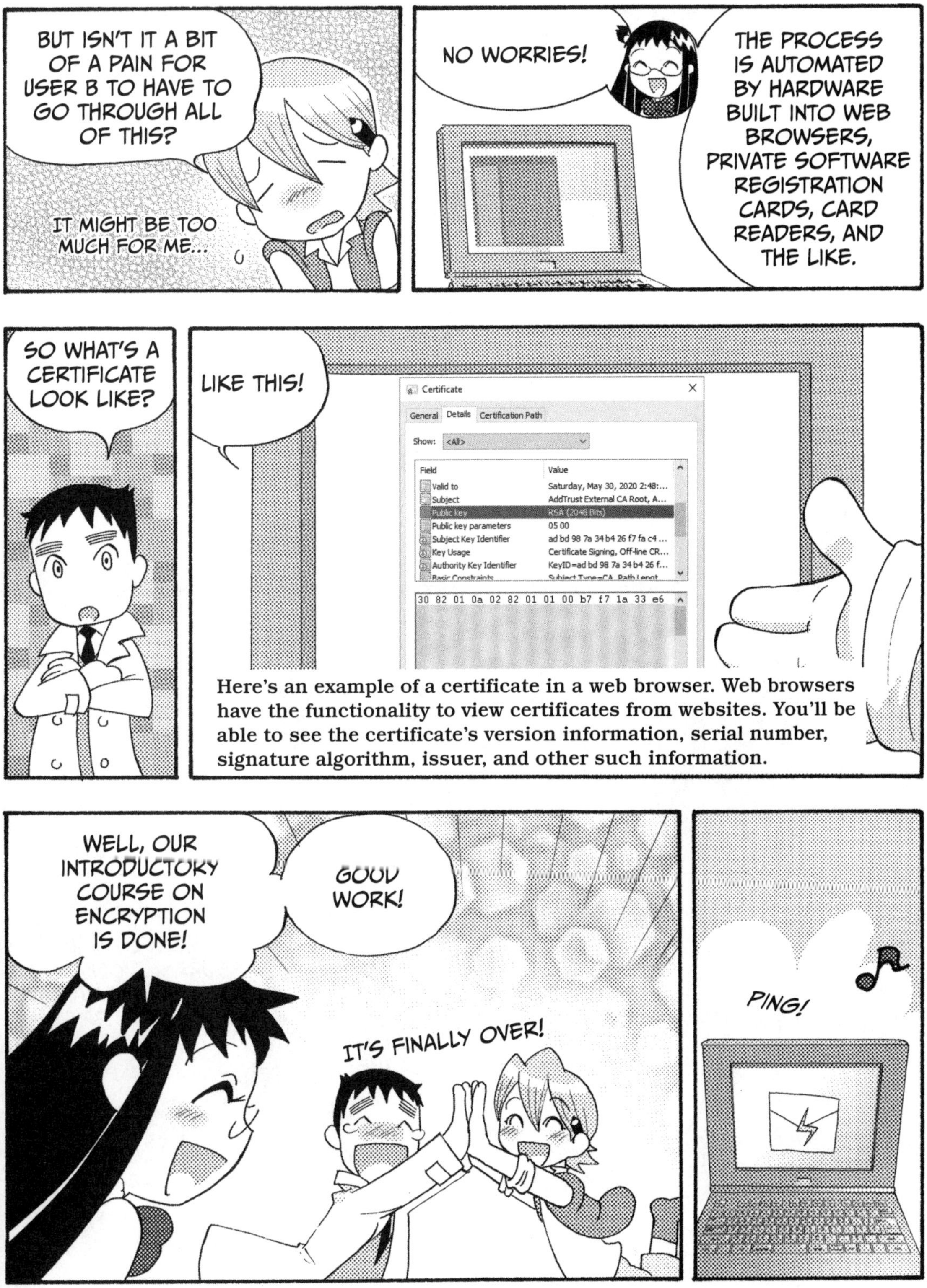
BUT ISN'T IT A BIT OF A PAIN FOR USER B TO HAVE TO GO THROUGH ALL OF THIS?
IT MIGHT BE TOO MUCH FOR ME...
NO WORRIES!
THE PROCESS IS AUTOMATED BY HARDWARE BUILT INTO WEB BROWSERS, PRIVATE SOFTWARE REGISTRATION CARDS, CARD READERS, AND THE LIKE.
SO WHAT'S A CERTIFICATE LOOK LIKE?
LIKE THIS!
Certificate
General
Details
Certification Path
Show: <All>
Field
Value
Valid to
Saturday, May 30, 2020 2:48:...
Subject
AddTrust External CA Root, A...
Public key
RSA (2048 Bits)
Public key parameters
05 00
Subject Key Identifier
ad bd 98 7a 34 b4 26 f7 fa c4 ...
Key Usage
Certificate Signing, Off-line CR...
Authority Key Identifier
KeyID=ad bd 98 7a 34 b4 26 f...
30 82 01 0a 02 82 01 01 00 b7 f7 1a 33 e6
Here's an example of a certificate in a web browser. Web browsers have the functionality to view certificates from websites. You'll be able to see the certificate's version information, serial number, signature algorithm, issuer, and other such information.
WELL, OUR INTRODUCTORY COURSE ON ENCRYPTION IS DONE!
GOOD WORK!
IT'S FINALLY OVER!
PING!

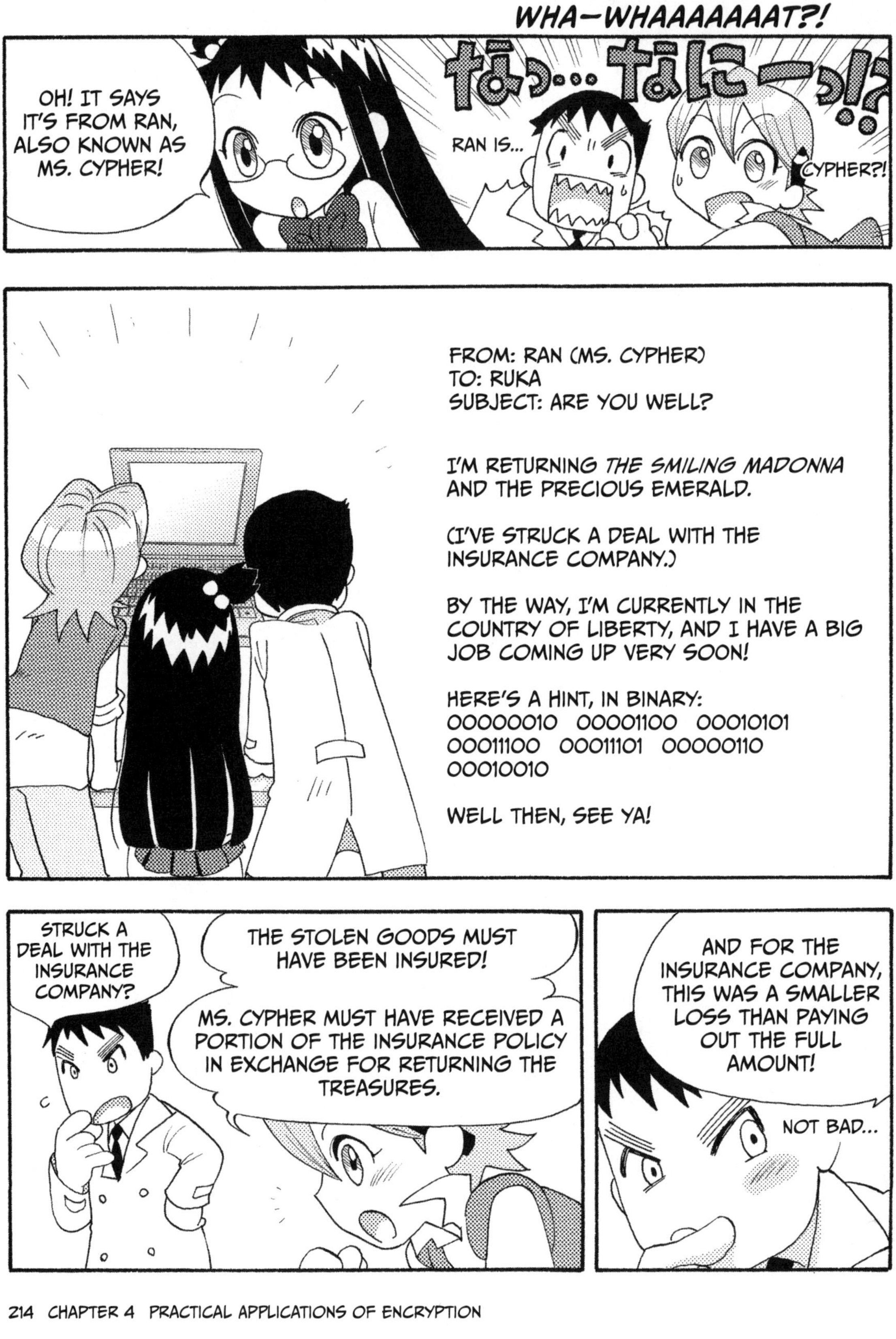
WHA-WHAAAAAAAT?!
OH! IT SAYS IT'S FROM RAN, ALSO KNOWN AS MS. CYPHER!
なっ…なにーっ!?
RAN IS...
CYPHER?!
FROM: RAN (MS. CYPHER)
TO: RUKA
SUBJECT: ARE YOU WELL?
I'M RETURNING *THE SMILING MADONNA* AND THE PRECIOUS EMERALD.
(I'VE STRUCK A DEAL WITH THE INSURANCE COMPANY.)
BY THE WAY, I'M CURRENTLY IN THE COUNTRY OF LIBERTY, AND I HAVE A BIG JOB COMING UP VERY SOON!
HERE'S A HINT, IN BINARY:
00000010 00001100 00010101 00011100 00011101 00000110 00010010
WELL THEN, SEE YA!
STRUCK A DEAL WITH THE INSURANCE COMPANY?
THE STOLEN GOODS MUST HAVE BEEN INSURED!
MS. CYPHER MUST HAVE RECEIVED A PORTION OF THE INSURANCE POLICY IN EXCHANGE FOR RETURNING THE TREASURES.
AND FOR THE INSURANCE COMPANY, THIS WAS A SMALLER LOSS THAN PAYING OUT THE FULL AMOUNT!
NOT BAD...

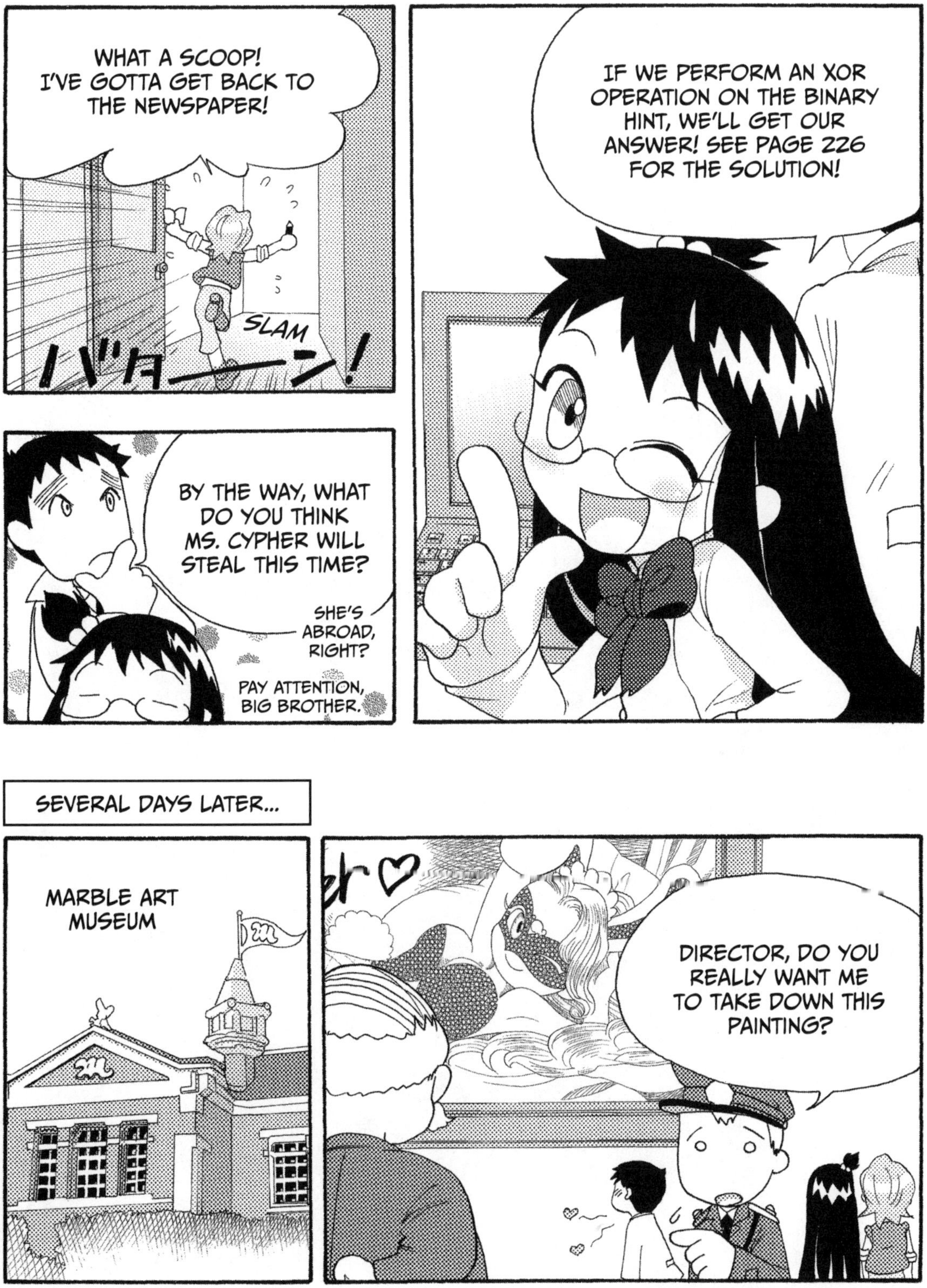
WHAT A SCOOP! I'VE GOTTA GET BACK TO THE NEWSPAPER!
SLAM
バターン!
BY THE WAY, WHAT DO YOU THINK MS. CYPHER WILL STEAL THIS TIME?
SHE'S ABROAD, RIGHT?
PAY ATTENTION, BIG BROTHER.
IF WE PERFORM AN XOR OPERATION ON THE BINARY HINT, WE'LL GET OUR ANSWER! SEE PAGE 226 FOR THE SOLUTION!
SEVERAL DAYS LATER...
MARBLE ART MUSEUM
DIRECTOR, DO YOU REALLY WANT ME TO TAKE DOWN THIS PAINTING?

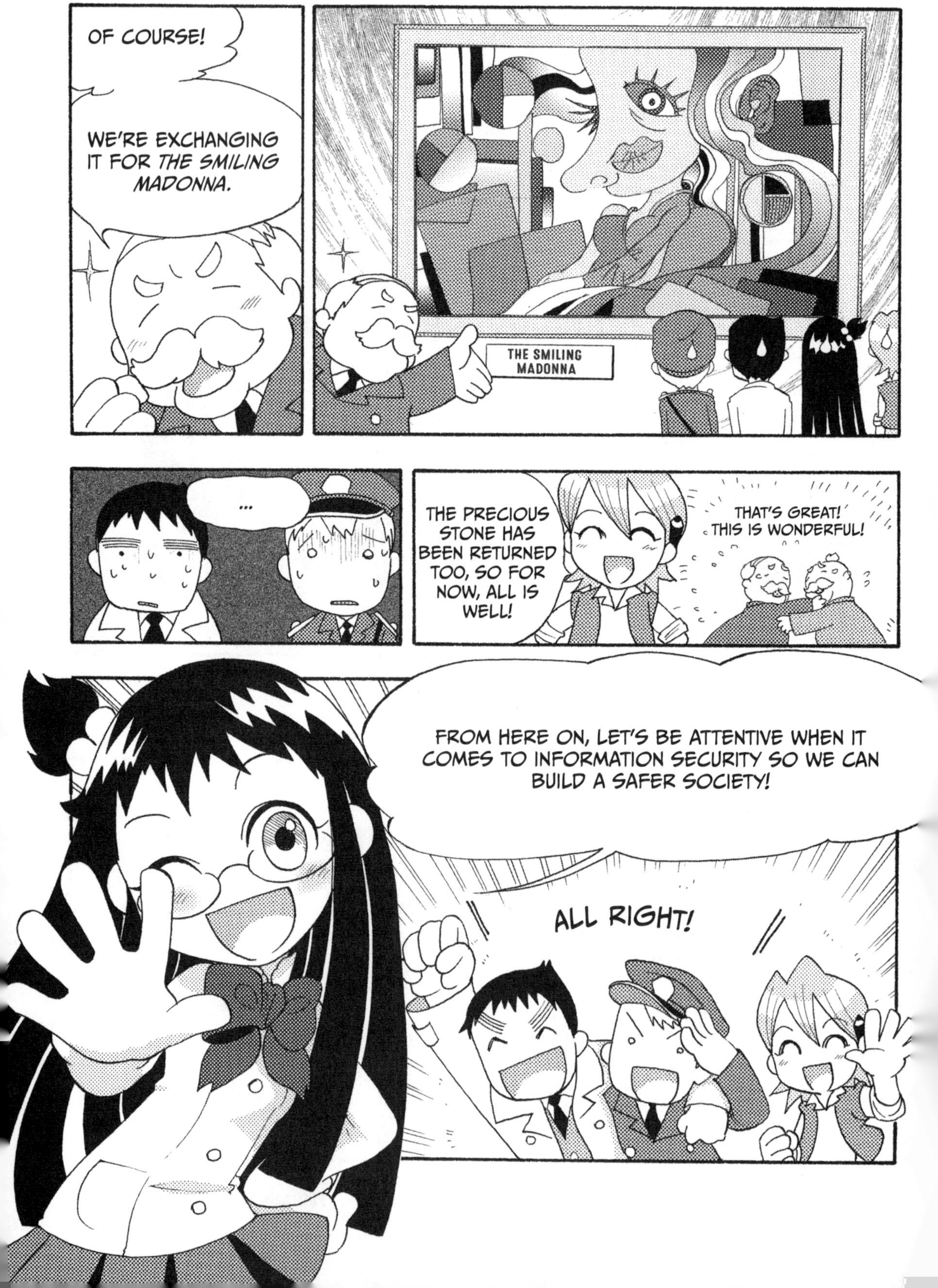
OF COURSE!
WE'RE EXCHANGING IT FOR THE SMILING MADONNA.
THE SMILING MADONNA
...
THE PRECIOUS STONE HAS BEEN RETURNED TOO, SO FOR NOW, ALL IS WELL!
THAT'S GREAT! THIS IS WONDERFUL!
FROM HERE ON, LET'S BE ATTENTIVE WHEN IT COMES TO INFORMATION SECURITY SO WE CAN BUILD A SAFER SOCIETY!
ALL RIGHT!

ZERO-KNOWLEDGE INTERACTIVE PROOF

In order to use a credit card, you need to share information to verify the authenticity of the card, but credit card theft is common. If your credit information is stolen while you are authenticating your card, you could be charged for items you don't recall purchasing (because you didn't purchase them!). In the same way, you risk revealing private information to outsiders whenever you need to verify your identity. Because of these risks, we need methods that ensure confidentiality can't be breached (also known as a *zero-knowledge protocols*) and methods that verify a person's identity to others (also known as *authenticity*).

In an effort to respond to these necessities, Goldwasser, Micali, and Rackoff introduced the concept of the *zero-knowledge interactive proof* in 1985. The zero-knowledge proof is a means by which a third party (for example, a credit card company) can verify the authenticity of an individual's card while ensuring that the private information attached to a card is not leaked. For example, a card has a randomized decimal password of more than 100 digits. To authenticate a card, a company or individual charging to the card would need to verify that the password is authentic without the ability to see the card's password. This might seem impossible, but we can do this using the mathematical theory behind encryption. Let's look at how this method works in detail by breaking the process down into two stages: the preparatory stage and the implementation stage.

PREPARATORY STAGE

The setup of a zero-knowledge proof first requires an honest *verifier* (such as a credit card company). Let's look at an example.

CREATE A COMPOSITE NUMBER N THAT IS PUBLICLY AVAILABLE TO ALL USERS

The verifier prepares two prime numbers (p, q) and calculates their product, the composite number N. That is, they use the following equation:

$$N = pq$$

The prime numbers p and q are secret. In actual practice, a proof would use large prime numbers comprising around 80 digits, but here, we'll use the two-digit prime numbers $p = 13$ and $q = 19$ for simplicity's sake. The product of these two prime numbers is

$$N = 13 \times 19 = 247$$

This is a three-digit composite number, but as noted, the factorization of N in practice would generate a number so large that it would be impossible for any computer to calculate. This very large composite number N is made available to all users.

REGISTER EACH USER'S ID WITH THE VERIFIER

Each user has an ID that is a publicly available numerical value associated with each user's public key. These IDs enable users to engage in one-to-one correspondence. Each user registers their ID with the verifier. In this book, we'll identify IDs with subscripts. For example, User A's ID is ID_A.

THE VERIFIER CALCULATES AND SENDS EACH USER A PRIVATE KEY

The verifier calculates the user's registered ID modulo the square root of N. When dealing with real numbers, calculating a square root is simple; however, because we need to use integers, the square root calculation is complex unless the prime numbers p and q of composite number N are known. The zero-knowledge proof is built upon this computationally complex calculation.

In this example, only the verifier knows the prime numbers 13 and 19, and since only the verifier can calculate the square root of each ID registered by the users, confidentiality is not breached. Let's look at an example in which ID_A is 101. In this case, the square root is 71.

$$\sqrt{101}\,(\text{mod } 247) = 71$$

When we calculate in reverse and square 71, we get 71^2 (mod 247) = 101. The value 71 is User A's private key (S_A), which is secretly delivered to User A. Generally, the following relationship exists between ID_A and private key S_A:

$$\sqrt{ID_A}\,(\text{mod } N) = S_A$$
$$(S_A)^2\,(\text{mod } N) = ID_A$$

In practice, the private key will be a number of more than 100 digits, so the private key isn't a number that User A can memorize. However, the purpose of the private key (S_A) is not to verify the identity of User A but rather to verify the authenticity of User A's card. Therefore, User A doesn't need to memorize S_A as one would memorize the PIN for an ATM card. Now that User A has a number to verify that their card is authentic, let's look at how User A would use this card.

IMPLEMENTATION STAGE (VERIFICATION PROCESS)

Now we'll demonstrate the verification process for when a *prover* such as User A wants to authenticate their identity to User B. If User A is trying to buy something with their credit card, this process shows that the card User A possesses is genuine.

USER A SENDS A VERIFICATION REQUEST TO USER B

First, User A selects a random number r_A, squares it, and divides it by the composite number N to find the remainder, y_A. In equation form, the remainder y_A is calculated as follows:

$$y_A = (r_A)^2\,(\text{mod } N)$$

The remainder y_A is sent to User B. Say for example that User A chooses the random number 50. The remainder y_A is calculated as follows:

$$y_A = 50^2 = 2{,}500 = 30\,(\text{mod } 247)$$

Thus, User A sends 30 to User B.

Next, User A takes the product of the private key S_A they received from the verifier and the random number r_A. Then User A divides the product by the composite number N to find the remainder, z_A.

$$z_A = S_A r_A (\text{mod } N)$$

Once User A calculates z_A, they send the value to User B. If we use the example where the random number r_A is 50, we get the following equation:

$$z_A = 71 \times 50 = 92 (\text{mod } 247)$$

And 92 is sent to User B.

USER B VERIFIES USER A'S AUTHENTICITY

User B squares the z_A they received from User A and divides by the composite number N to find the remainder v_A.

$$v_A = (z_A)^2 (\text{mod } N) = (S_A r_A)(\text{mod } N)$$

In our example, $z_A = 92$, so we get the following equation:

$$v_A = 92^2 = 8,464 = 66 (\text{mod } 247)$$

Next, User B calculates the value of v_A divided by y_A, which User B received from User A earlier in the process.

$$w_A = \frac{v_A}{y_A} (\text{mod } N) = v_A \times (y_A^{-1})(\text{mod } N)$$

All of the calculations are operations using the composite number N, and y_A^{-1} expresses the inverse element (reciprocal) of y_A. This means that y_A^{-1} is a value that satisfies the following equation:

$$y_A \times (y_A^{-1}) = 1(\text{mod } N)$$

In this example, $v_A = 66$, $y_A = 30$, and $y_A^{-1} = 30^{-1}$ (mod 247) = 140; therefore, we can calculate w_A as follows:

$$w_A = \frac{66}{30}(\text{mod } 247) = 66 \times 30^{-1}(\text{mod } 247) = 66 \times 140(\text{mod } 247) = 101$$

Lo and behold, this is User A's ID (ID_A).

Using this process, User B can verify the authenticity of User A's identity. We can find ID_A using this process because squaring User A's private key S_A yields ID_A. That is to say, we can derive $(S_A)^2$ using the previous equations as follows.

w_A is found by the equation $w_A = v_A / y_A \pmod{N}$.
Recall the equations found for v_A and y_A:

$$v_A = (z_A)^2 \pmod{N} = (S_A r_A)^2 \pmod{N}$$

$$y_A = (r_A)^2 \pmod{N}$$

Substitute these into the equation for w_A to get

$$w_A = \frac{(S_A r_A)^2}{(r_A)^2} = (S_A)^2 = ID_A$$

In other words, w_A is equal to User A's ID, ID_A, as you can see in Figure 4-1.

User A
User B
Sends y_A
$y_A = (r_A)^2 \pmod{N}$
Receives y_A
Sends z_A
$z_A = S_A r_A \pmod{N}$
(S_A: User A's private key)
Receives z_A
$w_A = \frac{(z_A)^2}{y_A} \pmod{N}$
The value w_A is calculated and then compared to User A's public ID (ID_A).

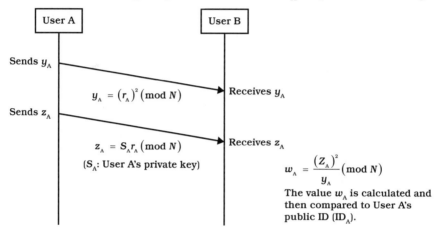

Figure 4-1: Verification process using a zero-knowledge interactive proof

METHODS OF IDENTITY FRAUD

Building on the same example, let's consider how User X, an attacker, might try to steal User A's identity. If User A can verify themselves to User X while ensuring that there is only a very small probability User X can learn anything about User A's secret key, then the scheme is a valid zero-knowledge protocol. Otherwise, the protocol is faulty.

The zero-knowledge protocol requires that the prover (in this case, User A or User X) know the secret key to be able to prove their identity to the verifier (User B), so the protocol protects against identity attacks in which the adversary doesn't have knowledge of the secret key. User X, the adversary trying to identify as User A, doesn't know anything about User A's private key S_A. In an attempt to trick User B, User X selects two numbers e and f that have the following relationship with ID_A:

$$e^2 = ID_A \times f \pmod{N}$$

We'll discuss this equation in more detail later.

In the scenario from Figure 4-1, the legitimate User A first sends User B y_A and z_A to initiate a verification request. When attempting identity fraud, User X mimics this verification request by sending f and e to User B as though they were User A's credentials.

Let's use $e = 25$ and $f = 82$ to see how User X would try to mimic User A's ID (ID_A).

Once User X sends e and f in place of z_A and y_A, respectively, User B uses e and f to calculate w_A as they would with a legitimate request. Because User X generated e and f to have a specific relationship with ID_A, w_A will be identical to User A's public ID ($ID_A = 101$), and User B will mistakenly authenticate User X as User A.

Let's see how User B's calculations work with e and f.

First, let's look at e's relationship with v_A. First, we know that $z_A = e$, so we can substitute z_A for e in the following formula:

$$v_A = (z_A)^2 (\text{mod } N)$$

We find this relationship:

$$v_A = e^2 = 25^2 = 131 (\text{mod } 247)$$

Next, we would substitute $v_A = e^2$ and $f = y_A$ into this equation:

$$w_A = \frac{v_A}{y_A} (\text{mod } N)$$

Doing so yields the following:

$$w_A = \frac{e^2}{f} = e^2 \times f^{-1} = v_A \times 82^{-1} (\text{mod } 247)$$

Here, from $82^{-1} (\text{mod } 247) = 244$, we get $w_A = 131 \times 244 (\text{mod } 247) = 101$.

Using this method, User X can commit identity fraud on User A's public ID_A without knowing User A's private key S_A or the random number r_A. This process is illustrated in Figure 4-2.

To get around the verification process in Figure 4-1, User X needs to find values that fulfill the relationship $f = e^2 (\text{mod } N)$ using only User A's public ID. To do this, User X squares e and divides by ID_A to find f:

$$f = \frac{e^2}{ID_A} (\text{mod } N)$$

Once User X calculates e and f, they can pretend to be User A without even knowing the random number r_A, committing a security breach. Let's look at a way to turn this protocol into one in which only User A, or someone with actual knowledge of the secret key S_A, can be verified as User A.

Legitimate User A
(ID_A = 101)
User B
Random number r_A = 50
Sends y_A
Receives y_A
y_A = 50^2 (mod 247) = 30
Sends z_A
Receives z_A
z_A = 71 × 50 (mod 247)
w_A = 92^2 / 30 (mod 247) = 101 = ID_A
Illegitimate User X
User B
Sends y_A
Receives y_A
y_A = 82
Thief has matched real ID_A and stolen User A's identity.
Sends z_A
Receives z_A
z_A = 25
w_A = 25^2 / 82 (mod 247) = 101 = ID_A

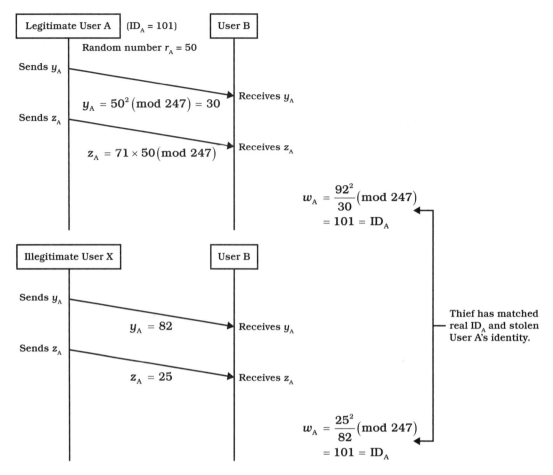

Figure 4-2: Example of identity theft

ANTI-IDENTITY FRAUD IN A ZERO-KNOWLEDGE INTERACTIVE PROOF

Our protocol is flawed because identity fraud is possible, so let's look at how one can defend against an attack. To do this, we'll incorporate a randomly chosen *challenge bit b* and modify the prover and verifier's protocol, as shown in Figure 4-3.

When User A delivers y_A to User B, User B randomly chooses a value of 0 or 1 as the challenge bit *b* and sends *b* to User A. The prover then sends z_A to User B, where $z_A = r_A \times (S_A{}^b)$. User B performs a check on the returned value to confirm whether the sender is a legitimate user. This check requires calculating $z_A{}^2$ using the two methods $z_A{}^2 = r_A{}^2 \times (ID_A{}^b)$ and $z_A \times z_A$ (where z_A is the value that User A sent). User B then compares the results of the two methods of calculating $z_A{}^2$ to determine whether they are equal: $z_A \times z_A = r_A{}^2 \times (ID_A{}^b)$? If they are equal, then the verifier accepts the prover's claim to be User A.

This entire protocol is run *t* times to ensure that the verifier trusts the prover, because if $b = 0$ (which occurs 50 percent of the time if User B chooses he challenge bit randomly), the prover may simply return r_A. This will trick the verifier into accepting the answer even though the prover doesn't have knowledge of S_A. The number of times the challenge bit check is performed depends on the level of secrecy one wants to achieve, where the probability a user will falsely impersonate someone is $1/(2^t)$. Performing the check $t = \log(N)$ times isn't uncommon.

As long as User X doesn't have the secret key S_A and we run this experiment enough times to satisfy the verifier, this protocol can authenticate a user and address the risk of identity fraud. The verifier also doesn't learn any information about S_A from the protocol because z_A is calculated from $S_A r_A \pmod N$, which multiplies S_A by a random number.

User A
User B
Sends y_A
$y_A = (r_A)^2 \pmod N$
Receives y_A
Sends challenge bit b (b randomly chosen to be 1 or 0)
$b = 0, 1$
Sends z_A
$z_A = r_A S_A^{\,b} \pmod N$
Performs the following:
$(r_A S_A^{\,b})^2 \pmod N = z_A z_A$
$y_A \mathrm{ID}^b = z_A z_A$
and accepts if they are equal
Protocol performed t times

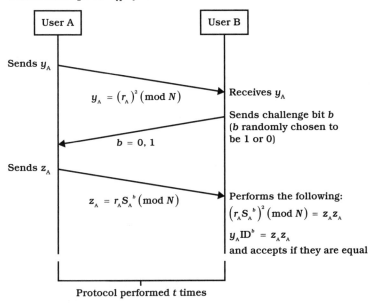

Figure 4-3: Valid verification process that prevents identity fraud

This protocol uses a small number of computations, so it's not uncommon to see this method on a token card of some sort.

WHAT NEXT?

Though we've covered the main concepts of cryptography in this book, we've forgone exploring several important topics, including the future of cryptography. If you're curious about where cryptography will develop from here or what areas you could explore next, the following sections will give you an idea of where to start.

PSEUDORANDOM NUMBERS AND ENCRYPTION SECURITY

A sequence of random numbers is one of the foundational pieces underlying security. For example, in public-key encryption, the key used to encrypt and decrypt information is generated using a random number. To ensure a good encryption scheme, one must use a random number generator whose results are impossible or very hard to predict (that is, one that generates a random number that can't be predicted based on previous numbers).

Pseudorandom numbers must be distinguished from the concept of *physically random numbers* (also called *truly random numbers*). Pseudorandom numbers are produced from a fixed formula (called a pseudorandom number generator), so they are deterministic or predictable by individuals with enough computing power. Some examples of pseudorandom number generators include the linear congruential generator, the middle square method, the M-series, the BBS (Blum-Blum-Shub) method, and the one-way hash function.

In contrast, a physically random number is generated based on a natural physical phenomenon, implements a perfectly random sequence of numbers, and can generate an infinite chaotic sequence of numbers. For example, a physical random number can be generated from the noise produced when electricity is distributed to a semiconductor circuit.

Despite the fact that most pseudorandom numbers are not secure, most systems use them instead of physically random numbers because many pseudorandom number generators require an inordinate amount of computing power to distinguish them from random number generators. In addition, the cost of using a truly random number generator is magnitudes higher than that of a pseudorandom number generator. We can't treat pseudorandom numbers as though they are truly random numbers, but in most cases, you can reasonably assume the adversary isn't capable of harnessing that much computing power, so pseudorandom generators suffice. Some top-secret or mission-critical systems may warrant the use of a random number generator, but these are rare.

PGP

The initials *PGP* stand for Pretty Good Privacy. PGP is a widely used type of encryption software that was invented in 1991 by Philip Zimmermann.

PGP is a vital piece of functionality in nearly all modern encryption software. It makes certificate generation possible in symmetric-key algorithms (AES, 3-DES, and so on), public-key encryption (RSA, ElGamal, and so on), digital signatures (RSA, DSA), and one-way hash functions (MD5, SHA-1, RIPEMD-160, and so on).

SSL/TLS

Communication protocols are used in online shopping and other forms of internet correspondence. When a protocol is used, a message authentication code certifies and authenticates the contents of a correspondence. Two security protocols that are often used for this purpose are *SSL* (*secure socket layer*) and *TLS* (*transport layer security*). For example, when a credit card number or other secure information is sent through a web browser, SSL or TLS is used to encrypt the data and prevent it from being intercepted. To determine whether you are using SSL/TLS in online communication, you can inspect the URL in your internet browser. Non-SSL/TLS URLs begin with *http://*, while URLs beginning with *https://* indicate SSL/TLS communication.

Like SSL/TLS, the protocols called SMTP (Simple Mail Transfer Protocol) and POP3 (Post Office Protocol) also encrypt emails using SSL/TLS to protect information. SMTP is used to encrypt mail that is being sent out, while POP3 is used for received mail.

QUANTUM CRYPTOGRAPHY

Quantum cryptography is considered an absolutely secure method of encryption. Quantum cryptography makes use of light pulses that contain more than 10,000 *photons*, which are the smallest unit of measurement for light. A single photon contains 1 bit of information, and the photon's polarity (the direction in which the electromagnetic waves oscillate) is used to distinguish whether the bit is a 0 or a 1. Photons follow *Heisenberg's uncertainty principle*, which states that a quantum system can't be observed without changing the system's state. This means the data contained in photons can't be copied by an attacker because, if a photon were observed by the attacker, the photon's polarization would be changed and any suspicious activity would be detected. This means that quantum encryption can't be intercepted. When quantum cryptography is combined with a one-time pad that uses a single-use encryption key, cryptographers can create fail-safe encryption.

BIOMETRICS

Biometrics are biological features unique to an individual that are used to confirm a person's identity. Some examples of biometrics include fingerprints, palm veins, facial structures, iris patterns, palm prints, DNA (genes), and so on. Verification systems are seeing more everyday usage, one prominent example being the fingerprint unlock mechanism in smartphones.

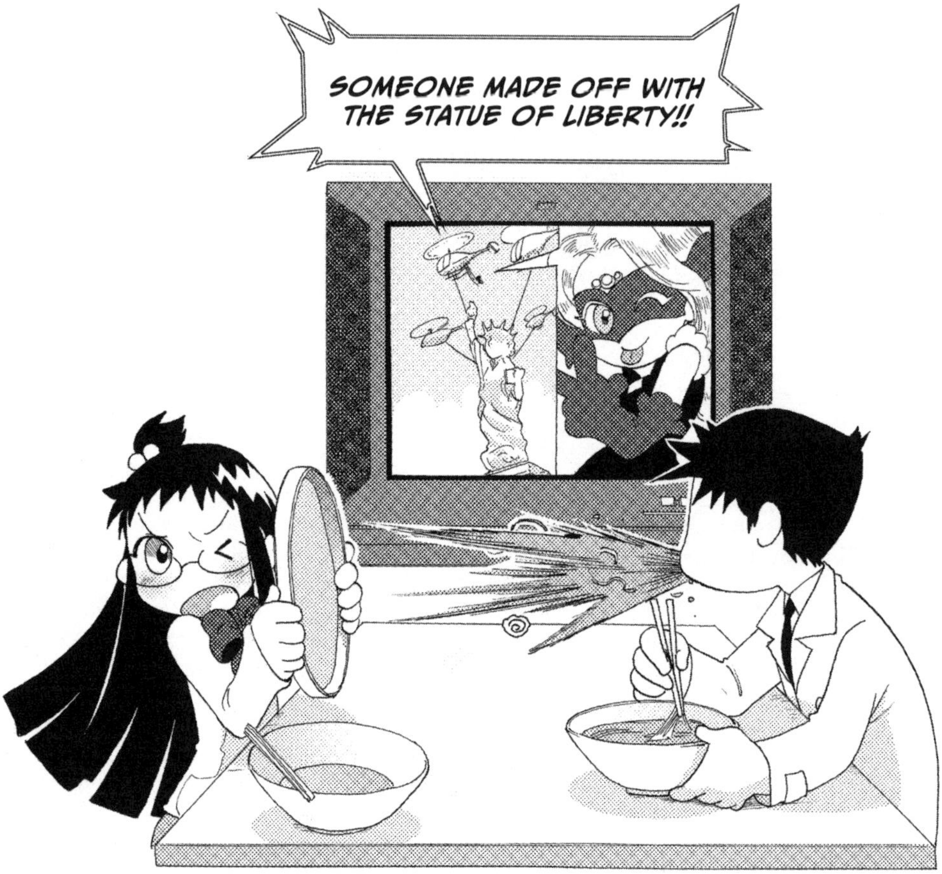
SOMEONE MADE OFF WITH THE STATUE OF LIBERTY!!

IF WE XOR THE HINT ON PAGE 214:

00000010 00001100 00010101 00011100 00011101 00000110 00010010

AND THE WORD *LIBERTY* IN ASCII BINARY:

01101100 01101001 01100010 01100101 01110010 01110100 01111001

WE GET

01101110 01100101 01110111 01111001 01101111 01110010 01101011

WHICH IS *NEWYORK* IN ASCII BINARY.

INDEX

G

H

I

J

K

L

M

MACs (message authentication codes), 195–199

man-in-the-middle attacks, 203–205

"A Mathematical Theory of Communication" article (Shannon), 19

MD5 hash function, 193

message authentication codes (MACs), 195–199

middle square method, 224

Miller-Rabin method (primality tests), 129

modulo operations, 134–137
addition, 137–138
associative property, 149
commutative property, 149
distributive property, 149
division, 143–147
fields, 149
multiplication, 140–143, 146–147
power table, 150–151
subtraction, 139

M-series pseudorandom number generator, 224

multiplication (modulo operations), 140–143, 146–147

N

National Security Agency (NSA) standards (DES ciphers), 75–76

natural numbers, 121, 181–182

nonnegative integers, 121

O

OFB (output feedback), 71

one-time pad, 37, 225

one-way functions, 115–118
discrete logarithm problem, 116

integer factorization problem, 115

output feedback (OFB), 71

P

padding (block ciphers), 69

parity check (DES ciphers), 75

PC–1 (permuted choice 1) (DES keys), 77, 101–102

PC–2 (permuted choice 2) (DES keys), 77, 102–103

perfectly secure encryption, 37–38

permutations, 32
final permutation, 95–96, 99
initial permutation, 91, 97

permuted choice 1 (PC–1) (DES keys), 77, 101–102

permuted choice 2 (PC–2) (DES keys), 77, 102–103

PGP (Pretty Good Privacy), 189, 224

photons (quantum cryptography), 225

physically random numbers (truly random numbers), 224

PKI (public-key infrastructure), 206–214

plaintext, 20. See also names of specific encryption methods
breaking classic encryption, 37–40
Caesar cipher, 24
converting into binary, 89
polyalphabetic cipher, 26
simple substitution cipher, 25
substitution cipher, 25
transposition cipher, 27

Poe, Edgar Allen, 35–36

polyalphabetic cipher, 26, 33–34

POP3 (Post Office Protocol), 225

power table (modulo operations), 150–151

preparatory stage (zero-knowledge interactive proof), 217–218

Pretty Good Privacy (PGP), 189, 224

primality tests, 129–133

prime numbers, 120–123
composite numbers and, 123–124
coprime numbers, 143
Euler's totient function, 156
primality tests, 155
primality tests, 129–133
sieve of Eratosthenes, 124–129

primitive roots, 174

private key
calculating and sending to user, 218
making, 167–168
RSA encryption
calculating, 182–183
generating, 165–168
verifying compatibility, 166

procedure words (codes), 18

proposition, 154

provers (zero-knowledge interactive proof), 218–219

pseudoprimes, 129, 155

pseudorandom number generator, 224

pseudorandom numbers, 66–67, 151, 155, 224

public key
making, 167–168
RSA encryption
generating, 165–168
verifying compatibility, 166

ABOUT THE AUTHORS

MASAAKI MITANI

Masaaki Mitani is from the town of Setoda, formerly known as Toyota, in Onomachi of the Hiroshima prefecture. He graduated in 1974 from the Department of Electrical and Electronic Engineering in the School of Engineering at the Tokyo Institute of Technology. After working as an assistant professor at his alma mater, he is now a professor at Tokyo Denki University's School of Engineering in the Department of Information and Communication Engineering. He specializes in digital signal processing engineering, communication engineering, and educational engineering. He has a PhD in Engineering.

PRINCIPAL WORKS

- *An Introduction to Digital Signal Processing* (Ohmsha, Ltd.)
- *Learning Digital Signal Processing using Scilab* (CQ Publishing)
- *A Friendly Introduction to Electronic Circuits, Introduction (I) to Diodes and Transistors* (Micronet)
- *Re-Learning Signal Mathematics* (CQ Publishing)
- *Immediately Applicable Fourier Transform* (Kodansha Ltd.)

SHINICHI SATO

Shinichi Sato is from the town of Date in the Fukushima prefecture. In 1990, he earned his masters degree in electrical engineering at Tokyo Denki University's graduate student program. He worked on designing imaging machinery at a private corporation before conducting research related to bionics in a private institution's medical faculty as an assistant researcher. He is now an assistant professor at Tokyo Denki University's School of Engineering in the Department of Information and Communication Engineering. He specializes in signal processing engineering and educational engineering.

PRODUCTION TEAM FOR THE JAPANESE EDITION

Production: Verte Corp.

Editing: Tsugumi Endo

DTP: Satoshi Arai

HOW THIS BOOK WAS MADE

The *Manga Guide* series is a co-publication of No Starch Press and Ohmsha, Ltd. of Tokyo, Japan, one of Japan's oldest and most respected scientific and technical book publishers. Each title in the best-selling *Manga Guide* series is the product of the combined work of a manga illustrator, scenario writer, and expert scientist or mathematician. Once each title is translated into English, we rewrite and edit the translation as necessary and have an expert review each volume. The result is the English version you hold in your hands.

MORE MANGA GUIDES

Find more *Manga Guides* at your favorite bookstore, and learn more about the series at *https://www.nostarch.com/manga/*.

THE MANGA GUIDE TO
STATISTICS

THE MANGA GUIDE TO
DATABASES

THE MANGA GUIDE TO
ELECTRICITY

THE MANGA GUIDE TO
PHYSICS

THE MANGA GUIDE TO
CALCULUS

THE MANGA GUIDE TO
LINEAR ALGEBRA

THE MANGA GUIDE TO
REGRESSION ANALYSIS

THE MANGA GUIDE TO
RELATIVITY

THE MANGA GUIDE TO
PHYSIOLOGY

THE MANGA GUIDE TO
MOLECULAR BIOLOGY

THE MANGA GUIDE TO
BIOCHEMISTRY

THE MANGA GUIDE TO
MICROPROCESSORS

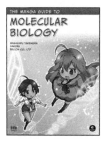